TROPICAL LEGUMES:

Resources for the Future

Report of an Ad Hoc Panel of the
    Advisory Committee on Technology Innovation
Board on Science and Technology for International Development
Commission on International Relations
National Research Council

NATIONAL ACADEMY OF SCIENCES
Washington, D.C.   1979

This report has been prepared by an ad hoc advisory panel of the Advisory Committee on Technology Innovation, Board on Science and Technology for International Development, Commission on International Relations, National Academy of Sciences—National Research Council. Program costs for the study were provided by the Office of Agriculture, Bureau for Development Support, Agency for International Development, under Contract AID/csd-2584, Task Order No. 17. Staff support was funded by the Office of Science and Technology, Bureau for Development Support, Agency for International Development, under Contract AID/csd-2584, Task Order No. 1.

Funding for this printing was provided by the Office of Agriculture, Bureau for Science and Technology, Agency for International Development, Washington, D. C., under Grant No. DAN-1406-G-SS-4001-00.

First printing, August 1979
Second printing, December 1979
Third printing, March 1981
Fourth printing, June 1984

Library of Congress Catalog Number 79-64185

Panel on Tropical Legumes

KENNETH O. RACHIE, Associate Director General Research, Centro Internacional de Agricultura Tropical, Cali, Colombia, *Chairman*

J. P. M. BRENAN, Director, Royal Botanic Gardens, Kew, Richmond, Surrey, England

JAMES L. BREWBAKER, Professor of Horticulture and Genetics, Department of Horticulture, University of Hawaii, Honolulu, Hawaii

JAMES A. DUKE, Chief, Plant Taxonomy Laboratory, Agricultural Research Station, United States Department of Agriculture, Beltsville, Maryland

E. MARK HUTTON, former Chief, Division of Tropical Crops and Pastures, Commonwealth Scientific and Industrial Research Organisation, St. Lucia, Queensland, Australia

THEODORE HYMOWITZ, Professor, Plant Genetics, Department of Agronomy, University of Illinois, Urbana, Illinois

RAYMOND J. JONES, Senior Principal Research Scientist, Davies Laboratory, Townsville, Queensland, Australia

ROBERT C. KOEPPEN, Plant Taxonomist, United States Forest Products Laboratory, Madison, Wisconsin

JEAN H. LANGENHEIM, Professor and Chairman, Division of Natural Sciences, University of California, Santa Cruz, California

JORGE LEÓN, Head, Plant Genetics Resources Center, Centro Agronómico Tropical de Investigación y Enseñanza, Turrialba, Costa Rica

JAMES C. MOOMAW, Director, Asian Vegetable Research and Development Center, Shanhua, Taiwan

B. N. OKIGBO, Deputy Director General, International Institute of Tropical Agriculture, Ibadan, Nigeria

A. M. PINCHINAT, Regional Director for Antillean Zone, Instituto Interamericano de Ciencias Agrícolas de la OEA, Santo Domingo, Dominican Republic

DONALD L. PLUCKNETT, Director of International Programs, Department of Agronomy and Soil Science, University of Hawaii, Honolulu, Hawaii

GUILLERMO SANCHEZ-RODRIGUEZ, Ingeniero agrónomo con especialidad en zootécnia, Banco de México, Ciudad Altamirano, Guerrero, México

SETIJATI SASTRAPRADJA, Director, Lembaga Biologi Nasional, Bogor, Indonesia

YUSUF N. TAMIMI, Professor of Soil Science, University of Hawaii, Agricultural Experiment Station, Hilo, Hawaii

CRAIG D. WHITESELL, Silviculturist, United States Forest Service, Honolulu, Hawaii

NOEL D. VIETMEYER, Professional Associate, National Academy of Sciences, Washington, D. C., *Staff Study Director*

MARY JANE ENGQUIST, Staff Assistant, National Academy of Sciences, Washington, D.C., *Staff*

iii

Preface

This report describes plants of the family Leguminosae, all of them greatly underexploited. Some are extensively used in one part of the world but unknown elsewhere; others are virtually unknown to science but have particular attributes that suggest they could become major crops in the future; a few are already widespread but their possibilities are not yet fully realized.

Most of the plants described in this book have the capacity to provide their own nitrogenous fertilizer through bacteria that live in nodules on their roots; the bacteria chemically convert nitrogen gas from the air into soluble compounds that the plant can absorb and utilize.* As a result, legumes generally require no additional nitrogenous fertilizer for average growth. This is advantageous because commercial nitrogenous fertilizers are now extremely expensive for peasant farmers. This report demonstrates how farmers in developing countries, by using leguminous plants, can grow useful crops while avoiding that expense. However, the plants to be discussed here should be seen as complements to, not as substitutes for, conventional tropical crops.

The panel that produced the report met at Kahului, Maui, Hawaii, in August 1976. Its objectives were:

- To identify leguminous plants, currently little known and underutilized, that could improve the well-being of people in developing countries;
- To select the species with the greatest inherent value; and
- To indicate what needs to be done to capitalize on these plants and to develop them to their potential.

Prior to the panel's meeting, a list of 150 neglected and seemingly promising legumes was mailed to plant scientists throughout the world. Each recipient was asked to "vote" for the species most worthy of inclusion in the panel's report. More than 150 scientists responded and, at the same time, nominated an additional 250 species for consideration. Furthermore, as the

---

*In the cases of some tree legumes described in the timber and ornamentals sections it is not yet known if they have either the root nodules or the bacteria necessary for this nitrogen "fixation" process.

study progressed, an additional 200 species with promise came to light. In a total of about 600 species, almost 300 received top ranking from at least one reviewer. From this wealth of candidates the panel selected the almost 200 species that are included in the 31 chapters of this book.

The choice is necessarily subjective, based as it is on the experience and judgment of the individuals making up the panel. However, the staff undertook extensive correspondence with researchers throughout the world to check out the merits of the species described in this report. For inclusion, a species had to satisfy certain general criteria, the most important of which were:

- Its potential to help improve the quality of life in developing countries;
- The lack of recognition of its potential; and
- Its need for greater attention from researchers and farmers, and for increased investment by organizations that fund research and development projects.

Other considerations were: Does the plant yield more than one product useful to a developing country? Can the plant improve the lives of the rural poor? Can it be grown in habitats where other plants grow poorly (for example, arid areas, swamps, slopelands, toxic soils)? If introduced to a new region, is the plant likely to become a pest? Little consideration was given to how much is known about the plant—if a species showed the requisite promise, it was included in the book even if it had been little studied in the past.

The object of this report is to show how little-known legumes can contribute to the economies of developing countries. Because most of these countries are tropical, the majority of the species discussed are adapted to warm areas. Nonetheless, there are huge areas of upland savanna and mountainous highlands throughout the developing world; therefore, plants like tarwi (*Lupinus mutabilis*) and honeylocust (*Gleditsia triacanthos*) that will grow in cooler regions are also included.

The report provides a brief introduction to the plants selected. It is intended neither as a textbook nor a comprehensive survey of tropical botany. For the convenience of the reader, most of the plants are presented in separate chapters, each arranged in the following general order:

- Description of the plant and of its advantages
- Limitations and special requirements
- Research needs

- Selected readings (significant reviews and general articles)*
- Research contacts (individuals or organizations known by the panelists to be involved in relevant research and who have agreed to provide advice and perhaps small amounts of seed to bona fide researchers; addresses are correct as of mid-1978).

The present book is one in a series that identifies unconventional scientific subjects with promise for developing countries. In each study, distinguished scientists pool their experience and knowledge and direct their recommendations to decision makers. Previous publications† dealing with legumes are:

- *The Winged Bean: A High Protein Crop for the Tropics*
- *Leucaena leucocephala: New Forage and Tree Crop for the Tropics*
- *Underexploited Tropical Plants with Promising Economic Value*

This last book describes 36 species and includes discussion of five legumes: winged bean (*Psophocarpus tetragonolobus*), *Acacia albida, Cassia sturtii,* tamarugo (*Prosopis tamarugo*), and guar (*Cyamopsis tetragonoloba*).

A companion report, *Firewood Crops: Shrub and Tree Species for Energy Production,* is in preparation. It describes woody species suited for fuelwood in rural developing areas, where firewood shortages are reaching a crisis point. Many of the species it describes will be legumes.

This report was made possible by a grant from the Office of Agriculture and Office of Science and Technology, Bureau for Development Support, Agency for International Development. Travel funds for Dr. Setijati Sastrapradja were provided by The Asia Foundation.

The panel is indebted to Professor Sheldon Whitney of the Maui Branch Station, Hawaii Agricultural Experiment Station, Kula, Maui, Hawaii, who made all arrangements for its meeting.

Without the hundreds of articles, books, and data bank searches obtained by the staff of the NAS Library this study could not have been accomplished. The panel gratefully acknowledges the invaluable help of James Olsen (head

---

*Although legumes are easily distinguished from other plant types, many are not easily differentiated from closely related species within the family. This leads to continual changes in the names designated by taxonomists. In the last decade, for example, almost all the species described in the pulse section of this report have had their names changed. Readers pursuing species described in this report should carefully note the synonymous names listed with each chapter. Many older references will use these synonyms.

†For information on how to order these and other reports, see page 329.

librarian), Celine Alvey, and Mary Jane Cochrane. Thanks are also due Professor J. P. M. Brenan and Dr. Bernard Verdcourt of the Royal Botanic Gardens, Kew, for checking and correcting taxonomic details.

The report was prepared for publication by F. R. Ruskin.

We also wish to acknowledge the courtesy of the Compania Shell de Venezuela for permitting use of the color plate of *Erythrina poeppigiana*, which appeared in the book *Arboles en Flor de Venezuela* (NV 1959), *Encyclopaedia Britannica*, for permission to adapt the article on leucaena, page 131, and Dr. C. G. G. J. van Steenis for permission to reproduce the map on page 218 showing the distribution of *Intsia* species.

Throughout this book the symbol "t" is used for metric ton and all quoted percentages of protein and other ingredients are based on dry weight rather than fresh weight. The figures quoted for diameters of tree trunks all refer to DBH, the diameter at breast height.

Comments on the report, especially if it has induced further research on the species described, should be sent to the staff officer, Dr. Noel Vietmeyer, National Academy of Sciences–National Research Council, 2101 Constitution Avenue, JH215, Washington, D.C. 20418, USA. Suggestions and information from readers about species not covered in this volume will be welcome; they might be included in a later publication.

Distribution of this book is made possible by a grant from the Office of the Science Advisor, Agency for International Development.

Table of Contents

Introduction and Summary

Of all plants used by man, only the grasses are more important than the legumes. However, while enormous resources have been expended in recent decades on grasses like rice, wheat, corn, sorghum, and barley, among the legumes only soybeans and peanuts (groundnuts) have received much attention. Yet it is the family Leguminosae that shows most promise for producing the vastly increased supplies of vegetable protein that the world will need in the near future. In developing countries especially, cultivation of legumes is the best and quickest way to augment the production of food proteins.

Leguminous plants are found throughout the world, but the greatest variety grows in the tropics and subtropics. Because tropical botany has been relatively neglected, there are thousands of promising species that await research and study. The wealth of untapped crop potential is exemplified in Mexico, where towns often have their own varieties of the common bean (*Phaseolus vulgaris*), quite distinct from those of neighboring towns. These varieties have never been disseminated outside their indigenous areas.

Of the thousands of known legume species, less than 20 are used extensively today. Those in common use include peanuts, soybeans, peas, lentils, pigeon peas, chick-peas, mung beans, kidney beans, cowpeas, alfalfa (lucerne), sweet clover (*Melilotus* species), other clovers (*Trifolium* species), and vetches. The remaining species are little used as yet, and many of them are almost unknown to science. Those that show greatest promise are described in later chapters.

The Family Leguminosae

With approximately 650 genera and 18,000 species Leguminosae is the third largest family of flowering plants (after Compositae and Orchidaceae). Its species are found in temperate zones, humid tropics, arid zones, highlands, savannas, and lowlands; there are even a few aquatic legumes.

1

The family is divided into three subfamilies:*

Caesalpinioideae. About 2,800 species, mainly trees of the tropical savannas and forests of Africa, South America, and Asia.

Mimosoideae. About 2,800 species, most conspicuous as small trees and shrubs of semiarid tropical and subtropical regions of Africa, North and South America, and Australia. Particularly numerous in the Southern Hemisphere. *Acacia* species are well-known examples.

Papilionoideae (alternative name, Faboideae). About 12,000 species, mainly herbs. Distributed worldwide.

All legumes bear pods, the characteristic by which they can most easily be recognized. The pods may be round, flat, or winged; long, short, thick, or thin; straight or coiled; papery or leathery; woody or fleshy. Some are not much bigger than a pinhead; one is the size of a tennis ball; others can be more than 1 m long. Usually the pod splits lengthwise, at one or both edges, to expose and release the seeds—from one to several dozen—that it contains.

Food Legumes

Legume seeds (also called beans, grain legumes, or pulses) are second only to cereals as a source of human and animal food. Nutritionally, they are 2–3 times richer in protein than cereal grains. Some—like soybeans, peanuts, and winged beans—are also rich in oil. Bean cultivation is very ancient; some species have been domesticated for as long as the major cereals and have been almost as basic to civilization's development.

Before the potato was introduced, beans constituted much of the diet of the poorer classes of Europe. Today, they remain as major foods in Latin America (especially the common bean, *Phaseolus vulgaris*), on the Indian subcontinent (especially lentils, *Lens esculenta*; pigeon peas, *Cajanus cajan*; and chick-peas, *Cicer arietinum*), and the Far East (especially soybeans).

There is a chronic protein deficiency in virtually every developing country. The "Green Revolution" has not increased the yields of pulses; indeed its emphasis on cereals has often led to decreased legume production. Only a similar revolution in the production of pulses can quickly eliminate protein malnutrition for the immediate future. A massive increase in vegetable protein supply in malnourished areas presents a less-difficult, less-expensive, and more energy-efficient prospect than boosting the supply of animal protein. Pulses are leading candidates, since they contain more protein than

*Sometimes treated as full families: Caesalpiniaceae, Mimosaceae, and Fabaceae (also known as Papilionaceae).

almost any other plant product. Many have protein contents between 20 and 40 percent. A few range between 40 and 60 percent. Thus, increased use of food legumes throughout the world should be encouraged.

Legumes offer a variety of edible products in addition to seeds. Many immature pods are edible during the 2 or 3 weeks before the fibers lignify and harden. At this stage they are still green and succulent and can be used as a green vegetable. Although they have less protein than the mature seed, they are rich in vitamins and soluble carbohydrates.

Leaves of leguminous plants are eaten in some parts of the world, particularly in the tropics. For example, *Pterocarpus* spp. are grown in southeastern Nigeria mainly for their leaves. However, this is always a local practice and, with few exceptions, has not yet been adopted widely. The use of edible legume leaves as food deserves increased study and promotion throughout the tropics.

Lesser-Known Uses of Legumes

Most people are unaware that legumes encompass far more than herbaceous annual crops grown only as table vegetables; and that they occur as vines, shrubs, and even as forest trees.

Many of the world's most exquisite flowering plants are legumes. In temperate climates, well-known examples include wisteria (*Wisteria* species), laburnum (*Laburnum* species), sweet peas (*Lathyrus odoratus*), and butterfly pea (*Clitoria ternatea*). But it is in the tropics that the largest number of different ornamental legumes is found. Indeed, some of the most characteristic plants of the tropics are legumes. These include the flamboyant or royal poinciana (*Delonix regia*), the golden shower (*Cassia fistula*), the pink-and-white shower (*Cassia nodosa*), pride of Barbados (*Caesalpinia pulcherrima*), orchid trees (*Bauhinia* species, especially *B. purpurea, B. variegata,* and *B. monandra*), cock's comb coral tree (*Erythrina crista-galli*), and the raintree (*Samanea saman*).

Some beautiful leguminous timbers (camwood from *Baphia nitida* and species of *Pterocarpus*, as well as various rosewoods from *Dalbergia* species, for example) have been in world markets for centuries and are among the lumbers most universally valued for cabinet work and carving. Indeed, a large number of leguminous tropical trees produce luxury timbers that command highest prices in international trade. But most of these are slow-growing trees and their cultivation in plantations remains untested. Accordingly, as the natural stands become logged out, these species can truly be labelled "vanishing timbers."*

*Examples include: *Afzelia* species, *Guibourtia* species, Rhodesian teak (*Baikiaea plurijuga*), purpleheart (*Peltogyne* species), *Acacia koa*, and partridge wood (*Vouacapoua americana*).

Other legume products include senna pods from *Cassia angustifolia* and related species, widely used for their laxative properties. Rotenone, an insecticide and fish poison, is extracted from species of *Derris, Lonchocarpus,* and *Tephrosia.* In Southeast Asia and India, twigs of several legumes are attacked by the tiny lac insect. Later, these twigs are collected and the sticky, resinous encrustations left by the insect are removed to produce shellac, long used as an electrical insulator and an ingredient in lacquer.

For several centuries the tonka bean (the seed of *Dipteryx odorata*) has been exported from South America as a spice to give vanilla-like scent to tobacco and foods, but recent concerns over the nutritional safety of coumarin, the active ingredient in the bean, have caused the trade's demise. The strongly scented seeds of fenugreek (*Trigonella foenum-graecum*) are also used as a spice to flavor curries, pickles, chutneys, imitation maple syrup, and other foods. They also contain diosgenin, a material used to synthesize oral contraceptives.

Some of the best copals—viscous resins famed for their toughness and durability in varnishes, paints, and lacquers—are produced from leguminous trees, particularly of the genera *Hymenaea* and *Copaifera.* A number of leguminous trees bear pods that provide a sweet pith that is eaten as a fruit.* And copaiba balsam, the oily liquid tapped from the heartwood of *Copaifera* species, is an ingredient still used in cough medicines and other preparations.

Many processed foods, for example mayonnaise and ice cream, contain gums from legumes such as *Acacia senegal* (gum arabic) or *Cyamopsis tetragonoloba* (guar). A common perfume ingredient is extracted from *Acacia farnesiana.* Licorice is extracted from the roots of a small leguminous herb, *Glycyrrhiza glabra.* The bark of *Acacia mearnsii* is a source of tannin for the world's leather industry.

Legumes are important to beekeepers, for they produce some of the finest honey in the world. Clover honey is famous in New Zealand, Australia, and the United States; alfalfa and mesquite (*Prosopis* species) honeys are also among the most valuable in the United States. Tropical tree legumes that make excellent bee pasture include *Pithecellobium* species, *Hymenaea courbaril, Inga* species, *Gliricidia sepium, Andira inermis,* and some *Acacia* species.

In previous centuries, when natural dyes were the only means of coloring fabrics, legumes were crucial in world commerce, and the quest for them played an important role in colonial development. Indigo, the brilliant blue dye (extracted from small shrubs of the genus *Indigofera*), was more widely used than any other. It became a major product of India, traded eastward to

---

*Including: West African locust beans (*Parkia biglobosa, Parkia clappertonia*), guaymochil (*Pithecellobium dulce*), raintree (*Samanea saman*), ice cream beans (*Inga* species), Tahiti chestnut (*Inocarpus fagiferus*), velvet tamarind (*Dialium guineense, D. indum,* and *D. ovoidum*), tallow tree (*Detarium senegalense*), namnam (*Cynometra cauliflora*), and courbaril (*Hymenaea courbaril*).

China and westward to Europe. More valued than spices, it was a major reason for establishing Portuguese, Dutch, and British colonies in India.*

In 1638 logwood (*Haematoxylon campechianum*), a small, gnarled leguminous tree, also stimulated the founding of British Honduras (now Belize). The purplish-red dye extracted from its heartwood had already been a major Spanish export from Central America for 100 years. Until late in the last century, British Honduras was still exporting over 100,000 t of it annually. Medical pathologists use it even today.

In South America, Portuguese traders found a small leguminous tree, *Caesalpinia echinata*, that yielded a wine-red dye virtually identical to bresil (from *Caesalpinia sappan*), a dye that Europe has been importing from Asia since the Middle Ages. It quickly became the most important product to be shipped to Portugal from the new land. The merchants and woodsmen eventually became known as bresilieros and the region as Brasil (Brazil). Today, the wood (known as Pernambuco) is used for violin bows.

Nitrogen Fixation

Legumes are crucial to the balance of nature, for many are able to convert nitrogen gas from the air into ammonia, a soluble form of nitrogen, which is readily utilized by plants. While a few other plant families include species with this ability, legumes produce the great mass of biologically fixed nitrogen.

The nitrogen contributions of legumes can be vital for maintaining soil productivity over long periods. A leguminous crop can add up to 500 kg of nitrogen to the soil per ha per year.†

Even today, cultivated legume crops add more nitrogen to the soil worldwide than do fertilizers. In Australia, the fertility increase effected by legumes has allowed vast areas to be brought into arable cultivation. Over 100 million ha have been planted in pasture legumes, principally to *Trifolium subterraneum* (subclover) and *Medicago tribuloides* (barrel medic) in the temperate areas, and *Stylosanthes humilis* (Townsville stylo) and siratro (*Macroptilium atropurpureum*) in the tropical areas. This is the first time that these species have been used in extensive agriculture. In addition, nitrogen from legumes (mostly from white clover, *Trifolium repens*) is the basis for New Zealand's exceptional pastoral economy. In the United States, legumes (especially alfalfa, soybeans, and peanuts) contribute about 2.4 million tons

---

*African or Yoruba indigo, still in widespread use for dyeing local prints in West Africa, is obtained from the leguminous tree *Lonchocarpus cyanescens*.

†National Academy of Sciences. 1977. *Leucaena: Promising Forage and Tree Crop for the Tropics*. To order see page 329.

of nitrogen a year, nearly one-fourth the amount of fertilizer nitrogen manufactured in the same period.

The conversion of atmospheric nitrogen to ammonia is actually accomplished by soil bacteria belonging to the genus *Rhizobium*. The bacteria infect
the legume root, and the plant, in reaction, forms swellings (nodules) on the
root surface. Within these nodules the rhizobia proliferate and thrive. There
they absorb air from the soil and, by processes not fully understood, "fix"
the nitrogen. The plant host absorbs much of the nitrogenous product and
uses it to produce protein, vitamins, and other nitrogen-containing compounds.

By using the nitrogen-fixing bacteria, legumes meet their needs for nitrogen without requiring fertilizer. Cereals, lacking this symbiotic arrangement,
have less seed protein and require soil nitrogen or fertilizer for satisfactory
growth.

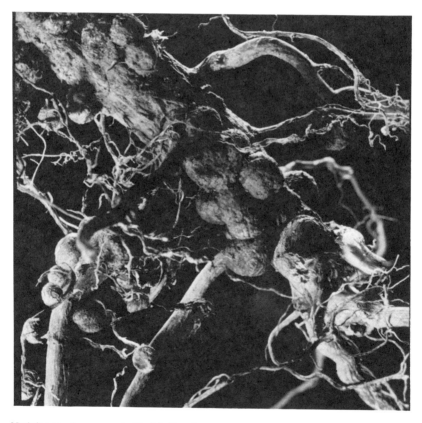

Nodules on a legume root. (Rodale Press)

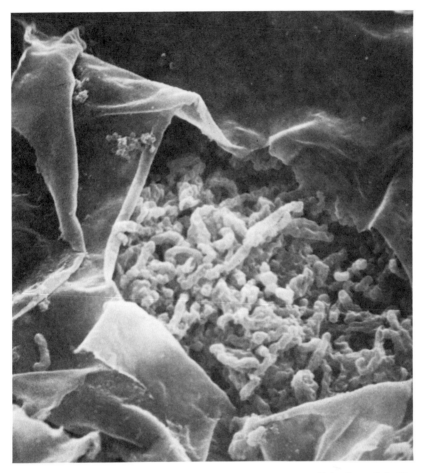

A legume root nodule opened to expose the dense mass of nitrogen-fixing bacteria inside. (W. J. Brill)

Most, but not all, legumes fix nitrogen. Although only one-tenth of the species have been checked, the results suggest that nodulation is fairly general in the Mimosoideae and Papilionoideae, but that only about 30 percent of Caesalpinioideae species bear nodules.

Inoculation

Leguminous plants only grow vigorously if they have functioning nodules, and this depends on their roots encountering appropriate *Rhizobium* strains in the soil. There are differences among *Rhizobium* strains. Some cannot infect the particular legume being grown; some invade the roots but bring no benefit to the host; others invade vigorously, producing effective nodules that continuously supply nitrogenous compounds to the plant.

In nature, the vigorously nodulating strains are usually found in soils where the particular legume species is native. When man introduces the plant to a region where it has never before been grown, the most effective nitrogen-fixing rhizobial strains may be lacking. Thus, when a legume is grown for the first time in a new area, it is crucial to ensure that appropriate rhizobia are likely to be present in the soil.

Some leguminous species accept and utilize a range of different *Rhizobium* strains, while in other cases a group of different legumes can all utilize the same *Rhizobium*. In these cases, the plant will grow well in soils of any location that previously supported a crop using a compatible *Rhizobium* strain. Luckily, this is a common situation, accounting for the widespread success in introducing leguminous plants to new regions.

For the major legume crops, appropriate strains of *Rhizobium* have been identified; cultures are available either commercially or from research institutions. The bacteria can be added directly to the soil, but usually the legume seed is coated with the culture so that, as the root emerges during germination, it is infected immediately.

Legumes and the Energy Crisis

The success of agriculture since World War II has depended on the availability of cheap, abundant energy that facilitated the use of fertilizers, pesticides, irrigation, and mechanization. Now, energy is no longer cheap nor abundant, and neither is fertilizer, especially nitrogenous fertilizer. Under pressures of population increases and shortages of energy and fertilizer, techniques that can increase food production without expending large quantities of energy are assuming great importance. Indeed, perhaps the most important task facing mankind today is to solve the problems of world hunger and malnutrition by methods that lessen exploitation of nonrenewable energy resources.

Atmospheric nitrogen is formed of twin atoms very tightly bound. It requires much energy to break them apart so that they can enter into compounds useful to living organisms. The Haber-Bosch process, the industrial process for splitting nitrogen, consumes large quantities of fossil fuel energy. Commercial fertilizer is now produced by first combining atmospheric nitrogen with the hydrogen of natural gas or the naphtha from oil fractionation. With fuel prices rising and gas production declining, fertilizer prices must increase.

The huge increase in fertilizer nitrogen costs in developing countries has perhaps been the most insidious effect of the recent energy crisis. A metric ton of fertilizer that cost $30 in 1972 had jumped to $140 by 1974. Under these conditions, legumes and biological nitrogen fixation take on new importance.

Legumes and Developing Countries

Malnutrition is usually prevalent where too few different plant foods are available. Animal protein is seldom affordable for the diets of the poor in developing countries, so legumes usually provide the chief—and sometimes the only—source of protein. A wider variety of food legumes can complement existing foods by providing additional protein and vitamins. There are useful species for almost every type of soil and climate; many species adapt well to a wide range of soils.

Legumes are especially important as a complement to carbohydrate staples such as rice, corn, and other cereals; and plantains, cassava, and other root and tuber crops. Pulses are proteinaceous foods that are as easily handled, stored, and transported as cereal grains. They are generally low in oil, but are important because of their high protein content and good protein quality.

Multipurpose plants abound in the Leguminosae. As noted in this report, many of them yield a multitude of end products. Such versatile crops offer important advantages to farmers in developing countries.

Toxins and Antinutritive Factors

Legumes contain a greater variety of toxic constituents than any other plant family. Some legume seeds are highly toxic; even among edible species some toxins occur. These compounds—flavonoids, alkaloids, nonprotein amino acids, and uncommon proteins—are often found in the leaves, pods, and seeds. Fortunately, many of the toxins can be neutralized in simple ways; for example, by soaking the seeds in water or by cooking them thoroughly. To avoid toxins, it is widespread practice in the Orient to treat pulses by fermentation (producing, for example, tempeh or soy sauce from soybeans), extracting the protein (as with tofu and soybean milk), or sprouting the seeds and eating the young seedlings. These processes produce wholesome, edible products essentially free of toxic materials.

Some compounds in legume seeds interfere with digestion without being truly toxic. Such metabolites occur in soybeans and many other pulses. They may inhibit the enzymes that digest protein or they may impede the absorption of amino acids from the digestive tract, both of which cause protein to be wasted. Dry beans also may contain compounds that cause flatulence and others that agglutinate certain blood types.

It is important that researchers take up the challenge of how best to neutralize the antinutrition factors and thus improve the food value of legume seeds. Promising lines of attack include genetic manipulation of the plants as well as processing the seeds by dehulling, milling away the seed coat, soaking, heating, and fermentation, or by treatment with acid, alkali, or sodium bicarbonate.

In legume protein the relative proportions of the essential amino acids are not as well balanced for human dietary requirements as in meat, milk, or fish. Nonetheless, legume protein usually contains more than adequate levels of some of the nutritionally important amino acids, such as lysine, that are deficient in most cereals and other edible plant groups. The combination of cereals and legumes provides a very good balance of amino acids, since the cereals usually supply adequate methionine.

*   *   *

A summary follows of the plants and topics selected by the panel for their promise.

Root Crops

Yam Beans (*Pachyrhizus* species). These plants of Central and South America produce large, swollen roots and have been feeding people since the dawn of history. Palatable, nutritious, and productive, they deserve the attention of modern science. (Page 21.)

African Yam Bean (*Sphenostylis stenocarpa*). This root crop from Africa produces a nutritious seed, as well as edible tubers and leaves. It can be grown in inherently infertile, weathered soils where the rainfall is extremely high. Although highly regarded among people of tropical Africa, the crop is virtually unknown elsewhere. It has received essentially no research attention or recognition from agricultural researchers. (Page 27.)

Other Root Crops. In some rural areas of the world, native tribes eat tubers harvested from wild legumes. Some tribes even cultivate tuber-producing legumes. Most of the species they use have been entirely neglected by science, though the few that have been analyzed show a remarkably high protein content—several times higher than that of the root crops now eaten throughout the tropics. The study and improvement of these little-known plants should provide exciting and valuable research. (Page 32.)

For an additional example of root crop species, see: Marama Bean, Page 68.

Pulses

Bambara Groundnut (*Voandzeia subterranea*). This African pulse is a rare example in which nature provides a complete food. Although its seeds have less oil and protein than peanuts, they do have more carbohydrate and make a well-balanced food with a calorific value equal to that of a high-quality cereal grain. The seeds taste good and Africans often prefer them to peanuts. While extensive research attention has been devoted to the peanut, the bambara groundnut has received almost none. Yet it can thrive in arid inferior soils where peanuts fail, it resists pests and diseases, and, if managed well, can give high yields. (Page 47.)

Jackbean and Swordbean (*Canavalia ensiformis* and *Canavalia gladiata*). Although their seeds are eaten in parts of the tropics, these hardy, vigorous, productive pulse crops are negligible contributors to the world's food supply because the seeds contain compounds that retard human and animal growth. If the growth-retarding toxins can be bred out or removed in cooking or processing, the jackbean and swordbean would produce high-quality protein in a wide range of climates and become major food sources for marginal regions where other pulses cannot be produced. (Page 54.)

Lablab Bean (*Lablab purpureus*). One of the most prolific of all leguminous herbs, this plant is widely used as animal feed and as a cover crop in plantations of coconut, rubber, and oil palm. But, despite its ubiquitousness, its nutritious, high-protein seeds remain a greatly underexploited source of human food. (Page 59.)

Marama Bean (*Tylosema esculentum*). Although it is a wild plant not previously cultivated, the plant's seeds have more protein than the peanut and more than twice the oil in soybeans. They also have a delicious flavor. The plant grows in the dry Kalahari region of southern Africa—and given much research it might become an important new oilseed crop for semiarid lands. In addition, it produces a huge, sugar-beet-sized, tuberous root that is sweet and probably nutritious. (Page 68.)

Moth Bean (*Vigna aconitifolia*). An exceptionally hardy South Asian legume that thrives in hot, dry, tropical conditions, the moth bean produces nutritious seeds and green pods, leafy forage for hay or pasture, and a soil-building "living mulch" to complement orchard crops and to protect and improve fallow land. Nonetheless, the moth bean remains virtually untouched by modern science and unknown outside the Indian subcontinent. It has characteristics that could make it valuable for torrid, semiarid regions throughout the tropics. It is likely to prove very useful in extending agricultural production into marginal regions—especially those bordering tropical arid zones. (Page 75.)

Rice Bean (*Vigna umbellata*). This very productive twining legume from India produces nutritious seeds. Although virtually unstudied heretofore, it seems to offer much potential for widespread exploitation throughout the wet tropics. A rapid-growing, fast-maturing plant, it can be sown in rice fields immediately following the rice harvest, where it will produce a crop of seeds before the next rice-planting season. (Page 80.)

Tarwi (*Lupinus mutabilis*). Although not a crop for tropical temperatures, tarwi has its native habitat in the high Andes straddling the equator. It is a vigorously growing, prolific lupin whose seeds are as rich as soybeans in protein and oil. Tarwi is not contributing to the world's food needs because toxic alkaloids are also present in the seed. Plant breeders have recently developed strains with almost no alkaloid. This opens the prospect for tarwi to rise from obscurity to become a crop for cool tropical highlands and for temperate zones. (Page 86.)

Tepary Bean (*Phaseolus acutifolius*). Although little known elsewhere, tepary bean has long been grown for food by the Indians of the southwestern United States and northwestern Mexico. It has the advantage of maturing quickly and of thriving in relatively arid and hot regions, as well as in sterile soil. (Page 92.)

Tropical Lima Bean (*Phaseolus lunatus*). Viny varieties of the lima bean are prolific and have been much used as a forage in the tropics. They also have potential importance as pulses, since they grow productively in tropical rainforest areas where the soils are highly weathered and are inherently of low fertility. (Page 97.)

Ye-eb (*Cordeauxia edulis*). This shrub, unknown outside the Horn of Africa, has an exciting potential as a profitable cash crop for tropical arid zones. Its seeds have a sweet, agreeable taste and have been compared with macadamia and pistachio nuts. During the Sahelian drought of recent years, ye-eb seeds were one of the few foods available in the Somali Desert; consequently, nomadic tribes (and their livestock) have devastated the few native stands remaining. Ye-eb is now threatened with extinction and deserves careful protection and detailed testing in cultivation. (Page 103.)

For additional examples of pulse species, see:

African Yam Bean Page 27
Velvet Bean   Page 293

Fruits

Carob (*Ceratonia siliqua*). The sugar-rich, mealy pulp contained in carob pods has for millenia been a favorite of people in hot, dry areas of the Mediterranean basin. The handsome, drought-tolerant carob tree deserves more research and widespread exploitation in semiarid areas, for in addition to pulp it provides a chocolate substitute, high-protein flour, and an industrial gum, as well as shade, beautification, erosion control, and forage. (Page 109.)

Tamarind (*Tamarindus indica*). India is the only country to extensively exploit this tall, spreading tree, a native of Africa now found scattered throughout the tropics. Though in commercial demand for centuries, with its products now exported by India all over the world, the tamarind remains a largely unimproved and little-cultivated crop. Up to half the weight of a tamarind pod is pulp with a sweet-sour taste, much in demand for use in sauces (e.g., Worcestershire sauce) and refreshing drinks. (Page 117.)

For additional examples of fruit species, see:

Erythrina	Page 257
Honeylocust	Page 129
Raintree	Page 202

Forage

Forage Shrubs and Trees. Woody plants that provide feed for livestock are now largely ignored in programs researching and developing improved forage for tropical regions. Yet browse shrubs and trees complement (and often benefit) herbaceous pasture species and can be crucial to the nutrition—even the survival—of animals, especially during drought, when shallow-rooted species shrivel to straw. Woody fodder species deserve much greater recognition and attention. Leguminous trees able to fix nitrogen, and with protein-rich foliage, pods, and seeds and general robustness, are likely to enormously benefit developing country livestock programs in the future. This chapter presents some promising species—others await discovery and exploitation. (Page 123.)

Acacia tortilis. This thorny, flat-topped bush is one of the most drought-tolerant trees of semiarid areas of Africa and the Middle East. Although now seldom cultivated, it could become an extremely useful species for semiarid areas worldwide, for it produces pods at a rapid rate that are eagerly snapped up by livestock and wildlife alike. It also stabilizes soil, reforests arid hillslopes, and provides lumber and excellent firewood. (Page 136.)

Other Forage *Acacias.* Species of *Acacia* are important as reserve fodder in several parts of the tropics and subtropics in arid regions. The leaves and the nutritive pods are browsed or the trees are lopped to provide fodder. They are also grown for shade trees and soil improvers and for binding sand dunes or controlling soil erosion. (Page 141.)

Prosopis **Species.** These trees or shrubs of the Americas are drought resistant and well adapted to light soils and arid regions of warmer climates. The young foliage, as well as the pods and beans, are relished by all farm animals and can be browsed or lopped without causing much damage to the trees. The wood is hard and valuable, and the flowers are an excellent honey source. (Page 153.)

For additional examples of forage species, see:

Fast-Growing Trees

Acacia auriculiformis. A rugged, robust, but little-known tree of the New Guinea area, this species has grown with exceptional vigor in Southeast Asia in problem soils such as eroding hillslopes, mining spoil, laterite, and sand, as well as in highly acid and alkaline sites. Although it produces crooked trunks of little value for timber, the wood is suitable for pulp and paper products. A fast-growing species that deserves much increased testing, especially in tropical savanna areas with long dry seasons and poor soils. (Page 165.)

Albizia **Species.** Species of the genus *Albizia* are distinguished from *Acacia* by small differences in floral structure. But whereas—as this report amply demonstrates—acacias provide a wealth of trees and shrubs with exceptional utility, *Albizia* species have received little research attention. Nonetheless, some members of this genus appear to have exceptional merits, and this chapter highlights some that grow with remarkable speed and provide softwood products, as well as others that grow more slowly and produce high-quality timbers. (Page 171.)

Sesbania grandiflora. This Southeast Asian tree grows exceptionally fast and provides an amazing range of products: edible leaves, flowers, and gum, as well as forage, firewood, pulp and paper, and green manure. It is also used as a shade tree, ornamental, nurse crop, and living fence. It has extraordinarily prolific nodulation and could become valuable for village use and for large-scale reforestation throughout much of the tropics. (Page 185.)

Other Fast-Growing Trees. Many woody legumes are pioneer species that colonize newly cleared sites. To outdo the competition, they grow fast and are very precocious and vigorous trees that nodulate well. With the desperate need for reforestation, erosion control, firewood, and paper, as well as other wood products in developing countries, many such leguminous trees are worth widespread testing. This chapter highlights nine exceptional candidates. (Page 193.)

For additional examples of fast-growing tree species, see:

Acacia pendula	Page 146
Acacia tortilis	Page 136
Leucaena leucocephala	Page 131
Moldenhauera floribunda	Page 259
Other Forage Acacias	Page 141
Peltophorum Species	Page 260
Pithecellobium grandiflorum	Page 261
Prosopis Species	Page 153

Luxury Timbers

Afrormosia (*Pericopsis elata*). This large, eye-catching tree produces a wood that rivals teak in quality. It deserves testing in plantations throughout the humid tropics. (Page 211.)

***Intsia* Species.** These trees from Southeast Asia and Melanesia produce highest-quality furniture woods that can be substituted for walnut. Demand for the wood already far exceeds the supply. Slow growing, but well worth testing in Africa, Latin America, Oceania, and elsewhere. (Page 216.)

***Pterocarpus* Species.** Philippine narra (*Pterocarpus indicus*), which gives prime-grade timber highly regarded in Southeast Asia, is large and straight trunked. Little is yet known about growth rates or general silviculture of this promising species. Other *Pterocarpus* species are native throughout the tropics, produce similar luxury timbers, and also deserve research. (Page 221.)

Rosewoods. Some of the classic furniture and finest veneer woods—renowned for vivid colors, striking grain, and exceptional technical properties—rosewoods come from species of *Dalbergia*, slow-growing leguminous trees that are being harvested to commercial extinction. This chapter highlights a dozen species from all parts of the tropics that deserve exploratory silviculture to find if they can be cultivated. (Page 231.)

Others

Ornamentals. Cleanliness and beauty can be important factors in leading people to take pleasure in, and thus respect, their environment. In this process, plants carefully chosen and positioned and well cultivated play an important role. This chapter describes some beautiful leguminous species that should be far more widely known and more extensively planted. (Page 239.)

For additional examples of ornamental species, see:

Acacia auriculiformis	Page 165
Acacia pendula	Page 146
Acacia senegal	Page 279
Acrocarpus fraxinifolius	Page 195
African Yam Bean	Page 27
Apios americana	Page 40
Calliandra callothyrsus	Page 197
Cassia sturtii	Page 124
Lablab Bean	Page 59
Pterocarpus Species	Page 221
Raintree	Page 202
Rosewoods	Page 231
Schizolobium parahyba	Page 204
Sesbania grandiflora	Page 185
Tipuana tipu	Page 205

Sunnhemp (*Crotalaria juncea*). Sunnhemp is grown for fiber or as a green manure. Because of its strong tap-root system, it thrives in poor soils and relatively arid regions. Sunnhemp fiber is valued and in great market demand, and intensive research on this crop could lead to marked expansion in its cultivation. (Page 272.)

Gums. Many legumes produce copious quantities of water-soluble mucilaginous carbohydrates. In some species such gums are found within the seeds, but in woody species (e.g., acacias) the gum exudes from the bark when it is damaged. For centuries these gums have been used in foods and medicines and today they are in great demand by food and cosmetics industries. Several species with exceptional promise as gum crops are highlighted in this chapter. (Page 278.)

For additional examples of gum species, see:

Acacia auriculiformis	Page 165
Acacia seyal	Page 150
Acacia victoriae	Page 148
Albizia Species	Page 171
Carob	Page 109
Sesbania grandiflora	Page 185
Tamarind	Page 117

Green Manure, Soil Reclamation, and Erosion Control. As already noted, *Rhizobium* bacteria in the root nodules confer on many legumes the power of nitrogen fixation. This allows legumes to survive, grow, and dominate other vegetation on refractory sites subject to erosion, low fertility, and similar adverse soil conditions. Legumes can help spearhead the fight to stop the erosion now prevalent in the tropics and can help rebuild the soils already damaged and degraded. Some exceptionally innovative and successful examples of using them this way are pictured in the chapter. (Page 292.)

Selected Readings

Allen, O. N., and E. Hamatova, compilers. 1973. *IBP World Catalogue of Rhizobium Collections*, F. A. Skinner, ed. International Biological Programme, Section P. P. (Production Processes). Knapp, Drewett and Sons, Ltd., Kingston-upon-Thames, London.

Asian Vegetable Research and Development Center. 1977. *Progress Report for 1976*. Shanhua, Taiwan. 77 pp.

Ayanaba, A., and P. J. Dart, eds. 1977. *Biological Nitrogen Fixation in Farming Systems of the Tropics*. John Wiley and Sons, New York. 378 pp.

Aykroyd, W. R., and J. Doughty. 1964. *Legumes in Human Nutrition*. Food and Agriculture Organization Nutritional Study No. 19. Food and Agriculture Organization of the United Nations, Rome. 138 pp.

The Bean Bag. A newsletter published quarterly by a volunteer team of legume specialists, contains information of interest to legume taxonomists. (Distributed by Richard Cowan, Division of Botanical Sciences, Smithsonian Institution, Washington, D.C. 20560, USA.)

The Bean Improvement Cooperative (c/o M. H. Dickson, Department of Seed and Vegetable Sciences, Hedrick Hall, New York State Agricultural Experiment Station, Geneva, New York 14456, USA). A voluntary and informal organization established to effect the exchange of information and materials among researchers working on edible legumes. The Cooperative's extensive annual report is a gold mine of new information.

Bulletin of the International Group for the Study of Mimosoideae. Secretary J. Vassal, Laboratoire de Botanique et Biogeographie, Université Paul Sabtier, 39 Alleés J. Guesde, 31077 Toulouse Cedex, France.

Burkart, A. 1952. *Las Leguminosas Argentinas*. Acme Agency, Buenos Aires.

Corby, H. D. L. 1974. Systematic implications of nodulation among Rhodesian legumes. *Kirkia* 9:301-329.

Douglas, J. S., and R. A. de J. Hart. 1976. *Forest Farming*. Watkins, London. 197 pp.

Food and Agriculture Organization of the United Nations. 1959. *Tabulated Information on Tropical and Subtropical Grain Legumes*. Plant Production and Protection Division, Food and Agriculture Organization of the United Nations, Rome. 367 pp.

Food and Agriculture Organization of the United Nations. 1970. *Amino-Acid Content of Foods and Biological Data on Proteins*. Food Policy and Food Science Service, Nutrition Division, Food and Agriculture Organization of the United Nations, Rome. 285 pp.

Goor, A. Y., and C. W. Barney. 1976. *Forest Tree Planting in Arid Zones*. The Ronald Press Company, New York. 504 pp.

Hall, N., R. W. Boden, C. S. Christian, R. W. Condon, F. A. Dale, A. J. Hart, J. H. Leigh, J. K. Marshall, A. G. McArthur, V. Russell, and J. W. Turnbull. 1972. *The Use of Trees and Shrubs in the Dry Country of Australia*. Department of National Development, Foresty and Timber Bureau, Canberra, Australia. 558 pp.

Harborne, J. B., D. Boulter, and B. L. Turner, eds. 1971. *Chemotaxonomy of Leguminosae*. Academic Press, London and New York. 612 pp.

Herklots, G. A. C. 1972. *Vegetables in South-East Asia*. Hafner Press, New York. 525 pp.

Herklots, G. A. C. 1976. *Flowering Tropical Climbers*. Wm. Sawson and Sons, Ltd, Folkestone, Kent, England; and Science History Publications, New York. 194 pp.

International Institute of Tropical Agriculture. 1973. *Proceedings of the First IITA Grain Legume Improvement Workshop 29 October-2 November 1973, Ibadan*. International Institute of Tropical Agriculture, Ibadan, Nigeria. 320 pp.

Jay, B. A. 1968. *Timbers of West Africa*. Timber Research and Development Association, Hughenden Valley, Bucks, England. 98 pp.

Jones, O., and F. R. Earle. 1966. Chemical analyses of seeds II: Oil and protein content of 759 species. *Economic Botany* 20:127-155.

Kay, D. E. 1978. *Food Legumes*. TPI Crop and Product Digest No. 3. Tropical Products Institute, London. 556 pp.

Kooiman, H. N. 1931. Monograph on the genetics of *Phaseolus*. *Bibliographiea Genetica* 8:295-413.

Menninger, E. A. 1962. *Flowering Trees of the World, for Tropics and Warm Climates*. Hearthside Press, Inc., New York. 336 pp.

Menninger, E. A. 1970. *Flowering Vines of the World*. Hearthside Press, Inc., New York. 410 pp.

Milner, M., ed. 1975. *Nutritional Improvement of Food Legumes by Breeding*. Wiley Interscience, New York. 400 pp.

Mors, W. B., and C. T. Rizzini. 1966. *Useful Plants of Brazil*. Holden-Day, Inc., San Francisco. 166 pp.

Nutman, P. S., ed. 1976. *Symbiotic Nitrogen Fixation in Plants*. Cambridge University Press, Cambridge. 584 pp.

Purseglove, J. W. 1968. *Tropical Crops: Dicotyledons I*. John Wiley and Sons, New York. pp. 199-332.

Quispel, A. 1974. *The Biology of Nitrogen Fixation*. North-Holland Publishing Co., Amsterdam.

Rachie, K. O., and L. M. Roberts. 1974. Grain legumes of the lowland tropics. In *Advances in Agronomy* 26:1-132. (Reprints available from the International Institute of Tropical Agriculture, P.M.B.5320, Ibadan, Nigeria.)

Rachie, K. O., and P. Silvestre. 1977. Grain legumes. In *Food Crops of the Lowland Tropics*, pp. 41-74. Oxford University Press, London.

Record, S. J., and R. W. Hess. 1972 (reprint of 1943 edition). *Timbers of the New World*. Arno Press, New York. pp. 227-336.

Rhizobium Newsletter, J. Brockwell, R. A. Date, and A. H. Gibson, eds., Microbiology Section. P.O. Box 1600, Canberra, A.C.T. 2601, Australia. Published twice a year. Provides abstracts and a forum for workers to exchange information and ideas about *Rhizobium*.

Schery, R. W. 1972. *Plants for Man*. Prentice-Hall, Inc., Englewood Cliffs, New Jersey. 657 pp.

Sinha, S. K. 1977. *Food Legumes: Distribution, Adaptability and Biology of Yield*. Plant Production and Protection Paper 3. Food and Agriculture Organization of the United Nations, Rome. 124 pp. (Describes chickpeas, cowpeas, lentils, other pulses, soybeans, peanuts. Order AGPC MISC/36.)

Skerman, P. J. 1977. *Tropical Forage Legumes*. FAO Plant Production and Protection Series No. 2. Food and Agriculture Organization of the United Nations, Rome. 609 pp.

Smartt, J. 1976. *Tropical Pulses*. Longman Group Ltd., London. 348 pp.

Smith, C. R., Jr., M. C. Shekleton, I. A. Wolff, and Q. Jones. 1959. Seed protein sources—amino acid composition and total protein content of various plant seeds. *Economic Botany* 13:132-150.

Sprague, H. B. 1975. *The Contribution of Legumes to Continuously Productive Agricultural Systems for the Tropics and Subtropics*. Technical Series Bulletin No. 12. Office of Agriculture, Technical Assistance Bureau, Agency for International Development, Washington, D.C. 42 pp.

Stanton, W. R., J. Doughty, R. Orraca-Tetteh, and W. Steele. 1966. *Grain Legumes in Africa*. Food and Agriculture Organization of the United Nations, Rome. 183 pp.

Terra, G. J. A. 1966. *Tropical Vegetables*. Department of Agricultural Research of the Royal Tropical Institute and Foundation, Netherlands Organization for International Assistance (NOVIB), Amsterdam. 107 pp.

Tropical Grain Legume Bulletin. Published quarterly by the International Grain Legume Information Centre, International Institute of Tropical Agriculture, P.M.B. 5320, Ibadan, Nigeria. Provides a forum for research and extension workers to exchange information and ideas about tropical grain legume research and development.

Vincent, J. M. 1970. *A Manual for the Practical Study of Roots-Nodule Bacteria*. IBP Handbook No. 15. Blackwell Scientific Publications, Oxford.

Vincent, J. M., A. S. Whitney, and J. Bose, eds. 1977. *Exploiting the Legume-Rhizobium Symbiosis in Tropical Agriculture*. College of Tropical Agriculture Miscellaneous Publication 145. Department of Agronomy and Soil Science, University of Hawaii, Honolulu 96822. USA. 469 pp.

Weber, F. R. 1977. *Reforestation in Arid Lands*. Volunteers in Technical Assistance (VITA), 3706 Rhode Island Avenue, Mt. Rainier, Maryland 20822, USA. 248 pp.

Westphal, E. 1974. *Pulses in Ethiopia, Their Taxonomy and Agricultural Significance*. Centre for Agricultural Publishing and Documentation, Wageningen, The Netherlands. 276 pp.

Whyte, R. O., G. Nilsson-Leissner, and H. C. Trumble. 1953 (reprinted 1966). *Legumes in Agriculture*. Food and Agriculture Organization of the United Nations, Rome. 367 pp.

I Root Crops

Yam Bean

Yam beans,* like potatoes, yams, and manioc, produce a fleshy underground tuberous root. But yam beans have the legume family advantage: the rhizobia in their root nodules make nitrogenous compounds available to the plants and even enrich the soil in which they are grown.

Yet yam beans remain a primitive crop. There has never been a concerted effort to advance it, despite the fact that root crops are much in demand throughout the tropics and that yam beans grow easily and resist pests. Further, they grow well in the difficult environment of the hot wet tropics (such as the Amazon Basin) and, with their succulence and crunchy texture, appeal to most palates. They are increasingly exported from Mexico to the United States in part to supplement scarce water chestnuts used in Chinese cooking and as a low-calorie snack food.

Two edible yam beans are known. *Pachyrhizus erosus* is native to southwestern Mexico, *Pachyrhizus tuberosus* to the Amazon headwater region of South America and to parts of the Caribbean. Centuries ago, *P. erosus* was carried to Asia with the Spanish galleons that annually voyaged from Mexico to the Philippines; it became a favorite crop of Chinese market gardeners throughout Asia. In 1889, the Royal Botanic Gardens at Kew distributed *P. tuberosus* widely throughout tropical British colonies, but today, though it is

*Pachyrhizus erosus (L.) Urban and *Pachyrhizus tuberosus* (Lam.) Spreng. Sometimes spelled *Pachyrrhizus.* Not to be confused with the African yam bean, *Sphenostylis stenocarpa* (see next chapter). Also known as Mexican yam bean, jicama (Mexico), ahipa (South America), dolique tubereux (French), pais patate (French), knollige bohne (German), fan-ko (Chinese), sankalu (India), sinkamas (Philippines). Subfamily: Papilionoideae.

Yam bean seller, Guanajuato Mexico. (Instituto Nacional de Investigaciones Agricolas SARH, Mexico)

a favorite food in the West Indies, it is apparently little known in Asia, Africa, Oceania, and most parts of Central America.

The two species differ only in size: *P. tuberosus* produces much larger roots (some botanists have speculated that it is perhaps only a variety of *P. erosus* selected for cultivation because of its large roots).

Yam bean plants are among the most vigorous-growing legumes. They are coarse, hairy, climbing vines that grow rapidly, can reach 5 m in length, and bear many beautiful white or violet flowers. Although they grow well in locations ranging from subtropical to tropical and dry to wet, for good yields they require a hot climate with moderate rainfall.* They tolerate some

*By starting the seeds indoors during the spring, yam beans have been grown successfully even in temperate climates (e.g., Massachusetts, USA).

Yam bean field, central Mexico. (C.A. Schroeder)

drought but are sensitive to frost. As with other root crops, the soil should be light and well drained so as not to restrict tuber growth or encourage fungal rot. The plants are easily propagated by seed and, except for good manuring of the soil before planting and then staking, require little attention.

When the plants are propagated from seed, 5-9 warm months are needed to produce large tubers, but propagating the crop using small tubers greatly reduces the growing time. In warmer parts of Mexico with light, rich soil, mature tubers are commonly harvested after only 3 months.

In some areas, to encourage large, sweet roots, the flowers are plucked by hand.* This doubles the yield of the roots. Yields average a respectable 40-50 t per ha throughout Mexico's Bajio region and Morelos State (where about 4,000 ha are planted each year).† In experimental plots, staggering yields of 80 or 90 t per ha have been reported from Mexico, the Philippines, and Indonesia.

The brownish tubers are either sugar-beet shaped or long and slender, weighing up to 3 kg. They have a thick, tough skin that peels off easily, exposing the white flesh beneath, which is crisp and succulent like that of an apple, with a sweet, pleasant flavor. Yam beans are often sliced thin and eaten raw in green salads (sometimes sprinkled with salt, chili pepper, and lemon juice) or in fruit salads (combined with such fruit as melon, watermelon, and papaya). They are also sometimes lightly cooked. Unlike most other root crops, the crunchy texture is retained even after cooking. In general, the tubers are handled, stored, and marketed like potatoes.

The plant forms clusters of irregularly shaped root nodules. It is associated with the general "cowpea-miscellany" rhizobia.

---

*In equatorial regions this appears unnecessary, for the tuber is already formed before flowering begins.
†Information supplied by J.A. Laborde C. and A. Díaz A. See Research Contacts.

Pachyrhizus tuberosus growing vigorously in the Amazon near Manaus, Brazil, (W. Kerr)

Limitations

Only the tuber is safe to eat. Leaves, stems, roots, ripe pods, and seeds possess insecticidal properties and can also be toxic to humans. In Central America immature pods are sometimes eaten,* but care and experience are necessary to avoid toxic effects.

Yam beans require well-drained soils and respond to applications of fertilizers. When they are planted in the same plot for several years, it is necessary to add compost or fertilizer to maintain productivity.

Some foliar diseases are known: bacterial spot and two fungal diseases have caused minor to severe damage in Mexico. Insect damage is very slight, possibly because of the presence of insecticidal compounds. In the field, the

---

*They are actually reported to be one of the most delicious green beans to be found in Philippine markets.

roots are sometimes attacked by boring insects. Storing the roots can be a special problem due both to shriveling and pests.

Although on a dry weight basis the roots contain 3–5 times the protein of other root crops (such as cassava, potato, sweet potato, and taro), the fresh roots have an unusually high moisture content, which decreases their nutritive value; the proportion of solids in fresh yam beans is only about half that in other tubers.

Research Needs

To provide the basis for the rational development of yam beans, a Latin American agricultural research institution should stimulate comprehensive germ plasm collections throughout Central and South America.

The plants now cultivated show a wide diversity of characteristics. Over the extensive geographical area where they are cultivated—from Mexico to the Andes—yam beans are produced in many different environments; from sea level to as high as 2,000 m; in semiarid and wet, humid regions; in poor soils and rich soils. It should be possible to take advantage of the yam bean's adaptive traits and—given a comprehensive germ plasm collection—to select varieties with superior yield, root characteristics, nutritive value, pest and disease resistance, and other agronomic characteristics.* Special attention should be given to differences in tuber-protein content and perhaps quality; it seems likely that types with exceptional protein levels will be found.

Because in tropical environments the seed remains viable for only 3 or 4 years, duplicates of all seed collections should be housed under controlled temperature and humidity at a modern seed bank (perhaps at the Centro Internacional de Agricultura Tropical in Cali, Colombia).

Methods used for growing yam beans throughout the Central and South American region should be reviewed, and concerted research programs organized to apply modern agronomic knowledge to yam bean production. Spacing, fertilization, irrigation, and other cultural trials are needed. The knowledge gained will have value for millions of peasant yam bean farmers throughout the hemisphere.†

Yam beans deserve to be more widely introduced in Africa, Asia, and Oceania. Agronomists in these areas are encouraged to communicate with the research contacts (page 26).

---

*A start on this has already been made in Mexico where two new cultivars, *Aguadulce* and *Cristalina*, are rapidly replacing the creole types formerly grown. Information supplied by J.A. Laborde C. and A. Díaz A. See Research Contacts.

†An extension pamphlet (in Spanish) for Mexican farmers that explains how to plant and cultivate yam beans is available from Instituto Nacional de Investigaciones Agricolas, Celaya, Mexico. See Research Contacts.

New World agronomists should also investigate *Pachyrhizus* species other than *P. erosus* and *P. tuberosus*. It is possible that useful varieties await discovery.

Their high moisture content makes yam beans shrivel and lose condition more quickly than other root crops. Improved storage and transportation methods are needed and perhaps cultivars with thicker epiderm.

The nodulation requirements of *Pachyrhizus* should be studied in detail.

Selected Readings

A yam bean bibliography, with more than 120 entries, is available from C. A. Schroeder, and a set of notes summarizing botanical and agronomic knowledge is available from J. A. Duke (addresses below).

Bautista, O. D. K., and T. G. Cadiz. 1967. Sinkamas in the Philippines. In *Vegetable Production in Southeast Asia*, eds., J. E. Knott and J. R. Deanon, Jr., pp. 301-305. University of the Philippines, College of Agriculture, Los Baños, Laguna, Philippines.

Boutin, F. C. 1974. Two jicamas, *Exogonium bracteatum* and *Pachyrrhizus erosus*. *California Horticultural Journal* 35(4):159-161.

Clausen, R. T. 1944. *A Botanical Study of the Yam Beans* (Pachyrrhizus). Memoir 264. Agricultural Experiment Station, Cornell University, Ithaca, New York. 38 pp.

Díaz, A., A. 1977. *El Cultivo de la Jicama en el Estado de Guanajuato*. Campo Agrícola Experimental, Bajio, Apartado Postal No. 112, Celaya, Guanajuato, Mexico.

Evans, I. M., D. Boulter, A. R. J. Eaglesham, and P. J. Dart. 1977. Protein content and protein quality of tuberous roots of some legumes determined by chemical methods. *Qualitas Plantarum/Plant Food for Human Nutrition* 27(3/4):275-285.

Heredia, Zepeda, A. 1971. Efecto de la desfloración de la jicama sobre el rendimiento. *Proceedings of the American Society for Horticulture Science, Tropical Region* 15:146-150.

Kay, D. E. 1973. *Root Crops*. Tropical Products Institute, 56/62 Gray's Inn Road, London WC1X 8LU, England. pp. 240-245.

Pinto Cortes, B. 1970. Cultivo de la jicama. *Novedades Horticolas* 15: 31-34.

Purseglove, J. W. 1968. *Tropical Crops: Dicotyledons I*. John Wiley and Sons, New York. pp. 281-284.

Schroeder, C. A. 1967. The jicama, a root crop from Mexico. *Proceedings of the American Society for Horticulture Science, Tropical Region* 11:65-71. (Reprints available from the author, see address below.)

Sinha, R. P., R. Prakash, and M. F. Haque. 1977. Genetic variability in yam bean (*Pachyrhizus erosus* Urban). *Tropical Grain Legume Bulletin* 7:21-23. (Published by the International Grain Legume Information Centre, see address below.)

Sinha, R. P., R. Prakash, and M. F. Haque. 1977. Genotypic and phenotypic correlation studies in yam bean (*Pachyrhizus erosus*). *Tropical Grain Legumes Bulletin* 7:24-25.

Srivastava, G. S., D. S. Shukla, and D. N. Awasthi. 1973. We can grow sankalu in the plains of Uttar Pradesh. *Indian Farming* 23(9):32.

The Tropical Grain Legume Bulletin often contains short articles and abstracts on yam beans. The *Bulletin* is available from the International Grain Legume Information Centre (see address below).

Research Contacts

Yam bean seeds (usually listed under the name jicama) are available from several large seed and nursery firms in the United States.

Centro Internacional de Agricultura Tropical, Apartado Aereo 67-13, Cali, Colombia (R. A. Luse and L. P. Song)

Department of Biology, University of California at Los Angeles, Los Angeles, California 90024, USA (Charles A. Schroeder)

Department of Botany, University of the Philippines at Los Baños, College, Laguna, Philippines (G. C. Lugod)

International Grain Legume Information Centre, International Institute of Tropical Agriculture, P.M.B. 5320, Ibadan, Nigeria

Instituto Nacional de Investigaciones Agricolas (INIA), Apartado Postal No. 112, Celaya, Guanajuato, Mexico (J. A. Laborde C. and A. Díaz A.)

Instituto Nacional de Pesquisas de Amazonia Caixa Postal 478, Manaus, Amazonas, Brazil (Warwick E. Kerr, Director, and H. Noda)

Mayaguez Institute of Tropical Agriculture, P.O. Box 70, Mayaguez, Puerto Rico 00708

National Botanic Gardens, Lucknow, Uttar Pradesh, India (G. S. Srivastava, D. S. Shukla, and S. N. Awasthi)

NifTAL Project, University of Hawaii, P.O. Box "O", Paia, Hawaii 96779, USA (S. Whitney and P. Woomer)

Plant Taxonomy Laboratory, Plant Genetics and Germ Plasm Institute, Beltsville, Maryland 20705, USA (James A. Duke, Chief)

Dr. M. R. Villanueva, Secretary, Philippine Root Crops Research and Training Center, 8 Lourdes St., Pasay City, Philippines

African Yam Bean

So little is known about the African yam bean* that virtually nothing has been written about it—or at least nothing more than a handful of sketchy summaries. Yet it is an important crop in much of western Africa. Below ground it produces small tubers that look like elongated sweet potatoes but that contain more than twice the protein in sweet potatoes or Irish potatoes and more than 10 times the amount in cassava roots (manioc). Above ground it produces good yields of edible seeds.

The plant is a vigorous vine that climbs and twines to heights over 3 m. With its prolific spattering of large flowers—pink, purple, or greenish white, depending on variety—it makes an attractive ornamental. The plant is found

*Sphenostylis stenocarpa (Hochst. ex A. Rich.) Harms. Known in Nigeria as girigiri. Subfamily: Papilionoideae.

African yam bean, southeastern Nigeria. *(D. L. Plucknett)*

growing wild through much of tropical Africa and is common in central and western Africa, especially in southern Nigeria. (Reportedly, it is also cultivated in the Ivory Coast, Ghana, Togo, Gabon, Congo, Ethiopia, and parts of East Africa.) It seems little affected by altitude and flourishes at elevations from sea level to 1,800 m. It grows well even on acid and highly leached sandy soils of the humid lowland tropics. Although slow to set seed (Nigerian genotypes average 86 days to first flowering and 140 days to first ripe pods), it flowers and forms its slightly woody pods (up to 30 cm long and containing 20–30 seeds) continually year-round after that. The seeds are delicious and in western Africa are often preferred over other grain legumes. The seeds have crude protein levels varying from 21 to 29 percent—lower than soybean (38 percent), but amino acid analyses indicate that the lysine and methionine levels in the protein are equal to, or better than, those of soybean (see Table 1). For example, lysine may comprise up to 8 percent of the protein, and methionine and cystine together may comprise 2.4 percent. The seed's carbohydrate content is about 50 percent, and fiber 5 or 6 percent. The dry beans are usually eaten alone, or with yams, maize, rice, or in soups.

TABLE 1

	Lysine	Methionine
African yam bean*	7.53	1.22
African yam bean**	8.02	1.07
African yam bean†	6.8	1.9
Soybean	6.6	1.1

Low concentrations of the amino acids lysine and methionine limit the nutritive value of many proteins. But in the seeds of the African yam bean they are at least as high as in soybeans. (All figures are expressed as g per 100 g of protein.)

*Evans and Boulter. 1975.
**Okigbo (see Research Contacts). Private communication.
†Busson. 1965.

It would seem that, with research, the African yam bean may yield as much seed as other pulses. From a germ plasm collection (63 lines) at the International Institute of Tropical Agriculture, Ibadan, Nigeria, the most productive line yielded 1,860 kg of seed per ha. At Nsukka, seed yields of 2,000 kg per ha have been recorded.

But it is the below-ground yield that is of greatest immediate interest. The spindle-shaped tubers are often small (5-7.5 cm long, weighing 50-300 g). Their white flesh is eaten raw or cooked like potato, which it resembles in taste. But whereas common potato varieties average 5 percent protein, tubers of the African yam bean vary from 11 to 19 percent.* The remaining components of the tubers combine to make them a highly nutritious food: carbohydrate comprises 63-73 percent and fiber 3-6 percent of the tuber.

Tuber yields vary between cultivars. Some produce none, others produce up to 0.5 kg per plant.†

The plant can be propagated both by seed or by tuber.

Limitations

Although little is known about the African yam bean, it seems to demand a humid tropical climate with well-drained soil.

The plant is normally grown on a support. African farmers use trellises or stakes, often the same stakes that support yam vines (*Dioscorea* species). However, some recent tests in Nigeria suggest that the plant grows and yields tubers satisfactorily even when unsupported.‡

*Both measured on a dry weight basis, to eliminate moisture differences between samples.
†Information supplied by B. N. Okigbo. See Research Contacts.
‡Information supplied by K. O. Rachie. See Research Contacts.

African yam bean tuber. (International Grain Legume Centre, Ibadan, Nigeria)

The tubers take from 5 to 8 months to mature to a size that justifies harvest. With current cultivars, yields are usually low, reaching about 4 t per ha under favorable conditions.

Before the dry beans can be eaten they must be softened by soaking for several hours in water; even then they may require a cooking time of many hours.

An unidentified yellow mosaic virus that attacks the plant has been observed at the International Institute of Tropical Agriculture, Nigeria. Fungal diseases are also known and, like most legumes, the plant is highly susceptible to nematode damage.

Research Needs

So little is known about the African yam bean that, to benefit the large numbers of Africans who grow and eat it, a commitment to research is essential. There appear to be many avenues of research that can help make the bean easier to grow, more productive, and more nutritious. For instance, nothing is known about natural varietal differences. Important opportunities for genetic improvement (particularly for increasing tuber size) thus remain untapped.

Germ plasm collections should be made throughout Africa, since farmers are gradually switching to crops that are given more agricultural extension than the African yam bean; without such collections the loss of valuable genotypes seems inevitable.

Because the African yam bean has not been subject to concentrated research, the only known way to manage it is by use of the method traditionally employed in Africa. Since this is always in mixed culture and scattered in small plots, it provides few guidelines for managing the crop more intensively. Agronomic trials to optimize production of the crop in the field are needed as well as information on planting, cultivating, pest and disease control, and harvesting.

Although little is known about the plant's environmental tolerances, it is recommended for small-scale trial cultivation in tropical regions outside its native habitat.

The long cooking time is a barrier to the plant's more widespread use as a pulse crop. Home economics research to reduce this, and to develop more recipes for both seeds and tubers, is much needed.

Selected Readings

Busson, F., P. Jaeger, P. Lunnen, and M. Pinta. 1965. *Plantes Alimentaires de l'Ouest Africain (Etude Botanique, Biologique et Chimique)*. Leconte, Marseille, France. pp. 245, 247-248, 252, 254-255.

Evans, I.M., and D. Boulter. 1974. Amino acid composition of seed meals of yam bean (*Sphenostylis stenocarpa*) and lima bean (*Phaseolus lunatus*). *Journal of the Science of Food and Agriculture* 25:919-922.

Evans, I. M., D. Boulter, A. R. J. Eaglesham, and P. J. Dart. 1977. Protein content and protein quality of tuberous roots of some legumes determined by chemical methods. *Qualitas Plantarum/Plant Food for Human Nutrition* 27(3/4):275-285.

Kay, D. E. 1973. *Root Crops*. Tropical Products Institute, 56/62 Gray's Inn Road, London WC1X 8LU, England. pp. 1-3.

Okigbo, B. N. 1973. Introducing the yambean *Sphenostylis stenocarpa* (Hochst. ex A. Rich.) Harms. In *Proceedings of the First IITA Grain Legume Improvement Workshop 29 October–2 November 1973, Ibadan*, pp. 224-238. International Institute of Tropical Agriculture, Ibadan, Nigeria. (Copies available from the author, see address below.)

The *Tropical Grain Legume Bulletin* often contains short articles and abstracts on African yam bean. The *Bulletin* is available from the International Grain Legume Information Centre (see address below).

Research Contacts

Department of Crop Science, University of Nigeria, Nsukka, Anambra, Nigeria (Prof. F. O. C. Ezedinma and Dr. J. N. C. Maduewesi)

E. V. Doku, Crop Science Department, University of Ghana, Legon, Ghana

International Grain Legume Information Centre, International Institute of Tropical Agriculture, P.M.B. 5320, Ibadan, Nigeria (E. N. O. Adimorah, Documentalist)

S. N. Lyonga, P.M.B. 25, Buea, Cameroon

B. N. Okigbo, Deputy Director General, International Institute of Tropical Agriculture, P.M.B. 5320, Ibadan, Nigeria

K. O. Rachie, The Rockefeller Foundation, 1133 Avenue of the Americas, New York, New York 10036, USA

Other Root Crops

Many legumes that produce edible tubers grow in the humid tropics and subtropics. Most are wild plants whose cultivation has never been attempted, though some palatable species or varieties may have been selected by indigenous peoples. It seems probable that, with research, at least some of these legumes could become valuable food crops. To agronomists and nutritionists they offer exciting and interesting research challenges.

Tuberous legumes provide useful, edible products in situations unfavorable to fruit and seed crops. This is especially important in the humid lowland tropics where constant rain and humidity provide ideal conditions for insect pests and diseases, which often prevent fruit or seed from developing. For example, virtually all pulses (see next section) flower and fruit poorly during rainy humid weather.

Another advantage of root crops is that their harvest can sometimes be extended over a long period, thereby reducing or eliminating storage problems.

Nonleguminous roots such as cassava (manioc), sweet potatoes, and yams are staple foods, particularly in humid tropical lowlands. Nutritionally they provide energy and some minerals, but are seriously deficient in protein. This lack has tragic consequences, especially for weanling children. The abrupt change from breast milk to root crops and other starchy staples deprives them of the protein needed for developing brains and bodies to their fullest and healthiest potential.

But legume tubers reap the benefit of nitrogen fixation: they are protein rich. Thus, the exploitation of leguminous tubers offers a way to integrate into established root-crop diets tubers that are much more nutritious.

Of the legume tubers now in use, most are unknown outside their native habitats.* Many are decreasing in use because newly introduced root crops— the beneficiaries of much research—are more easily cultivated and more productive. The legumes' protein contributions are being displaced largely because of the neglect of the research community.

Tubers included in this chapter have barely been subjected to the most basic analysis; the few that have been studied show protein contents at least double that of standard varieties of potato and sweet potato (see page 39). The winged bean has tubers with 4-10 times the protein of conventional root crops.

Literature reports (mostly anthropological) suggest that the tubers are not toxic and that, though they may be fibrous, most are not acrid or unpalatable.

Many of these plants survive in the wild in leached, infertile soils and have promise as crops for marginal areas.

The whole topic of leguminous root crops calls for concentrated research by anthropologists, botanists, agronomists, plant breeders, nutritional biochemists, and food scientists. The potential for increasing protein supplies in the tropics through such research is compelling.

A selection of species† that seem to warrant vigorous research attention follows.

---

*This chapter includes leguminous tubers that are (or were) basic foodstuffs of North American Indians, New Guinea highlanders, other Melanesians, hill tribes of northern India, and Ambos (Namibia). The marama bean (see page 68), a multipurpose legume with tuberous root, is harvested by several peoples of the Kalahari region of southern Africa. The root of the common runner bean (*Phaseolus coccineus*) is often eaten by Central American Indians.

†All species mentioned in this chapter belong to the subfamily Papilionoideae.

The Winged Bean

The outstanding promise of this plant,* a native of New Guinea and Southeast Asia, has been dealt with in detail in a companion report.† Above ground, it produces edible leaves, shoots, flowers, and pods as well as seeds whose composition virtually duplicates that of soybeans. But the winged bean also provides a root vegetable. Not all its varieties produce tubers big enough to merit cultivating, but edible winged bean tubers are common in both Burma and the central highlands of Papua New Guinea.

The tubers are like early-season potatoes. Their flesh is white and firm, and is neither acrid nor fibrous. As traditionally prepared in Papua New Guinea (roasted in embers), they have a pleasant, slightly nutty flavor.

The most impressive feature of winged bean tubers is their protein content. Cassava averages 1 percent protein and potatoes, sweet potatoes, and yams 3-7 percent, whereas winged bean tubers average 20 percent.

Tuber yields equivalent to over 11,000 kg per ha have been measured in highland village plots in Papua New Guinea.‡

Vigna vexillata

A twining vine or prostrate herb, the widely distributed *Vigna vexillata*§ is found in tropical Africa, Asia, and Australia. It produces large, thickened edible tubers. Although well regarded as a pasture cover crop, green manure and erosion control plant, its cultivation as a root crop has not been attempted; tubers are now collected entirely from wild specimens. No detailed study of the distribution, ecology, life cycle, or economic potential has ever been published. But it could become a valuable vegetable in areas where the growing season is too short or rainfall too low for cassava, taro, potato, and other slowly maturing root crops. It could also prove useful for the vast tropical areas having lateritic soils. The study of this plant is wide open; it could provide many exciting and valuable student research projects.

In Africa, the tubers are used particularly in times of scarcity, from Senegal to South Africa. In Australia the plant‖ grows in the far northern monsoon regions with heavy summer rainfall (1,250-1,500 mm) followed by

---

Psophocarpus tetragonolobus (L.) DC.
†National Academy of Sciences. 1975.
‡Khan, Bohn, and Stevenson. 1977.
§ *Vigna vexillata* (L.) A. Rich. The plant has been classified under at least 15 different botanic names including *Vigna capensis* auctt. non (L.) Walp. and *Vigna senegalensis* A. Chev.
‖ Though this plant appears to have the characteristics of *Vigna vexillata* it has not yet been formally classified by taxonomists. (Information supplied by N. B. Byrnes and C. Dunlop. See Research Contacts.)

Winged bean tubers in a roadside market, Mt. Hagen, Papua New Guinea. (N.D. Viet-meyer)

Protein-rich tubers of *Vigna vexillata*. (National Bureau of Plant Genetic Resources, New Delhi, India)

months of drought. It is common near Darwin, and thrives in lateritic, acid, and aluminous soils that are very infertile. It is a traditional and highly prized food of Aboriginals. In Asia, *Vigna vexillata* (known as "wild mung") is plentiful between 1,200 and 1,500 m altitude in the Himalayas and in the hills of eastern and northeastern India. The tubers are eaten by tribes in the region.*

Vigna vexillata tubers have a soft, easily peeled skin and creamy, edible, tasty flesh inside. They can be eaten raw or boiled like sweet potato or cassava. Particularly rich in protein, tubers analyzed in India have shown a 15-percent protein content.*

The plant resembles an intermediate form between a cowpea and a mung bean. It has long pods profusely covered with hairs that appear to repulse pod-boring insects, major pests in the humid tropics. It yields dark green seeds the size of large mung beans. The roots develop abundant nodules and the plants are excellent pioneers for sterile land. They cover the ground quickly and are thus useful for erosion control.

Other *Vigna* Species

Although several other species of the genus *Vigna* furnish edible tuberous roots, little is known about any of them, and we can present little more than the following brief list.

Vigna lanceolata Benth. A perennial legume that grows in alluvial areas throughout tropical and subtropical Australia. The sweet, mealy, parsnip-like root (30–40 cm long) was said to be one of the best indigenous vegetables available to early European settlers. The foliage is palatable to livestock. The tubers are still much eaten by Aboriginals.

Vigna lobatifolia Baker (sometimes called *Vigna dinteri* Harms). This little-known perennial vine is native to Namibia (South West Africa), Angola, and extends into the central Kalahari in Botswana. It has seldom been collected by botanists and has never been studied by agronomists. Yet *Vigna lobatifolia* grows long, narrow-branched roots (up to 60 cm long) along which are spaced potato-sized swellings. These fleshy swellings are widely eaten by the Bushmen and Ovambo peoples. They are edible raw or cooked and are mild-flavored, crisp, have some fibers, and make a pleasant and satisfying food. *Vigna lobatifolia* tuber is remarkably rich in protein—15 percent.† This is a plant whose cultivation seems worth attempting.

*Chandel, Arora, and Joshi. 1972.
†Wehmeyer, Lee, and Whiting. 1969.

Vigna marina (Burm.) Merrill (also known as *Vigna lutea*[Sw.] A. Gray). Very widely distributed in tropical Asia, northern Australia, and Oceania. In north Queensland Aboriginals roast and eat the tubers.

Vigna ambacensis Welw. ex. Bak. Native to tropical Africa. Tubers are reportedly eaten in Zaire.

Vigna fischeri Harms. Cameroon to Kenya, Sudan to Zambia and Malawi. Tubers are reportedly eaten in Malawi.

Vigna reticulata Hook. f. Tropical Africa and Madagascar. Tubers are reportedly eaten in Malawi and Zaire.

Flemingia vestita

Found growing wild along the length of the Himalayan hills (between 1,500 and 1,800 m), *Flemingia vestita** has been brought under cultivation by native peoples of Meghalaya (Assam) in northeastern India. Its small, somewhat juicy tubers (3-6 cm long) can be found in the local markets in the Khasi and Jaintia hills of Meghalaya (1,500-1,800 m), where it is grown as a rain-fed crop. Its delicate skin is easily washed off, exposing the smooth, soft, creamy white flesh that has a sweet, nut-like flavor. The tuber is a rich source of iron and phosphorus and contains more than 3 times the protein of cassava, the most widely grown root crop in the tropics.

Reported as being exclusively wild a century ago, it is now so relished and sought after by tribal people in Meghalaya that it has become a cultivated cash crop of the area. The tubers take 7 months to mature; yields of over 3,000 kg per ha have been reported.†

Despite the increasing demand for this crop in recent years, it has been so neglected by agronomists and economic botanists that in all the literature there is only one research paper that deals with it specifically.† Like the other leguminous root crops in this chapter, this is a plant whose cultivation deserves thorough testing under controlled conditions.

Psoralea Species

In central Australia are found two species of *Psoralea*‡ that grow in the most adverse, dry conditions. Each produces edible tubers with agreeable

---

**Flemingia vestita* Benth. ex Bak. (also known as *Moghania vestita* [Benth. ex Bak.] O. Kuntze).
†Singh and Arora. 1973.
‡*Psoralea patens* Lindl. and *Psoralea cinerea* Lindl.

Tubers of *Flemingia vestita*. (R.K. Arora)

flavor and texture. Tubers of *Psoralea patens* contain 5 percent protein, and those of *Psoralea cinerea* 5-7 percent protein (dry weight). Both deserve research. Germ plasm should be collected and exploratory cultivation trials conducted.

In the midwestern region of North America early white settlers discovered the value of the tubers of *Psoralea esculenta*,* which many Indian tribes considered a special delicacy. An early explorer sent samples back to France, convinced that, like the potato, it would become an important cultivated crop in Europe.

The tubers, often called prairie potatoes, are usually the size of hen's eggs, though they can grow the the size of a large carrot. The Indians utilized them as we use potatoes today. Dug when the tops began browning, the tubers were peeled and then boiled or baked. Prairie Indians used the plant extensively because the flesh of the tuber dries quickly in the sun, producing

*Psoralea esculenta Pursh. Also called breadroot, Indian turnip, Dakota turnip, pomme blanc.

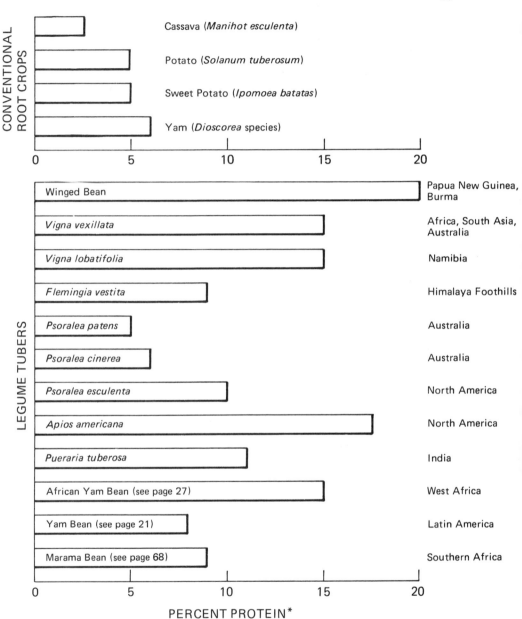

CONVENTIONAL ROOT CROPS

Cassava (*Manihot esculenta*)

Potato (*Solanum tuberosum*)

Sweet Potato (*Ipomoea batatas*)

Yam (*Dioscorea* species)

LEGUME TUBERS

Winged Bean	Papua New Guinea, Burma
Vigna vexillata	Africa, South Asia, Australia
Vigna lobatifolia	Namibia
Flemingia vestita	Himalaya Foothills
Psoralea patens	Australia
Psoralea cinerea	Australia
Psoralea esculenta	North America
Apios americana	North America
Pueraria tuberosa	India
African Yam Bean (see page 27)	West Africa
Yam Bean (see page 21)	Latin America
Marama Bean (see page 68)	Southern Africa

PERCENT PROTEIN*

*All figures are based on dry weight, and represent crude protein content. Figures for the conventional root crops are those of the cultivars in common use.

Protein content of legume tubers.

The prairie turnip, *Psoralea esculenta*. (H.H. Marshall)

a hard cake that can be stored safely for long periods. Ground into a flour, this product was used year-round for thickening soups and for making bread. The white flesh of the tuber is not strongly flavored; it is firm, chewy, and palatable both raw and cooked. A recent analysis found a protein content of 7.4 percent.* Analyses published 40 years ago record protein contents of 7.7 and 13.1 for *Psoralea esculenta* tubers from Nebraska.†

Although the plant will grow on marginal soils, it is difficult to propagate by vegetative means and seedlings grow slowly, taking several years to produce useful-size tubers. Research is needed to overcome this drawback.

Apios Species

The sweet, starchy tubers of the North American plant *Apios americana*‡ were once much esteemed by native Americans. Early European settlers called them groundnuts, potato beans, or Indian potatoes, and they ate them as well. Captain John Smith, leader of the Jamestown colony of 1607, described them as being "good as potatoes." They were eaten boiled, roasted, or fried.

*Information supplied by H. H. Marshall. See Research Contacts.
†Yanovsky, E., and R. M. Kingsbury. 1938. *Journal of the Association of Official Agricultural Chemists* 21:648-665.
‡*Apios americana* Medikus. Also called *Apios tuberosa* Moench or *Glycine apios*.

Tubers of *Apios americana*. (N.D. Vietmeyer)

The tubers are perennial and can be harvested at any season as an emergency food supply. The Pilgrims in New England survived their first few winters by living on them.

During the potato famine of 1845, when the potato was plagued by disease, *Apios americana* was introduced to Europe. Its cultivation as a food crop was abandoned when potato growing again became feasible.

The plant is still widely distributed in eastern Canada and the United States,* often at ancient Indian campsites, especially in low, wet soil and along river banks. Round or oval tubers (2–8 cm diameter), brown-skinned, white within, occur as swellings spaced along a slender rootstock found just beneath the surface of the soil.

An attractively flowered climbing plant reminiscent of wisteria, *Apios americana* also makes a useful, sweet-scented ornamental.

---

*Neither *Apios americana* nor *Psoralea esculenta* (see above) are tropical plants. Yet both grow over a wide range of climates and the southern extremes of their range are subtropical. (*A. americana*, for example, produces well in southern Florida.) They certainly deserve further testing in subtropical zones.

The plant has been so neglected that little is known about the composition and nutritive quality of its tubers. The only published analysis* records a remarkable protein content of 17.5 percent. Research into this and into *Apios* cultivation seems well warranted. The plant is very fast growing and its roots are well nodulated. Its viny nature complicates its cultivation, but bush-like mutants may well be found in nature. The plant also may make a useful forage.

Other *Apios* species deserve consideration. *Apios priceana*,† the only other North American species, produces a large single tuber that is edible, but the plant is so rare that it is classified as an endangered species. *Apios fortunei*‡ is already cultivated in some remote areas of China, Japan, and Taiwan, but no investigation of its cultivation has yet been reported.

Miscellaneous

Other legumes with edible tubers include:

Periandra mediterranea (Vell.) Taub. A sweet-tasting root used as a substitute for licorice, common in Central Brazil.

Phaseolus adenanthus G.F.W. Meyer. Pantropical.

Phaseolus coccineus L. (*Phaseolus multiflorus* Willd.). Scarlet runner bean. Commonly grown in temperate countries for its green pods, but in its native Central American highland habitat this plant is sometimes grown for its fleshy tubers. Deserves research to determine the genetics and physiology of tuber formation. The plant is also a promising pulse for tropical highlands and temperate areas.

Phaseolus heterophyllus. Central America.

Pueraria lobata Ohwi (formerly *Pueraria thunbergiana*). Kudzu. Starch extracted from the tuberous roots (which can be 2 m long and weigh 30 kg) in Japan is now sold as a health food worldwide. This exceptionally vigorous vine has become a major weed in southeastern United States.

Pueraria phaseoloides. Tropical kudzu, puero. Now grown or tested in most tropical countries for fodder, soil cover, green manure, or erosion control, this plant bears tuberous roots that can be eaten. Nothing has been

*Yanovsky, E., and R. M. Kingsbury. 1938. *Journal of the Association of Official Agricultural Chemists* 21:648-665.
†*Apios priceana* Robinson.
‡*Apios fortunei* Maxinowicz.

reported on palatability, varietal differences, yields, toxins (if any), or other aspects of this plant's potential as a root crop.

Pueraria tuberosa. Indian kudzu. Large tubers weighing up to 35 kg are eaten in parts of northern India. They taste like licorice and are said to be eaten raw or boiled. An 11-percent protein content and yields up to 7.5 t per ha have been reported.*

Selected Readings

Winged Bean

Hymowitz, T., and J. Boyd. 1977. Origin, ethnobotany and agricultural potential of the winged bean–*Psophorcarpus tetragonolobus. Economic Botany* 31:180-188.

Khan, T. N., J. C. Bohn, and R. A. Stevenson. 1977. Winged beans: Cultivation in Papua New Guinea. *World Crops* 29(5):208-214.

National Academy of Sciences. 1975. *The Winged Bean: A High Protein Crop for the Tropics.* National Academy of Sciences, Washington, D.C. 43 pp.

The Winged Bean Flyer. A newsletter devoted solely to this plant, and the progress of research on it, is available from Prof. Russ Stephenson, Department of Agriculture, University of Papua New Guinea, University, Papua New Guinea.

Vigna vexillata

Chandel, K.P.S., R.K. Arora, and B.S. Joshi. 1972. *Vigna capensis* Walp. [*V. vexillata*] – an edible root legume. *Current Science* 41:537.

The *Tropical Grain Legume Bulletin* often contains short articles and abstracts on *Vigna vexillata.* The *Bulletin* is available from the International Grain Legume Information Centre (see address below).

Other *Vigna* Species

Evans, I. M., D. Boulter, A. R. J. Eaglesham, and P. J. Dart. 1977. Protein content and protein quality of tuberous roots of some legumes determined by chemical methods. *Qualitas Plantarum/Plant Food for Human Nutrition* 27(3/4):275-285.

Wehmeyer, A. S., R. B. Lee, and M. Whiting. 1969. The nutrient composition and dietary importance of some vegetable food eaten by the Kung Bushmen. *South African Journal of Nutrition* 5(4):1529-1530. (*Vigna lobatifolia*).

Flemingia vestita

Singh, H. B., and R. K. Arora. 1973. Soh-phlong, *Moghania vestita* a leguminous root crop of India. *Economic Botany* 27:332-338.

Psoralea esculenta

Harrington, H. D. 1967. *Edible Native Plants of the Rocky Mountains.* University of New Mexico Press, Albuquerque, New Mexico. pp. 203-206.

*Anonymous. 1969. *Wealth of India: Raw Materials*, Vol. 8. Council for Scientific and Industrial Research, New Delhi, India. pp. 316-317.

Apios americana

Seabrook, J. A. E., and L. A. Dionne. 1976. Studies on the genus *Apios*. I. Chromosome number and distribution of *Apios americana* and *Apios priceana. Canadian Journal of Botany* 54:2567-2572.

Miscellaneous

Baudet, J. C. 1973. Notes sur quelques especes africaines du genre *Eriosema* (DC) Desv. (Papilionaceae). *Bulletin du Jardin Botanique National de Belgique/Nationale Plantentiun Van Belgie* 43:17-32.

Research Contacts

Winged Bean

Lists of research contacts, as well as suppliers of winged bean seed and inoculum, can be found in the *Winged Bean Flyer* (see Selected Readings).

Vigna vexillata

N. B. Byrnes, Queensland Herbarium, Meiers Road, Indooroopilly, Queensland 4068, Australia

C. Dunlop, Scientific Service Division (Botany), Animal Industry and Agriculture Division, P.O. Box 5150, Darwin, Northern Territory, Australia

International Grain Legume Information Centre, International Institute of Tropical Agriculture, P.M.B. 5320, Ibadan, Nigeria

National Bureau of Plant Genetics Resources, Indian Agricultural Research Institute, New Delhi 110012, India (R. K. Arora, K. P. S. Chandel, and K. L. Mehra)

K. O. Rachie, The Rockefeller Foundation, 1133 Avenue of the Americas, New York. New York 10036, USA

Vigna lobatifolia

M. A. N. Müller, Officer-in-charge, South West Africa Herbarium, Private Bag 13184, Windhoek, Namibia (South West Africa)

R. Story, c/o CSIRO, Box 109 City, Canberra, A.C.T., Australia

A. S. Wehmeyer, National Food Research Institute, Council for Scientific and Industrial Research, Scientia P.O. 395, Pretoria 0001, South Africa

Flemingia vestita

National Bureau of Plant Genetic Resources, Indian Agricultural Research Institute, New Delhi 110012, India (R. K. Arora and K. L. Mehra)

Psoralea Species

J. R. Maconochie, Curator, Herbarium of the Northern Territory, Department of the Northern Territory, Alice Springs, N.T. 5750, Australia

H. H. Marshall, Research Station, P.O. Box 3001, Morden, Manitoba, ROG 1JO, Canada

Apios americana

Angus Gholson, P.O. Box 96, Chattahoochee, Florida 32324, USA

Lawrence Kaplan, Professor of Biology, University of Massachusetts/Boston, Boston, Massachusetts 02125, USA

Robert Kral, Department of Biology, Box 1705, Station B, Vanderbilt University, Nashville, Tennessee 37235, USA

R. T. Mohlenbrock, Department of Botany, Southern Illinois University, Carbondale, Illinois 62901, USA

J. A. E., Seabrook, Department of Biology, University of New Brunswick, Fredericton, New Brunswick, Canada E3B 5A3

N. D. Vietmeyer, National Academy of Sciences, 2101 Constitution Ave., Washington, D.C. 20418, USA

II Pulses

Bambara Groundnut

Although it produces a nutritious food and is cultivated throughout Africa—from Senegal to Kenya and from the Sahara to South Africa and Madagascar—the bambara groundnut* remains one of the crops most neglected by science. Stigmatized a "poor man's crop," the plant has never been accorded a large-scale breeding and research program. Yet empirical evidence and fragmentary research results suggest that it is a crop with much promise. As one of the two most drought-tolerant cultivated legumes, it deserves to be taken far more seriously. Furthermore, despite the lack of research, its commercial use in Africa is increasing.

One of the most popular pulses among Africans (along with cowpeas, peanuts, pigeon peas, and common beans), the bambara groundnut is little known in other parts of the world.

Like the peanut, it forms pods and seeds on, or just beneath, the ground. To achieve this the flower stalk elongates, and as its bulbous tip penetrates the soil, it creates a tunnel through which the fertilized flowers, attached a few centimeters behind the tip, are drawn into the soil. The pods are round and wrinkled and each contains one or two seeds. The seeds are round (up to 1.5 cm diameter), smooth, and when dried, very hard. They may be cream, brown, red, mottled, or black-eyed.

Voandzeia subterranea (L.) Thouars var. *subterranea*. Also known as Congo goober, earth pea, baffin pea, Njugo bean (South Africa), Madagascar groundnut, voandzou (Madagascar), epi roui (Yoruba), okpa otuanya (Ibo), juijiya (Hausa), nzama (Malawi), nlubu, nyimo (Rhodesia), njugu mawe (Swahili). Sometimes spelled bambarra groundnut. Subfamily: Papilionoideae.

Bambara groundnut, *Voandzeia subterranea*. (Agriculture Research Institute, Ukiriguru, Mwanza, Tanzania)

The plant itself occurs in both erect and prostrate types. It grows best in climates similar to those used for growing peanuts, maize, or sorghum. It needs bright sunshine, high temperatures (at least 4 frost-free months), and frequent rains in the period between sowing and flowering. But the bambara groundnut is one of the most adaptable of all plants and tolerates harsh conditions better than most crops. For example, it yields food under conditions too arid for peanuts, corn, or sorghum. (Bambara is actually a district near Timbuktu on the Sahara Desert's southern fringe.) Thus the bambara groundnut is a legume particularly suited for hot, dry regions where growing other pulses is risky.

The plant will also grow in rainforest areas and also grows in cool, moist highlands in Rhodesia.

The bambara groundnut tolerates (some researchers say "prefers") poor soils. On worn-out soils it can yield more than peanuts. In fact, nitrogen-rich soils are to be avoided because they stimulate the plant to produce too much leaf at the expense of the pods and seeds.

The plant has a reputation for resisting pests and diseases. It is less susceptible to diseases than peanuts, perhaps because it has been grown only in isolated, backyard gardens in mixed cultivation with other similarly isolated plants. Since the bambara groundnut buries its fruits in the soil, they are safe from attack by the flying insects that severely limit or destroy pulses like cowpeas and beans whose pods remain in the air. Rodents and crickets may damage the plant, however.

Though widely assumed to be a low yielder, there is substantial evidence to show that, with good management, the bambara groundnut can match yields with even the most productive legumes.*

The crop is cultivated with methods similar to those used for growing peanuts. It takes 3-6 months to mature, depending on climatic conditions and cultivar type.† The timing of harvest is less critical than with peanuts; bambara groundnuts can be harvested early or late without serious loss. However, when mature, the seeds are too hard to be eaten raw. Usually they are eaten immature (i.e., before becoming too hard), but when roasted or boiled even the mature beans are edible. Ripe or immature, they are sweet and pleasant to eat and contain 14-24 percent protein and about 60 percent carbohydrate. Sometimes the roasted seeds are ground into a nutritious flour that can be incorporated into many dishes. The seed protein has more methionine (nutritionally an essential amino acid) than is found in other grain legumes.

The plant is also useful in crop rotations, for it contributes nitrogen to the soil, which benefits subsequent crops.

In summary, this is a nutritious, rugged plant for growing where other crops do poorly—in hot, disease-laden regions where soil fertility and rainfall patterns are variable.

---

*Apparently the quoted yields reflect low-density populations because African farmers intercrop bambara groundnut with other crop plants. Johnson, 1968 (see Selected Readings), reports yields in excess of 2,000 kg of shelled seeds per ha. These were from six independent trials in several Central African countries. A 1969 report from Ukiriguru Experiment Station, Tanzania (see Research Contacts), records yields up to 2,600 kg per ha. Various other documents refer to experimental yields in excess of 3,000 kg per ha.
†Highest yields seem to be produced mainly by slow-maturing (140-150 days) cultivars. Information supplied by P. Silvestre, IRAT.

Limitations

Bambara groundnuts contain 6-12 percent oil, less than half the amount found in peanuts. They are therefore not useful as oilseeds.

Unripe seeds are eaten fresh; ripe seeds are hard and indigestible and must be boiled or ground to be edible.

Like the cowpea, the bambara groundnut nodulates freely, but specific *Rhizobium* strains that are exceptionally effective in promoting growth have been found in experiments at NifTAL in Hawaii.* For best growth, it also requires high temperatures and abundant sunshine. Good soil drainage is essential, and the crop has to be planted in loose, light soils to facilitate the *Rhizobium* in its small, spherical root nodules and to enhance development of the buried seeds. Careful cultivation is needed; the flower stalks are weaker than those of peanut and cannot penetrate a hard soil crust. Loose soils also make it easier to dig up the pods.

The plant should be harvested during dry spells and precautions taken to ensure dry safe storage; during storage, the seeds can mold or become infested with insects. The seeds can be harvested when the plant is green, at which time the pods do not shatter and the nutritious foliage can be fed to livestock.

Despite the plant's general healthiness, some disease organisms known to attack it are fusarium wilt, leaf spot, root-knot nematode, and a virus. These infestations are usually serious only in seasons or areas of high rainfall.

Though the crop can be found in vastly different environments in Africa, there are indications that individual cultivars are not in themselves very adaptable. High-yielding types from one location may fail when grown elsewhere. Tanzanian cultivars have yielded poorly in Zambia, for example. Indeed, some from northwestern Tanzania have proved unsatisfactory in the drier climate and different soils of central Tanzania. The most effective research on this crop in a given African locality may therefore be that which concentrates on selecting and improving *local* cultivars. Researchers outside Africa should ensure that any cultivars tested come from appropriate climates.†

Research Needs

The bambara groundnut is so important to the rural poor in most of Africa, and potentially so important elsewhere in the tropics, that the improvement of its germ plasm (for higher yield, protein and digestibility) and the agronomy of its production both deserve intensive study.

The cultivars that now exist have arisen by casual selection during traditional cultivation. They have only very localized distribution. Cultivars that

*See Research Contacts.
†Information supplied by R. V. Billington. See Research Contacts.

differ in leaf shape and size, as well as in seed color, size, and hardness, have been observed. Primitive cultivars have a trailing habit; the better selected cultivars are self-standing, which facilitates cultivation and harvesting.

Collecting and comparing bambara groundnut germ plasm from all over Africa is one of the most important research needs. It is particularly necessary to collect in Upper Volta, Togo, the middle belt of Nigeria, Tanzania, and Zambia, where the greatest variation is thought to occur. This could be a good project for the Association for the Advancement of Agricultural Sciences in Africa to coordinate.

To determine yield and the feasibility of commercial bambara groundnut production, an agronomist should conduct trials using superior cultivars in semiarid areas where peanuts yield poorly because of drought. It is important to do this in Africa, but the plant is well worth testing in similar regions elsewhere.

Efforts should also be made to improve the management of the crop in the field. Further trials using and adapting modern methods of intensive peanut farming should be undertaken.

Bambara groundnut in a market at Bamako, Mali. (B.N. Okigbo)

So far, the bambara groundnut has been cultivated only in small plots, but it has good potential as a field crop. Investigations are justified of mechanized cultivation, harvesting, shelling and processing (especially canning), and of the plant's potential as a cash crop for processed foods and world trade.

Although the crop is relatively free of pathogens and pests, research to identify cultivars that resist its known diseases is needed. Searches should also be made for highly effective *Rhizobium*, both from available lines and from rhizobia associated with the plant in its native habitat.

Research into the bambara groundnut's nutritional effectiveness is needed. There are indications that the protein digestibility is inhibited by antinutritive factors in the seeds.

A closely similar plant, the groundbean or Kersting's groundnut,* also deserves research. The leaves of *Kerstingiella geocarpa* are broader than those of the bambara groundnut and the plant is less robust; though the pods develop underground like those of peanuts and bambara groundnuts, the seeds resemble common beans (*Phaseolus vulgaris*) and are usually white, brown, black, or speckled in color. Their protein is rich in the essential amino acids lysine (6.2 percent) and methionine (1.4 percent) and it occurs in good quantity (19–20 percent).† Grown in both high-rainfall and savanna areas in tropical Africa, the groundbean is grown in even drier areas than the bambara groundnut and is even less known scientifically. Although the seeds are tasty, they are small and yields are poor, disadvantages that probably could be corrected with appropriate research.

Selected Readings

A bibliography of the world literature on bambara groundnut is being prepared by the International Grain Legume Information Centre. (For address, see Research Contacts.)

Amuti, K., and C. J. Pollard, 1974. Studies on the bambarra ground nut (*Voandzeia subterranea*) seeds. *Journal of the West African Science Association* 19:85-90.

Bakhareva, S. N. 1975. Voandzeia–a valuable legume crop. *Trudy po Prikladnoi Botanike, Genetike i Selektsii* 54(3):164-169.

Busson, E., and B. Bergeret. 1958. Contribution à l'étude chimique des graines de *Voandzeia subterranea* Thouars. *Acta Tropica* 15:246-250.

Doku, E. V., and S. K. Karikari. 1971. Bambarra groundnut. *Economic Botany* 25(3):255-262.

Hepper, F. N. 1963. The bambara groundnut (*Voandzeia subterranea*) in West Africa. *Kew Bulletin* 16:398-407.

Hepper, F. N. 1970. The bambara groundnut. (*Voandzeia subterranea*). *Field Crops Abstracts* 23:1-6.

Jacques-Felix, H. 1950. Pour une enquête sur le Voandzou. *Agronomie Tropicale* 5:62-73.

Johnson, D. T. 1968. The bambarra groundnut, a review. *Rhodesia Agricultural Journal* 65:1-4.

Kerstingiella geocarpa Harms or *Macrotyloma geocarpum* (Harms) Marechal & Baudet.
†Information supplied by M. L. Genevois. See Research Contacts.

Karikari, S. K. 1971. Economic importance of bambarra groundnut. *World Crops* 23: 195-196.

Kay, D. E. 1978. *Food Legumes.* TPI Crop and Product Digest No. 3. Tropical Products Institute, London. pp. 24-33.

Lartey, B. L. 1976. The canning of bambara groundnut (*Voandzeia subterranea*). In *Proceedings of the Symposium on Grain Legumes*, pp. 119-126. University of Ghana and the Council for Scientific and Industrial Research, Accra, Ghana.

Masefield, G. B., S. G. Harrison, and M. Wallis. 1969. *Oxford Book of Food Plants.* Oxford University Press, London.

Pollack, S. B. 1973. The bambara groundnut: Its morphology, culture and nutritional deficiency symptoms. M.S. Thesis, University of Florida, Gainesville. (Advisor D. E. McCloud, see address below.)

Purseglove, J. W. 1968. *Tropical Crops: Dictoyledons I.* John Wiley and Sons, New York. pp. 329-332.

The *Tropical Grain Legume Bulletin* sometimes contains short articles and abstracts on bamabara groundnut. The *Bulletin* is available from the International Grain Legume Information Centre (see address below).

Research Contacts

Agricultural Research Institute, Ukiriguru, P.O. Box 1433, Mwanza, Tanzania (Mrs. M. A. Mussa)

R. V. Billington, 14 Cassiobury Park Avenue, Watford, Herts, England

Jean C. Baudet, Chaussee de Tournai 230, B-7340 Tertre, Belgium

Chibero College of Agriculture, Private Bag 901, Norton, Zimbabwe-Rhodesia (J. Mkandla)

H. D. L. Corby, University of Rhodesia, Department of Botany, P.O. Box MP167, Mount Pleasant, Salisbury, Zimbabwe-Rhodesia

Department of Agriculture, Research Branch, Mount Makulu Research Station, P.O. Box 7, Chilanga, Zambia

Department of Crop Science, University of Ghana, Legon, Ghana (K. Amuti [also Kersting's groundnut], E.V. Doku, and S. Sinnadurai)

D. L. Ebbels, Plant Pathology Laboratory, Hatching Green, Harpenden, Herts AL5 2BD, England

F. O. C. Ezedinma, Department of Crop Science, University of Nigeria, Nsukka, Nigeria

M. Louis Genevois, 18 rue Duban, 75106 Paris, France

W. Godfrey-Sam-Aggrey, Head, Crop Production, University of Botswana and Swaziland, P.O. Luyengo, Swaziland

F. N. Hepper, Royal Botanic Garden, Herbarium, Kew, Richmond, Surrey, England

IRAT, Institut de Recherches Agronomiques Tropicales et des Cultures Vivrières, 110 rue de l'Universite, 75007 Paris, France

Institute for Crops and Pastures, Private Bag X116, Pretoria 0001, South Africa (J. W. Snyman)

Institute of Agricultural Research, Samaru, Zaria, Nigeria (Ono Leleji and C. Harkness)

International Grain Legume Information Centre, International Institute of Tropical Agriculture, P.M.B. 5320, Ibadan, Nigeria

S. K. Karikari, University of Ghana, Agricultural Research Station, P.O. Box 43, Kade, Ghana

B. L. Lartey, Food Research Institute, P.O. Box M20, Ministry Post Office Branch, Accra, Ghana

Magoye Regional Research Station, P.O. Box 11, Magoye, Zambia (G. C. H. Hill, Acting Principal Research Officer)

Darrell E. McCloud, Department of Agronomy, University of Florida, Gainesville, Florida 32601, USA

NifTAL Project, University of Hawaii, P.O. Box "O", Paia, Hawaii 96790, USA (S. Whitney and P. Woomer)

B. N. Okigbo, International Institute of Tropical Agriculture, P.M.B. 5320, Ibadan, Nigeria

Jackbean and Swordbean

These two robust, high-yielding, closely related species* produce nutritious pods and high-protein seeds. They are capable of providing food in marginal areas where other pulses fail and they can provide a plentiful green manure and forage. Although they are already widely eaten—particularly in Asia—their full potential is limited by growth-inhibiting proteins that must be carefully detoxified before the seeds are edible.

Yet these plants, growing under extremely difficult conditions, offer a means for extending protein production to marginal areas, particularly to tropical lowlands with depleted soils and to areas with unpredictable climate or varying soil types, high altitudes, and pest infestations.

The jackbean is a New World plant that was grown in the drought-ridden regions of Arizona and Mexico in ancient times—seeds as much as 1,000 years old have been found by archaeologists. The swordbean is of prehistoric Old World origin and is widely cultivated in the humid tropics of Africa and Asia, especially in India.

Both plants produce flat, straight, scimitar-shaped pods that are among the largest of any domesticated legumes. In the jackbean, they can reach 30 cm long and 3½ cm wide; in the swordbean, they can reach 40 cm long and 5 cm wide. The jackbean is usually an erect, somewhat shrubby annual about 1 m tall, though climbing varieties are also known. Swordbean cultivars are woody, high-climbing, twining perennials, with runners as long as 10 m. The two can also be distinguished by differences in seed color (jackbean seeds are white, swordbean seeds are red) and pod shape, as well as in flower size and color.

The hardiness of these plants is shown by the range of conditions under which they can be cultivated:

• *Temperature*. Jackbean has been grown successfully where average annual temperatures range from 14°C to 27°C, from warmer parts of the tem-

*Jackbean: *Canavalia ensiformis* (L.) DC., also known as horsebean, gotani bean, feve Jacques, pois sabre. Swordbean: *Canavalia gladiata* (Jacq.) DC. Subfamily: Papilionoideae.

perate zone to hot, tropical, rainforest areas. Yet both jackbeans and sword-beans have promise for areas where early frost shortens the growing season, because even if the foliage gets frostbitten, the beans themselves remain unaffected.

• *Rainfall*. The jackbean has been reported to grow well where rainfall is as high as 4,200 mm and as low as 700 mm. A deep root system allows both plants, once established, to draw on stored soil moisture and to survive dry conditions.

• *Sunlight*. Although both plants require full sun for optimum growth, they can also grow well in shade.

• *Soils*. Both plants tolerate a wide range of soil textures and fertility; among pulses only jackbean, swordbean, and lima beans (see page 97) grow really well on the highly leached, nutrient-depleted, lowland tropical soils. They grow well on acid soils (pH 4.3-6.8) and they are far less affected by waterlogging and salinity than other pulse crops.

• *Altitude*. Although generally grown in the lowlands, they can also be grown at elevations at least as high as 1,800 m.

In addition to their uncommon adaptability, jackbean and swordbean are relatively fast-growing, usually producing a crop in 3-4 months. They germinate readily and are easily cultivated by use of methods similar to those for the cowpea. Both plants are virtually immune to most pests; though insect, fungus, and bacterial and viral infestations have been recorded, they do not seriously reduce the plant vigor or yields. A stem borer and a fungal root disease sometimes cause more serious losses, however. The seeds are also highly resistant to infestation during storage.

Both beans are highly productive pulse crops and on fertile soils their yields equal those of cowpeas. Production as high as 4,600 kg of dry seed per ha has been recorded in experiments—a remarkable yield—but throughout the tropics, most farm plots average 800-1,000 kg per ha. In many areas where cowpeas and common beans fail, the jackbean and swordbean continue to produce useful yields.*

Young leaves and pods are edible, but they must first be cooked. The pods are gathered when half grown, i.e., before the seeds inside them swell. Served as a boiled green vegetable like snap beans, they are reportedly "exceedingly tender and little, if any, inferior to the French bean."† Although commonly consumed in tropical Asia and Japan, they seem to be unpopular elsewhere.

Inside the pods 10-30 large, turgid seeds develop. They contain 22-29 percent protein and have a good amino acid balance. The full-grown but still

---

*Information supplied by K. O. Rachie. See Research Contacts.
†Hedrick, U. P., Ed. 1919. *Sturtevant's Notes on Edible Plants*. J. B. Lyon Company, State Printers, Albany. p. 131. However, the fiber content is more like that in string beans of some decades ago rather than in the highly bred snap beans of today.

Jack bean, *Canavalia ensiformis*. (E.N.O. Adimorah)

green, moist, and soft seeds are eaten as a cooked vegetable. The dry, fully mature seeds are also edible, but only after extensive boiling with one or two changes of the cooking water and peeling of the seed coat. They can also be detoxified by fermentation to "tempeh," as is done with soybeans in Asia.

The jackbean and swordbean are valuable green manure and cover crops. Yields of 40–50 t of green vegetation per ha can be produced. The jackbean has also been extensively grown as a source of plant nutrients and soil cover for tobacco, sugarcane, cacao, citrus, coconut, and pineapple plantations in the southeastern United States, Hawaii, and Indonesia. The vegetation of both species yields a good leaf meal for use in animal feeds.*

*Information supplied by R. Bressani. See Research Contacts.

Limitations

The promise of the jackbean and swordbean is limited by the growth-inhibiting compounds they contain. These are the proteins canavalin, concanavalin A and B, the enzyme urease, and the amino acid canavanine. Concanavalin A (Con A) is a protein that mimics an antibody. As such, it aggulinates certain viruses and spermatozoa, as well as normal, embryonic, and transformed cells. Recently, Con A has been used by biochemists to isolate blood group substances (immunoglobulins and glycoprotein), thus becoming an important tool in medical analysis. There is now speculation that Con A is a plant antibody (lectin) that protects these beans against diseases caused by microorganism infections.* Jackbean and swordbean toxicity seems largely due to Con A, which binds to the mucosal cells living in the intestine and thus reduces the body's ability to absorb nutrients from the intestine.

The urease extracted from jackbeans and swordbeans is used also in analytical laboratories. It converts urea into carbon dioxide, water, and ammonia and is used as a reagent for determining urea concentrations.

Unlike the other pulses in this report, there are no rich, diverse, gene pools of "folk varieties" of jackbean and swordbean available. Only highly inbred strains that are found almost exclusively in experiment stations are readily obtainable. Jackbeans are not a traditional crop of any cultural group; swordbeans are traditional in a few parts of Southeast Asia, but they too are mostly disseminated by agricultural experiment stations.

Wider use of jackbeans and swordbeans is also limited by local food preferences. The cooked seeds have little flavor and a coarse, mealy texture.

Research Needs

There has been little agronomic development of these plants. Cultivars have been selected for low toxicity, but it is likely that types exist—or can be developed—that will overcome major restrictions to their wider use. A worldwide collection of germ plasm is needed, to be followed by mass screening for types free of Con A and other toxic constituents.

Another important line of research is the study of all aspects of the utilization of these plants. One promising development is processing of the beans to produce a protein concentrate for use in formulated foods.† Researchers at INCAP in Guatemala have shown that jackbean protein can be isolated in

---

*It seems possible also that the presence of such lectins in a plant root can be detected by *Rhizobium* bacteria, which use it as a signal that the plant is a suitable nodulating host.
†Molina *et al.* 1974.

high yield without the toxins. Development of this process could extend the production of high-protein formulated foods to new geographical areas.

Because the plants are already used despite their limitations, there is important agronomic development to be done over and above detoxification. Methods now used for planting, fertilizing, and harvesting are nearly always traditional ones that should be subjected to modern analysis or improvement. Breeding to enhance desirable characteristics would also contribute to the welfare of those who already grow the beans and would lay the groundwork essential for capitalizing on low-toxicity cultivars as they become available.

There are two other *Canavalia* species that have been cultivated since ancient times but which are now close to extinction. In Peru some specimens of *Canavalia plagiosperma* Piper still remain, but *Canavalia regalis* Dunn, an African cultigen, is probably extinct.* Botanists in Peru and West Africa are alerted to the importance of searching for these plants and preserving their germ plasm.

Selected Readings

Kay, D. E. 1978. *Food Legumes.* TPI Crop and Product Digest No. 3. Tropical Products Institute, London. pp. 261-272, 487-494.

Molina, M. R., D. E. Argueta, and R. Bressani. 1974. Extraction of nitrogenous constituents from the jack bean (*Canavalia ensiformis*). *Journal of Agricultural and Food Chemistry* 22:309-312.

Molina, M. R., and R. Bressani. 1974. Protein-starch extraction and nutritive value of the jack bean and jack bean protein isolate. In *Nutritional Aspects of Common Beans and Other Legume Seeds as Animal and Human Foods*, ed. W. G. Jaffe. pp. 153-163. Proceedings of a meeting held in Ribeirão Preto, November 1973. (Copies of the article are available from the authors, see address below.)

Piper, C. V. 1920. *The Jack Bean.* United States Department of Agriculture Circular No. 92. United States Department of Agriculture, Washington, D.C.

Purseglove, J. W. 1968. *Tropical Crops: Dicotyledons I.* John Wiley and Sons, New York. pp. 242-244.

Sauer, J., and L. Kaplan. 1969. Canavalia beans in American prehistory. *American Antiquity* 34:417-424.

The *Tropical Grain Legume Bulletin* often contains short articles and abstracts on *Canavalia.* The *Bulletin* is available from the International Grain Legume Information Centre (see address below).

Westphal. E. 1974. *Pulses in Ethiopia, Their Taxonomy and Agricultural Significance.* Centre for Agricultural Publishing and Documentation, Wageningen, The Netherlands. pp. 72-84.

Research Contacts

I. J. Goldstein, Department of Biological Chemistry, University of Michigan, Ann Arbor, Michigan 48104, USA (Biochemical studies)

*Information supplied by J. Sauer. See Research Contacts.

Grain Legume Improvement Program, International Institute of Tropical Agriculture, P.M.B. 5320, Ibadan, Nigeria (P. R. Goldsworthy, Assistant Director)

Instituto de Nutrición de Centro America y Panama–INCAP, Apartado Postal 1188. Carretera Roosevelt Zona 11, Guatemala City, Guatemala, Central America (R. Bressani and M. R. Molina)

I. E. Liener, Department of Biochemistry, College of Biological Sciences, University of Minnesota, St. Paul, Minnesota 55101, USA (Toxicological studies)

International Grain Legume Information Centre, c/o International Institute of Tropical Agriculture, P.M.B. 5320, Ibadan, Nigeria

Legume Improvement Programme, Agriculture Faculty, University of Papua New Guinea, University, Papua New Guinea (R. Stephenson and W. Erskine)

Lembaga Biologi Nasional, Bogor, Indonesia (S. Sastrapradja and I. Lubis)

Mayaguez Institute of Tropical Agriculture, P.O. Box 70, Mayaguez, Puerto Rico 00708

NifTAL, P.O. Box "O", Paia, Maui, Hawaii 96790, USA

K. O. Rachie, The Rockefeller Foundation, 1133 Avenue of the Americas, New York, New York 10036, USA

J. Sauer, Department of Geography, University of California, Los Angeles, California 90024, USA (no germ plasm)

E. Westphal, Laboratory for Plant Taxonomy and Geography, University of Agriculture, 37 General Foulkesweg, Wageningen, The Netherlands

Lablab Bean

The lablab bean* is already widespread throughout the tropics, but it has so many uses, so many varieties, and such wide adaptability that, in most countries, it has by no means reached its potential. Indeed, outside of India, very little lablab research has been undertaken in the last decade.†

There are myriad uses for the lablab bean. One region may use it only for forage, while another capitalizes on its food uses. In the United States it is

---

Lablab purpureus (L.) Sweet. The literature contains at least 26 separate botanical names for what now seem to be different forms of this plant. Many articles published in recent decades use the names *Dolichos lablab* L. or *Lablab niger* Medik. There are also many common names—almost every country (indeed every province in India) uses a different one. Among these are: bonavist, chicharos, chink, Egyptian bean, Indian bean, hyacinth bean, pharao, lubia bean, seem, and val. Subfamily: Papilionoideae.

†Of the 39 lablab bean papers published since 1969, 30 were from India, four from Australia, and one each were from Egypt, Uganda, Chad, Switzerland, and Burma.

marketed solely as an ornamental—for its long, showy, violet-purple blossoms. In the Sudan it is the main green manure used in the highly successful Gezira project. But the plant offers each tropical and subtropical country a wealth of different products and uses.

Food

- Young pods make an excellent table vegetable.
- Dried seeds are a wholesome, palatable food, either cooked and eaten directly, processed to bean cake (tofu) or fermented to tempeh.
- Leaves and flowers are cooked and eaten like spinach.
- Sprouts are comparable to soybean or mung bean sprouts.
- Protein concentrate can be made from the seeds.

Forage

- The plant is grazed by cattle, sheep, goats, and pigs.
- Lablab bean hay is palatable and (if cut at a young, leafy stage) is chemically comparable to alfalfa, though less digestible. It also makes good silage.
- Incorporating this crop into grass pastures improves the quality, palatability, and digestibility of the pasture.

Miscellaneous Uses

- It makes excellent green manure.
- It is effective for erosion control and soil protection.
- It can be used as a nitrogen-fixing crop grown alone, interplanted with field crops, or, grown in rotation with these crops, it may be grazed after the primary crop is harvested.
- It makes a good cover crop in coffee and coconut plantations, fruit orchards, etc.
- It is often planted as a second crop in rice fields after the harvest of paddy.

Varieties

Lablab bean occurs in two botanical types. The garden type is twining and has to be grown on supports. It is late maturing and is used mainly as a green vegetable. The field type is erect and bushy. It matures earlier but cannot be used as a green vegetable because the green pods are fibrous and have an unpleasant smell. Over 200 genotypes are recognized. Their variable characteristics include:

- Pods differing in size, shape, texture, or color (green, white, purple, for example);
- Seeds differing in size, shape, color (white, yellow, black and red-purple), and attachment within the pod;
- Flowers differing in abundance, fragrance, corolla size or penduncle length, and color;
- Leaves differing in size, shape, hairiness, or color (green to purple); and
- Physiological differences (seedling vigor, drought tolerance, day-length sensitivity, flowering time, maturation time, disease and pest resistance, and seed viability).

Despite the wealth of available germ plasm, only a handful of registered commercial varieties are known in the countries that now cultivate the lablab bean.

Adaptability

The lablab bean is remarkably adaptable. Its various strains thrive in a number of different areas and under diverse conditions. There are varieties for:

- Arid, semiarid, and humid regions (that is, for a range of 200–2,500 mm of annual precipitation);
- Warm-temperate, subtropical, and humid rainforest regions where mean summer temperatures range from 22° to 35°C (some new, early-flowering varieties can be grown in frost-prone regions because the seeds mature before the onset of frosts in the fall);
- Lowlands and highlands (it is grown widely up to 2,100 m altitude in the New Guinea highlands);
- Many types of soils, including some of the poorest and most toxic soils (e.g., it has been reported growing well in soils ranging from acid to alkaline, pH 4.4–7.8) as well as in aluminous soils;*
- Both mechanized, large-scale farming and labor-intensive, small-farm agriculture; and
- Field agriculture and home gardens (the Government of Guyana encourages city dwellers to grow it along fence lines as an ornamental hedge that also provides protein for the family table).

Cultivated in Asia since ancient times, the lablab bean plant looks a little like cowpea, but its stems are stronger and more fibrous, and it is more resistant to the root diseases common in cowpea. Single plants have been

*Information supplied by C.D. Foy. See Research Contacts.

reported to produce twice the herbage of cowpea. In cooler climates the plant dies at the end of the growing season, but in the tropics it will persist for 2 or 3 years, though, unless ample moisture is available, it produces progressively fewer leaves and more stem. It nodulates easily either with lablab or cowpea-type *Rhizobium*, common in soils worldwide. Thus its growth is generally unaffected by low soil-nitrogen content. Seed pods are generally 5–8 cm long, flat, broad, and scimitar shaped. Many varieties are nonshattering and their mature pods shed seed only when threshed.

The plant establishes easily. It is drought tolerant, but good soil moisture is needed to get the crop established. Its dense growth suffocates most weeds; in most cases it will propagate by self-seeding, especially if the soil is reculti-vated to bury the seeds. A well-established plant has a deep root system,

Lablab bean, Highworth variety. This interesting variety, newly developed in Queensland Australia, is quick maturing and yields well in widely differing environments. Its pods are nonshattering, mature at much the same time, and grow above the foliage at the top of the stems so that harvesting them is easy. High forage yields are reported (2.5 t per ha of hay produced under rain-fed conditions in 54 days), and, "very high daily live weight gains have been recorded with steers grazing mature and ripening pods." (Wildin, 1974, see Selected Readings).

often penetrating to water sources more than 2 m below the soil surface, permitting luxurious growth to persist long into dry seasons. Thus the lablab bean has a long production season and can provide food, fodder, and soil protection when many other herbaceous plants have become desiccated.

Dried seeds of lablab bean contain 20-28 percent crude protein (for nutritional composition, see Appendix A); some types are tasty and are eaten like other beans. Their amino acids are moderately well balanced, with an especially high lysine content (6.1 percent). The seeds complement cereal diets well.

Lablab bean leaves are also rich in protein (up to 28 percent), and among legumes they are one of the best sources of iron (155 mg per 100 g of leaves, dry weight).

Yields are unknown for most cultivars. However, the lablab bean appears to yield well. In trials in northern Australia, four accessions yielded over 4 t of dry seed per ha.* One of these, a commercially registered Australian variety called Highworth, consistently provides over 1.5 t of seed per ha in commercial use.† In addition, yields of 5-11 t (dry matter) of forage—with protein content between 13.5 and 22 percent depending on season—can be expected. In Queensland, Australia, lablab bean pastures are ready for grazing 60-80 days after planting, when optimum stocking with cattle is about 1.5 animals per ha.

In Tamil Nadu, India, one cultivar (Co.9) has been bred as a green vegetable crop. It yields an average of 7,500 kg of pods per ha. It is quick maturing (120 days) and the pods are broad and flat, with attractive light-green color and good flavor, aroma, and texture.‡

Limitations

Lablab cultivars are generally reported as being fairly pest resistant, but soil, leaf, pod, and flower insect pests have proved very serious in north Queensland. Some cultivars are susceptible to a bean rust and fungal rot may also occur.§ Root-knot nematodes and, in some areas, parasitic weeds (*Striga* spp.) can seriously affect the crop.

Some strains are so variable that even their growth form can be influenced by the time of planting. In Queensland, "Highworth" develops as a twining

---

*Information supplied by I. M. Wood. See Research Contacts.
†See illustration page 62.
‡Information supplied by Y. B. Morachan. See Research Contacts.
§In Queensland, Australia, farmers reports that "Highworth" tolerates brief waterlogging better than any other forage legume including cowpeas. (Information supplied by J. H. Wildin.)

Harvesting the Highworth lablab bean. Yield: 2.5 t of clean seed per ha. (J. H. Wildin)

creeper if planted in spring, but grows erect if planted in late summer or autumn.*

The mature seeds (especially dark-colored ones) must be boiled to become edible, for they contain a trypsin inhibitor that is broken down by heat and a toxic cyanogenetic glucoside that is soluble in the cooking water. Their hard seed coat necessitates a longer cooking time than common beans.

When first introduced to lablab bean, cattle take about a week to adapt. After that they eagerly graze its leaves, flowers, young and mature pods, and soft stems; coarse stems are not eaten. In dairy cattle, it sometimes imparts a slight odor to the milk, easily removed by pasteurization. Unlike perennial pasture legumes, the lablab bean requires annual replanting (or supplementary seeding), though self-seeding may often maintain a heavy crop.

Research Needs

Because of its many outstanding qualities, the plant is recommended for immediate use in tropical areas as a pulse, green vegetable, green manure, forage, or as a ground cover for erosion control. With the very large number

---

*Apparently, this is because the short day lengths initiate flowering, which curtails the plant's vegetative growth. (Most lablab genotypes require short days to initiate flowering.)

of different lablab bean cultivars scattered through the Indian subcontinent and the tropics, it is imperative that a comprehensive germ plasm collection be made.

Researchers in many regions may wish to avail themselves of germ plasm suited to their needs and environment, so it is also important that a series of indicator trials be undertaken in areas of widely differing climates. Comparing the properties of many cultivars under different conditions will lead to strains with known adaptability and qualities; these strains can then be introduced to new countries with improved chances for their successful establishment and ready adoption by local farmers. Because strains already growing in a given location may have become adapted to local conditions by natural selection, agronomists should first screen the types in their immediate area for desirable strains.

Lablab bean as forage, Queensland Australia. (Wright Stephenson & Co. [Aust.] Pty. Ltd.)

Despite the wide occurrence of lablab beans, little agronomic improvement has been reported. There is need for research into genetics and breeding for faster, uniform maturing varieties with higher, more dependable yields and resistance to pests, diseases, and adverse soils and weather.

For forage types, attention should be given to:

- Dry matter yield and its distribution through the year;
- Palatability and feeding value; and
- Compatability as an intercrop with other forages.

For existing varieties, research and testing of management practices, including fertilizer requirements, time of planting, and plant populations for specific products (seed, forage, hay, or green manure) are needed.

Research into the feeding value of the seeds for humans and livestock (including poultry and pigs) is also needed. Methods to reduce or remove the antinutrition factors and the hard seed coat either by processing or by plant breeding need developing.

Although the lablab bean now finds its greatest use in small-scale agriculture, its potential for large-scale mechanized production of protein seems impressive. In the monsoonal tropics, where other large-scale grain legumes (such as soybean) grow poorly, the lablab bean thrives. The Highworth variety shows that the lablab bean can be suited to mechanical harvesting and production. Research along these lines is needed.

Such aspects as processing the seeds into protein concentrates for livestock, poultry, and human foods, and the functional and chemical properties of the protein all deserve attention.

Because of the bean's ability to survive in marginal environments, varieties should be further tested for tolerance to aridity and to acid, alkaline, saline, high-alumina, and nutrient-deficient soils. Its nodulation and the amount of nitrogen it can fix and transfer to the soil also deserve early attention.

Selected Readings

Cassidy, G. J. 1975. Lablab bean for autumn grazing. *Queensland Agricultural Journal* 101:37-40.

Joshi, S. N. 1971. Studies on genetic variability for yield and its components in Indian beans *Dolichos lablab* var *lignosus*. *Madras Agricultural Journal* 58:367-371.

Kay, D. E. 1978. *Food Legumes.* TPI Crop and Product Digest No. 3. Tropical Products Institute, London, pp. 246-260.

Luck, P. E. 1965. *Dolichos lablab*, a valuable grazing crop. *Queensland Agricultural Journal* 91:308-309.

Magoon, M. L., A. Singh, and K. L. Mehra. 1974. Improved field bean for dryland forage. *Indian Farming* 24(2):5-7.

Purseglove, J. W. 1968. *Tropical Crops: Dicotyledons I.* John Wiley and Sons, New York. pp. 273-276.

Rangaswani, G. N., and K. K. Krishnam. 1935. Studies on *Dolichos lablab* (Roxb.) L., the Indian field and garden bean, II. *Proceedings of the Indian Academy of Science* 2(1):74-79.

Skerman, P. J. 1977. *Tropical Forage Legumes*. FAO Plant Production and Protection Series No. 2. Food and Agriculture Organization of the United Nations, Rome. 609 pp.

von Schaafhausen, R. 1963. *Dolichos lablab* or hyacinth bean, its uses for feed, food, and soil improvement. *Economic Botany* 17:146-153.

Westphal, E. 1974. *Pulses in Ethiopia, Their Taxonomy and Agricultural Significance*. Centre for Agricultural Publishing and Documentation, Wageningen, The Netherlands. pp. 91-104.

Wildin, J. H. 1974. Highworth, a new lablab cultivar. *Queensland Agricultural Journal* 100:281-284. Reprinted as Advisory Leaflet No. 1252, Queensland Division of Plant Industry, Department of Primary Industries, William Street, Brisbane, Queensland 4000, Australia.

Wilson, G. P., and G. J. Murtagh. 1968. *Lablab, Annual Forage Crop for the North Coast*. Bulletin P232, Division of Plant Industry, New South Wales, Department of Agriculture (available from the authors, see addresses below).

Research Contacts

Agricultural Research Station, Grafton, N.S.W. 2560, Australia (G. P. Wilson)

Central Arid Zone Research Institute, Jodhpur, India (H. S. Mann, Director)

Department of Primary Industries, P.O. Box 689, Rockhampton 4700, Queensland, Australia (J. H. Wildin)

Division of Tropical Crops and Pastures, Commonwealth Scientific and Industrial Research Organisation, Mill Road, St. Lucia, Brisbane 4067, Queensland, Australia (R. J. Williams and I. M. Wood)

Food Industries Service (AGSI), Food and Agriculture Organization, Via delle Terme di Caracalla, 00100 Rome, Italy (H. A. B. Parpia)

Lembaga Biologi Nasional, Bogor, Indonesia (N. W. Soetjipto)

Mayaguez Institute of Tropical Agriculture, P.O. Box 70, Mayaguez, Puerto Rico 00708

National Bureau of Plant Genetic Resources, Indian Agriculture Research Institute Campus, New Delhi 110012, India (K. L. Mehra, Director)

Queensland Department of Primary Industries, Research Station, Walkamin 4872, Queensland, Australia (I. B. Staples and J. M. Hopkinson)

Queensland Department of Primary Industries, William Street, Brisbane, Queensland 4000, Australia (D. G. Cameron)

Reimar von Schaaffhausen, Caixa Postal 12.633, Santo Amaro, 04745 São Paulo, Brazil

Tamil Nadu Agricultural University, Coimbatore 641 003, India (Y. B. Morachan)

United States Department of Agriculture, Beltsville, Maryland 20705, USA (Harold F. Winters, Germplasm Resources Laboratory, and C. D. Foy, Plant Physiology Institute)

Wollongbar Agricultural Research Center, Wollongbar, N.S.W. 2480, Australia (G. J. Murtagh)

Some collections of lablab seed are maintained by the U.S. plant introduction program. For information contact George A. White, Agriculture Research Service, Beltsville, Maryland 20705, USA

Marama Bean

Of all the plants described in this book, the marama bean* is perhaps the least developed. It is a wild plant that has not been introduced to cultivation. However, with research, particularly breeding, the plant could become a valuable crop for semiarid lands. Below ground, it produces a tuber often larger than a sugar beet, while above ground, it produces seeds whose composition and nutritive value rival those of the peanut or soybean.

Native to the Kalahari and neighboring sandy regions of southern Africa, the marama bean is a staple in the diet of some Khoisan peoples (Bushmen and Khoi-khoi) and is a well-known delicacy of the Herero, Tswana, and other Bantu-speaking peoples. The plant is a rich source of protein and energy and nourishes man in regions where few conventional crops can survive. Adapted to a wide range of climatic conditions, the marama bean grows in some areas that receive up to 800 mm annual rainfall, and in other areas where rainfall is so slight and erratic that in some years almost no rain falls at all.

In Botswana and Namibia (South West Africa), the marama bean is an important component of the diet in remote settlements and among nomadic "hunter-gatherers." It is also found in South Africa (northern Cape Province and Transvaal), usually in undulating grass-veld (savanna). In deep, loose, sandy soils the plant sometimes forms characteristic "craters" where the soil is stony. These hollows, sometimes more than 1 m across, are often ringed with stones that appear to have been forced to the surface by the tuber beneath. In some areas, marama bean occurs in scattered stands several kilometers across.

The plant is not a climber; it grows prostrate, sending long viny stems (up to 6 m long) creeping out over the soil surface in several directions. The vines

---

Tylosema esculentum (Burchell) A. Schreiber. Also known as *Bauhinia esculenta* Burchell. Commonly called tsi or tsin bean (Kung Bushman names); braaiboontjie (Afrikaans); gemsbok bean; tamami or thamani berry; marama, marami, or morama (Tswana names); ombanui (Herero name); or gami (Khoi-khoi name). Subfamily: Caesalpinioideae.

Kalahari bushmen collecting marama bean, Botswana. (L.K. Marshall)

carry double-lobed leaves that are soft and red-brown when young, and turn leathery and gray-green with age. Golden yellow blossoms develop in midsummer (December in southern Africa) and the fruits ripen in late autumn (April). Each fruit comprises a broad woody pod with 1-6 large chestnut-brown seeds inside. Though hard, the woody shell is thin, brittle, and is easily cracked. The normally spherical seeds are roughly the diameter of a thumbnail and weight about 2-3 gm. Their inner flesh is firm, cream colored, oily, and almost without fiber.

The uncooked seeds are usually nearly tasteless but they have an unpleasant, slimy texture and are never eaten raw. After roasting they have a delicious nutty flavor that has been compared with that of roasted cashew nuts or coffee beans. Europeans in southern Africa grind the roasted seeds and use them as a culinary substitute for almonds. Africans often boil them with cornmeal or grind or pound them to a powder that is boiled in water to make either a porridge or cocoa-like beverage. The raw seeds store well and remain edible for years.

The marama bean analyses so far reported record protein contents of 30, 34, and 39 percent, respectively,* a range roughly comparable to that of soybean, 37-39 percent. Oil content is reported as 36-43 percent of the dry seed by weight. Thus, the marama seed has a protein content that rivals that of soybean, and its oil content, about twice that of soybean, approaches that of

*Bray, G. T. 1921. Gemsbok Beans. *The Analyst* 46:401-402; Department of Agriculture, South Africa, 1924. Wehmeyer, Lee, and Whiting. 1969 (see Selected Readings).

Marama beans. (B. Maguire)

the peanut (see page 305). The seeds have less than half the fiber of peanuts and are a source of nutritionally important minerals. Like most legume proteins, marama bean protein is rich in lysine (5 percent) and deficient in methionine (0.7 percent).*

A clear golden-yellow oil is extracted from the seeds by conventional presses or solvent extraction. The oil has a pleasant nutty odor and agreeable taste and is similar to almond oil in consistency and appearance. It appears suitable as an edible oil for use in cooking and foods. It is a good source of linoleic acid, one of the nutritionally essential fatty acids. The meal remaining after oil extraction has a remarkable 52-percent protein content.

During cooler months, stems of the marama bean die back, but the underground tuber remains viable and, with returning warmth, produces new stems. The red-brown tuber, shaped like a giant top, can attain a weight of over 10 kg. Inhabitants of the Kalahari region dig up young tubers when they weigh about 1 kg. Baked, boiled, or roasted whole they have a sweet, pleasant flavor and make a good vegetable dish.† The succulent tuber contains much moisture (sometimes 90 percent by weight); in arid and semiarid regions it is an important emergency source of water for humans and animals. The plant probably survives droughts by drawing on water stored in the tuber, which shrinks greatly in dry years.

*Information supplied by A. S. Wehmeyer.
†Tubers more than 2 years old become fibrous and are not suitable as food. W. J. Burchell, an Englishman who traveled the Kalahari in the 1820s and who made the first botanical records of the plant, reported that the tuber was astringent. Apparently he ate tubers that were either over-mature or from a poor strain.

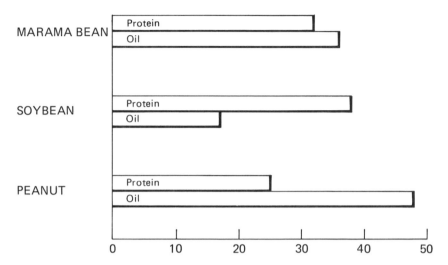

Though virtually unknown to science, the marama bean rivals soybeans and peanuts in oil and protein content.

Like other legume tubers (see pages 21, 27, and 32) the tubers of marama beans are rich in protein (9 percent dry weight).*

Although there has been no concerted research effort to domesticate the bean, it was reported in the early 1960s that, for 20 years, farmers near Barberspan (Western Transvaal) had cultivated the plant just by sowing it (in October) directly into sand without any preliminary plowing.†

Limitations

This plant is so neglected that the very lack of knowledge about it is a major limitation. Before large-scale cultivation can be undertaken, information is needed on its adaptability to cultivation and on all aspects of its agronomy.

Even its limitations and special requirements are unknown. Some writers have reported that the seeds can taste slightly bitter and that the hard pod that surrounds them is a hindrance to their use as oilseeds.

Although not yet tested, it is possible that the tubers grow slowly, perhaps taking 2-4 years to reach a marketable size. Some tubers also have a tough, leathery skin.

*Wehmeyer, Lee, and Whiting. 1969.
†Story, R. Undated. Fodder report from the Kuruman District. Unpublished Notes, No. 3528. Botanical Research Institute, Pretoria, South Africa. (For author's address, see Research Contacts.)

Marama bean tuber. (A.S. Wehmeyer)

While the plant has a wide distribution, it occurs patchily in very localized stands, perhaps indicating that it has special soil requirements.

Research Needs

As is evident, research on the marama bean is badly needed. Among agronomic features that need investigating are the plant's requirements for altitude, temperature, moisture, soil types, fertilization, and latitude. In addition, trials are needed for learning how to manage the plant as a crop. Such cultural practices as germination, spacing, planting, weeding, and pest and disease control all need study and evaluation, as do harvesting, storage, and processing of the seed.

Genetic improvement needs particular attention. Wild stands offer a wealth of different germ plasm. But they are being exterminated in many areas because the land has been ploughed up and planted with corn or sunflower, or because the seeds have been relentlessly harvested for village use and for sale to white farmers. Another threat to the plant is that cattle ranching now extends into the Kalahari region. Livestock eagerly devour the plant's leaves and runners.

Germ plasm collections should be made immediately and desirable strains selected. Initially, strains should be selected on the basis of yield; to date, no single yield, measured or estimated, has been reported. Vigorous strains that produce large numbers of pods, bigger seeds, or more seed per pod are needed. Furthermore, strains that yield under adverse conditions should be sought.

Because of this plant's special importance for semiarid climates, botanists could provide useful information by detailing the mechanisms that allow it to survive extreme heat and desiccation. Temperatures sometimes reach 50°C in its native habitat and surface water is usually available only for 8 weeks a year (though in the fine-grained sandy soils water may remain in the root zone for as long as 2 months after a rainfall).

The extent of its nodulation and nitrogen fixation also needs investigation; the plant belongs to subfamily Caesalpinioideae whose members often fail to nodulate and fix nitrogen.

In the 1920s, the seeds were reported to be free of alkaloids and cyanogenetic glucosides, but analysis for these and other antinutritional factors should be made with sensitive modern instruments.

The tubers warrant particular attention: composition, growth rate, occurrence of nonastringent types, and production potential in small plots should all be investigated.

Related species may also be worth agronomic attention.

*Tylosema fassoglense.** Grows from the Transvaal northwards through East and Central Africa to the Sudan. A sprawling vine, it, too, bears edible seeds and a tuber.

Bauhinia petersiana.† A small shrub that grows together with the marama bean in open grasslands (as well as in sandy bushveld and woodlands) in

---

Tylosema fassoglense (Schweinf.) Torre and Hillcoat. Also known as *Bauhinia fassoglensis* Kotschy ex Schweinfurth.

†*Bauhinia petersiana* Bolle subsp. *serpae* (Ficalho & Hiern) Brummitt & Ross. Also known as *Bauhinia macrantha* Oliv.

Transvaal, Namibia (South West Africa), and Botswana, as well as in Angola and Zambia. The seeds can be eaten green, but ripe seeds are usually roasted, peeled, and pounded into a pleasant-tasting, coarse meal. The plant has been cultivated as an ornamental in South Africa and, given research, might also become a useful food crop for arid zones.*

Selected Readings

Anonymous. 1924. Bauhinia esculenta *Burch., Economic Plants of South Africa*. Notes from the National Herbarium and Museum, Series No. 2, Department of Agriculture, Pretoria, South Africa. 3 pp.

Engelter, C., and A. S. Wehmeyer. 1970. Fatty acid composition of oils of some edible seeds of wild plants. *Journal of Agricultural and Food Chemistry* 18:25-26.

Marshall, L. 1976. *The !Kung of Nyae Nyae*. Harvard University Press, Cambridge, Massachusetts.

Story, R. 1958. Some plants used by the Bushmen in obtaining food and water. *Botanical Survey of South Africa Mem. 30*. (Obtainable from Department of Agricultural Information, Private Bag X144, Pretoria 0001, Republic of South Africa.)

Wehmeyer, A. S., R. B. Lee, and M. Whiting. 1969. The nutrient composition and dietary importance of some vegetable foods eaten by the ?Kung bushmen. *South African Journal of Nutrition* 5(4):1529-1530.

Research Contacts

Megan Biesele, Kalahari Peoples' Fund, Box 4973, Austin, Texas 78751, USA

Botanical Research Institute, Private Bag X101, Pretoria 0001, South Africa

A. C. Campbell, Director, Botswana National Museum, Gaborone, Botswana

N. A. Coetzee, 72 Julius Jeppe Street, Waterkloof 0181, Pretoria, South Africa

H. D. L. Corby, Department of Botany, University of Rhodesia, P.O. Box M.P. 167, Mount Pleasant, Salisbury, Zimbabwe-Rhodesia

Department of Agricultural Research, Private Bag 003, Gaborone, Botswana

Department of Botany, University of Pretoria, Pretoria 0002, Republic of South Africa (P. J. Robbertse and L. A. Coetzer)

Brian Maguire, Bernard Price Institute for Palaeontological Research, University of the Witwatersrand, Jan Smuts Ave., Johannesburg, South Africa

Lorna Marshall, 4 Bryant Street, Cambridge, Massachusetts 02139, USA

M. A. N. Muller, Officer in Charge, South West Africa Herbarium, Private Bag 13184, Windhock, Namibia (South West Africa)

George B. Silberbauer, Senior Lecturer, Anthropology and Sociology, Monash University, Clayton, Victoria, Australia

Geoffrey Stanford, Agro-City Incorporated, Rt. 1, Box 861, Cedar Hill, Texas 75104, USA

Robert Story, c/o CSIRO, Box 109 City, Canberra, A.C.T., Australia

A. S. Wehmeyer, National Food Research Institute, Council for Scientific and Industrial Research, P.O. Box 395, Pretoria 0001, South Africa

Marjorie Whiting, 407 5th St., S.W., Washington, D.C. 20003, USA

*Story. 1958.

Moth Bean

The moth bean* has been so neglected that it has inspired only a handful of original research papers in the past 5 years; the last review article appeared in 1925. Yet the information available shows that this plant, now cultivated as a pulse only in India, could substantially increase the food or forage available to arid and semiarid lands throughout the tropics, subtropics, and even some warm-temperate areas.

Reportedly the most drought-tolerant pulse crop grown in India,† the moth (a Hindi word pronounced "mat" or "mote") bean is already cultivated on about 1.5 million hectares, mainly on arid, sandy tracts of Rajasthan, India's driest state.

A hot-weather legume, the moth bean thrives where temperatures are high. It survives with little moisture; if it is planted near the end of the rainy season the moisture remaining in the soil is often enough to mature a crop, which takes 2-3 months, with little or no additional rainfall or irrigation.

Growing only about 25 cm tall, the plant forms a mat across the soil surface. The stem of each plant radiates horizontal branches (0.5-1.5 m long), producing an expanding circlet of densely matted, ground-hugging vegetation. A living mulch, the moth bean shields soil from the sun's heat, prevents cracking and crust formation, reduces soil moisture and organic matter losses, and retards soil erosion. Livestock avidly graze its pods and foliage. The pods, when young, are eaten as a table vegetable; the tiny beans they contain are high in protein and other nutrients and are a valued pulse for dry regions. The plant is an annual that can be used as a second crop, to follow winter crops (grain, hay, vegetables) and increase the year-round productivity of the land.

Found growing wild from the Himalayas to Sri Lanka, from sea level to 1,500 m altitude, the moth bean is a well-established commercial crop on the Indian subcontinent. Annual seed production is about 360,000 t.‡

Vigna aconitifolia (Jacq.) Marechal, known until recently as *Phaseolus aconitifolius* Jacq. Also known as mat, matki, math, or mout bean. Subfamily: Papilionoideae.
†Indian Council for Agricultural Research. 1970.
‡Information supplied by S.B.S. Tikka. See Research Contacts.

The plant's climatic requirements are like those of cowpea, but the moth bean prefers an even warmer environment (40-45°C daytime temperatures). It is often planted with other hot-weather crops such as sorghum or millet. It tolerates widely different soil textures but grows best in light soils ranging from sand to sandy-loam. Soil fertility is not crucial and the moth bean can grow vigorously and yield heavily even in fairly poor soils. Numerous small, spherical nodules cover its root system and its rhizobial microsymbiont is of the cowpea type.*

The crop requires little care. At the monsoon's onset it is sown broadcast into virtually untilled soil and is given little or no weeding after that.

Food

Each of the moth bean's numerous bright-yellow flowers develop into a short, narrow, yellowish-brown pod. When green and immature, these pods make an appealing and nutritious vegetable. Each contains from 4 to 9 seeds not much larger than a fat grain of rice (5 mm long, 2 mm wide).

Seed yields averaging 1,800 kg per ha have been measured at Davis, California, and 1,600 kg per ha at Ibadan, Nigeria. Though tiny, the seeds are rich in protein (22-24 percent) and other elements and make an excellent supplement to cereal diets. The plant holds the seed well; the pods have little tendency to shatter (drop seed) even when dried out, so not many seeds are wasted on the ground.

In India, the seed is used, either whole or split, as a pulse. Fried in a little oil it is the basis for *dal moth*. It is also used in a salted snack called *bhujia* which looks like broken macaroni.

Forage

In addition to all its other potential, the moth bean shows good promise of supplying quality forage under arid and semiarid conditions.

Fields of moth bean make valuable pastures and have been cultivated for this purpose in India, California, and Texas. At the end of the hot season, when other crops have succumbed to the heat, the leaves and vines are still green—even after the seeds and pods are ripe—and they remain succulent until the arrival of cold weather. They are palatable and are relished by livestock. Yields of over 60 t per ha of green forage have been achieved.

Moth bean hay is also readily eaten by livestock and has a feeding value almost equal to that of alfalfa hay (see Appendix A). The stems are small and the leaves do not easily fall off when the plant is dried; few legumes retain their leaves as well. A California extension bulletin (Kennedy and Madson,

*Information supplied by P. Woomer. See Research Contacts.

A moth bean plant showing its mat-like form of growth. (P.S. Kennedy and B.A. Madson)

1925, see Selected Readings) projects that yields of 7–10 t of hay per ha can reasonably be expected. In India, moth fodder recently proved superior to cowpea and guar in digestible dry-matter yield, the researchers concluding that it is the best leguminous fodder for summer use in Haryana state.*

Limitations

Lack of information on its potential and cultivation is limiting the bean's spread and utilization. Even today there is no modern literature to guide growers.

The plant is notable for its pest and disease resistance,† but a yellow mosaic leaf virus, certain nematodes, and witch weed (*Striga* species) are known to affect it. In storage, the seed can be infested by bean weevils.

Because the vines lie close to the ground, it is more difficult to harvest moth bean for hay than the more upright legumes and grasses. Moreover, the

*Das *et al.* 1975.
†In part, this may reflect the environment in which it is grown; aridity is not conducive to growth of pest and disease organisms.

A trailing branch of a mature moth bean plant. (P.S. Kennedy and B.A. Madson)

small size of the pods and seeds makes them somewhat difficult to handle and process.

Despite Indian farmers' casualness in planting moth bean, to achieve high germination the seed bed must be carefully prepared: the seedlings are so tiny that weeds smother them easily, and a slight soil crust can block their emergence.

The plant needs high temperatures throughout the growing season. The literature contains conflicting statements on its ability to tolerate wet conditions, but it grows poorly in waterlogged soils because root development is retarded.

Research Needs

To help the moth bean reach its potential as a valuable global crop, plans should be made to:

• Assemble, explore, evaluate, and maintain the world germ plasm resources of the species. In particular, Indian researchers should gather the germ plasm of Maharashtra, Uttar Pradesh, Rajasthan, and Haryana states.

• Explore the ecological limits and optimal management factors for the crop, both in mixed and monoculture systems.

• Study the pest and disease problems of the crop and devise practical controls.

• Breed types to correct any proclivity to pests and diseases.

• Breed types with an upright, non-viny (determinate) habit.

• Breed types with superior nutritive value—richer in protein and the limiting amino acids, poorer in the trypsin inhibitor that now renders some of the protein unavailable.

• Investigate the nutritional aspects of the seeds and green pods—biochemical analyses, food-preparation studies, and feeding trials are all needed.

Despite these research needs, the widespread use of the plant by peasant farmers in some of the most difficult growing conditions in India shows that it already has much to contribute. Small-scale trials in tropical and subtropical areas beset by long dry seasons seem warranted. In these areas, moth bean may well become a valuable reserve forage for use during long, hot, late-summer days. It also may prove useful for protecting soil from dry, desiccating summer winds when other herbaceous vegetation has succumbed to drought.

Selected Readings

Biwas, M. R., and S. Dana. 1976. *Phaseolus aconitifolius* x *Phaseolus trilobus*. *Indian Journal of Genetics and Plant Breeding* 36:125-131.

Das. B., S. K. Arora, R. S. Paroda, P. S. Gill, and Y. P. Luthra. 1975. Nutritive parameters of summer legume forages in relation to phosphorus levels and irrigation regimes. *Indian Journal of Dairy Science* 28:190-195.

Faroda, A. S. 1972. Effects of seeding rates and row spacings on fodder production of moth bean (*Phaseolus aconitifolius*). *Annuals of Arid Zone* 11:183-186.

Indian Council for Agricultural Research. 1970. *Pulse Crops of India*. Indian Council for Agricultural Research, New Delhi. pp. 156-158.

Kay, D. E. 1978. *Food Legumes*. TP1 Crop and Product Digest No. 3. Tropical Products Institute, London. pp. 357-364.

Kennedy, P. S., and B. A. Madson. 1925. *The Mat Bean*, Phaseolus aconitifolius. California Agricultural Experiment Station Bulletin No. 396. University of California, Berkeley, California. 33 pp.

Purseglove, J. W. 1968. *Tropical Crops: Dicotyledons I*. John Wiley and Sons, New York. pp. 286-287.

Tikka, S. B. S., J. P. Yadavendra, P. C. Bordia, and S. Kumar. 1976. A correlation and path coefficient analysis of components of grain yield in *Phaseolus aconitifolius* Jacq. *Genetica Agraria* 30:241-248.

Tikka, S. B. S., and S. Kumar. 1976. Association analysis *Vigna aconitifolia* (Jacq.) Marechal. *Science and Culture* 42:182-184.

The *Tropical Grain Legume Bulletin* often contains short articles and abstracts on moth bean. The *Bulletin* is available from the International Grain Legume Information Centre (see address below).

Research Contacts

Agriculture Research Station, Gujarat Agricultural University, Maktampur (Broach), Gujarat, India (S. B. S. Tikka, Cotton Breeder and Officer in Charge)

Department of Genetics and Plant Breeding, Agricultural Experiment Station, University of Udaipur, Udaipur, India (Sudhir Kumar)

Dry Farming Research Station, Sholapur, Maharashtra, India (The Director)

ECHO, R.R. 2, Box 852, North Fort Myers, Florida 33903, USA

Haryana Agricultural University, Hissar, Haryana, India (A. S. Faroda, Department of Agronomy; R. S. Paroda, Department of Forage Research)

International Grain Legume Information Centre, International Institute of Tropical Agriculture, P.M.B. 5320, Ibadan, Nigeria (P. R. Goldsworthy, Assistant Director; E. N. O. Adimorah, Documentalist)

National Botanic Gardens, Lucknow, India (T. N. Khoshoo, Director)

National Bureau of Plant Genetic Resources, Indian Agricultural Research Institute, New Delhi 110012, India (K. L. Mehra, Director)

K. O. Rachie, The Rockefeller Foundation, 1133 Avenue of the Americas, New York, New York 10036, USA

R. C. Sharma, Division of Agricultural Botany, S.K.N. College of Agriculture, University of Udaipur, Jobner: 303329 (Janipur) Rajasthan, India

Paul Woomer, NifTAL Project, University of Hawaii, P.O. Box "O", Paia, Hawaii 96779, USA (Moth bean inoculum)

Some collections of moth bean seed are maintained by the U.S. plant introduction program. For information, contact George A. White, Agriculture Research Service, Beltsville, Maryland 20705, USA

Rice Bean

The rice bean* is adapted to high temperature and humidities as well as to heavy soils—few other pulse crops tolerate such conditions. Furthermore, it grows and matures quickly, is relatively free from major insect and disease problems, and produces easily cooked, good-tasting seeds. Yet today it is an important crop only in tribal areas of northeastern India. Once it was important to farmers throughout South and Southeast Asia. Planted in rice fields after the harvest, certain varieties could produce a prolific crop of nutritious seeds before rice planting recurred. The bean benefited the rice by improving the nitrogen and humus contents of the paddy soil. But multiple cropping of rice—the modern technique—leaves no time for rice bean cultivation between crops. The bean has been dispossessed by changing technology. Yet on its own merits it is a potentially valuable crop, one that deserves increased testing throughout the tropics.

*Vigna umbellata (Thunb.) Ohwi & Ohashi. Called, until recently, Phaseolus calcaratus Roxb. Also known as Japanese rice bean, red bean, climbing mountain bean, mambi bean. Subfamily: Papilionoideae.

Rice bean. (National Bureau of Plant Genetic Resources,
New Delhi, India)

The nutritive value of the bean is high (see Appendix A); it is rich in
protein and contains high amounts of calcium, iron, phosphorus, and the
vitamins thiamine, niacin, and riboflavin. Because of the protein's nutritional
quality, the rice bean has been ranked as one of the best of all pulses and its
use is highly recommended in nutritional programs in the Philippines.* In
addition, the immature pods and seedlings are excellent green vegetables, and
the plant makes forage that is eagerly consumed by livestock.

There are many types and cultivars of rice bean.† Types are known that
produce black, red-violet, greenish, brownish, or mottled seeds. Cultivars vary
from short-stemmed, erect plants to twining ones that may grow up to 3 m
long and need stakes or other supports for maximum yield. The plant is an

*Information supplied by R. M. Lantican. See Research Contacts.
†It is a measure of the neglect accorded this plant by researchers that the most recent
comprehensive classification was made in 1897.

annual that bears clusters of 5–20 bright-yellow flowers that produce narrow pods (often in clusters of up to 12) containing 7–10 seeds.

Because the rice bean grows well in the hottest climates and in high humidity (though it is also moderately drought resistant), it seems ideally suited to the low-altitude tropics, a zone where crop growing is most difficult. Seedlings grow vigorously, establish themselves early, and smother weeds. The plant is covered with hairs, which may help protect it, for it is remarkably resistant to insect pests. In recent tests at the Asian Vegetable Research and Development Center (AVRDC), rice bean proved to be the pulse least attacked by bean fly. Furthermore, the plant is generally resistant to the common leguminous diseases: AVRDC has discovered lines resistant to powdery mildew, damping off, and bacterial leafspot.*

In equatorial climates the rice bean can mature in as little as 60 days (this has been recorded in Angola, for example). All the pods on a plant mature simultaneously and the whole crop can be harvested at one time. Cowpeas and most little-known pulses ripen seeds at different times and must be harvested in several pickings.

Rice beans are native to South and Southeast Asia (from the Himalayas to South China and Indonesia) and they are cultivated in the same way as the more familiar Asian pulse, the mung bean. Despite their special importance for the lowland humid tropics, most rice bean cultivars are also well adapted to drier conditions and thrive where cowpeas grow well. They tolerate soil textures from light to heavy and are known to thrive at altitudes as high as 1,500 m.

Yields are reported to be low, but small-plot trials have shown that they can be as high as with most of the better-known pulses.†

The dried seeds, like other pulses, are usually boiled and eaten with, or sometimes instead of, rice. They contain 16–25 percent protein, but less than 1 percent oil.

In eastern parts of India, the plant is grown both as a pulse and a forage. It is particularly valuable in that it provides forage at a time when other sources are scarce. Yields of over 33 t of green forage per ha have been reported.‡ The foliage, green pods, immature seeds, and flowers are all readily eaten by animals. The rice bean also makes a useful green manure and cover crop. Usually grown as a garden or household hedge in Indonesia, it provides privacy as well as a handy supply of leaves, pods, and seeds for the family meals.

*Information supplied by Hyo-Guen Park. See Research Contacts.

†Chaudhuri and Prasad, 1972 (see Selected Readings), report average seed yields of 1,850 kg per ha from their experiments in West Bengal; Tropical Products Institute, 1962 (see Selected Readings), reports up to 2,000 kg of dry seed per ha in experiments in Northern Rhodesia (Zambia); Vieira, 1971 (see Selected Readings), reports seed yields from 1,300 to 2,500 kg per ha from his experiments in the state of Minas Gerais, Brazil (subtropical climate).

‡Chaudhuri and Prasad, 1972, and Vieira, 1971. See Selected Readings.

Limitations

The rice bean is very sensitive to day length: flowering and seed set are initiated only when days are short. When grown in equatorial areas this is no limitation, but in the subtropics the rice bean matures seeds only during the cooler seasons when days are short (and, unfortunately, growth is slow). When planted at other times the crop produces masses of vegetation but little seed. In these seasons the rice bean can be grown only for forage. Even in warm temperate climates of the southern United States it is used for this purpose.

The plant is susceptible to attack by root-knot nematodes. However, the water in a rice paddy eliminates them and makes it safe for subsequent rice bean crops even if soil nematodes infest the surrounding area. It should be noted, however, that the rice bean itself cannot withstand waterlogged conditions.

The viny growth and seed-shattering habit (dried pods drop their seed) make the rice bean difficult to harvest mechanically.

Although the plant usually matures rapidly, the actual maturing time depends on variety, climate, latitude, and season. In adverse cases it can take as long as 140 days just to get flower initiation.

The seeds are free of toxic cyanogenic compounds, but must be cooked before being eaten. They lack the strong taste of common beans (*Phaseolus vulgaris*); though an advantage in some societies, this may limit their acceptance where common beans are a staple (such as in Latin America).

Research Needs

The rice bean deserves trial introduction to those tropical regions where it is now little known. Although only Asians now use the crop extensively, it will grow well elsewhere; in Fiji and Mauritius it is a commercial market-garden product and it has also been grown successfully in Queensland and East Africa.

As with the other legumes discussed in this book, the obscurity of the rice bean means that there are many things to learn about its potential and its limitations. For the most rational attack on this scientific unknown, researchers should have available a wide assortment of different varieties. Without a germ plasm collection the extent of the plant's properties will be unappreciated. Plant scientists should survey the status of the crop throughout the southern and eastern regions of Asia and should begin collecting seeds and

comparing lines because, as rice multiple-cropping expands, formerly cultivated rice bean cultivars are being lost.*

To advance the rice bean as a crop, the most urgent research need is the
production of cultivars that stand erect and that are insensitive to differences
in day length. Other objectives include selecting or breeding quick-maturing,
high-yielding, and nonshattering varieties. The possibility for breeding a
nematode-resistant rice bean should also be explored.

Along with the varietal testing, research into the most effective methods
for cultivating rice beans is needed. Such aspects as planting density, staking,
fertilizer requirements, and time of planting require analysis.

The flowers are self-fertile, which facilitates breeding, but some natural
outcrossing occurs and the plant will cross even with other legume species.
This makes the rice bean a potential source of disease resistance for crops like
the mung bean (green gram).†

Studies of the nutritional qualities of rice bean seeds, leaves, and green
pods are needed. Checks should be made for nonnutritional amino acids and
other potential antinutritional factors.

As is common among legumes, the plant invariably forms fewer pods than
there are flowers on the inflorescence. Usually only the lower flowers form
pods, while the upper ones abort. It is important to study the causes of this,
for if they can be overcome seed yields would improve dramatically.

Selected Readings

Ahn, Chang-Soon. 1976. Interspecific hybridization among four species of the genus
    Vigna savi. Ph.D. dissertation, Department of Horticulture, University of Hawaii,
    Honolulu. 96 pp.
Anonymous. 1962. The nutritional value of the rice bean, *Phaseolus calcaratus* Roxb.
    from Northern Rhodesia. *Tropical Science* 4:163.
Arora, R. K., K. P. S. Chandel, B. S. Joshi, and K. C. Pant. In Press. Rice bean—a tribal
    pulse of northeastern India. *Economic Botany*.
Chaudhuri, A. P., and B. Prasad. 1972. Flowering behaviour and yield of rice-bean (*Phase-
    olus calcaratus* Roxb.) in relation to date of sowing. *Indian Journal of Agricultural
    Science* 42:627-630.
Chaudhuri, A. P., and B. Prasad. 1973. Grow rice bean—an excellent fodder legume for
    the scarcity period. *Indian Farmers' Digest* 6:27-30.
Herklots, G. A. C. 1972. *Vegetables in South-east Asia*. Hafner Press, New York. pp.
    257-248.
Kay, D. E. 1978. *Food Legumes*. TP1 Crop and Product Digest No. 3. Tropical Products
    Institute, London. pp. 468-475.

---

*A start on this has been made by India's National Bureau of Plant Genetic Resources,
which recently obtained 400 collections mostly from Northeastern and South India.
Information supplied by K.P.S. Chandel. See Research Contacts. The AVRDC has collected 79 lines from 12 Asian nations, Information supplied by Hyo-Guen Park. See
Research Contacts.

†Ahn. 1976.

Majumdar, B. R., S. Sen, and S. R. Roy. 1968. Raise rice bean for nutritious fodder. *Indian Farming* 18:29-30.

Purseglove, J. W. 1968. *Tropical Crops: Dicotyledons I.* John Wiley and Sons, New York. pp. 294-295.

Sastrapradja, S., and H. Sutarno. 1977. *Vigna umbellata* (L.) D.C. in Indonesia. *Annales Bogorienses* 6:155-167. (Copies available from the authors, see address below.)

The *Tropical Grain Legume Bulletin* often contains short articles and abstracts on rice bean. The *Bulletin* is available from the International Grain Legume Information Centre (see address below).

Tropical Products Institute. 1962. The nutritional value of the rice bean, *Phaseolus calcaratus* Roxb. from Northern Rhodesia. *Tropical Science* 4:163.

Vieira, C. 1971. Nota sôbre o comportamento de variedades de *Phaseolus calcaratus* Roxb., em Viçosa, Minas Gerais. *Revista Ceres* 18:303-307. (Copies available from author, see address below.)

Research Contacts

Asian Vegetable Research and Development Center, P.O. Box 42, Shanhua, Tainan 741, Taiwan (Hyo-Guen Park)

Bidhan Chadra Krishi Viswa Vidyalaya, P.O. Kalyani, District Nadia, West Bengal, India (B. N. Chatterjee, Professor of Agronomy; S. Dana, Department of Cytogenetics and Plant Breeding)

International Grain Legume Information Centre, International Institute of Tropical Agriculture, P.M.B. 5320, Ibadan, Nigeria

The International Rice Research Institute, P.O. Box 933, Manila, Philippines

Tanveer Khan, Department of Agriculture, South Perth 6151, W.A., Australia

R. Lantican, University of the Philippines at Los Baños, College, Laguna, Philippines

Legume Improvement Programme, Agriculture Faculty, University of Papua New Guinea, University, Papua New Guinea (R. Stephenson and W. Erskine)

Lembaga Biologi Nasional, Bogor, Indonesia (S. Sastrapradja, Director; Hadi Soetarno)

B. R. Majumder, Salbani Fodder Farm, P.O. and District Midnapore, 721 101, West Bengal, India

National Bureau of Plant Genetic Resources, Indian Agricultural Research Institute, New Delhi 110012, India (K. P. S. Chandel)

S. Sen, B. 8/62 3rd Street, Kalyani, West Bengal 741 235, India

C. Vieira, Professor of Agronomy, Universidade Federal de Viçosa, Viçosa, Minas Gerais, Brazil

Some collections of rice bean seed are maintained by the U.S. plant introduction program. For information contact George A. White, Agriculture Research Service, Beltsville, Maryland 20705, USA.

Tarwi

Although practically unknown outside South America's Andean region, tarwi* produces seed whose content of protein (up to about 50 percent) is among the highest of any legume seed. In addition, the seed contains 14–24 percent oil, and the combination of high protein and oil means that tarwi seeds have a composition similar to soybeans. Tarwi thus would appear to be a ready source of high-protein meal for food and feed as well as of cooking oil, margarine, and other edible-oil products.

But tarwi does not enjoy widespread use because of bitter-tasting and toxic alkaloids in the seeds. However, it is known that alkaloid-free, sweet-tasting types can be developed by conventional breeding methods, and given further research such cultivars could make tarwi a major crop for cool, tropical highlands and for a number of temperate regions.

Tarwi is a lupin native to western South America, mainly Peru, but it also grows in Ecuador, Bolivia, and Chile. Pre-Inca people domesticated it at least 1,500 years ago, and it became a significant protein contributor to the region's food supply. Indians still grow it to a limited extent in the Andean highlands.

The genus *Lupinus* is very diverse, with about 200 different species in the New World and a smaller number in the Mediterranean region. Other than tarwi, all agriculturally important lupins derive from Mediterranean species: the New World lupins are so greatly neglected that tarwi is the only one that has gained appreciable use. The seed of Mediterranean lupins were rendered free of toxic alkaloids in the late 1920s and 1930s by the German researcher, R. von Sengbusch, who isolated low-alkaloid ("sweet") strains. These sweet lupins are now used as feed and fodder in Europe (especially the Soviet Union and Poland), the United States, Australia, and South Africa.

An erect annual, growing 1–2.5 m tall, tarwi is a decorative plant with showy, multicolored purple, blue, and yellow flowers held high above the leaves. To attract pollinating insects, the flowers exude an extremely pleasant-smelling nectar.

Lupinus mutabilis Sweet or *Lupinus tauris* Hook. Also known as tarhwi, taura, tarin, tarhui, altramuz, chocho, pearl lupin. Subfamily: Papilionoideae.

Field of tarwi high in the Andes, near Chiara, Department of Cuzco, Peru. (D.W. Gade)

Tarwi pods contain bean-like seeds that are white, speckled, mottled, banded, or black. The plant is native to tropical latitudes (1°N–22°S) but occurs mainly in cool valleys and basins at high altitudes (1,800–4,000 m). Thus it is a crop for cool climates (tropical highlands and temperate regions), not for the humid or arid tropics.

Tarwi seeds are soft-skinned and germinate rapidly, producing vigorous, quick-growing seedlings. Robust vegetative growth continues through the plant's life.

On forming the first inflorescence, the main stem develops lateral branches. These also form flowers and, in turn, produce more lateral branches, the process continuing indefinitely, producing flowers, pods, seeds, and leaves whose numbers increase in geometrical progression.*

Tarwi is semi-hardy, with some resistance to frost and an ability to withstand drought. It is also tolerant of sandy and acid soils. Many forms resist the fungus *Phomopsis leptostromiphormis* that sometimes kills livestock fed on lupin fodder (lupinosis)† and is resistant to the lupin mildews and rots caused by species of *Erysiphe, Fusarium*, and *Rhizoctonia.*‡

---

*In experiments in the Soviet Union the plant produced 50 t per ha of vegetation containing 1.75 t of protein per ha. Brücher, 1968 (see Selected Readings), reports that the green matter production considerably exceeds that of European lupin species.
†Van Jaarsveld and Knox-Davies. 1974.
‡Information supplied by K. W. Pakendorf. See Research Contacts.

Tarwi is an adaptable plant that will flower both in the short (12-hour) tropical days and in the longer summer days in temperate zones. It has been grown in experiments in England, France, Central Europe, the Soviet Union, South Africa, and Australia, but it matures very late in temperate latitudes.

When von Sengbusch and others set out to improve some of the Mediterranean lupin species, a major problem was seed-shattering: dry pods of unselected forms split and shed their seed on the ground. This problem does not exist in tarwi, probably because early Indian cultivators selectively grew plants whose pods held seed longest.

Protein and oil make up more than half the seed's weight. In a survey of seed from a large number of varieties, protein content varied from 41 to 51 percent (average 46 percent),* while oil content varied (in roughly inverse proportion) from 14 to 24 percent (average 20 percent).† Removing the seed coat and grinding the remaining kernel yields a flour that contains over 50 percent protein. Tarwi protein has adequate amounts of the essential amino acids lysine and cystine, but has only 25–30 percent of the methionine required to support optimal growth in animals. The protein digestibility and nutritional value are reportedly equivalent to those of soybean.‡

Tarwi oil is light colored and acceptable for household use. It is relatively rich in unsaturated acids, including the nutritionally essential linoleic acid. Fiber content is not excessive (see Appendix A) and the seed is thought to be a good source of nutritionally important minerals.§ The soft seed coat makes for easy cooking.

Like other lupins, tarwi is an excellent green manure crop (see page 292). able to fix as much as 400 kg of nitrogen per ha. Much of this becomes available in the soil to succeeding crops. With the high prices and shortages of this essential element, tarwi could become very important in crop-rotation systems.

Limitations

The alkaloids in the seeds are tarwi's most serious liability. Mature seeds of most cultivars are toxic to livestock and humans if eaten raw. Today's Indians, like the ancient Inca, steep the seeds in water for several days to leach out the soluble alkaloids. This lengthy process, and uncertainty over the amount of insoluble alkaloids that remain, now preclude tarwi's introduction as a pulse crop to areas outside the Andes.

*Brücher. 1968.
†Information supplied by R. Gross. See Research Contacts. These are results from testing over 300 different genotypes.
‡Ortiz, Gross, and Von Baer, 1975; Brücher, 1968.
§Pakendorf, Van Schalkwyk, and Coetzer. 1973.

Because there has been little agronomic improvement of tarwi, the available cultivars are primitive. They often take 5–11 months to mature seeds. The multiple tiers of flowers, though they produce exceptional yields, mean that all the pods do not ripen together. For a small farmer in a developing country it means a continuing source of food, but it greatly hinders mechanized harvesting.

Compared with other lupin species (e.g., *Lupinus angustifolius* or *Lupinus luteus*), tarwi is more stemmy (i.e., its leaf to stem ratio is lower), and compared to other pulse crops, it produces fewer seeds than would be expected from such a mass of vegetation.

Tarwi cross-pollinates so readily that to preserve specific cultigens, such as low-alkaloid types, may require a sophisticated system of seed production and distribution.

Research Needs

Eliminating the bitter alkaloids is the first prerequisite for tarwi's advancement as a world crop. Low-alkaloid cultivars would have great practical and economic value. Fortunately, there are excellent prospects for minimizing alkaloid content. In the mountains of South America exist numerous wild

Tarwi seeds. (E. Ampuero P.)

and domesticated cultivars with an impressive diversity of forms; improvements can be made by selecting nontoxic strains from the germ plasm now available. A screening method that uses specially prepared reagent paper is already available.*

Indeed, naturally occuring genotypes and radiation-induced mutants that are low in alkaloids have already been discovered.† The challenge now is to make them "stable," so that the low alkaloid content is inherited uniformly by succeeding generations.

Many flowers fail to set seed and research is needed into pollination and fertility to allow the plant to approach its potential yield.

More details of the composition of both protein and oil are needed. This should be supplemented by breeding to improve the level of sulfur-containing amino acids. Practical tests of tarwi seed's potential in the food-processing industry should also be encouraged.

In addition, there is a need to select and breed cultivars in which all the pods ripen synchronously. This would facilitate mechanical harvesting and would also improve the efficiency of manual harvest.

Tarwi now requires a long growing season to fully ripen its seeds. In any breeding program, high priority should be given to selecting quick-growing, early-maturing varieties for cultivation where growing seasons are short, for example in temperate latitudes and in semiarid areas with long dry seasons. These should also suffer less from disease. Mutants that flower only once rather than continuously might be particularly useful.

Tarwi easily crosses with North American lupin species such as *Lupinus ornatus, Lupinus douglasi*, and *Lupinus pubescens* to yield fertile hybrids that offer a means for improving tarwi itself.‡

Research is needed into the technology of removing bitterness from tarwi seeds on a large scale. In this regard, a pilot plant—sized to process 7,000 t of seeds per year into vegetable oil and protein concentrate—is soon to be constructed in Peru.§

Adaptability trials should be conducted in different parts of the world. Other cultivated lupins are fairly specific in their temperature and soil requirements and tarwi might also prove to have limited adaptability.

Selected Readings

Aguilera, J. M., and A. Trier. 1978. The revival of the lupin. *Food Technology* 32:70-76.
Brücher, H. 1968. Die genetischen reserven Südamerikas für die kulturpflanzenzüchtung. *Theoretical and Applied Genetics* 38:9-22.

*Information supplied by E. Nowacki. See Research Contacts.

†By Von Sengbusch in the 1920s. Also by Brücher (1968) and Pakendorf (1974). See Selected Readings. Also von Baer, Oram, and Golobchenko (personal communications). See Research Contacts.

‡Information supplied by E. Nowacki. See Research Contacts.

§Information supplied by R. Gross. See Research Contacts.

Brücher. H. 1970. Beitrag zur domestikation proteinreicher und alkaloidarmer lupinen in Südamerika. *Angewandte Botanik* 44:7-27.

Castillo, R. 1965. Estudio sobre Lupinus (chocho) en el Ecuador. *Archivos Venezolanos de Nutricion* 15:87-93.

Eckardt, W. R., and W. Feldheim. 1974. Lupinen, eine neue ölfrucht für Südamerika? (The lupine, a new oil plant for South America?) *Zeitschrift für Lebensmittel-Untersuchung und -Forschung* 155:92-93.

Gade, D. W. 1969. Vanishing crops of traditional agriculture: the case of tarwi (*Lupinus mutabilis*) in the Andes. *Proceedings of the Association of American Geographers* 1:47-51.

Gladstones, J. S. 1970. Lupins as crop plants. *Field Crop Abstracts* 23:123-148.

Gross, R., and E. von Baer. 1975. Die lupine, ein beitrag zur nahrungsversorgung in den Anden. 1. Allgemeine gesichtspunkte. (Lupines, a contribution to nutrition maintenance in the Andes. 1. General aspects.) *Zeitschrift für Ernährungswissenschaft* 14:224-228.

Hackbarth, J., and K. W. Pakendorf. 1970. *Lupinus mutabilis* Sweet, eine kulturpflanze der zukunft? (*Lupinus mutabilis* Sweet, a cultivated plant of the future?) *Zeitschrift für Pflanzenzüchtung* 63:237-245.

Hackbarth, J., and H. J. Troll. 1961. Lupinen als körnerleguminosen und futterpflanzen. In *Handbuch der Pflanzenzüchtung* 2nd ed., Vol 4, eds. Kappert and Rudorf, pp. 1-51. Verlag Paul Parey, Berlin and Hamburg.

Masefield, G. B. 1975. A preliminary trial of the pearl lupin in England. *Experimental Agriculture* 11:113-118.

Masefield, G. B. 1976. Further trials of pearl lupins in England. *Experimental Agriculture* 12:97-102.

Ortiz, C., R. Gross, and E. von Baer. 1975. Die lupine, ein beitrag zur nahrungsversorgung in den Anden. 2. Die proteinqualität von *Lupinus mutabilis* im vergleich zu *Lupinus albus, Lupinus luteus* and *Soja max*. (Lupines, a contribution to food supply in the Andes. 2. Protein quality of *Lupinus mutabilis* compared to *Lupinus albus, Lupinus luteus* and soybeans.) *Zeitschrift für Ernährungswissenschaft* 14:230-234.

Pakendorf, K. W. 1974. Studies on the use of mutagenic agents in Lupinus II. Some mutants of *Lupinus mutabilis* after the application of gamma irradiation. *Zeitschrift für Pflanzenzüchtung* 72:152-159.

Pakendorf, K. W., D. J. Van Schalkwyk, and F. J. Coetzer. 1973. Mineral element accumulation in Lupinus II. Variation of mineral element concentration in plant components and growth stages of various lupin species. *Zeitschrift Acker- und Pflanzenbau* 138:46-62.

Torres-Tello, F. 1976. *Lupinus mutabilis* Sweet—a potent food source from the Andean region. *The American Journal of Clinical Nutrition* 29:933.

Van Jaarsveld, A. B., and P. S. Knox-Davies. 1974. Resistance to lupins to *Phomopsis leptostromiformis*. *Phytophylactica* 6:55-60.

von Baer, E., O. Blanco, and R. Gross. 1977. Die lupine—eine neue kulturpflanze in den Anden. *Zeitschrift für Acker- und Pflanzenbau* 145:317-324.

von Baer, E., and R. Gross. 1977. Auslese bittersloffarmer formen von *Lupinus mutabilis*. *Zeitschrift für Pflanzenzüchtung* 79:52-58.

von Baer, E., and R. Gross. 1978. Selection of low-alkaloid forms of *Lupinus mutabilis* as an alternative to the soya bean. In *Plant Research and Development*, vol. 7, pp. 60-66. Institut für Wissenschaftliche Zusammenarbeit, Landhausstrasse 18, Tübingen, Federal Republic of Germany.

Research Contacts

E. Ampuero, Director General, Instituto Nacional de Investigaciones Agropecuarias, Apartado 2600, Quito, Ecuador

E. S. Bunting, Plant Breeding Institute, Marris Lane, Trumpington, Cambridge, England

D. W. Gade, Department of Geography, Old Mill Building, University of Vermont, Burlington, Vermont 05401, USA

R. Gross, Institutos Nacionales de Salud, Instituto de Nutrición, Jirón Tizón y Bueno No. 276, Lima 11, Peru

Instituto de Investigaciones Tecnológicas, (INTEC-CHILE), P.O. Box 667, Santiago 1, Chile (J. M. Aguilera and A. Trier)

M. Lenoble, Institut National de la Recherche Agronomique, Station D'Amélioration des Plantes Fourragères, 86600 Lusignan, France

Museo de Historia Natural "Javier Prado," Universidad Nacional Mayor de San Marcos, Au. Arenales 1256, Apartado 1109, Jesús María, Lima 1, Peru (O. Tovar S.)

E. Nowacki, Department of Physiology and Biochemistry, Institute of Soil Science and Cultivation of Plants, Pulawy, Poland

R. N. Oram, Division of Plant Industry, CSIRO, P.O. Box 1600, Canberra City, A.C.T. 2601, Australia

K. W. Pakendorf, Chief, Wheat Breeding, Small Grain Centre, Private Bag X29, Bethlehem 9700, South Africa

K. Rohrmoser, Institut für Grundlandwirtschaft, Futterbau und Futterkonservierung, Bundesallee 50, D-3300 Braunschweig, Federal Republic of Germany

Felix Torres Tello, Association Peruana de Nutricion, Apartado 4297, Lima, Peru

Universidad Nacional Agraria, La Molina, Apartado 456, Lima 100, Peru (F. Camarena M. and A. Cerrate V.)

E. von Baer, Semillas Baer, Campo Experimental, Casilla 943, Gorbea, Chile

W. Williams, Department of Agricultural Botany, University of Reading, Whiteknights, Reading, Berks RG6 2AS, England

Tepary Bean

A drought-tolerant crop, the tepary bean* thrives in arid and semiarid regions. Withstanding heat and dry atmospheres, it can produce large quantities of edible dry beans and often survives in climates too arid for other beans. In addition, tepary beans contain as much or more protein than most edible legume crops. Yet the plant remains virtually unknown outside its North American homeland.

Phaseolus acutifolius A. Gray. Cultivated varieties are classified as part of var. *latifolius* Freeman. Also known as tepari, yori muni, and pavi; numerous other Amerindian names are in local use in parts of Mexico, Guatemala, and the United States. Subfamily: Papilionoideae.

The tepary bean was brought under cultivation in Mexico, more than 5,000 years ago. Since then, both the domesticated varieties and the wild ones, still found throughout much of North America, have been harvested by American Indians.

The wild varieties are vines, sometimes up to 3 m high, that often climb up desert shrubs. They sprout quickly—immediately after a rainfall—and pass through their brief life cycle while the moisture remains in the soil.

Domesticated varieties are either semi-viny or bushy, self-standing plants that can be grown as a field crop or in small gardens. Many domesticated cultivars differing in taste, seed color, and other characteristics were developed by Indian farmers. Most of these were lost early in this century when they abandoned traditional subsistence farming and turned to irrigated cash crops.

The plant has small, pointed leaves and small pods with seeds often resembling miniature navy beans. The ephemeral nature of their wild ancestors endows domesticated tepary varieties with quick maturation. Indian farmers in the Sonoran desert harvested their crop just 60–90 days after planting the seed. If irrigation water is available, two crops can be produced before cool weather ends the growing season.

The plant needs ample moisture to germinate seed and advance its growth to the onset of flowering, but after that, scanty desert rainfall or even no rain at all may suffice to mature the crop. Floodwaters from a single rain are enough to complete the whole process if the soil is deep and retains moisture. Teparies are therefore suited to semiarid farming with minimal irrigation or runoff agriculture* as well as to dry-land, rain-fed farming.

On dry soils, teparies seem to outproduce most other field legumes. Today, by using fertilizer and moderate irrigation methods, commercial growers have harvested 1,100–2,200 kg of cleaned seed per ha. The record yield is over 4,000 kg for tepary beans grown in California under minimal irrigation.†

Their high protein content (23–25 percent)‡ makes tepary beans (seeds) nutritionally comparable to most economic legumes (see Appendix A). They are eaten like other dry beans—first soaked and then boiled or baked. Some Indians also parch teparies and grind them to a meal that can be added to boiling water for "instant beans." In northern Mexico teparies are also popular as a base for soups and stews.

---

*For a discussion of runoff agriculture, see a companion report: National Academy of Sciences. 1974. *More Water for Arid Lands: Promising Technologies and Research Opportunities.* To order see page 329.

†Hendry, G.W. 1918. Bean culture in California. *University of California Agricultural Experiment Station Bulletin* 294:285–348.

‡Protein contents as high as 32.9 percent have been recorded, for example, see Earle, F.R., and Q. Jones. 1962. Analyses of seed samples from 113 plant families. *Economic Botany* 16(4):221–250.

Tepary bean field planted in bare sand dunes near Hotevilla, Arizona. In this dry region, where conventional crops cannot be grown without irrigation, Hopi and Papago Indians still produce their traditional tepary beans without turning on a tap. (G.P. Nabhan)

In addition to the seeds, the leaves and young pods provide edible forage for livestock. Tepary hay is comparable to alfalfa (lucerne) in composition, and in dry parts of the southwestern United States when irrigation water is not available, the tepary sometimes outproduces alfalfa. *Rhizobium* strains that nodulate lima beans and *Canavalia* species (see pages 97 and 54) also cause nitrogen fixation in tepary beans.*

Limitations

Some accessions of the tepary bean are so resistant to common bean blight that plant breeders have used them to increase the resistance of other bean

*Information supplied by G.P. Nabhan (see Research Contacts) and J. Burton.

crops by interspecific hybridization. But it is only mildly resistant to most other diseases and pests. Furthermore, it is sensitive to salty soils and water, which often exist in semiarid areas.

Teparies produce poorly and grow aberrantly in climates more humid than the semiarid habitats in which they originated. The plant cannot tolerate waterlogged soils or frost. In temperate latitudes (long day length) flowering is delayed; the tepary bean is a crop for the tropics and subtropics (short day length conditions).

The nutritional quality of teparies, like that of other beans, is limited by the sulfur-containing amino acids and tryptophan. In comparisons with pinto beans, preliminary tests have shown teparies to be relatively deficient in methionine and lysine, yet nutritionally their amino acids are a nearly perfect complement to those of cereal grains.

Reluctance to adopt tepary beans as a food staple may be due to their small size, their tendency to cause flatulence, and the longer cooking time they require in comparison with more common beans.

Research Needs

Teparies seem eminently suited for dry-land farming in semiarid lands throughout the tropics and subtropics. Trial introductions to Australia,

Tepary beans. (N.D. Vietmeyer)

Africa, South America, Asia, the Middle East, and arid islands in Oceania and the Caribbean are recommended. In particular, the plant's value as a dry-land forage crop should be tested.

Since the spread of agriculture into the traditional habitat of the tepary bean, many of the plant's locally adapted ecotypes have fallen out of cultivation; indeed, several varieties are near extinction. Germ plasm should be collected throughout the bean's former growing areas, particularly in Mexico and Guatemala.

Testing is needed to determine the range of genetic variability within the species. The use of both wild and domesticated teparies in new breeding efforts could produce cultivars with higher yields and greater pest resistance and environmental tolerance.

The precise water requirements and nutritive value of different varieties are yet to be determined.

Teparies have long been adapted to floodwater agriculture during hot, briefly intense monsoon seasons. They have been introduced into modern irrigated agriculture, but little is known about the optimal time for supplying them with water. With properly phased irrigation, they may prove suitable for cultivation in other horticultural and agronomic environments.

Through interspecific breeding, the tepary bean's heat and drought tolerance may provide useful characteristics to other *Phaseolus* species. Through an interspecific hybrid breeding program, it may be possible to develop common bean (*Phaseolus vulgaris*) cultivars for use in the hot, semiarid tropics and subtropics.

Selected Readings

Calloway, D. H., R. D. Giauque, and F. M. Costa. 1974. The superior mineral content of some American Indian foods in comparison to federally donated counterpart commodities. *Ecology of Food and Nutrition* 3:203-211.

Freeman, G. F. 1918. Southwestern beans and teparies. *University of Arizona Agricultural Experiment Station Bulletin* 68:1-55.

Kay, D. E. 1978. *Food Legumes.* TPI Crop and Product Digest No. 3. Tropical Products Institute, London, pp. 494-503.

Nabhan, G. P. 1976. Teparies and other native beans (*Phaseolus*) in southwestern North America. *Journal of the Arizona Academy of Science* 11:18-19.

Nabhan, G. P., and R. S. Felger. 1978. Biogeography and ethnohistory of teparies (*Phaseolus acutifolius*) in southwestern North America. *Economic Botany* 32:2-19.

Waines, J. G. 1978. Protein contents, grain weights and breeding potential of wild and domesticated tepary bean. *Crop Science* 18:587-589.

Research Contacts

F. Crosswhite, Boyce-Thompson Southwestern Arboretum, Superior, Arizona 85273, USA

R. S. Felger, Arizona-Sonora Desert Museum, Route 9, Box 900, Tucson, Arizona 85704, USA

G. F. Freytag, Mayaguez Institute of Tropical Agriculture, P.O. Box 70, Mayaguez, Puerto Rico 00708

H. S. Gentry, Desert Botanical Garden, Box 5415, Phoenix, Arizona 85010, USA

L. Hudson, Regional Plant Introduction Station, Washington State University, Pullman, Washington 99163, USA

L. Kaplan, Department of Biology, University of Massachusetts, Harbor Campus, Boston, Massachusetts 02125, USA

G. P. Nabhan, Department of Plant Sciences, University of Arizona, Tucson, Arizona 85721, USA

N. D. Vietmeyer, National Academy of Sciences, 2101 Constitution Avenue, Washington, D.C. 20418, USA

J. G. Waines, Department of Plant Sciences, University of California, Riverside, California 92521, USA

Seeds can still be bought at markets and stores in northwestern Mexico and on some Indian reservations in Arizona. A 1976 plant explorations project of the U.S. Department of Agriculture, implemented through the University of Arizona, has located and conserved numerous stocks of both domesticated and wild teparies. A similar collection is maintained at the Department of Plant Sciences, University of California, Riverside, California. Seeds are available through the appropriate contacts listed above.

Tropical Lima Bean

There are few pulse crops so well adapted to the lowland tropics—especially the highly leached, infertile soils of the more humid regions—as certain varieties of the lima bean.*

Lima beans are one of the most widely cultivated pulse crops, both in temperate and subtropical regions. But in recent experiments in Africa, some little-known cultivars have given extraordinarily high yields in a lowland tropical rainforest region. This is a particularly difficult environment in which to grow crops—especially pulses—because the extreme heat and humidity foster pests and diseases, suppress growth, or kill the plant outright. Yet it is an

---

Phaseolus lunatus L. (syn. *Phaseolus limensis* Macf.; *Phaseolus inamoenus* L.). Commonly known as sieva, butter, Madagascar, sugar, and towe bean.

environment where malnutrition is often widespread and the need for nutritious crops is great.

Over the decades, researchers have expended much effort in breeding bushy lima bean plants because, with their strong stems, they are self-standing and can be planted without expensive stakes. But the varieties that performed so well in the African heat and humidity were the unselected, viny type.

Unlike other promising plants for the humid lowland tropics, the lima bean is a familiar crop about which much is known. The challenge is to apply knowledge gained from the vast cultivation of commercial lima beans to growing the "primitive viny varieties" in this difficult environment.

Indigenous to tropical America, undomesticated lima bean varieties can still be found growing wild in the Caribbean area as well as in Central and South America. The plant was already in widespread cultivation among American Indians in Pre-Columbian times, and seeds from crops grown 4,500 years ago have been found by archaeologists working in Peru. Europeans first met the plant 400 years ago in the vicinity of Lima. Today the lima bean is the predominant bean throughout much of the American tropics. It is also a major pulse crop in Liberia, Nigeria, and Burma. In poor soils of the lowland humid tropics, it is better adapted and gives more reliable yields than common beans (*Phaseolus vulgaris*).

In recent decades plant geneticists have improved the lima bean enormously, and a number of early-maturing, vigorous, disease- and pest-resistant, non-toxic cultivars are widely available commercially. This effort has focused on non-viny types and on varieties for growing outside the humid lowland tropics. Thus, the available varieties yield poorly in temperatures above 27°C and succumb to the onslaught of diseases and pests fostered by heat and humidity.

It is in experiments in the tropical lowlands of southeastern Nigeria that the neglected viny types became laden with pods along their whole length, with seed yields that are extraordinary for any pulse crop. They often yielded 3,000 kg of dry seed per ha, sometimes even producing 5,000 kg per ha.*

Usually the harvest can be made within 5 months of planting, but growing conditions cause this to vary from 3 to 9 months. The seeds are harvested either just as the green color of the pods begins to fade, which gives succulent seeds that are cooked and eaten as a vegetable, or after the pods have completely dried out, giving a dry bean that can be stored and used as a pulse. In either case, the seeds have high food value (see Appendix A).

Although green seeds and dry seeds are the main products from lima beans, both the pods and the leaves can be eaten as a pot herb when they are young and tender.

*Information supplied by K.O. Rachie. See Research Contacts.

The plant itself is valuable for restoring soil fertility; throughout its growth, it sheds copious leaves, which decay rapidly and enrich the soil.

With humid lowland plantation crops such as rubber, the viny lima bean can be employed as a green manure and as a cover plant to protect soil from the ravages of heavy rainfall. At CIAT in Colombia it has been found that

Tropical lima beans, Central Nigeria. (E.N.O. Adimorah)

viny lima beans grown in association with corn can yield 2 t of beans and 5 t of corn per ha.*

The Nigerian experience has been that the viny limas are notably free of serious diseases and pests. Also, unlike those of most pulse crops, the pods are nonshattering, i.e., the seeds do not naturally fall from the dry pod onto the ground.

Even though the viny limas are admirably suited to humid tropical lowlands, it should not be assumed that this is the only environment where they grow well. Indeed, they have been grown successfully at elevations up to about 2,400 m and, once established, are highly resistant to drought. Some lines appear to be more cold tolerant than common beans.

Limitations

The main deterrent to the greater use of viny limas is the general ignorance of their potential, range of adaptation, and of the practical aspects of their cultivation and use.

As with most locally untried plants, regional preferences and cooking methods pose a problem, since other pulses like cowpeas, common dry beans (*Phaseolus vulgaris*), pigeon peas, or mung beans have longer traditions of use throughout the tropics. The lima's longer cooking time, especially as compared with cowpeas, may be a particular drawback.

The plants prefer well-drained, well-aerated, neutral (pH 6–7) soils. With their viny growth, they must be supported (that is, on other crops, trees, poles, trellises, wires, fences, or walls). Planting is done at the beginning of the rains. Although the plant accepts the widespread cowpea type of *Rhizobium*, a specific rhizobial inoculum is available.

Although they are widely eaten, limas are one of the few pulses that can contain toxic amounts of cyanide-producing glucosides. Usually the white-seeded types are safe, but some dark-seeded ones are bitter tasting and must be thoroughly boiled and the cooking water discarded.

Lima bean plants are less affected by disease than most other pulses, but they do suffer from certain diseases. Particularly serious are some of the leaf diseases such as cercospora and rust, as well as root-knot nematodes, viruses, and insect pests. Moreover, lima bean plants can become a reservoir of diseases and pests that can spread to other crops, especially to other pulses.

Research Needs

The most urgent need in raising the status of the lima bean is to increase the recognition of its potential, especially for the more humid lowland trop-

*Information supplied by K.O. Rachie. See Research Contacts.

ics. The lima bean can often be used interchangeably with or as a substitute for the major tropical pulses like the common bean, cowpea, mung bean, and peanut in the humid, fertility-depleted areas where the incidence of pests and diseases is high. The tropical lima bean deserves intensive efforts applied toward:

- Assembling, exploring, and evaluating an extensive germ plasm collection;
- Determining the range of ecological conditions to which the lima bean can adapt and the management factors needed for economical production;
- Developing effective controls for major pests and diseases, emphasizing the use of the plant's natural resistance and cultural practices;
- Developing types with better seed qualities such as white or light-green, sweet-tasting, and quick-cooking seeds;
- Crossing pest- and disease-resistant varieties with high-yield varieties and those with better seed qualities;
- Developing new genetic stocks of both viny and bush limas, widely adapted to hot climates; and
- Improving cooking methods to make lima beans more palatable and nutritious and reduce the fuel required.

Intensive research is also needed on the symbiotic nitrogen-fixation process in the plant and in the plant's growth processes, biochemical properties, and protective mechanisms.

Improved genetic stocks deserve agronomic trials over a broad range of tropical environments, not only in the humid lowlands.

Bush strains of lima beans are available, but in the tropics they perform poorly compared with the viny climbers. Nevertheless, many farmers would grow this crop more extensively if well-adapted, high-yielding, disease-resistant, short-duration tropical bush limas became available.

Selected Readings

A set of brief, but comprehensive, notes on the lima bean is available from James A. Duke, Chief, Plant Taxonomy Laboratory, Plant Genetics and Germplasm Institute, United States Department of Agriculture, Beltsville, Maryland 20705, USA

Kay, D. E. 1978. *Food Legumes.* TP1 Crop and Product Digest No. 3. Tropical Products Institute, London. pp. 302-326.

Kernick, N. D. 1961. *Agricultural and Horticultural Seeds.* Study No. 55. Food and Agriculture Organization of the United Nations, Rome. pp. 272-277.

Mackie, W. W. 1943. Origin, dispersal and variability of the lima bean, *Phaseolus lunatus. Hilgardia* 15:1-29.

Otoul, E. 1976. Spectres des acides aminés chez *Phaseolus lunatus* L., chez quelques espèces apparentées et chez l'amphidiploïde *P. lunatus* L. x *P. polystachyus* (L.) B.X. et P. *Bulletin des Recherches Agronomiques de Gembloux* 11(1-2):207-220.

Purseglove, J. W. 1968. *Tropical Crops: Dicotyledons I*. John Wiley and Sons, New York. pp. 296-301.

Rachie, K. O., and L. M. Roberts. 1974. Tropical grain legumes. *Advances in Agronomy* 24:1-132.

Stanton, E. R. 1966. *Grain Legumes in Africa*. Food and Agriculture Organization of the United Nations, Rome. pp. 111-113.

Thompson, H. C., and W. C. Kelly. 1968. *Vegetable Crops*, 5th ed. McGraw-Hill Book Co., New York. pp. 454-458.

The *Tropical Grain Legume Bulletin* often contains short articles and abstracts on tropical lima beans. The *Bulletin* is available from the International Grain Legume Information Centre (see address below).

Westphal, E. 1974. *Pulses in Ethiopia, Their Taxonomy and Agricultural Significance*. Centre for Agricultural Publishing and Documentation, Wageningen, The Netherlands. pp. 140-151.

Research Contacts

Chaire de Phytotechnic des Regions Chaudes, Faculté des Sciences Agronomique de l'Etat, Gembloux, Belgium (R. Marechal, Chef de Travaux; E. Otoul; J. C. Baudet; and M. Le Marchand)

E. V. Doku, Crop Science Department, University of Ghana, Legon, Ghana

International Grain Legume Information Centre, International Institute of Tropical Agriculture, P.M.B. 5230, Ibadan, Nigeria (D. Nangju, Agronomist; C. Wien, Physiologist; D. Allen, Pathologist; S. R. Singh, Entomologist; F. E. Cavenes, Nematologist; and W. M. Steele, Botanist)

K. O. Rachie, The Rockefeller Foundation, 1133 Avenue of the Americas, New York, N.Y. 10036, USA.

Rodale Press, 222 Main Street, Emmaus, Pennsylvania 18049, USA (R. Harwood)

C. L. Tucker, Department of Agronomy and Range Science, University of California, Davis, California 95616, USA

E. Westphal, Laboratory for Plant Taxonomy and Geography, University of Agriculture, 37 General Foulkesweg, Wageningen, The Netherlands

Ye-eb

The ye-eb,* a small bush native to the arid, semi-desert border region between Somalia and Ethiopia, produces a nutritious and tasty nut with a chestnut-like flavor, in a region with rainfall sometimes as low as only 150-200 mm per year.

The ye-eb is such a hardy shrub that during drought it is sometimes the only food left for nomads. Its food value has at times enabled destitute Somalis to rely on it alone for subsistence. Yet until recently it has never been grown outside its native habitat and the agronomic improvement of the legume has not yet begun. Nonetheless, the plant may provide a valuable food—and perhaps export item—for hot, dry regions, especially with low, uncertain rainfall. It may well prove useful on sandy soils in many tropical countries where irrigation is not possible and where rainfall is too low for the cultivation of more conventional crops.

In the arid hinterland of Somalia the ye-eb used to grow profusely. In 1929 it was reported to constitute up to half the woody vegetation in many areas. Today it is much reduced, and it is threatened even further by regional droughts and war. A dwarfed, many-stemmed shrub, usually about 1.6 m tall, it grows up to 2.5 m tall in favorable locations. Long roots allow the plant to tap deep soil moisture and it remains green year-round. Ye-eb reseeds itself well but grows slowly, especially in the seedling stage while it is establishing its massive root system.

In its native habitat, the ye-eb is found in open bush savanna at altitudes of 300-1,000 m. The red sandy soils are extremely poor. It is a frost-free region, with two rainy seasons, and an annual rainfall of 250-400 mm, though it is often below 250 mm.

Before age 3, a young plant may bear a few pods, but once 3-4 years old it will yield prolifically (under favorable conditions). Inside the pods are from one to four round or ovoid seeds the size of a small macadamia nut or

---

Cordeauxia edulis Hemsl. Also known as jeheb-nut, yeeb, hebb, ye'eb, yi-ib, or yehib. In Somali pronunciation, the word's central syllable is a guttural sound. This is represented by the letter C, in the new Somali orthography, and so the plant's name is now spelled jicib in Somalia. Subfamily: Caesalpinioideae.

a large filbert (hazelnut). These can be cooked or eaten raw and have a smooth consistency and taste that one author likens to that of cashews.

When in season, the ye-eb is a staple of the poorer people living in the Somali hinterland. It is much relished, often being preferred to the usual diet of rice and dates. Relatively few of the nuts ever enter commercial trade, but each year sacks of them are brought to market in Somali coastal towns.

The seeds alone make an unusually nourishing and balanced diet. Although their protein and carbohydrate contents are less than those of most other pulses, the seeds contain both fat and sugar. They contain starch (37 percent), sugar (24 percent), protein (13 percent), fat (11 percent), and various minerals,* and have a high energy value (see Appendix A).

The most recent work on the ye-eb nut's nutritional value† indicates that its protein contains amino acids in similar proportions to those found in other pulse crops. For example, it is rich in lysine and deficient in methionine. Trypsin inhibitors occur in proportions similar to those in lablab beans (see page 59), but no trace of phytohemagglutinins, whose toxicity is more serious, was found.

Ye-eb leaves contain a brilliant red dye that stains the hands. Livestock are fond of them and the bones of goats fed ye-eb foliage become stained a bright orange. Leaf extracts are vividly colored, form fast and insoluble dyes with some metals, and have been used as mordants to dye fabrics.

Limitations

The ye-eb is a wild plant whose domestication is only now beginning. Some 50 young shrubs are under cultivation at the Central Agricultural Research Station, Afgoi, Somalia, where they have grown slowly but nonetheless flower and provide fruit abundantly. In Kenya, some 30 plants have been under cultivation at Voi since 1957 and 400 seedlings were recently planted at the Galana Ranch.

Seed germination of over 80 percent has been achieved, but plantation establishment is slightly less. The seedlings quickly develop a thin but tough tap root, which in the wild improves access to soil moisture and increases chances of survival, but the tap root is a serious complication in the nursery production of seedlings. Researchers now feel that seeding the fields directly is probably the most satisfactory way to establish plantations.

Although the shrub is essentially free of insect pests, ye-eb nuts themselves are attacked by weevils and moth larvae. To combat this, Somalis roast or

---

*These figures, given by Greenway, 1947 (see Selected Readings), differ slightly from those in Appendix A.

† Miège and Miège. In Press. See Selected Readings.

The bushlike ye-eb, near Belet Uen, Somalia. (J.J. Norris)

boil the freshly picked nuts to kill insects and to harden the shells and make them less penetrable. This makes it particularly difficult to get viable seed for planting. Even under the best of conditions the seeds retain their viability for only a few months.

Like other tree and bush crops, the ye-eb is slow to mature and takes 3–4 years to bear seeds.

Research Needs

Since few nutritious plants survive in the ye-eb's native habitat, it is always much exploited—animals graze the foliage, people remove virtually all seeds—but the last decade has seen many years of drought, which has led to severe overexploitation of the plant. During the extreme drought years 1973–1976, the bushes survived but failed to flower or set fruit. Furthermore, the Ogaden region has recently been a war zone and this combination of adverse circumstances puts the ye-eb in great danger of extinction.

To preserve the species, selected stands must be protected from grazing and from overexploitation and seed orchards need to be established both in Somalia and elsewhere.* In addition, germ plasm should be collected and rushed to safekeeping in a temperature- and humidity-controlled seed-storage facility.

It is recommended that agronomists in both Somalia and Ethiopia establish ye-eb plantations for comparing varieties. Botanical and agronomic

---

*It is heartening to learn that the Somali government has made an initial start on this by fencing off a small patch of ye-eb between Belet Uen and Dusa Mareb and a 25-ha area at Salah Dhadhaab.

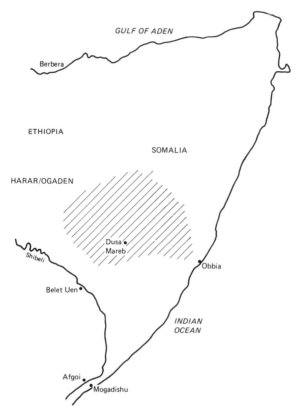

Ye-eb nut native habitat in the Horn of Africa.

studies of the plant in the wild are also recommended. Perhaps wild-stand yields can be improved by fencing or by micro-catchments for rainfall-runoff water.* This work will, in turn, provide more information on the plant and its requirements. The ye-eb should also be tested in comparable semiarid regions elsewhere in the world.

Selected Readings

Bally, P. R. O. 1966. Miscellaneous notes on the flora of Tropical East Africa. 29. *Candollea* 21(1):3-11.

Greenway, P. J. 1947. Yegeb. *The East African Agricultural Journal* 12:216-219.

Hemming, C. F. 1972. *Ecological and Grazing Survey of the Mudugh Region, Somalia Democratic Republic.* Food and Agriculture Organization of the United Nations,

*For an explanation of this and other similar techniques, see a companion report: National Academy of Sciences. 1974. *More Water for Arid Lands: Promising Technologies and Research Opportunities.* To order see page 329.

Rome. (AGP:DP/Som/70/512 Working Paper, available from S. R. Risopoulos, Plant Production and Protection Division, Food and Agriculture Organization of the United Nations, 00100 Rome, Italy.)

Miège, J., and M.-N. Miège. In Press. *Cordeauxia edulis* A. Caesalpinaceae of arid zones of East Africa, Caryologic, blastogenic and biochemical features. Potential aspects for nutrition. *Economic Botany.*

Westphal, E. 1974. *Pulses in Ethiopia, Their Taxonomy and Agricultural Significance.* Centre for Agricultural Publishing and Documentation, Wageningen, The Netherlands. 276 pp.

Research Contacts

Mohamed M. Awaleh, National Range Agency, P.O. Box 1759, Mogadisho, Somalia

Peter R. O. Bally, P.O. Box 14084, Nairobi, Kenya

Central Agricultural Research Station, Afgoi, Somalia

Department of Natural Resources, Hargeisa, Somalia

East African Herbarium, Box 45166, Nairobi, Kenya (C. H. S. Kabuye and J. B. Gillett)

C. Hemming, Centre for Overseas Pest Research, College House, Wright Lane, London W8, England

J. Miège, Director, Conservatoire et Jardin Botaniques, Boite postale 60, CH-1292 Chambésy-Geneve, Switzerland

National Range Agency, Somalia (S. M. A. Kazmi)

J. J. Norris, School of Natural Renewable Resources, University of Arizona, Tucson, Arizona 85721, USA

III Fruits

Carob

On steep slopes and in semiarid lands where plowing is not practicable, tree crops can often yield valuable harvests. One such crop is the carob,* which holds special promise in hot and Mediterranean-type regions with extended dry seasons. Noted for its drought resistance, the plant is especially useful where irrigation is impractical or rainfall unreliable.

Although for centuries this legume has contributed to the economy of the Mediterranean basin, it has seldom been farmed elsewhere. Yet millions of hectares of land in the dry subtropics seem suited to its culture; in these areas, too, the carob could become commercially important.

Carob provides a wealth of products including food, forage, and industrial gum, and it is useful for shade and erosion control. Its pods contain more sugar than sugar beets or sugarcane. Its value was recognized by the ancient Greeks, who brought it from its native Mid-East to Greece and Italy, and by the Arabs, who disseminated it along the North African coast and up into Spain. In the time of the Pharaohs, Egyptians fed their cattle on it and made wine from its fruits. Today it is widely cultivated in the Levant (the region stretching from Egypt to Greece), in Southern Europe, on Mediterranean islands, and throughout North Africa. Carob is a substantial crop in Spain, Portugal, Crete, Sardinia, and Sicily, and the beans are principal exports of Cyprus and Syria. Cyprus alone exports 45,000 t of crushed, deseeded carob pods annually; Western Europe, the United Kingdom, and the United States

---

Ceratonia siliqua L. Known in Arabic as "al kharoubah," which, in other languages, has given rise to similar names such as: kharuv (Hebrew), caroube (French), algarroba (Spanish), carruba (Italian). Subfamily: Caesalpinioideae.

are the main consuming nations. Export prices have shown an upward trend in recent years.

In the Levant, carob is one of the trees growing in dry areas on hillsides and in water courses; there are over 250,000 carob trees in Israel's forests.

The carob is a handsome tree, reaching over 10 m and having rich, glossy, evergreen foliage and branches that are often contorted fantastically. Its tiny red flower buds expand into greenish, or cream-colored flowers that eventually convert into thick, broad pods 10–30 cm long. When ripe, the pods turn brown and begin to fall; those that fail to drop are easily shaken off or knocked down with a pole. Each one contains 5–15 very hard seeds* embedded in a sweet, mealy pulp.

The tree is less exacting in its soil requirements than most fruit trees. It survives in a wide variety of soils, sometimes clinging to hillsides that seem to be almost pure rock, and grows in stony areas unsuited to other crops provided its roots can penetrate crevices. (In Cyprus, holes have been blasted in rocky surfaces [kafkalla] to expose the soil below; carobs and olives planted there grew successfully.) In addition carob can adapt to slightly alkaline soils. But it cannot withstand waterlogged soils, nor can it be grown in wet ground or in hard clay with poor drainage. The carob is commonly planted on hillsides above orange groves. The two crops have much the same temperature requirements, but the carob needs far less water.

Carobs are usually started from seed, but can also be propagated by cuttings, suckers, layers, and air-layering. For fast-growing and high-yielding trees, buds from a high-yielding variety are grafted to 3- to 4-year-old seedlings in the field.

The tree coppices well, and carob wood makes reasonable fuel.

In Cyprus, carob plantations usually have a density of about 90 trees per ha, and yields of 1.5-4 t of pods per ha are achieved if the plants are grown under good conditions and are well tended.† Elsewhere, much higher yields have been reported, and in a good year a single large tree may produce a ton of seed. In Israel in 1958, irrigated groves yielded 12 t per ha, whereas good, fully bearing nonirrigated groves, where rainfall exceeds 550 mm, yielded about 7 t per ha.‡

Feed

Carob pods make excellent fodder. In the Mediterranean region, where animals have been raised on them for several thousand years, the pods are voraciously consumed by many kinds of livestock. Goatherds, for example, often beat down the pods with sticks.

*The seeds have been used as weights by jewelers and apothecaries and are believed to be the original goldsmith's carat (a corruption of carob) weight.
†Davies. 1970.
‡Goor, Ticho, and Garmi. 1958.

Carob tree. (Tate and Lyle Ltd, Group Research and Development)

In food value, carob pods are almost equal to many cereal grains; livestock fatten and thrive on them. They were the feed that sustained Wellington's cavalry horses during the campaign against Napoleon's forces in Portugal and Spain, since no other feedstuff grew in the dry, rocky battle region. Today, thousands of tons of carob pods (with seeds removed) are exported to Britain, where, like molasses, their sweetness is used to increase palatability of dairy feeds. Carob-pod meal can constitute up to 10 percent of the diet of calves, kids, and dairy goats without adversely affecting their growth. The meal has a low energy content, but animals compensate for this by eating more. An Israeli variety [variety AA2 (Aaronsohn's Plot)] has special promise for pastureland because its pods fall off naturally and can be grazed by livestock.

Food

Carob seeds and the sweet pulp from carob pods are supposedly the "locusts and wild honey" eaten by John the Baptist in the wilderness. About half the weight of the pulp is sugar, and today it is sometimes sold as a dried confection called St. John's bread. Although usually eaten like candy, it can be converted to syrup and fermented to a wine or liquor. It is also widely used to flavor chewing tobacco, and the pods can be ground and used as a flavorful chocolate substitute in cakes, bread, breakfast cereals, and candy. In

Carob pods. (Ministry of Agriculture and Natural Resources, Nicosia, Cyprus)

Germany and elsewhere, roasted carob seeds have been used as a substitute for coffee.

Carob seeds contain up to 21 percent protein, but they comprise only about 10 percent of the weight of the pod. When the whole pod is ground, the resulting edible powder is about 7 percent protein, 30 percent sugar, and 9 percent fiber. Fat contributes only 1–2 percent of the pod's weight, making the carob a comparatively low-energy food (180 calories per 100 g).

Gum

By weight, about one-third of the carob seed consists of a mucilaginous gum* that is widely used as an emulsion stabilizer and thickener in ice cream, cheese, and salad dressings. It is also used in cosmetics, pharmaceuticals, textiles, paper, and other industrial products. Carob gum, a neutral galactomannan like other legume gums (see page 278), is commercially valuable because it is especially viscous and is low in starch and other impurities. The gum, present as an inner vitreous coating of the seeds, can be used in place of some expensive gums, including tragacanth (see page 284) and karaya. Carob gum is mainly used in Europe; however, Japan imports increasing quantities.

---

*Variously known as carob gum, carob seed gum, locust bean gum, locust kernel gum, tragasol, gum hevo, and gum gatto.

Forestation and Soil Conservation

In semiarid regions soils are particularly vulnerable. If agricultural practices are careless, the vegetation cover succumbs to drought, leaving the soil exposed to sun and wind and subject to rainfall runoff and devastating erosion.

In suitable areas, the carob tree offers a way to control erosion, conserve soil, and reclaim land at the same time it is producing a commercial crop. Established plants survive drought and heat. In Australia, carob has been used to reforest eroded land in New South Wales and is recommended for windbreaks in the hot northern districts of Victoria. Few other crop plants can provide a cover of protective vegetation under such trying conditions. However, unless irrigated, the fruits are dried and shrivelled, have little commercial importance, and the yields are very low.

Shade and Beautification

Throughout much of the Mediterranean basin the carob, with its spreading crown, is an indispensable shade tree. It is also commonly used to beautify cities, and in Southern California thousands of carob trees line residential streets.

Limitations

The carob, like most tree crops, matures slowly and most cultivars now available do not begin to bear commercial quantities of fruit for 6-7 years after planting. When budded trees are planted, the harvests can begin in 5-6 years. The yields gradually increase, reaching perhaps 45 kg in a tree's 12th year* and, as previously noted, a mature tree in good soil may produce as much as 1,000 kg. Some trees have a productive life of 100 years or more.

The carob tends toward alternate bearing and yields most abundantly every second year. This is most pronounced when growing conditions are poor.

The crop needs a dry climate characterized by hot, dry summers and cool, wet winters. Although drought resistant, carob trees do not bear commercial crops unless they get enough rainfall. In Israel a minimum average rainfall of about 550 mm is needed to ensure a profitable crop. Two or three summer irrigations will greatly aid the plant's establishment, hasten fruiting, and increase yield. Where annual rainfall is less than 400 mm, the crop requires supplemental irrigation or a planting arrangement that exploits water harvesting.†

---

*Coit, J. E. 1949. *Carob Culture in the Semi-Arid Southwest*. Privately published by W. Rittenhouse, San Diego, California.
† See National Academy of Sciences. 1974. *More Water for Arid Lands: Promising Technologies and Research Opportunities*. To order see page 329.

Another limiting climatic factor is dew. Frequent wetting of the leaves enhances the spread of leaf diseases, which leads to poor crops, and the carob fails as a commercial crop in areas with more than 220 dew nights per year.

The crop is limited to regions where temperatures are suitable for growing olives or oranges. Although withstanding light frost, the trees are killed (or fruiting retarded) by temperatures below $-7°C$. Young trees are more frost susceptible than old ones.

Most carob trees are either male (staminate) plants that produce pollen or female (pistillate) plants that produce the pods.* Plantations are composed of female plants interspersed with 5-percent well-placed male ones that provide the necessary pollen even though they contribute no pods. In some cases a male branch is grafted to a female tree to provide pollen *in situ.* In street-border plantings only female plants are generally used, as the male flowers have an unpleasant smell.

The seeds require a simple treatment (using acid, boiling water, or sand-paper) to encourage germination. But the tree itself demands little care, requires almost no pruning once it is well established, and does not need frequent attention. So far, it has shown little susceptibility to serious disease, except where the roots are in damp soil, when root rot and root-knot nematode can cause damage. Two carob pests, a red scale fungus and the carob moth, also damage citrus crops. Furthermore, in humid or summer-rainfall areas, the leaves and fruit get infected with powdery mildew fungus, though resistant varieties are known. In storage, the pods are attacked by a number of insect pests.

In Israel, carob cultivation has become unprofitable in recent years due to high wage rates and the amount of labor needed to pick the pods by hand.

Research Needs

The carob has been established in Australia, Argentina, the United States, Mexico, Malawi, Rhodesia, and South Africa. One report states that it is one of the few promising exotic species for the savanna-woodland zone of Ghana.† Thus it seems to have more widespread utility than is generally recognized. Many regions that have warm, dry weather in late summer and fall when the pods mature seem suited to carob culture. These include large areas in southern, eastern, and sub-Sahelian Africa; Persian Gulf countries; Australia; Latin America; Pakistan and northern India; southern South America; and Mexico and the southwestern United States. In these areas, the carob may prove a dependable source of forage, withstanding drought better

---

*A few carry both male and hermaphrodite flowers and are self-pollinating.
†Streets, R. J. 1962. *Exotic Forest Trees in the British Commonwealth.* Clarendon Press, Oxford.

than some grasses and annual pasture legumes, and trials on the plant should be started.

Centuries of cultivation have given rise to a large number of varieties differing in size and quality of pods, vigor, productiveness, and adaptability to various soils. A project is needed to compare and classify the characteristics of the most useful varieties grown in Mediterranean countries.

Although the carob can grow well in poor soils, no one has demonstrated that it nodulates and is able to obtain nitrogenous nutrients by nitrogen fixation. Research is needed to resolve this question.

Trial plantings of new clones and the selection of promising varieties are basic research requisites for evaluating the carob's potential in any specific area.

Improved control of the storage pests of carob is needed.

Research is needed to test and improve the synchronization of pollen production on staminate trees with the receptivity of pistillate trees.

Israeli researchers report the successful use of purified sewage water to irrigate carobs.* This important discovery needs further testing and development. Wastewater is a promising new source for arid-land irrigation,† and carob appears to tolerate moderate amounts of some of the mineral salts it contains.

Selected Readings

A set of notes summarizing carob tree data in the files of the Royal Tropical Institute, Amsterdam, is available from the International Centre for Research on Agroforestry, c/o H. J. von Maydell, Leuschnerstrasse 91, 2050 Hamburg 80, West Germany.

Anonymous. 1972. Saving the locust bean harvest in Cyprus. *Tropical Science* 14(4): 374-375.

Artaud, J., J. Estienne, and M. Cas. 1976. Progrès récents dans l'analyse des gommes et colloides végétaux naturels hydrosalubles. II. Farine de caroube. *Annales des Falsifications et de l'Expertise Chimique* 69(737):23-45.

Ashman, F. 1965. *Interim Report on a Study in Cyprus of Insect Infestation in Stored Carobs.* Ministry of Overseas Development, London, England. (mimeo)

Charalambous, J., ed. 1966. *The Composition and Uses of Carob Bean.* Cyprus Agricultural Research Institute, Nicosia, Cyprus. 50 pp.

Davies, W. N. L. 1970. The carob tree and its importance in the agricultural economy of Cyprus. *Economic Botany* 24:460-470.

Davies, W. N. L., P. I. Orphanos, and J. Papaconstantinou. 1971. Chemical composition of developing carob pods. *Journal of the Science of Food and Agriculture* 22:83-86.

Goor, A. Y., and C. W. Barney. 1976. *Forest Tree Planting in Arid Zones*, 2nd ed. Ronald Press Co., New York. 504 pp.

Goor, A., R. J. Ticho, and I. Garmi. 1958. *The Carob.* Agricultural Publications Section, Ministry of Agriculture, Israel.

Karschon, R. 1960. *Studies in Nursery Practice for Carob* (Ceratonia siliqua *L.*). Israel Department of Forestry Leaflet 14. Forestry Department, Tel Aviv, Israel. 8 pp.

*Goor, Ticho, and Garmi. 1958.
†National Academy of Sciences. 1974. Reusing water. In *More Water for Arid Lands: Promising Technologies and Research Opportunities*. pp. 45-53. National Academy of Sciences, Washington, D.C. To order see page 329.

Loock, E. E. M. 1940. The carob or locust tree (*Ceratonia siliqua* L.). *Journal of South African Forestry Association* 4:78-80.

Louca, A., and A. Paras. 1973. The effect of different proportions of carob pod meal in the diet on the performance of calves and goats. *Animal Production* 17:139-146.

Orphanos, P. I., and J. Papaconstantinou. 1969. *The Carob Varieties of Cyprus.* Technical Bulletin 5. Cyprus Agricultural Research Institute, Ministry of Agriculture and Natural Resources, Nicosia, Cyprus. 27 pp.

Rol, F. 1959. Locust bean gum. In *Industrial Gums*, ed. R. L. Whistler, pp. 361-375. Academic Press, New York.

Sekeri-Pataryas, K. H., K. A. Mitrakos, and M. K. Georgi. 1973. Yields of fungal protein from carob sugars. *Economic Botany* 27(3):311-319.

Smith, J. R. 1953 (reprinted 1977). *Tree Crops—A Permanent Agriculture.* Devin-Adair Publishing Company, Old Greenwich, Connecticut, USA.

Toth, J. 1965. The forest aspect of a plantation in the Sahara. *Revue Forestière Française (Nancy)* 17:674-695.

Research Contacts

Agricultural Research Institute, Ministry of Agriculture and Natural Resources, Nicosia, Cyprus

E. Alumot, Director, Department of Animal Nutrition, Agricultural Research Organization, P.O. Box 6, Bet Dagan, Israel

F. Ashman, British Development Division in Southern Africa, P.O. Box 30059, Lilongwe 3, Malawi

Department of Animal Science, Faculty of Agriculture, University of Stellenbosch, Stellenbosch 7600, South Africa (F. J. van der Merwe)

Department of Fruit Growing, Ministry of Agriculture, Hakirya, Tel Aviv, Israel (Sigler Tomy)

Forestry Division, Agricultural Research Organization, Ilanot, D. N. Lev Hasharon, Israel (R. Karschon, Director)

Institut Universitaire de Technologie, rue des Geraniums, 13337 Marseille, Cedex 3, France (J. Artaud)

Ministry of Commerce and Industry, Nicosia, Cyprus

A. W. Owadally, Conservator of Forests, Ministry of Agriculture, and Natural Resources, and the Environment, Forestry Service, Curepipe, Mauritius

Reforestation Service, Keren Kayemet, BP 45, Kiryat Haim, Haifa, Israel (S. Weitz, Director)

C. A. Schroeder, Department of Biology, University of California, Los Angeles, California 90024, USA

A. J. Vlitos, Group Research & Development, Tate and Lyle, Limited, P.O. Box 68, Reading, RG6 2BX, England

Bee Williams Carob Nursery, 2025 San Miguel Dr., Walnut Creek, California 94596, USA

The carob collection of the late Eliot Coit is located in Vista, California. Although it is perhaps the most extensive bank of carob germ plasm ever assembled and includes some 600 fully mature trees of different genotypes, it is likely to soon be lost to the bulldozer because the site is planned for housing development. Researchers should take advantage of this resource while it is still available. (Information supplied by D. M. Yermanos, Department of Agronomy, University of California, Riverside, California 92502, USA)

Tamarind

The tamarind* is native to the dry savannas of tropical Africa; Senegal's capital city is named after the tree, whose local name is "dakar." In ancient times the tree was introduced to Asia by Arab traders, and with its pleasant, acidic tasting fruit, it was so enthusiastically adopted, especially on the Subcontinent, that today the plant's botanic and common names both point up its association with India.†

Long ago the tamarind reached the New World, probably brought with the first shipments of slaves from West Africa. In Caribbean and Latin American countries the plant is much appreciated, as in Africa and Asia, for the succulent, sweet-sour pulp that fills its pods. Nevertheless, India remains the only country to exploit the tamarind extensively: over 250,000 t are harvested there annually, 3,000 t of which are exported to Europe and North America for use in meat sauces and beverages.

Although it has been in commercial demand for centuries,‡ there has been no research to improve the tamarind as a crop plant. Throughout much of the tropics the plants grow untended along roadsides, in backyards, and on wasteland. These untended, unimproved tamarind trees are nonetheless commercially exploited, and a number of countries—Costa Rica and Puerto Rico, for example—produce canned tamarind pulp and juice. The Mexican government has recently planted large areas with tamarind in the state of Guerrero, but to date the only mature plantations are those in India.

The tamarind has an attractive commercial future for producing drinks, jams, and confections on an industrial scale. The tree is so well adapted to both dry savanna regions and monsoon areas with well-drained soils that it deserves greater research attention with extensive organized plantings.

Tamarindus indica L. Subfamily: Caesalpinioideae.
†The name tamarind derives from the Arabic *tamar-u'l-Hind*, which means "date of India." Also known as tamarindo (Spanish and Portuguese) and tamarin, tamarinier, tamarindier (French).
‡Marco Polo recorded it in 1298, Arab traders made it an important commerical item in Medieval Europe, and New England sea captains commonly carried preserved tamarind from the Caribbean to Boston in the 18th and 19th centuries.

Tamarind tree, Karnataka, India. (Central Food Technological Research Institute, Mysore)

A handsome, short-trunked tree with a spreading frame of branches that may reach 25 m in height, the tamarind has a great, dome-shaped crown of graceful, airy leaves. It is a long-lived tree, sometimes still productive after 200 years. It is drought resistant and is frequently seen in sandy soils near the seashore. It tolerates widely different soils, growing best where soils are deep, but with little or no cultivation it can flourish in poor soils, and even in rocky terrain. Its strong, supple branches are little affected by wind, and it is known as a hurricane-resistant tree.

Showy clusters of pale-yellow, pink-veined blossoms turn into long, flat, rust-colored pods that are usually slightly curved, sometimes with constrictions in the spaces between the seeds they contain. At maturity, the shell becomes brittle and is easily cracked open to expose dark-brown, pasty pulp that encloses hard, shiny, brown seeds.

About half the pod weight consists of pulp, which has a sweet-sour flavor, for it contains both sugars (30–40 percent) and organic acids such as citric, tartaric, acetic, and ascorbic (vitamin C). The pulp is a rich source of vitamins and important minerals and contains more calcium than most fruits. Though reputed to be richer in sugar than any other fruit, the pulp usually has an acid taste. However, there is much variability between fruits from different trees; some are almost acid free.

The fully ripe, unshelled fruit has exceptional keeping qualities and is often sold in native markets. The pulp can be pressed into flavorsome loaves, balls, or cakes (often with sugar added), for local sale or export. Average annual yields from an adult tree are very large—150–200 kg of fruits per tree, or about 12–16 t per ha.*

The pulp is often eaten fresh, directly from the pod. But it is also used to season many foods, for example, chutney, curries, preserves, confections, ice cream, and syrups. When mixed with sugar and water, it becomes a refreshing drink, widely sold throughout Latin America. In Guatemala and Mexico, it is carbonated. European and North American countries import tamarind pulp mainly for use in condiments such as Worcestershire and barbecue sauce.

Although the pulp is by far the most important tamarind product, the tree is also used for other purposes. Young leaves, flowers, and immature pods are edible. All are agreeably sour and are used to season rice, fish, or meat in curries, soups or stews. The flowers can be an important source of honey. Tamarind seeds, now largely wasted, can be ground up to make a palatable livestock feed and can be processed to prepare a purified pectin-like gum (see page 278) used for jelling fruit juices and stabilizing other processed foods. This is also used for sizing textiles, paper, and jute products. In addition, the seeds yield an amber-colored oil suitable for food or industrial use.

The dark, purplish-brown tamarind heartwood, while hard to work, is strong and termite-proof and takes a fine polish. It is excellent for turnery, toys, tool handles, decorative paneling, and furniture and has been sold in North America as "Madeira Mahogany." Tamarind wood is also valued as a fuel. When burned, it gives off intense heat, and in India it is a choice wood for firing brick kilns. Tamarind charcoal is of such high quality that it has been used to make gunpowder and was a major fuel for producer-gas (gasogen) units that powered Indian cars and trucks during World War II.

Tamarind is also a useful species for beautifying and shading parks, backyard gardens, city avenues, and country roads. In India, it is particularly common as an avenue shade tree. Around the trees the ground is usually bare because of shading by the dense canopy, and in India tamarind is planted in strips among forest plantations to act as firebreaks. In the United States it has recently been hailed as a splendid new tree for indoor beautification.

Tamarind is easy to propagate by direct seeding or by transplanting. Its seeds remain viable for months and germinate rapidly.

Limitations

Tamarind is suitable for growing only in regions that have extended spells of dry weather. In the humid tropics, where rain falls evenly year-round, the tree refuses to bear and fails to grow unless the soil is well drained. The tree is also sensitive to frost and requires protection when small.

*Information supplied by the Royal Tropical Institute, Amsterdam.

Tamarind fruit. (N. D. Vietmeyer)

The tamarind is slow growing and late to reach bearing age. Commonly, it grows between 0.5 and 0.8 m per year and takes 10–12 years to mature and yield fruit. Quick-maturing varieties have not yet been selected.*

In some areas, if tamarinds are left too long on the tree (and are not eaten by monkeys or other creatures) they become infested with small beetles. This can also happen in storage.

The pedicels that hold the fruit to the tree are very tough; they cannot be broken off by hand without damaging the fruit and must be clipped off.

Research Needs

The tamarinds now growing throughout the tropics are not the products of any careful agronomic selection—they derive from seeds picked up at random in Africa or India. There is excellent potential for markedly improving the crop. For example, odd trees bear exceptionally large pods well-filled with

---

*However, some seedlings from a sweet tamarind grown in limestone soils at Homestead, Florida, in the 1960s grew relatively fast and bore first fruit in 6–8 years. (Information supplied by C. W. Campbell, see Research Contacts.)

pulp; some are much less acid than others and are referred to as "sweet." Superior types like these can be successfully reproduced by air-layering and grafting and bear fruit at a much younger age than seedlings. However, none of these findings has yet been exploited commercially.

Germ plasm collections need to be made in a region that stretches from Senegal across sub-Sahelian Africa to the Sudan. Collections of Indian tamarind types also need to be made, and there are interesting genetic types in Thailand and elsewhere in Southeast Asia. From such a collection of germ plasm, more plants with sweeter and juicier pulp are likely to be developed, as well as quicker-growing varieties.

Tamarind's commercial promise merits plantation trials in many parts of the tropics. If the best available varieties are selected, the plant should prove to be a profitable crop that, once established, requires little or no care and will bear for many decades.

Since nothing is known of the tamarind's nodulation and its ability to take advantage of nitrogen fixation by *Rhizobium*, research is needed in this area.

Efficient harvesting techniques also need to be devised.

Selected Readings

A tamarind bibliography is available from Service de Documentation, Institut Français de Recherches Fruitieres Outre-Mer, 6 rue du Général Clergerie, 75116 Paris, France.

Anonymous. 1976. *Tamarindus indica.* In *The Wealth of India* (Raw Materials Series), Vol. X:144-122. Council of Scientific and Industrial Research, New Delhi.

Benero, J. R., A. C. de Rivera, and L. M. I. de George. 1974. Studies on the preparation and shelf-life of soursop, tamarind and blended soursop-tamarind soft drinks. *Journal of Agriculture of the University of Puerto Rico* 58(1):99-104.

Benero, J. R., A. J. Rodriguez, and A. C. de Rivera. 1972. A mechanical method for extracting tamarind pulp. *Journal of Agriculture of the University of Puerto Rico* 56(2):185-186.

Lefevre, J.-C. 1971. Revue de la littérature sur le tamarinier. *Fruits* 26(10):687-695.

Morton, J. F. 1958. The tamarind (*Tamarindus indica* L.), its food, medicinal and industrial uses. *Proceedings of the Florida State Horticultural Society* 71:288-294. (Copies available from author, see address below.)

Morton, J. F. 1960. Se elaboran confites con tamarindo y maranones. *La Hacienda* 55(7):44, 46.

Rao, P. S. 1959. Tamarind. In *Industrial Gums*, ed. R. L. Whistler, pp. 461-504. Academic Press, New York.

Savur, G. R. 1956. Tamarind pectin industry of India. *Chemistry and Industry* 13: 212-214.

Research Contacts

Devendra B. Amatya, Forest Research Officer, Forest Survey and Research Office, Department of Forestry, Babar Mahal, Kathmandu, Nepal

Assistant Conservator of Forests (Silviculture and Research), Forest Department. P.O. Box 1017, Kingston, Georgetown, Guyana

C. W. Campbell, University of Florida, Agricultural Research and Education Center, 18905 SW 280th Street, Homestead, Florida 33030, USA

Central Food Technological Research Institute, Mysore-2 (A), Karnataka, India (Y.S. Lewis)

Food Technology Laboratory, University of Puerto Rico, Agricultural Experiment Station, P.O. Box H, Rio Piedras, Puerto Rico 00928 (M. A. Gonzalez, Technical Director)

Forestry Research Institute of Nigeria, P.M.B. 5054, Ibadan, Nigeria (G. O. A. Ojo)

Institut d'Elevage et de Médicine Vétérinaire Tropicaux, 10 rue Pierre Curie, 94700 Maison-Alfort, France

H. B. Joshi, Editor, Indian Forest Research Institute and Colleges, P.O. New Forest, Dehra Dun, Uttar Pradesh, India

Mayaguez Institute of Tropical Agriculture, P.O. Box 70, Mayaguez, Puerto Rico 00708

Andree Millar, Director, National Capital Botanic Gardens, 4677 University P.O., Port Moresby, Papua New Guinea

Ministry of Agriculture and Forestry, Forest Department, P.O. Box 31, Entebbe, Uganda (P. K. Karani, Deputy Chief Forest Officer)

J. Morton, Morton Collectanea, University of Miami, Box 248204, Coral Gables, Florida 33124, USA

A. W. Owadally, Conservator of Forests, Ministry of Agriculture, Natural Resources, and the Environment, Forestry Service, Curepipe, Mauritius

K. Vivekanandan, Research Officer (Silviculture), Office of the Conservator of Forests, P.O. Box 509, Colombo 2, Sri Lanka

IV Forages

Forage Shrubs and Trees

In the tropics, uncertain supplies and increasing costs of feed, fertilizer, and food, coupled with projected population increases, are giving leguminous trees whose foliage is browsed by animals a status they have never previously enjoyed.

In large measure, the current underproduction of animal protein in the developing world is caused by lack of forage. Trees and shrubs play a dual role in the forage supply, serving both as shade for grasses and as forage themselves. In dry savannas in particular, shrubs and trees are very precious; without them, stock raising would probably be impossible, for pasture grasses die when upper soil layers lose their moisture, but the trees' roots exploit deep underground moisture and they continue to flourish. During the dry season trees and shrubs provide green fodder—leaves, flowers, and fruit—often rich in protein, vitamins, and minerals. In their absence, animals have only straw from native grasses. This poor feed causes avitaminosis, mineral deficiencies, and severe debilitation.

The shrubs and trees can be interplanted with grasses, thus increasing the carrying capacity of pastoral areas and often supplying the only grazing during drought or periods of the year when other food is normally scarce. Indeed, in savannas everywhere livestock and wildlife would barely survive a bad season were it not for the native leguminous browse shrubs and fodder trees. During the severe 6-month dry season in Brazilian savannas, for example, cattle obtain as much as 60 percent of their forage from leguminous shrubs and trees.

Thanks to their rhizobia, many of these trees and shrubs can grow in the most barren terrain. A number of them (as well as a few nonlegumes) can provide fixed nitrogen that benefits grasses and other ground-level forages. In addition, they provide shade to the livestock, enabling the animals to graze during the heat of the day. The trees can also be used for firewood, charcoal, or sometimes food (leaves and fruit).

With their extensive root system, trees and shrubs adapt to steeply sloping lands where both grazing and crop production foster erosion; they can often grow in sites unsuited for food production from conventional crops. In doing so, they may stabilize sandy and eroding soils and can protect them from torrential downpours and tropical windstorms.

Yet compared with the massive research efforts on pasture grasses, research on forage production from shrubs and trees is almost nonexistent. The subject falls between the traditional training and purviews of livestock researchers and foresters and therefore receives scant attention from either. Tree and bush forages have been accorded so little attention that many pastoralists regard them as noxious weeds and deliberately destroy them to allow grasses more room. At best, the utilization of edible trees is haphazard. During droughts, entire stands are often decimated for feed. At other times, the trees are destroyed by indiscriminate scrub clearing.

The purpose of this chapter is to introduce some leguminous shrubs and trees that have exceptional promise as animal feeds.*

Negev Desert, Israel. *Cassia sturtii* growing well on sand dunes without irrigation in an area receiving only 150 mm rainfall annually. Before planting, city garbage was ploughed into the sand to increase its organic matter and water retention. (M. Forti)

*See also chapters on *Acacia tortilis* (page 136), other forage acacias (page 141), *Acacia senegal* (page 279), *Prosopis* species (page 153), *Sesbania grandiflora* (page 185), tamarind (page 117), and carob (page 109).

Cassia sturtii

Considered unimportant as forage in its native Australia, *Cassia sturtii** is providing nutritious forage in experimental projects in Israel's arid region.†

Awassi ram at Beer-Sheva, Israel. *Cassia sturtii* is the most palatable browse species selected in Israel. (M. Forti)

*Subfamily: Caesalpinioideae.
†The promise of this plant is described in more detail in National Academy of Sciences. 1975. *Underexploited Tropical Plants with Promising Economic Value.* pp. 118-122. To order see page 329.

Under the conditions of the Negev Desert, it has demonstrated better year-round palatability than any bush yet tested. It also has good grazing resistance and the leaves have a protein content of about 12 percent with dry-matter yields (in two grazing periods) of about 1,000 kg per ha in a semiarid (200 mm rainfall) area.

The plant yields well in areas of 200-250 mm of winter rainfall, but also thrives in areas of greater rainfall. It will grow in a variety of soils, including those that are sandy and slightly alkaline, but does best in loamy soils.

The plant is also a valuable ornamental for dry areas.

Desmanthus virgatus

The genus *Desmanthus* comprises several dozen species, some of which may prove to be exceptional forage sources. *Desmanthus virgatus** is the only one investigated so far. It is a small shrub, 2–3 m tall, native to tropics and subtropics of the New World from Florida to Argentina and roughly resembling leucaena (page 131) in appearance. As a browse shrub it has proved to be very palatable, aggressive, persistent, and tolerant of heavy grazing because its regrowth is rapid.

This plant's climatic requirements are similar to those of leucaena. Its foliage has a lower protein content (leaves: 22 percent, foliage with stems: 10-15 percent) than that of leucaena and its yields are lower (7.6 t dry matter per ha per year has been measured at Sigatoka, Fiji, up to 70 t of green foliage per ha per year at Kununurra, northern Australia). Nevertheless, it deserves more widespread testing because, unlike leucaena, it is not toxic to livestock. Also, its pithy stems are more easily harvested than leucaena's woody ones.

Desmanthus virgatus fixes nitrogen well. It is so resilient that it can be mowed four times a year. Constantly mowed plants develop a broad root crown that may sprout as many as 50 slender stems.

Because of its vigor and prolific seeding, this plant can become a troublesome weed in cultivated fields.

Desmodium Species

Species of *Desmodium*† are so palatable and make such nutritious forage plants that they have been termed "alfalfas of the tropics." Livestock of all kinds relish both the leaves and young branches so much that many species

Desmanthus virgatus (L.) Willd. Also known as *Mimosa virgata* L. Subfamily: Mimosoideae.
†Subfamily: Papilionoideae.

are being entirely eliminated by overgrazing.* Yet *Desmodium* species have been accorded little attention in forage research in the tropics; most remain wild plants and many probably still await discovery as forage crops. For example, four little-known shrubs that deserve increased attention are *Desmodium discolor, Desmodium distortum, Desmodium gyroides,* and *Desmodium nicaraguense.*

Desmodium discolor. This vigorous, perennial shrub† (growing as tall as 3 m) is native to subtropical regions of Brazil (Sao Paulo, Mato Grosso), Argentina (Misiones), and Paraguay. Its clover-like leaves are extremely palatable to livestock and the plant makes especially useful supplementary grazing in the late summer and fall when grasses have lost their feed value. The foliage can be grazed or mowed (up to 5 cuts per year) and makes excellent hay and silage. Its protein content is about 15 percent, and annual productions of about 30 t of green forage per ha have been recorded in Brazil.

Desmodium discolor bushes nodulate freely and grow well in pastureland both in the tropics and subtropics. It has been introduced to southern Africa, as well as to Fiji and Colombia. In southern Africa it has been used to upgrade natural pastures by sowing seed into strips harrowed through rough veld just before the onset of the rainy season. It can also be planted together with corn; the corn yield is unaffected and the vulnerable *Desmodium discolor* seedlings are protected from desiccation and soil crusting. During the first year the foliage is too sparse for grazing, but after that the bushes dominate the weeds and provide a permanent source of high-quality feed. The plant grows best in deep fertile, loamy soils but will grow on many types from acid sandy soils to loams.

Desmodium distortum. A native of Venezuela and neighboring areas, *Desmodium distortum*‡ produces good crops of fodder (7 t of dry matter per ha per year have been measured in Zambia, for instance).

A many-branched perennial bush growing to 2 m high, it has a coarse, stemmy appearance, but its foliage is relished by cattle. Mature leaves have a crude protein content of 22-24 percent.

It is an especially promising forage crop for the vast tropical areas with acid soils. In replicated field trials on an acid soil (pH 4.1) in Colombia, *Desmodium distortum*, harvested only 3 months after planting, yielded 1.4-1.9 t of green forage per ha; 2 months later a second harvest yielded 2.8 t per ha.§

*Whyte *et al.* 1953.
†*Desmodium discolor* Vog. Known as horse marmalade (South Africa), marmelade de cavalo (Brazil), and discolored clover.
‡*Desmodium distortum* (Aubl) Macbride.
§ Information supplied by J. Halliday. See Research Contacts.

*Desmodium gyroides.** Indigenous to South and Southeast Asia, this bushy shrub (reaching about 4 m tall) is very leafy and cattle graze it readily. Although used as a shade crop for young cocoa and coffee plants, *Desmodium gyroides* has had only limited testing as a forage crop. It deserves wider trials, for it establishes readily from seed, grows vigorously even in poor soils (both acid and alkaline), and thrives at altitudes ranging from sea level to 1,000 m. Although it appears to have slight drought tolerance (it remains fairly leafy through a 3-month drought), the plant tolerates waterlogging well and probably has great value for wet sites in the tropics and subtropics.

The foliage and succulent new shoots are palatable to cattle, water buffalo, and goats. The woody stems usually prevent the plant from becoming too heavily grazed; however, they are brittle and large grazing animals can damage the plant. The plant coppices and regenerates branches readily, so that it can be cut and the forage carried to the animals. However, the bushes should be well established before being harvested or grazed; otherwise, they become prostrate. No evidence of toxicity was found in trials conducted by the Commonwealth Science and Industrial Research Organisation in northern Australia.†

Apparently *Desmodium gyroides* has no problem nodulating in new sites. It produces abundant nodules with cowpea inoculant and, at least in Belize, it nodulates readily with native *Rhizobium* strains.‡

Like leucaena (see below), *Desmodium gyroides* may well have importance as green manure because of its abundant leaf fall.

Desmodium gyroides germ plasm should be collected and promising strains selected for high yield, stem suppleness, and tolerance to dry and wet soils.

One year old *Desmodium gyroides*. Belize, Central America. (J. Lazier)

Desmodium gyroides (Roxb. ex Link) DC. Also known as *Codariocalyx gyroides* (Roxb. ex Link).
†Unpublished results of the late W. W. Bryan.
‡Information supplied by J. Lazier. See Research Contacts.

Nutritional content needs to be analyzed in detail. Animal feeding trials should follow.

Desmodium nicaraguense.* This shrub, a native of Central America's Pacific slope from Mexico to Nicaragua, is so nourishing to livestock that in Guatemala and El Salvador it is known as "engorda caballo" (horse fattener) or "engorda cabras" (goat fattener). Its leaves and young branches are eaten by livestock of all kinds and are locally considered excellent forage. The plant grows wild and in abundance, both in wet or dry thickets and on rocky hillsides. It grows up to 6 m tall, but livestock usually keep it cropped back. Although the shrub recovers quickly after grazing, it is killed outright if cropped too close. The foliage contains about 22 percent crude protein and can be harvested for hay or silage (up to 7 cuttings a year have been achieved in Costa Rica). The crop is easily established by direct sowing, seedling transplants, or cuttings, and the plants can sustain heavy competition from grasses and other vigorous plants.

Honeylocust

Native to hardwood forests of eastern North America, the honeylocust† is one of the hardiest, most adaptable, and most interesting fodder trees known. Its plump pods, borne in profusion, can be filled with sweet, succulent pulp relished by humans and animals alike. They constitute excellent livestock feed, especially when ground or crushed to make digestible the high-protein seeds, which are embedded in the pulp. Furthermore, the plant is deciduous and sheds leaves during autumn when other forage is scarce. These, too, are eagerly consumed by animals. In addition, its open fern-like foliage is translucent enough for plants such as pasture grasses or other crops to thrive beneath its canopy—a two-story agriculture that makes efficient use of space.

A wide-spreading, flat-topped tree, the honeylocust may reach 45 m in height. Although some bisexual types are known, most specimens are either male (pollen producing) or female (fruit producing). Trunks and limbs of wild trees usually bear branching thorns, but thornless forms have been isolated for use in cultivation.

Easily grown from seed, suckers, or cuttings, the trees grow fairly fast and will bear pods from their fourth or fifth year. The giant pods can be up to 45 cm long and 5 cm wide. Top-yielding, superior cultivars may produce an astounding 450 kg of dry pods per tree per year. During the 1920s and 1930s,

---

Desmodium nicaraguense Oerst.
†*Gleditsia triacanthos* L. (sometimes spelled *Gleditschia*). Subfamily: Mimosoideae.

Honeylocust. (Tennessee Valley Authority)

several American scientific organizations sponsored contests to find the sweetest honeylocust trees. Winning entries produced pods with as much as 39 percent sugar.

Few tree species are as widely adaptable as the honeylocust. In its native habitat it thrives in cold-temperate to subtropical climates. It is also well established in the Russian steppes, South African veld, and the Australian Outback. The tree is known in Tunisia and it seems probable that honeylocust will adjust to many new, untried locations. Its climatic limits are unknown. It is, however, very frost hardy, can be grown at least up to 1,500 m elevation, and seems particularly worth testing as a new crop for tropical highlands such as in Nepal, northern Thailand, Central Africa, and Latin America. Although moist soil is needed for good growth, the honeylocust's deep roots make it drought tolerant where deep soil moisture is available and it can grow well in semiarid regions. The tree also grows best in

130

deep, sandy loam, but tolerates almost all soil types: acid to alkaline, slightly saline, and sand to clay.

Useful for a wide range of purposes in addition to supplying forage, the honeylocust makes an attractive ornamental or shade tree for hedges, shelter belts, avenues, or rangeland. It puts out suckers, coppices vigorously, and can be used for erosion control. Honeylocust wood is heavy, strong, and of good quality for furniture, structural work, and general utility. It also makes excellent fuel. For ornamental purposes fruitless cultivars are available.

Any use of honeylocust must employ thornless types; the thorns are sharp, hard, and can injure animals' hooves. Thornless, high-sugar-yielding varieties have been selected. Thornlessness is a genetically dominant trait, and these types breed true without reverting to thorniness. Today, however, high-yielding trees have to be produced vegetatively by budding or grafting, which retards the widespread utilization of the species.

Extreme care must be taken when testing the species in new locations. It has a habit of forming dense thickets and has become a pest in Queensland, Australia, for example.

Leucaena

This species,* a native of Central America, occurs both as a many-branched shrub and tall single-trunked tree.†

Cattle feed on the leaves and stems of the bushy variety of leucaena in Australia. (R.J. Jones)

*Leucaena leucocephala. Subfamily: Mimosoideae.
†This plant and its use for forage, timber, and other purposes is detailed in National Academy of Sciences. 1977. *Leucaena: Promising Forage and Tree Crop for the Tropics.* To order see page 329.

In the lowland tropics, much protein can be produced efficiently and economically from leucaena grown on well-drained, fertile soils and harvested regularly as hay or forage. A leucaena pasture is almost 2 m high. Cattle are lost among the bushes, only the tops of their heads being visible. But this gives a leucaena pasture an added dimension; cattle find forage from ground level to eye level. Sunlight penetrates through the plant's open feathery leaves, reaching the lowest branches and grasses beneath the bushes so that they, too, provide healthy, vigorous forage. A field of leucaena is a block of forage rather than a conventional sward-like pasture.

Cattle relish the leaflets and young stems and often leave the bushes stripped bare. But leucaena quickly regrows new foliage, and within 2 weeks a "bare" field can be ready for grazing once more. So resilient is the plant that pastures near Brisbane, Australia, have been browsed almost continuously for about 20 years without requiring replanting.

Leucaena leaves, similar to alfalfa in digestibility, protein content, and nutritional value, are particularly palatable to dairy cows, beef cattle, water buffalo, and goats. Under favorable conditions one hectare of leucaena can produce 10-20 t of edible dry matter, compared with 8-9 t for alfalfa.

However, leucaena forage has a drawback. Mimosine, an uncommon amino acid, comprises about 5 percent of the weight of the leaflets. If taken in excess, mimosine causes cattle to produce less than normal quantities of thryoxine, a thyroid hormone. Eventually, the cattle lose tail and rump hair and in extreme cases become completely debilitated with goiter. To avoid this, leucaena must always be fed in combination with grass or other feeds and kept to no more than one-third of the diet. New low-mimosine leucaena varieties, now in advanced development, hold great promise as worry-free tropical feedstuffs.

Nonetheless, two decades of research have shown that leucaena complemented with grass can produce extraordinary weight gains in cattle, and can do so over extended periods with little or no adverse effect. Cattle feeding on leucaena near Brisbane gained an average of almost 1 kg each day for more than 200 days. This performance included a winter period when the growth of the leucaena slowed. During warm months, weight gains of more than 1 kg a day were recorded.* Such growth is about twice what is normally expected from animals grazing in tropical pastures; it approaches the weight increases normally obtained only in feedlots.†

*Information supplied by R. J. Jones, CSIRO Davies Laboratory, Townsville, Queensland 4810, Australia.
†This section adapted from Vietmeyer, N. D. 1978. Leucaena: new hope for the tropics. In *Yearbook of Science and the Future*, Encyclopaedia Britannica Inc., Chicago. pp. 238-247.

Selected Readings

Bene, J. G., H. W. Beall, and A. Côté. 1977. *Trees, Food, and People: Land Management in the Tropics.* International Development Research Centre, Box 8500, Ottawa, Canada. 52 pp. (Order No. IDRC-084e)

Dougall, H. W., and A. V. Bogdan. 1958. Browse plants of Kenya. *The East African Agricultural Journal* 23:236-245.

Everist, S. L. 1969. *Use of Fodder Trees and Shrubs.* Division of Plant Industry Advisory Leaflet No. 1024. Queensland Department of Primary Industries, George Street, Brisbane, Queensland, Australia. p. 24.

Imperial Agricultural Bureaux. 1947. *The Use and Misuse of Shrubs and Trees as Fodder.* Joint Publication No. 10. Imperial Bureau of Pastures and Field Crops, Aberystwyth; Imperial Forestry Bureau, Oxford; and Imperial Bureau of Animal Nutrition, Aberdeen. 258 pp.

Le Houérou, H. N. 1974. *The Useful Shrubs of the Mediterranean Basin and the Arid Tropical Belt South of the Sahara.* Food and Agriculture Organization of the United Nations, Rome. 20 pp. (Order No. AGPC:MISC/24)

Skerman, P. J. 1977. *Tropical Forage Legumes.* FAO Plant Production and Protection Series No. 2. Food and Agriculture Organization of the United Nations, Rome. 609 pp.

Cassia sturtii

National Academy of Sciences. 1975. *Underexploited Tropical Plants with Promising Economic Value.* National Academy of Sciences, Washington, D.C. pp. 118-122.

Desmanthus virgatus

Skerman, P. J. 1977. *Tropical Forage Legumes.* FAO Plant Production and Protection Series No. 2. Food and Agriculture Organization of the United Nations, Rome. pp. 494-495.

Desmodium Species

Squibb, R. L. 1945. Desmodiums—"alfalfas of the tropics." *Agriculture in the Americas* 5:151-153.

Whyte, R. O., G. Nilsson-Leissner, and H. C. Trumble. 1953 (reprinted 1966). *Legumes in Agriculture.* Food and Agriculture Organization of the United Nations, Rome. pp. 268-272.

Desmodium discolor

Boultwood, J. N. 1964. Two valuable perennial legumes—horse marmalade (*Desmodium discolor*) and kuru vine (*D. intortum*). *Rhodesia Agriculture Journal* 61:70-72.

Otero, J. de R. 1952. *Informacoes Sobre Algunes Plantas Forrageires.* Directora de Estatistica da Produccao, Rio de Janeiro.

Skerman, P. J. 1977. *Tropical Forage Legumes.* FAO Plant Production and Protection Series No. 2. Food and Agriculture Organization of the United Nations, Rome. pp. 496-500.

Desmodium distortum

Skerman, P. J. 1977. *Tropical Forage Legumes.* FAO Plant Production and Protection Series No. 2. Food and Agriculture Organization of the United Nations, Rome. pp. 500-501.

Honeylocust

A comprehensive honeylocust bibliography is available from F. S. Santamour, see address below.

Jurriaanse, A. 1973. *Are they Fodder Trees?* Pamphlet 116. Department of Forestry, Private Box X93, Pretoria, South Africa. 32 pp.

Podems, M., and B. Bortz. 1975. *Ornamentals for Eating.* Rodale Research and Development Report No. 2. Rodale Press, Inc., 33 East Minor St., Emmaus, Pennsylvania 18049, USA.

Santamour, F. S. 1978. Where are the sweet honeylocusts today? *Bulletin of the Association of Arboreta and Botanic Gardens* 12(1):24-28. (Reprints available from the author, see address below.)

Smith, J. R. 1977. *Tree Crops, A Permanent Agriculture.* Devin-Adair Publishing Company, Old Greenwich, Connecticut. pp. 65-79.

Leucaena leucocephala

National Academy of Sciences. 1977. *Leucaena: Promising Forage and Tree Crop for the Tropics.* National Academy of Sciences, Washington, D.C. 115 pp.

Research Contacts

Cassia sturtii

Charleville Pastoral Laboratory, Charleville 4470, Queensland, Australia

Desert Botanical Garden, P.O. Box 5415, Phoenix, Arizona 85010, USA

M. Forti, Research and Development Authority, Ben-Gurion University of the Negev, P.O. Box 1025, Beer-Sheva, Israel

Herbarium of the Northern Territory, Animal Industry and Agriculture Branch, Department of the Northern Territory, Alice Springs, N.T. 5750, Australia

Los Angeles State and County Arboretum, Arcadia, California 91006, USA

Desmanthus virgatus

James L. Brewbaker, Professor of Horticulture and Genetics, Department of Horticulture, University of Hawaii, Honolulu, Hawaii 96822, USA

R. Burt, CSIRO, Davies Laboratory, Private Bag, Townsville, Queensland, Australia

Chitedze Agricultural Research Station, P.O. Box 158, Lilongwe, Malawi

CSIRO Division of Tropical Agronomy, Cunningham Laboratory, St. Lucia, Queensland 4067, Australia

Msekara Regional Experiment Station, Fort Jameson, Zambia

W. J. A. Payne, 63 Half Moon Lane, London SE24 9JX, England

José Ramírez Bermúdez, Instituto Técnico de Agricultura, Ministerio de Agricultura, Guatemala City, Guatemala

Makato Takahashi, 2810 Kinohou Place, Honolulu, Hawaii 96822, USA

Desmodium discolor

Director of Agriculture, Suva, Fiji
Katapola Farm Institute, Chipata, Zambia
Mount Makalu Research Station, P.O. Box 7, Chilanga, Zambia
For seed sources in Brazil and South Africa, see Skerman, 1977, cited above.

Desmodium distortum

Beef Production Program, Centro Internacional de Agricultura Tropical (CIAT), Apartado Aereo 67-13, Cali, Colombia (Jake Halliday, Soil Microbiologist). *Rhizobium* inoculant available.
CSIRO Division of Tropical Agronomy, Cunningham Laboratory, St. Lucia, Queensland 4067, Australia
Department of Agriculture, Srisomrong Street, Bangkok, Thailand
Federal Experiment Station, Penang, Malaysia
Indian Veterinary Research Institute, Isantnagar, India
Rubber Research Institute, Haadyai, Thailand

Desmodium gyroides

IDRC-Belize Pasture and Forage Legume Program, Central Farm, Cago District, Belize, Central America (R. H. Neal)
J. Lazier, c/o Soil Science, University of the West Indies, St. Augustine, Trinidad, West Indies
R. J. Williams, CSIRO, Cunningham Laboratory, St. Lucia, Queensland 4067, Australia

Desmodium nicaraguense

Dirección General de Investigaciones Agronomía, Nueva San Salvador, El Salvador
J. Halliday, Centro Internacional de Agricultura Tropical, Cali, Colombia
   D. distortum for forage, a closely similar species.)

Honeylocust

Frank S. Santamour, Jr., U.S. National Arboretum, U.S. Department of Agriculture, Washington, D.C. 20002, USA
Gregory Williams, Route 1, Gravel Switch, Kentucky 40328, USA

Leucaena leucocephala

An extensive list of research contacts is given in the NAS report on this plant, listed above.

Acacia tortilis

The umbrella thorn,* one of the most distinctive and widespread of African acacias, supplies fodder, fuel, shade, and shelter in most of semiarid Africa and the Middle East.† It is very resilient, often being the first tree to colonize arid regions and the last survivor in the face of encroaching desert. Even in the absence of all other feed, the pods of this plant are said to be sufficient to fatten sheep and other livestock. Throughout much of Africa, during the dry season when the pods fall they often provide the main forage for cattle, sheep, goats, and wildlife.

Acacia tortilis, Senegal. (Centre Technique Forestier Tropical)

Surviving in the most refractory sites, the umbrella thorn is a promising species for afforesting dry, rocky, and sandy areas. For example, over the past

Acacia tortilis (Forsk.) Hayne. Commonly called Israeli babool (India), umbrella thorn (Africa), haak-en-steekdoring (South Africa). Subfamily: Mimosoideae.
†It is found in sub-Saharan countries from Mauritania to Sudan and in East African countries from Ethiopia to South Africa. Also found in Egypt, Israel, Saudi Arabia, and Yemen.

15 years it has proved to be the best multipurpose tree (out of 228 species tested) for growing in the arid and semiarid regions of the state of Rajasthan, India, becoming "a boon to the people of the desert who suffer from shortage of fuel, fodder, and timber."*

Acacia tortilis is usually a medium-size tree (4–20 m tall), sometimes with several trunks that spray upwards and outwards and that support a flat-topped umbrella of foliage. The foliage is feathery and typically acacia-like. Two kinds of thorns occur on the trunk and branches: long, straight, white thorns and small, curved, brown ones. The fragrant white or pale-yellow flowers are borne in round clusters, and the ripe fruits—yellowish-brown pods (8–10 cm long)—are spiralled like a coil spring.

The plant has four distinct subspecies that exist in different geographical zones.† They are:

subspecies *tortilis*	Sudan, Egypt, Arabia
subspecies *raddiana*	North Africa, tropical Africa
subspecies *spirocarpa*	eastern and southern tropical Africa
subspecies *heteracantha*	southern and northern Africa

Although it thrives where annual rainfall is 1,000 mm, umbrella thorn is also extremely drought resistant and can survive in climates with less than 100 mm annual rainfall and long, erratic dry seasons. The plant is so drought hardy that specimens are sometimes found isolated in otherwise treeless arid environments. In northern Sudan, as the desert expands southwards *Acacia tortilis* is the last surviving woody plant to form stands on sandy soils adjoining the desert.

It does well, too, in hot climates with maximum temperatures as high as 50°C, and it grows where minimum temperatures are close to 0°C. The tree favors alkaline soils, but grows well in sand dunes, sandy loam, rocky soils, and other soils that drain well.

Pods are produced prolifically. They fall to the ground and are devoured by wild herbivores, camels, cattle, and other domestic livestock. They are the main sustenance for much of East Africa's wildlife. The foliage, too, is palatable. It is, for example, the major fodder for sheep and goats in the semi-desert areas of northwestern Sudan.

Wood from *Acacia tortilis* is dense and is used for fence posts and for manufacturing small implements and articles. It has high calorific value (4,360 Cal per kg) and makes superior firewood and charcoal. With the chronic and increasing fuel shortages in arid regions, this is a vitally important

*Roy, Kaul, and Gyanchand. 1973. The test included 56 acacias and 104 eucalyptus species.
†Brenan. 1957. Some taxonomists maintain that subspecies *raddiana* is distinct enough to be designated a separate species, *Acacia raddiana* Savi.

property.* In Rajasthan, India, *Acacia tortilis* plantations are being established for fuelwood. It is projected that the trees will be harvested on a 10-year rotation. The plant coppices well,† so that there is no need to replant trees after every harvest for fuelwood.

Acacia tortilis is excellent for soil stabilization. In Rajasthan, over 800 ha of shifting sand dunes have been stabilized by planting the species. The seed is now being distributed to other parts of India (including Haryana, Gujarat, Tamil Nadu, and Andhra Pradesh). In the comparison trials at the Central Arid Zone Research Institute, Jodhpur, India, it was noted that *Acacia tortilis* grew twice as fast as indigenous acacias and that the plant withstood arid conditions better than *Acacia nilotica*, *Acacia senegal*, and the local *Prosopis* species (see page 153).

With its dense, spreading, flat crown, the umbrella thorn also makes an attractive decorative tree that provides shade almost year-round.

Limitations

Acacia tortilis is a plant best adapted to hot, dry lowlands (below 1,000 m rainfall) in the tropics. It will grow fairly well in shallow soils, though it then develops long lateral roots that can become a nuisance in nearby fields, paths, and roadways. In shallow soil the plants remain shrubby and must be widely spaced to allow for this lateral root growth.

Plants less than 2 years old are damaged by frost and require protection.

Acacia tortilis should not be introduced to new areas where grazing and firewood are in adequate supply, as it is likely that the species will grow out of control and become a nuisance. This is particularly so in humid to sub-humid areas.

Acacia tortilis seeds are very hard, and a simple treatment (dipping in hot water and soaking overnight) is needed to ensure quick and uniform germination. Given this treatment, the percentage of seeds that germinate is very high; furthermore, the seedlings can be established in plantations with little loss. However, the seeds are very susceptible to attack by larvae of bruchid beetles.

The tree is usually slow growing. Its long thorns can be a nuisance.

---

*See forthcoming companion report: *Firewood Crops: Shrub and Tree Species for Energy Production*. To order see page 329.
†Bosshard, W. C. 1966. *Forest Research and Education Project Pamphlet No. 17*. Ministry of Agriculture, Khartoum, Sudan.

Research Needs

Acacia tortilis is recommended for trial plantings in semiarid areas that face severe shortages of forage and fuel, particularly where soil erosion, desertification, or sand stabilization are problems.

Research should begin with searches throughout East Africa and the Middle East for *Acacia tortilis* germ plasm. Plant explorers should look for thornless types that grow rapidly. Needed are types with single trunks (for wood production) and others with branches low enough for browsing.

There have been some unconfirmed allegations that *Acacia tortilis* foliage can become toxic to domestic livestock.* This needs investigation and the germ plasm should be screened for types without toxic principles.

In some East African game reserves (for example, Tanzania's Lake Manyara Park), elephants that eat *Acacia tortilis* bark are destroying the trees so rapidly that the species is likely to become extinct in those areas, and some protection is needed.

The pods are heavily injured by pest attacks. Investigation of control treatments could aid higher production.

Acacia tortilis is a particularly promising species for use with water-harvesting techniques that use basins or ridges to concentrate rainfall run-off.† Trials with different systems are highly recommended.

Selected Readings

Brenan, J. P. M. 1957. Notes on Mimosoideae: III. *Kew Bulletin* 12:86-89.

El Amin, H. M. n.d. *Sudan Acacias.* Forest Research Institute Bulletin No. 1. Forest Research Institute, Khartoum, Sudan.

Gupta, R. K., and G. S. Balara. 1972. Comparative studies on the germination, growth and seedling biomass of two promising exotics in Rajasthan desert, *Prosopis juliflora* (Swartz) DC. and *Acacia tortilis* (Forsk.) Hayne ssp. *tortilis. Indian Forester* 98(5): 280-285.

Karschon, R. 1975. *Seed Germination of* Acacia raddiana *Savi and* A. tortilis *Hayne as Related to Infestation by Bruchids.* Leaflet No. 52. Agricultural Research Organization, Division of Scientific Publications, Bet Dagan, Israel.

Kaul, R. N. 1970. Indo-Pakistan. In *Afforestation in Arid Zones*, ed. R. N. Kaul. Monographiae Biological Vol. 20, pp. 155-210. Dr. W. Junk N.V. Publishers, The Hague.

Puri, D. N., K. D. Muthana, D. P. Handa, and M. Singh. 1973. Study on the comparative growth and establishment of *Acacia tortilis* (Forsk.) and *Acacia senegal* in rocky habitats. *Annals of the Arid Zone* 12:167-171.

Mariaux, A. 1975. A dendroclimatology trial on *Acacia raddiana* in the Sahelian climate. *Bois et Forets des Tropiques* 163:27-35.

---

*Dalziel, J. M. 1948. *Useful Plants of West Tropical Africa.* Crown Agents for the colonies, London. pp. 209-210; and Watt, J. M., and M. G. Breyer-Brandwick, 1962. *Medicinal and Poisonous Plants of Southern and Eastern Africa*, 2nd Ed. Longman, New York. p. 551.

†See National Academy of Sciences. 1974. *More Water for Arid Lands.* To order see page 329.

Roy, A. D., R. N. Kaul, and Gyanchand. 1973. Israeli babool—a promising tree for arid and semi arid lands. *Indian Farming* 23(8):19-20.

Research Contacts

Agricultural Research and Training Project, El-Kod/Giar, P.O. Box 1188, Aden, South Yemen (National Coordinator on Forest Genetic Resources)

M. Baumer, 446 rue de la Combe caude, 34000 Montpelier, France

L. Boulos, National Research Centre, Tahrir Street, Awgaf Post Office, Dokki, Cairo, Egypt

M. Evenari, Botany Department, Hebrew University of Jerusalem, Jerusalem, Israel

M. Forti, Research and Development Authority, Ben-Gurion University of the Negev, P.O. Box 1025, Beer-Sheva, Israel

Forestry Division, Agricultural Research Organization, Ilanot, D. N. Lev Hasharon, Israel (R. Karschon, Director)

ICAR, Central Arid Zone Research Institute, Jodhpur, Rajasthan, India (H. S. Mann, Director; R. N. Kaul; and K. S. Muthana)

P. K. Karani, Deputy Chief Forest Officer, Ministry of Agriculture and Forestry, Forest Department, P.O. Box 31, Entebbe, Uganda

M. Kassas, Botany Department, Faculty of Science, Cairo University, Giza, Cairo, Egypt

H. F. Lamprey, UNEP-MAB Integrated Project in Arid Lands, UNESCO, Regional Office for Science and Technology for Africa, P.O. Box 30552, Nairobi, Kenya

H. N. Le Houérou, FAO Regional Adviser—Coordinator for Range Development in Northern Africa, Casier Postal Orvu, Rabat—Chellah, Morocco

National Bureau of Plant Genetic Resources, IARI Campus, New Delhi 110012, India (K. L. Mehra, Director)

Officer in Charge, National Herbarium and National Botanic Garden, P.O. Box 8100, Causeway, Salisbury, Zimbabwe-Rhodesia

Reforestation Service, Keren Kayemet, BP 45, Kiryat Haim, Haifa, Israel (S. Weitz, Director)

Royal Botanic Gardens, Kew, Richmond, Surrey TW9 3AE, United Kingdom (J. P. M. Brenan and G. E. Wickens)

A. G. Seif-el-Din, Gum Research Officer, Agricultural Research Corporation, Gum Research Division, P.O. Box 429, El Obeid, Sudan

K. K. Wachiira, Department of Geography, Kenyatta University College, P.O. Box 43844, Nairobi, Kenya

Other Forage Acacias

The untapped potential of browse shrubs and fodder trees has been out-lined (see page 123). In addition to the umbrella thorn, several other species of *Acacia** are among the most promising and are discussed in this chapter.†

There are about 800 species of the genus *Acacia*. They are abundant in savannas and arid regions of Australia, Africa, India, and the Americas. Many are exceedingly robust and grow under the most severe conditions. The amount of protein in their edible tissues is often high. Although the leaves, pods, or young shoots of some species are toxic to animals, many provide the main browse for wildlife and have fair-to-excellent palatability for domestic livestock such as cattle, sheep, goats, donkeys, and camels.

The great promise of forage acacias is for dry regions where pasture grows poorly or only seasonally. Many acacias have a fast-growing tap root that enables them to utilize moisture stored in lower soil layers and to remain green long into the dry season. They are often found in seasonally dry, sandy valleys and ravines; on gravelly plains, they are the chief source of dry-season fodder in many regions. Both the foliage and the pods are potentially edible, though in some species only one or the other is accepted by livestock. The bark and fresh young stems of some species are also relished by certain animals.

Most acacias grow vigorously, coppice readily, and withstand heavy brows-ing. The leafy branches can also be cut for fodder, within reason, without significant damage to the plants. Many acacias are important to arid-land grazing because of the shade they provide to livestock. In addition, the na-tural fall of leaves and the large quantities of animal dung and urine return to the soil much of the nitrogen fixed by the *Rhizobium* in the acacia's nodules, and the humus improves the soil's fertility and physical properties. This, in turn, improves subsequent crops of grasses that share the soil. In addition, certain palatable, low-growing species that die in the open thrive in the acacia's shade and protection. Thus grasses and acacias tend to be compatible and to grow well in combination when the trees are widely spaced.

*Subfamily: Mimosoideae.
†See also *Acacia senegal*, page 279.

Acacias are also grown to control erosion, to stabilize sand dunes, and to reclaim land lost to unpalatable grasses. In some cases, they can be cropped for forage as an additional benefit.

Acacia flowers are favorites of bees. Honey production can often supplement forage production. Some say that acacia nectar is unequalled in the tropics for producing honey.

Discussion follows of some promising forage acacia species.

Acacia albida

A most valuable plant, *Acacia albida** is native to Africa's dry savannas and riverine basins. It deserves to be better known in similar environments

Acacia albida, Niger. (Centre Technique Forestier Tropical)

Acacia albida Del. Also known as *Faidherbia albida* (Del.) A. Chev., applering acacia, ana tree, and winter thorn. This species is described in more detail in a companion report: National Academy of Sciences. 1975. *Underexploited Tropical Plants with Promising Economic Value.* pp. 111-114. To order see page 329.

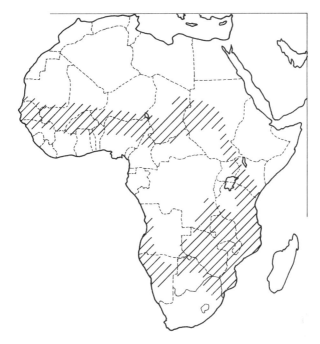

Native distribution of *Acacia albida*. (G. E. Wickens)

elsewhere; even in Africa, its greater protection and use should be encouraged.

Contrary to usual tree behavior, *Acacia albida* retains its leaves through the dry season and sheds them just as the rainy season begins. This has a number of economic benefits:

- Forage is available throughout the off-season when other trees are leafless;
- At the end of the dry season, when feed is often desperately scarce, the protein-rich pods are maturing and drop off in huge quantities;
- During hot months, the tree's dense foliage provides cool shade for livestock;
- The tree's leafy crown protects the soil when most grasses have succumbed to drought, leaving the ground vulnerable to wind erosion;
- The leaf drop and continuous presence of livestock near the trees greatly enrich the soil, making it more suitable for growing crops among the scattered trees;
- The tree's foliage falls off just when food crops are being planted, perfectly timed for providing soil nutrients when they are most needed (the heat and humidity at the rainy season's onset fostering quick decay of the leaflets and rapid release of their nutrients); and

- The tree's lack of leaves during the rainy season enables sunlight to reach the crops planted around it.

Found mainly in the wetter areas of Sahelian savannas, from Senegal to the Sudan, *Acacia albida* also grows along the rivers in eastern Africa as far south as northern Transvaal and Botswana. Stands also occur in coastal areas of Namibia and Angola, as well as in Israel and Lebanon. Because of its drought tolerance, the tree is often the only one of any size to be found. A large tree, growing as high as 30 m, it has pairs of short white thorns tipped with reddish-brown and a crown of blue-green foliage. Although it prefers deep sandy soils and an annual rainfall of 650 mm, if deep groundwater is available, *Acacia albida* also thrives where rainfall is only 300 mm. After the roots reach water, it is one of the fastest growing savanna trees.

Acacia albida has the unusual habit of growing new foliage during the dry season and dropping its leaves in the wet season. African farmers take advantage of this and feed and shade livestock beneath the trees during the dry season when the foliage is available. Then they grow crops beneath the leafless trees during the wet season. The accumulated manure remarkably increases crop yields. The picture shows sorghum growing beneath *Acacia albida* in Sahelian Africa. (International Development Research Centre)

Avidly eaten by sheep, goats, camels, and cattle, the leaves, small branches, and twisted pods make excellent fodder and are much prized. Niger's dry farmlands normally support only 10 cattle per km^2, but 18-20 cattle per km^2 are possible where *Acacia albida* grows. The pods can be dried and stored for later use (which is not feasible with other acacia pods because they split apart and disintegrate). Yields of 125-135 kg of pods on a single tree have been recorded.[*] However, yields of 400-600 kg of pods per ha are more usual in the scattered trees in Sahelian savannas.

Where *Acacia albida* grows, the land is favored for growing crops. Peanuts grown beneath the tree have yielded twice as much as those grown further away;[†] millet yield has increased five times when the crop is planted beneath the trees.

In reforestation projects in Senegal, Upper Volta, Niger, and Chad, large areas are being planted with *Acacia albida* on a village and community level.

Acacia albida can attain a trunk diameter of 1.5 m, and it produces timber useful for general construction. In the Sudan, this wood has been widely used for school furniture, roofing, and boxmaking. The trees grow quickly; *Acacia albida* is recognized as the fastest growing acacia in South Africa. Trees have reached 6.5 m after 4 years and 10.5 m (with a 9.4 cm diameter) after 7.5 years.

Acacia albida also makes a most useful ornamental and shade tree for gardens and avenues. Further, the plant's spreading root system offers excellent protection to the banks of water courses.

Acacia aneura, Mulga

Mulga[‡] is an outstanding Australian fodder tree. It is found in abundance in the states of Queensland and Western Australia and is especially important where annual rainfall is only 200-500 mm. Seen from a distance, mulga's pendant blue-green foliage creates the characteristic grayness of the dry grassland areas of the Australian Outback. In these areas pastoralists have high regard for mulga and manage the trees as a reserve fodder source for use during drought. The leaves and branches are lopped off or pushed down with a tractor. A daily ration of 1.4 kg of mulga leaf (12 percent protein, 3 percent fat, 20 percent fiber) supplies sheep with sufficient protein, calcium, and vitamin A. The mulga diet alone provides adequate protein but insufficient sulfur and phosphorus, and to maintain healthy sheep, supplements should be available. An evergreen, mulga provides year-round fodder and shade.

At least 12 different forms of this species are known, and they differ in their palatability to grazing animals. Some are straight-trunked trees reaching

[*]Information supplied by C. Dancette and G.E. Wickens. See Research Contacts.
[†]Wickens. 1969.
[‡]*Acacia aneura* F. Muell. ex Benth.

Sheep eating foliage of *Acacia aneura* (mulga). (N.P. McMeniman)

9 m tall, but in arid areas the plant is reduced to a shrub. Mulga grows on a variety of soils including lateritic soils, friable clay loams, and even sand.

Mulga wood has striking color, with pale-yellow sapwood contrasting sharply with the brown and black heartwood. For this reason it is much used to make small objects, especially souvenirs, which are widely sold in Australia. In addition, mulga wood (one of the hardest woods in the world) is much sought for fencing, pit-props in mines, and other roundwood uses. The wood also makes useful fuel, though it burns quickly and leaves no coals.

Acacia pendula, Weeping Myall

The weeping myall,* a strikingly attractive tree with drooping branches resembling those of a weeping willow, is one of the most graceful of all acacias. Its silvery-white foliage is readily eaten by sheep and cattle and is thought to be more palatable and nutritious than that of mulga (*Acacia aneura*). In many areas uncontrolled grazing has exterminated this species. In the interior savanna woodlands of New South Wales and Queensland, the myall makes an excellent standby fodder for drought years.†

The tree reaches heights of 6-12 m (with trunk diameter up to 30 cm) and makes a fine shade tree on farms. It is also excellent for windbreaks, ornamental plantings, and fencing. It prefers good soils (clays or black soils) with access to groundwater. But it is exceptionally robust, and in its native habitat summers are often extremely hot and annual rainfall is only 400-650 mm.

Acacia pendula A. Cunn. ex G. Don. Also called boree.
†Recently introduced in Israel, the weeping myall is proving a valuable species for gardening and landscaping under dry conditions, but preliminary grazing trials indicate that other legume shrubs are preferred by cattle. Information supplied by M. Forti. See Research Contacts.

Acacia pendula. (N. Hall)

Myall wood has a peculiar violet-like odor. It has a rich, dark color, beautifully patterned. The wood is smooth, closely grained, and makes excellent fuel.

Acacia victoriae*

This is a fodder shrub widespread in semi-desert areas in inland Australia. Its leaves are readily eaten by sheep and cattle; its foliage, though not produced in large quantities, is a valuable forage supplement during dry seasons, for the plant retains leaves year-round except during extreme droughts. The shrub has shown excellent growth and survival characteristics in arid test plots in Israel, with good palatability during the winter growing season and excellent ability to recover after "being grazed in the most severe and merciless way."†

In its native habitat, *Acacia victoriae* tolerates a wide range of climates and soils ranging from sands to heavy clays. It even grows on saline soils. Its branches and twigs often exude quantities of a clear, tasteless gum (see page 278). Though analyzed for the first time in 1978, it seems to have outstandingly good qualities for use in foods and industry. Solutions of it are frequently colorless, a very desirable property.‡

Some forms of this plant are very prickly. But types that completely lack thorns or that have only a few small thorns are known, and only these should be selected for forage use.

Acacia victoriae, in bloom, Northern Territory, Australia. (J.R. Maconochie)

Acacia victoriae Bench. Formerly referred to as *Acacia sentis* F. Muell. Known commonly as gundabluey or narran in Australia.
†Information supplied by M. Forti. See Research Contacts.
‡Information supplied by D. M. W. Anderson. See Research Contacts.

Limitations

The vigor and adaptability of acacias make them potential weeds. They may encroach on poorly grazed and poorly managed pastures, becoming noxious pests.

Many acacias have long, sharp thorns or hooked prickles and are not readily eaten by livestock except in extreme drought. However, some have thorns only when young, and they mature into trees suitable for browsing. Most Australian acacias are thornless.

Generally, acacias are easily propagated by seed and adapt well to cultivation. The seeds have hard coats but germinate well after simple treatment by standard horticultural methods that use hot water or sulfuric acid. However, the seedlings' long roots complicate nursery production, and establishment in the field is made difficult by livestock and wildlife, which relish the tender seedlings.

Dry-land acacias thrive in coarse, well-drained soils, while riverine species can withstand prolonged waterlogging on heavy clays. Although extremely hardy when mature, many species are frost sensitive when young.

It is important to grow palatable grasses among the fodder trees. Without such supplemental feed, the trees alone may be inadequate as feedstuffs. Finding compatible grasses is a major research challenge.

When cut for fodder, the trees have to be lopped carefully. Cutting and breaking large branches reduces yields in succeeding years. It has also been found that dead branches left dangling enable otherwise harmless grass fires to engulf the trees.

The toxicity of some acacias is caused by cyanogenetic glucosides. Their palatability to livestock can vary with location. This may be due to changes in toxic or other compounds resulting from differences in climate, season, or locale. The palatability of acacias also varies during the year; it is usually lower at the end of the dry season when the leaves and pods have matured and dried out. The pods of some species give an odor to cow's milk and cannot be fed immediately before milking time.

Although they usually cause little problem, the pests and diseases of acacias are numerous. Defoliation can be caused by beetles, looper caterpillars, and the wattle bagworm. Other potential pests are scale insects, sapsucking bugs, termites, nematodes, and fungi. The pods are often heavily infested with bruchid beetles.

Research Needs

These forage acacias deserve trials in suitable arid habitats throughout the world. The trials should test the relative merits of the different species under various rainfall, soil, altitude, and other environmental conditions. Forage value and toxicity should also be monitored.

Methods should be devised for keeping the shrubs producing optimally and for getting maximum utilization from them; this could include consideration of spacing, water harvesting, and inoculation, and the effects of fertilization, severity of grazing, efficient manual and mechanical foliage harvesting methods, and drying (processing) and storage of whole foliage versus leaflets alone.*

It is also important to develop combinations of acacia shrubs, natural grasses (or other edible low-growing vegetation), introduced forage grasses, and various grazing animals. By interplanting the crops, it should be feasible to develop combinations that greatly increase stocking rates while still protecting the fragile arid environment and providing balanced nutrition, extended grazing seasons, and shade. The goal should be to create a planned and managed grazing system that avoids the seasonal crisis of the pastoral industry in arid locations, something easier said than done.

If great care is taken, forage acacias can be introduced to new regions. However, their potential for escaping and becoming weedy pests must be guarded against and the plants must be destroyed if necessary. This is a special concern where, in the absence of grazing and periodic fires, impenetrable, useless acacia thickets may develop.

Different provenances of many acacia species have different palatability and degrees of thorniness. Care must be taken to select the most useful types.

Some other *Acacia* species worth testing in exploratory research projects are:

Acacia seyal Del. variety *fistula.* Considered the plant with the best fodder value in northern Nigeria and large parts of the Sahelian savannas—where it grows in quantity on all types of soil, even heavy clay—this small tree is a major source of dry-season fodder for sheep and goats. Leaves, pods, and flowers are all important feedstuffs. The plant is also found in the Middle East. Its hard, dark wood (shittim wood) was used by ancient Egyptians for pharoahs' coffins. *Acacia seyal* also produces a low-grade gum.

Acacia senegal. Primarily known as the main source for gum arabic (see page 279). Grows on poor, sandy soils, in natural stands as well as in plantations. Leaves and pods provide valuable fodder. A suitable tree for agroforestry systems under arid conditions.

---

*Some of these acacias could prove to have promise equivalent to that of leucaena. Ideas for tests to conduct can be gleaned from a companion report: National Academy of Sciences. 1977. *Leucaena: Promising Forage and Tree Crop for the Tropics.* To order see page 329.

Acacia gerrardii **Benth.** ssp *negevensis* **Zoh.** A species discovered in Israel only in the 1960s.* Fairly cold tolerant and grows in Sinai and the Negev up to heights of about 800 m where other indigenous species such as *Acacia tortilis* (see page 136) cannot survive. Given research and testing this species could become important for afforestation and animal feeding at higher tropical altitudes than other *Acacia* species.†

Selected Readings

Skerman, P. J. 1977. *Tropical Forage Legumes.* FAO Plant Production and Protection Series No. 2. Food and Agriculture Organization of the United Nations, Rome. 609 pp.

Acacia albida

Anonymous. n.d. Acacia albida. *The Miracle Tree of the Sahel Zone.* Canadian International Development Agency, 122 Bank Street, Ottawa, Canada, K1A 0G4. 11 pp. (mimeo)

Catinot, R. 1974. Contribution du forestier à la lutte contre la désertification en zones sèches. *Revue Bois et Forêts des Tropiques* 155:3-13.

Dancette, C., and J. F. Poulain. 1969. Influence of *Acacia albida* on pedoclimatic factors and crop yields. *Sols Africains (Paris)* 14:43-84.

Felker, P. 1978. *State of the Art:* Acacia albida *as a Complementary Permanent Intercrop with Annual Crops.* University of California, Riverside, California. 133 pp. (A review of the *Acacia albida* literature together with site-by-site analysis of the plantings of this tree and interviews with African farmers who grow it. Available from P. Felker, see Research Contacts.)

Giffard, P. L. 1971. Recherches complementaires sur *Acacia albida* Del. *Revue Bois et Forêts des Tropiques* 135:3-20.

Kerr, G. R. C. 1940. *Gawo.* The ideal farm tree. *Nigerian Forester* 1:72-75.

Laurie, M. V. 1974. *Tree Planting Practices in African Savannas.* Food and Agriculture Organization of the United Nations, Rome. pp. 42-43.

Pelissier, P. 1966. *Les paysans du Sénégal.* Fabrege Saint Yrieix, Haute Vienne, France.

Touzeau, J. 1973. *Les Arbres Fourragers de la Zone Sahélienne.* Ecole Nationale Veterinaire, Toulouse, France.

Wachiira, K. K. 1975. *Kenya's Lowland Acacias: Strong Case for New Approaches to Forestry.* (mimeo) (Available from author, see address below.)

Weber, F. R. 1977. *Reforestation in Arid Lands.* Volunteers in Technical Assistance (VITA), 3706 Rhode Island Avenue, Mt. Rainier, Maryland 20822, USA. 248 pp.

Wickens, G. E. 1969. A study of *Acacia albida* Del. (Mimosoideae). *Kew Bulletin* 23:181-200.

Acacia aneura

A bibliography containing over 130 *Acacia aneura* references is available from N. P. McMeniman, see Research Contacts.

Anonymous. 1973. The mulga lands of Australia. *Tropical Grasslands* 7:1-170.

*See Zohary, M. 1972. *Flora Palaestina,* part two. Israel Academy of Sciences and Humanities, Jerusalem, Israel.
†Information supplied by M. Evenari.

Anson, R. J., and J. R. Childs. 1972. *Mulga Feeding in South-west Queensland.* Advisory Leaflet No. 724. Division of Animal Industry, Department of Primary Industries, Brisbane, Queensland, Australia.

Everist, S. L. 1969. *Use of Fodder Trees and Shrubs.* Advisory Leaflet No. 1024. Division of Plant Industry, Department of Primary Industries, Brisbane, Queensland, Australia. 44 pp.

Hall, N., R. W. Boden, C. S. Christian, R. W. Condon, F. A. Dale, A. J. Hart, J. H. Leigh, J. K. Marshall, A. G. McArthur, V. Russell, and J. W. Turnbull. 1972. *The Use of Trees and Shrubs in the Dry Country of Australia.* Forestry and Timber Bureau, Department of National Development, Canberra, Australia. 558 pp.

McMeniman, N. P. 1975. Machine for stripping leaves from fodder trees. *Acacia aneura. Queensland Journal of Agriculture and Animal Science* 32:91-94.

Weller, M. C. 1974. Mulga, *Acacia aneura* as drought feed for cattle. *Queensland Agriculture Journal* 100:530-538.

Research Contacts

Acacia albida

M. Baumer, 446 rue de la Combe caude, 34000 Montpellier, France

Centre National de Recherches Agronomiques de Bambey, B.P. 41, Bambey, Senegal (C. Dancette, M. Mbodj, and M. Pocthier)

Centre National de Recherches Forestières, B.P. 2312, Dakar-Hann, Senegal (O. Hamel)

Centre Technique Forestier Tropical, 45 BIS Avenue de la Belle Gabrielle, 94130 Nogent-sur-Marne, France (P. L. Gifford and R. Catinot)

Conservator of Forests, Ministry of Animal and Forest Resources, Private Mail Bag No. 3022, Kano, Nigeria

Department of Plant Science, University of California, Riverside, California 92521, USA (P. Felker and G. Chanell)

R. W. Fishwick, Western Africa–Projects Department, A203, The World Bank, 1818 H Street, N.W., Washington, D.C. 20433, USA

D. Gates, TA/AGR 414B SA-18, Agency for International Development, Department of State, Washington, D.C. 20523, USA

ICRISAT, B.P. 3340, Dakar, Senegal

Institut für Weltforstwirtschaft, Leuschnerstrasse 91, 2050 Hamburg 80, Germany (H. J. von Maydell)

P. K. Karani, Deputy Chief Forest Officer, Ministry of Agriculture and Forestry, Forest Department, P.O. Box 31, Entebbe, Uganda

H. F. Lamprey, UNEP-MAB Integrated Project in Arid Lands, UNESCO, Regional Officer for Science and Technology for Africa, P.O. Box 30552, Nairobi, Kenya

H. N. Le Houérou, Programme du Sahel, Centre International Pour l'Elevage en Afrique (ILCA), B.P. 60, Bamako, Mali

M. McGahuey, CARE/Chad, c/o Agency for International Development, American Embassy, N'djamena, Chad

Officer in Charge, National Herbarium and National Botanic Garden, P.O. Box 8100, Causeway, Salisbury, Zimbabwe-Rhodesia

A. W. Owadally, Conservator of Forests, Ministry of Agriculture, and Natural Resources, and the Environment, Forestry Service, Curepipe, Mauritius

G. Poulsen, Sr., Research Advisor (Forestry), IDRC-Regional Officer of East and Central Africa, P.O. Box 30677, Nairobi, Kenya

S. A. Radwanski, 4 rue Georges Bergere, Paris 17e, France

Service des Eaux, Forêts et Chasses, Ministère du Développement Rural et de l'Hydraulique, B.P. 1831, Dakar, Senegal (El Hadji Sène, Directeur)

K. K. Wachiira, Department of Geography, Kenyatta University College, P.O. Box 43844, Nairobi, Kenya

G. E. Wickens, The Herbarium, Royal Botanic Gardens, Kew, Richmond, Surrey TW9 3AE, England

Acacia aneura, Acacia pendula, and Acacia victoriae

D. M. W. Anderson, Department of Chemistry, University of Edinburgh, West Mains Road, Edinburgh EH93JJ, Scotland (gum chemistry)

Animal Industry and Agriculture Branch, Herbarium of the Northern Territory, Alice Springs, N.T. 5750, Australia (J. R. Maconochie)

Department of Primary Industries, Charleville Pastoral Laboratory, Charleville, Queensland 4470, Australia (N. P. McMeniman, I. Beale, and W. Burrows)

Desert Botanical Garden, P.O. Box 5415, Phoenix, Arizona 85010, USA (*A. aneura* and *A. victoriae*)

M. Forti, Ben-Gurion University of the Negev, P.O. Box 1025, Beer-Sheva, Israel

J. E. D. Fox, Department of Biology, Western Australian Institute of Technology, Hayman Road, South Bentley 6102, Western Australia, Australia

Queensland Department of Primary Industries, Brisbane, Queensland, Australia (J. P. Ebersohn and J. R. Childs)

Seed Section, Division of Forest Research, P.O. Box 4008, Canberra, A.C.T. 2600, Australia (J. C. Doran)

Prosopis Species

Forty-four species of *Prosopis* are recognized. At least three are aggressive weeds that cause great devastation to subtropical grasslands. However, there are six species that can produce useful forage and wood, where all other crops fail, on the poorest soils in low-rainfall areas, and these are highlighted in this chapter. Several other species are potentially valuable, though they are now used only in a very localized way.

The three major weedy species are *Prosopis glandulosa* Torrey* (a native of northern Mexico and southwestern United States), *Prosopis ruscifolia* Grisebach (native to the Gran Chaco region from eastern Bolivia and Paraguay

---

*In North America, the common name mesquite is used for several *Prosopis* species, whereas in South America the name algarrobo is used commonly. Algarrobo is actually the Old World name for carob (see page 109); the Conquistadores applied it to *Prosopis* species because of a carob-like appearance.

Prosopis taxonomy is very confusing. In most of the general literature *Prosopis glandulosa* is designated as *Prosopis juliflora*. This chapter follows findings of the recent in-depth study by A. Burkart (see Selected Readings).

Subfamily: Mimosoideae.

to north-central Argentina), and *Prosopis juliflora* (a native of Central America and the West Indies).* These species can spread rapidly due to their easy propagation and remarkable ability to withstand both the adverse conditions that reduce the competitiveness of neighboring plants and heavy grazing.

Other *Prosopis* species lack the exceptional aggressiveness of the weedy types but retain many of the desirable features. In general, their value lies in redeeming semiarid land that would otherwise remain economically worthless; *Prosopis* trees are very drought resistant and are well adapted to the heat and poor soils of dry regions. Various species of *Prosopis* were once the staff of life for Indians in the warm deserts of North America, providing food, fodder, fuel, wood, weapons, tools, shade, and shelter. In the Atacama and Gran Chaco Deserts of South America, they were also once of great value, providing timber and other products for which no other source was available. Consequently, the natural stands were logged out.

Plants of *Prosopis* are medium-size shrubs or spreading, short-trunked trees, though with water available they can develop into trees 20 m tall with trunks more than 1 m in diameter. Most have spines on the branches, but spineless forms of each of the important species are known to occur naturally. The leaves, like those of so many leguminous trees, are compounded of numerous small leaflets and have a feathery appearance. Flowers are small and are usually clustered in elongated spikes or spherical heads.

Although generally growing along water courses, *Prosopis* species often form dense spreading thickets. They can tolerate, and even grow rapidly in, barren wastelands if there is sufficient subterranean water. They usually need annual rainfall of 250 mm, but some specimens have been found well established where annual rainfall is an incredibly low 75 mm. They easily withstand protracted droughts and can be relied on to survive and even produce a crop of pods (though at reduced yields) during a drought year.

Usually found on poor land, *Prosopis* trees thrive in light sand or rocky soils. Some species are remarkably salt tolerant (see below). At least several of the species have nitrogen-fixing root nodules that support their growth in nitrogen-poor soils. In most semiarid locations, a *Prosopis* tree's growth is unaffected by pest or disease; however, weevil-like insects can invade the pods, sometimes consuming much of the seed crop.

Because the plants grow readily from seeds and regenerate by suckers or coppice shoots, the trees show remarkable survival. In addition to a considerable spreading network of lateral roots, taproots in search of groundwater often penetrate 10 m of soil, sometimes reaching depths over 20 m.†

*Cultivated in northeastern Brazil, Peru, the Sudan, several Sahelian countries, South Africa, and India, this plant is a highly esteemed tree for shade, timber, and forage. But in the Caribbean region it has become a despised aggressive weed.

†The deepest plant roots ever recorded were those of a *Prosopis velutina* specimen near Tucson, Arizona, recovered from an open-pit copper mine at a depth of 53 m.

Prosopis pods are very palatable to livestock. Merino sheep, South Africa. (F.J. van der Merwe)

Prosopis pods are among the earliest foods known to have been used by prehistoric man in the New World, and up to modern times they have been a source of carbohydrate and protein for many inhabitants of North American deserts.* Pods are produced hanging on small stalks in clusters of up to 12. Usually about 20 cm long, they are either flat or coiled into a spiral and contain several seeds embedded in a sweet, dry, yellow pulp. The amount of pulp (mesocarp) in a pod varies widely from tree to tree; in some, it constitutes half the pod's weight. The pulp is largely sucrose, and this sugar alone often comprises one-third the weight of the whole pod in some species. In others the amount of pulp is slight and seeds make up the bulk of the pod's weight. Livestock relish the pods; cattle, sheep, horses, mules, donkeys, goats, and wildlife all eat them avidly.

Produced in profusion†—sometimes twice a year—the pods fall to the ground when mature and are unusual among legume fruit in that they do not split open on drying, so that neither the pulp nor seeds are lost. The pods from *Prosopis* groves in Hawaii, Peru, Argentina, and Chile have sustained animals for a month or two each year without any other feed available. Alternatively, the pods can be gathered and stored for later use. With a feed value roughly comparable to that of barley or corn, the pods, with their sweet pulp and protein-rich seeds (34–39 percent protein, 7–8 percent oil), are nutritious and are of great benefit to livestock in dry seasons when little comparable feed is available.‡

*Today, flour products made from the pods remain popular, although only sporadically prepared by Indian peoples in Southern California and Arizona; Sonora, Mexico; and parts of South America.

†Yields have been estimated to be well over 2,000 kg per ha in 10-year-old Southern California plantations receiving 250–500 mm rainfall annually (Felker and Waines, 1977, see Selected Readings). Even higher figures have been reported from South Africa (Jurriaanse, 1973, see Selected Readings), Hawaii, Chile, and India.

‡In some species the seeds are digestible only after grinding.

Some *Prosopis* species also yield edible foliage, but this seldom becomes an important feed. However, forage grasses grow well in combination with the trees; indeed, the nitrogen and shade provided by the *Prosopis* is often evident in the color and vigor of grasses growing nearby.*

In addition to being attractive to livestock, *Prosopis* species are favorites of bees. Nectar gathered from the flowers yields a honey with superior flavor.

Prosopis wood is usually sinewy, irregular (unless plantation grown), and of little use as lumber. It varies in color from marbled yellow to the red of a smouldering fire. It takes a high polish, and with its striking grain it has been equated with walnut, rosewood (see page 231), or mahogany.† Because most available trees are small, crooked, and often hollow, only small wood pieces can be obtained. Nonetheless, they are in great demand because they can be made into beautiful parquet floors, furniture, and turnery items. Durable in contact with the ground, the wood is much sought for fenceposts and small pilings. Blocks of *Prosopis* wood were the first street paving used in San Antonio, Texas. Furthermore, until 30 years ago major avenues of Buenos Aires, Argentina, were "cobblestoned" with cubes of *Prosopis* wood set on sand and coated lightly with tar. The resulting road surface was smooth and noise absorbent and lasted 10–15 years.

The wood's greatest use is as fuel. In the past it was used to power steam locomotives and industrial boilers (notably in Argentina, as recently as World War II). Today it is still in demand in rural areas for cooking stoves and heating. It has high calorific value, produces little ash, and yields charcoal of gunpowder quality. The rootwood is very hard, has little sapwood, and in many localities is laboriously excavated for household or restaurant cooking. It is much sought after for barbecues because it burns with little smoke and imparts a delectable flavor to meat.

An unusual use of *Prosopis* wood is as a substrate for producing single-cell protein. Much experimental work has been done on this in Texas, and several microorganisms can be grown on the wood to produce potentially valuable animal feeds.‡

Species of *Prosopis* are prime candidates for erosion control, for stabilizing shifting desert or coastal sand dunes, for windbreaks, for shelter belts, and for reforesting dry wastelands. For example, in India erosion caused by careless farming is advancing the Rajputana (Thar) Desert eastwards towards New Delhi. To check the menace, a *Prosopis* belt 3 km wide and 650 km long is being established.§

The following six species of *Prosopis* show particular merit:

*Soil beneath *Prosopis* trees can be three times richer in nitrogen than soil more distant from the plant (Felker and Waines, 1977, see Selected Readings).
†Dobie, J.F. 1943. The conquering mesquite. *Natural History Magazine* 51:208-217.
‡For information contact D. W. Thayer, Department of Biological Sciences, Texas Tech University, Lubbock, Texas 79409, USA.
§Douglas, J.S. 1967. 3-D forestry. *World Crops* 19:20-24.

Prosopis affinis **Sprengel.** A flat-topped, spiny, subtropical tree, 2–8 m tall; irregularly branched; trunk short and up to 60 cm diameter. Native to and important in the savannas of Paraguay, eastern Argentina, western Uruguay, and the extreme southwest of Rio Grande do Sul (Brazil). Cut on an 8–10 year rotation, it yields valuable feed and fenceposts of great durability. Many ranches (*estancias*) ration its use. In open stands it enables vigorous grasses to grow up beneath it. It also shelters the livestock and provides them nutritious pods, especially during summer when little forage is available.

Prosopis alba **Grisebach.** A round-crowned tree 5–15 m tall, sometimes with a straight trunk as large as 1 m in diameter and as high as 10 m. A very important native tree in arid (250–500 mm annual rainfall) subtropical plains of Argentina, Uruguay, Paraguay, southern Bolivia, northern Chile, and Peru, where it is cultivated to some extent. In northeastern Argentina, it is called *el arbol*, the tree, because of its usefulness and abundance. Valuable for windbreaks and roadside planting, it is also valued as a fodder and timber tree, especially in afforesting dry and saline soils. The fruit is milled into flour from which cakes are made for human consumption. It furnishes timber of high value for construction, doors, and other uses.

Prosopis chilensis **(Molina) Stuntz emend. Burkart.** A round-topped, fast-growing tree native to arid regions of Peru, Bolivia, central Chile, and northwestern Argentina where it provides a staple cattle feed. Found at elevations

A thornless *Prosopis chilensis* growing in a commercial nursery in Riverside, California, USA. This variety is in much demand for landscape use in southwestern United States. (P. Felker)

Prosopis nigra, Gran Chaco Desert, Argentina. (O.T. Solbrig)

to 2,900 m, the tree is important for shade, timber, fuel, forage, and food. It is sometimes cultivated in plantations in Argentina and Chile. Specimens that lack thorns are known.

Prosopis nigra **(Grisebach) Hieronymus.** A round-topped tree 4-10 m tall. A valuable timber tree of the Gran Chaco Desert, native to southern Bolivia, Argentina, Paraguay, and western Uruguay. Much used for furniture, barrels, firewood, forage, food, shade, and ornament in this dry region. Nowhere is it regarded as a weed.

Prosopis pallida **(Humboldt and Bonpland ex Willdenow) H.B.K.** A tree 8-20 m tall (but shrubby on sterile soil), native to the drier parts of Peru, Colombia, and Ecuador, especially along the coast. Also found naturalized in Hawaii and Puerto Rico. In Hawaii, 10-20 percent of the trees are spineless. Very valuable in arid conditions for shelter, timber, fuel, and forage.

Prosopis tamarugo **F. Philippi.** A tree* reaching 18 m tall, native to Chile's northern desert plateau region, where it is the only tree that survives on arid

---

*This species is described in more detail in a companion report: National Academy of Sciences. 1975. *Underexploited Tropical Plants with Promising Economic Value.* To order see page 329.

Prosopis pallida, Piura, Peru. In the dry coastal region of Peru, *Prosopis* pods are commonly fed to cattle, donkeys and other livestock. They are also added to soups and are made into "algarrobina," a sweet syrup used to prepare cocktails and fruit drinks. (C. López-Ocaña)

salt flats. The region is called Pampa del Tamarugal after it. As it produces the only available forage, lumber, and firewood, natural stands have been devastated. In the 1960s, an afforestation program using this species began transforming tens of thousands of hectares of Chile's northern salt desert into dense forests planted especially for raising sheep and angora goats, which feed on the falling leaves and pods. Each tamarugo tree yields up to 160 kg of pods, leaves, and small twigs, which layer the soil beneath and provide year-round feed.

The region receives only 100–200 mm rainfall annually and sometimes gets no rain for years on end. During rains, the flats turn into salty marshes that later evaporate, leaving a crust of salt crystals. Yet thousands of seedlings, nursed in seedbeds, are annually planted out into this fearsome landscape. In 1970, near Iquique, at least 100,000 seedlings were being raised and each month 150 ha of desert were planted with this tree.

Prosopis tamarugo, Atacama Desert, Chile. (M. Sarquis)

Limitations

The aggressive invaders, *Prosopis glandulosa, Prosopis ruscifolia*, and *Prosopis juliflora* should never be introduced to new locations, for they can too easily become pests. *Prosopis glandulosa* (mesquite) is already considered a nuisance, competing with grass for water and reducing the livestock-carrying capacity of 30 million hectares of rangeland in the southwestern United States. In addition, great caution must be exercised with other species. They are plants for problem sites—arid and/or salty—where safer crops, for example, *Acacia tortilis* (page 136), will not succeed. *Prosopis* species are *not* recommended for good soils or moist locations.

Prosopis thorns can be hard enough and sharp enough to puncture a tire, and care should be taken to propagate only spineless lines of any species selected.

When pods of *Prosopis pallida* or *Prosopis glandulosa* are fed as the exclusive diet, cattle become malnourished and develop "jaw and tongue trouble," with loss of weight and difficulty in chewing. This does not seem to occur with *Prosopis tamarugo*.* Furthermore, in recent studies the *Prosopis* species (thought to be *Prosopis juliflora*) growing in South Africa has proved to provide a fairly well balanced, highly digestible diet for sheep even when the pods were fed exclusively.† Whether toxicity occurs with other species has not been reported, but livestock grazing *Prosopis* pods should always be managed so that other feeds balance the diet.

Protein constitutes 60 percent or more of the seed kernel's weight, a remarkable proportion.‡ But for animals to benefit from this, the seed (or

*See Pak *et al.* 1977.

†Kargaard and van der Merwe. 1976.

‡Felker, P., and R.S. Bandurski. 1977. Protein and amino acid composition of tree legume seeds. *Journal of the Science of Food and Agriculture* 28:791-797.

whole pod) must be crushed or ground; otherwise it passes the digestive tract unused. Grinding is made difficult by the sticky pulp surrounding the seeds. When livestock feed on the whole pods, the seeds that escape digestion spread the trees from pasture to pasture, which may not be desirable.

Although the plants establish well and grow rapidly, seed bearing does not begin for at least 2–3 years after planting.

Research Needs

In their natural habitat, *Prosopis* species occur in many genotypes. Variation occurs in stature (shrub or tree); spines; size, taste, and yield of pods; number of leaflets; and other features. It is important that researchers—especially those in Argentina, Paraguay, and Uruguay, where several useful species are native—collect germ plasm and begin initial improvement by selecting fast-growing, high-yielding types. In particular, it is important for forage work that the lines collected and propagated be spineless and have large seeds with little pulp surrounding them, to balance the proportions of protein and sugar.

It is known that hybrids between species occur naturally,* so that breeding for desirable traits appears promising.

Superior spineless strains of *P. affinis, P. alba, P. chilensis, P. nigra, P. pallida*, and *P. tamarugo* should be cultivated and tested at experiment stations in arid and semiarid countries. Selections can then be made for use in local afforestation programs.

Agronomic aspects of harvesting pods, spacing plants, minimizing insect predation, and other factors of cultivation need to be worked out.

Selected Readings

Burkart, A. 1976. *A Monograph of the Genus* Prosopis *(Mimosoideae)*. (Reprinted from *Journal of the Arnold Arboretum* 57:216-249, 450-525.) The Arnold Arboretum, Harvard University, Cambridge, Massachusetts. 113 pp.

Contreras, D. 1978. *Estado actual de conocimiento de tamarugo* (Prosopis tamarugo Phil.). Mimeographed report with many photographs. 28 pp. Copies available from M.A. Habit. See Research Contacts.

Elgueta, H. S., and S. S. Calderón. 1971. *Estudio del Tamarugo Como Productor de Alimento del Ganado Lanar en la Pampa del Tamarugal*. Informe Técnico No. 3. Instituto Forestal, Santiago, Chile.

Felker, P. J. 1976. Potential utilization of leguminous trees for minimal energy input agriculture. Ph.D. Thesis, Michigan State University, E. Lansing, Mich. Available from University Microfilms, Ann Arbor, Michigan 48106, USA. Order No. 77-18.478.

*See, for example, Hunziker *et al.* 1975.

Felker, P. J., and G. Waines. 1977. Potential use of mesquite as a low energy water and machinery requiring food source. In *Proceedings, Energy Farms Workshop, Sacramento, California, July 14, 1977*. Available from Publications Unit, Energy Resources Conservation and Development Commission, 1111 Howe Ave., Sacramento, California 95825, USA.

Figueirdo, A. A. 1975. Lebensmittelchemische relevante in haltstoffe der schoten der algarobeira. Ph.D. Thesis, Julius-Maximilians-Universität, Wurzburg, Germany.

Griffith, A. L. 1961. Acacia *and* Prosopis *in the Dry Forests of the Tropics*. Food and Agriculture Organization of the United Nations, Rome. 149 pp. (mimeo)

Hunziker, J. H., L. Poggio, C. A. Naranjo, R. A. Palacios, and A. B. Andrada. 1975. Cytogenetics of some species and natural hybrids in *Prosopis* (Leguminosae). *Canadian Journal of Genetics and Cytology* 17:253-262.

Jurriaanse, A. 1973. *Are They Fodder Trees?* Pamphlet 116. Department of Forestry, Private Bag X93, Pretoria, South Africa. 32 pp.

Kargaard, J., and F. J. van der Merwe. 1976. Digestibility studies with *Prosopis juliflora* (mesquite thorn) pods. *South African Animal Science* 6:35-39.

Latrille, L., X. Garcia, J. G. Robb, and M. Ronning. 1971. Digestibility, total digestible nutrient and nitrogen balance studies on tamarugo (*Prosopis tamarugo* Phil.) forage. *Journal of Animal Science* 33:667-670.

Pak, N., H. Araya, R. Villalon, M. A. Tagle. 1977. Analytical study of tamarugo (*Prosopis tamarugo*) an autochthonous Chilean feed. *Journal of the Science of Food and Agriculture* 28:59-62.

Schuster, J. L., ed. 1969. *Literature on the Mesquite* (Prosopis L.) *of North America, an Annotated Bibliography*. Special Report No. 26. International Center for Arid and Semi-Arid Studies, Texas Tech University, Lubbock, Texas. 84 pp.

Simpson, B. B., ed. 1977. *Mesquite—Its Biology in Two Desert Scrub Ecosystems*. US/IBP Synthesis Series. Dowden Hutchinson and Ross, Inc., Stroudsberg, Pennsylvania.

Smith, J. R. 1953 (reprinted 1977). *Tree Crops—A Permanent Agriculture*. Devin-Adair Publishing Company, Old Greenwich, Connecticut.

Weber, F. R. 1977. *Reforestation in Arid Lands*. Volunteers in Technical Assistance (VITA), 3706 Rhode Island Avenue, Mt. Rainier, Maryland 20822, USA. 248 pp.

Wiley, A. T. 1977. Mesquite—A possible source of energy. *Forest Products Journal* 27(7):48-51.

Research Contacts

General

Department of Animal Science, The University of Stellenbosch, Stellenbosch, Cape Province, South Africa (J. Kargaard and F. J. van der Merwe)

P. J. Felker, Department of Plant Sciences, University of California, Riverside, California 92521, USA

Forestry Research Institute, P.O. Box 658, Khartoum, Sudan

M. C. Johnston, University of Texas, Austin, Texas 78712, USA

B. B. Simpson, Division of Botanical Sciences, U.S. National Museum, Smithsonian Institution, Washington, D.C. 20560, USA

O. T. Solbrig, Gray Herbarium, Harvard University, Cambridge, Massachusetts, 02138, USA

C. W. Weber and G. Nabhan, Nutrition and Food Sciences, University of Arizona, Tucson, Arizona 85721, USA

Prosopis affinis, Prosopis alba, Prosopis nigra

Botanical Gardens, Faculty of Agronomy, Av. San Martin 4453, Buenos Aires, Argentina
A. L. Cabrera, Instituto de Botanica Darwinion, Labarden 200, San Isidro, 1640 Martinez, Argentina
Departamento de Ciencias Biológicas, Facultad de Ciencias Exactas y Naturales, Universidad de Buenos Aires, Buenos Aires, Suc. 28, Argentina (L. Bravo de Palacios, J. H. Hunziker, L. Poggio, C. A. Naranjo, and R. A. Palacios)
Laboratorio de Genética, Facultad de Agronomía, Universidad Nacional de Tucumán, Ayacucho 482, San Miguel de Tucumán, Argentina (A. B. Andrada)
Los Angeles State and County Arboretum, Arcadia, California 91006, USA (*P. alba* only)
H. R. Mangieri, Jefe Division Dasologia, Instituto Forestal Nacional, Secretaría de Estado de Recursos, Naturales y Ambiente Humano, Buenos Aires, Argentina
Instituto Argentinio de Investigaciones de las Zonas Aridas, Casilla de Correos 507, (5500) Mendoza, Argentina
M. Rolfo, Pablo de María 1057 Ap. 104, Montevideo, Uruguay
Servicio Nacional Forestal, Investigaciones Forestales, Departamento de Dasología, Pueyrredon 2446-3 P.B., Buenos Aires, Argentina

Prosopis chilensis

Agricultural Research and Training Project, El-Kod/Giar, P.O. Box 1188, Aden, South Yemen (National Coordinator on Forest Genetic Resources)
Arid Zone Forestry Research, Forestry Research Institute, P.O. Box 658, Khartoum, Sudan (H. A. R. Musnad)
Banco Nacional de Semillas Forestales, Servicio Forestal y de Caza, Ministerio de Agricultura, Natalio Sanchez 20-Jesús María, Lima, Peru
F. A. Roig, Guido Spano 164, 5519-San José, Mendoza, Argentina

Prosopis pallida

J. L. Brewbaker, Department of Horticulture, University of Hawaii, Honolulu, Hawaii 96822, USA
D. L. Plucknett, Deputy Director, Board for International Food and Agriculture Development, Agency for International Development, Washington, D.C. 20523, USA
Y. N. Tamimi, University of Hawaii, Agricultural Experiment Station, 461 W. Lanikaula Street, Hilo, Hawaii 96720, USA

Prosopis tamarugo

Corporación de Fomento de la Producción (CORFO), Departamento de Ganaderia, Santiago, Chile
Mario A. Habit, Oficial Regional de Producción y Protección Vegetal para América Latina, F.A.O., Casilla 10095, Santiago, Chile
H. M. Hull, Renewable Natural Resources, 325 BioSciences East, University of Arizona, Tucson, Arizona 85721, USA
Carlos Lopez, Universidad Nacional Agraria, Apartado 456, La Molina, Lima, Peru
Harold A. Mooney, Department of Biological Sciences, Stanford University, Stanford, California 94305, USA
M. Ronning, Department of Animal Science, University of California, Davis, California 95616, USA
Mario Sarquis (ex-Generente de Desarrollo CORFO), Isabel La Catolica 4827 (Las Condes), Santiago, Chile
Fusa Sudzuki, Escuela de Agronomía, Departamento Botánica, Campus Antumapu, Santiago, Chile

V Fast-Growing Trees

Acacia auriculiformis

Native to the savannas of Papua New Guinea, to islands of the Torres Strait, and to northern areas of Australia, *Acacia auriculiformis** is a resilient, vigorously growing small tree. It deserves much increased testing throughout tropical areas, especially those with dry seasons as long as 6 months. The tree's outstanding quality is its ability to grow on poor soils where few other trees can survive. Its greatest potential seems to be as a source of paper pulp, but it is also promising for fuel, roundwood, checking soil erosion, and reclaiming wastelands now lost to useless weedy grasses.

In its native habitat, *Acacia auriculiformis* is a colonizing species. It provides the initial ground cover and shading for the establishment of rainforest species, but is then itself unable to regenerate in the shade beneath the closed rainforest canopy. An evergreen with dense foliage and an open, spreading crown, *Acacia auriculiformis* can reach a height of 30 m, with a trunk up to 60 cm in diameter. It is a very adaptable plant, and with practically no maintenance it will grow in a wide range of deep or shallow soils, including sand dunes, mica schist, compacted clay, limestone, podsols, laterite, and lateritic soils. These problem soils are often poor in nutrients, but the plant produces profuse bundles of root nodules and can often survive on land very low in nitrogen and organic matter where most eucalyptus and other species fail.

At Rum Jungle in northern Australia, the tree grows on alkaline (pH 9.0) sand dunes as well as on acid (pH 3.0) spoil from uranium mining. It is the

---

**Acacia auriculiformis* A. Cunn. ex Benth. (Formerly spelled *A. auriculaeformis.*) Subfamily: Mimosoideae.

Avenue of *Acacia auriculiformis*, Petaling Jaya, Malaysia. (M. Ratnasabapathy)

only native woody plant adaptable enough to colonize these uranium spoil heaps, and even on 20-year-old heaps it is the only tree to be found. In Malaysia, *Acacia auriculiformis* has grown well on the spoil heaps left after tin mining. In Indonesia, it has been successfully planted on steep, unstable slopes for erosion control, and it is recommended for planting on the poorest soils in national forests. It is also planted along roadsides and—on large scale—in privately owned fuelwood plantations.

Because of its ability to grow on difficult sites, the species is now being tested in Papua New Guinea, the Solomon Islands, Indonesia, Malaysia, India, Nigeria, and Tanzania. For example, in a recent 10-year trial in northern Papua New Guinea, 19 tree species were planted on a degraded grassland with low soil fertility and poor drainage. The region had been abandoned for agricultural use, but *Acacia auriculiformis* and *Eucalyptus tereticornis* have grown so outstandingly that this extremely difficult site has become a productive forest. "The plantations are now a distinctive feature in an otherwise nearly treeless landscape. Not only have they shown that this unwanted agricultural land is capable of producing rapid tree growth, but they have been an important boost to extension plantings in the district."[*]

Acacia auriculiformis is equipped to grow on dry, exposed sites. It thrives in hot climates with mean annual temperatures from 26° to over 30°C. It has

*Lamb. 1975.

Five-year-old *Acacia auriculiformis*, Papua New Guinea. This vigorous stand is located on former farm land abandoned due to infertility. Of 19 tree species tested, *Acacia auriculiformis* was one of two that could survive. Now this barren area is thickly forested and productive once more. (For more information see text.) (K.J. White)

a thick, leathery "leaf" (actually a flattened and expanded leaf stalk) that withstands heat and desiccation.

Although well adapted to drought, *Acacia auriculiformis* is also suited to climates with annual rainfall up to 1,800 mm. Although native to low altitudes in Indonesia, it is recommended for planting in areas too high for leucaena* to grow satisfactorily.

Under optimal conditions its growth rate is unknown, but in the Papua New Guinea trials mentioned before, trees established on small mounds (to improve drainage around the seedlings) grew 6 m tall in 2 years (diameter 5 cm) and up to 17 m in 8 years. In Malaysia, transplanted seedlings on clay soils have reached a height of 9–12 m after 3 years; on nutrient-poor, sandy soils they grew to 6 m in 3 years. In Zanzibar, on a shallow coral soil, the trees topped 9 m (13 cm diameter) in 8 years; in deep sand they reached 11 m (30 cm diameter) in 6 years.† In Indonesia, the species has shown a

*See National Academy of Sciences. 1977. *Leucaena: Promising Forage and Tree Crop for the Tropics.* To order see page 329.

†Streets, J.R. 1962. *Exotic Trees in the British Commonwealth.* Clarendon Press, Oxford. p. 137.

moderate growth rate with a production of 17–20 m^3 per ha per year at rotations of 10–12 years. However, on very poor, eroded lateritic soils where many other trees will not grow, volume increments of about 10 m^3 per ha per year have still been obtained.*

Acacia auriculiformis seedlings grow so vigorously that they can, if properly tended during their first years, outgrow and smother dense *Imperata* grass. This is an important finding because millions of hectares of tropical hill land are lying useless, lost to this pernicious grass weed.

Poor soils are enriched by the ability of *Acacia auriculiformis* to fix nitrogen and by its prolific leaf-litter—unpalatable to livestock—that is rich in plant nitrogen and builds both fertility and tilth.

As its trunk is generally crooked, the tree is not good for sawed timber.† However, the wood is well suited for fuelwood: it has a specific gravity of 0.6–0.75 and a calorific value of 4,800–4,900 Cal per kg. It is already established in fuelwood plantations in Indonesia. The wood also yields excellent charcoal.

However, the principal promise of *Acacia auriculiformis* is as a source of wood pulp. Recent tests conducted in Australia have shown that 10-year-old trees grown in a Papua New Guinea plantation can be pulped easily by the sulfate process and that a high yield of pulp is obtained. Both the sulfate and NSSC (neutral sulfite semi-chemical) process produced "pulp with high strength properties that can be used to manufacture a wide range of paper and paper-board products. Of the many Papua New Guinea plantation species tested for pulpwood to date *Acacia auriculiformis* is the most promising."‡

The plant can withstand root competition from nearby trees and adapts well to plantation cultivation. It is easily grown, flowers profusely and at an early age, and continues fruiting almost continually so that its natural seedlings are always plentiful. The species is shade intolerant, so it can only be regenerated in the open. Plantings can be established by direct seeding or by seedlings transplanted from a nursery. The seedlings are hardy; plantations require no extensive site preparation other than clearing vegetation. However, during the early years weeds must be controlled.

---

*At Pursowari, Java, on soils only 25–50 cm deep and suffering over 3 cm erosion per year, *Acacia auriculiformis* production is still 9.5 m^3 per ha per year. No other vegetation grows on these heavily eroding slopes. (Information supplied by K.F. Wiersum. See Research Contacts.)

†In Papua New Guinea straight-stemmed specimens have recently been discovered and staked out for seed collection. (Information supplied by J.R. Luton. See Research Contacts.) For a related species that grows with a straight trunk, see *Acacia mangium*, page 194.

‡Using only 13 percent total alkali, delignification to kappa numbers below 20 was achieved with 55 percent yield of screened sulfate pulp. The pulp had high bonding strength with breaking length and tearing resistance satisfactory for papermaking. NSSC pulps also had strength levels similar to those expected of good quality sulfate pulp. (Information supplied by A.F. Logan and F.H. Phillips. See Research Contacts.)

The trees can be grown in coppice rotations, and natural regeneration of cut-over stands by seedlings is also facile.

With its dense foliage—which remains through the hot season—*Acacia auriculiformis* makes a useful shade tree and soil cover crop. It is an attractive ornamental that withstands city heat better than most broad-leaved trees and requires little attention. In Malaysia, it is being planted as an avenue tree along many roads. It is popular also for shading factory grounds, school compounds, playgrounds, and parks.* In the Darwin area of Australia, it is being used more and more as a quick-growing shade tree for parks and roadsides.

Limitations

Acacia auriculiformis has poor form for a lumber species. It can grow very large lateral branches that often begin low on the trunk. It is, however, easily pruned. Branches break easily in strong winds.

It is said to be less fire resistant than eucalyptus.

Although it is drought tolerant, *Acacia auriculiformis* cannot withstand as severe drought as can some hybrid eucalyptus, probably because its roots are closer to the soil surface.

Research Needs

Acacia auriculiformis has much wider potential in forestry than has been hitherto recognized. This tree's qualities—especially its capacity to enrich poor soils and to produce good fuelwood even in areas with an extended dry season—make it a very worthwhile species for large-scale exploitation as a fuelwood species. It has proven its ability to grow with practically no maintenance on many types of soil—from tin-mine tailings to compacted clay. But extensive experience with it is limited to Indonesia, Malaysia, and Papua New Guinea. Trial plantings on difficult sites in other lowland tropical regions are warranted. Trial sites could include barren soils, newly cleared building sites or excavations where top soil has been removed, spoil dumps, eroding slopes, laterite, sand, clay, and other soils whose texture and properties make silviculture and agriculture difficult.

When the tree's bark is wounded a polysaccharide gum exudes. Although now unknown to commerce it has unusually high viscosity and molecular weight as well as clear color, solubility in water, high acidity, and a protein content of about 7 percent. These are remarkable properties for a

*Ratnasabapathy. 1974.

gum; with further investigation it may prove to have considerable economic value.*

More information is needed on the quality of the pulp and paper from *Acacia auriculiformis* grown in different areas and from different provenances. Searches should be made throughout northern Australia, Papua New Guinea, West Irian, and islands of the Torres Strait for straight-stemmed genotypes suited to the production of timber and other wood products.†

In Papua New Guinea's Western Province, *Acacia crassicarpa* and *Acacia aulacocarpa* occur together with *Acacia auriculiformis*. Neither has been studied, although each provides an attractive timber for furniture and cabinet-making.‡ Exploratory planting and pulping trials are recommended.

Selected Readings

Banerjee, A. K. 1973. Plantations of *Acacia auriculaeformis* (Benth.) A. Cunn in West Bengal. *Indian Forester* 99:533-540.

Lamb, D. 1975. *Kunjingini Plantations 1965-1975*. Tropical Forestry Research Note Sr. 24. Department of Forests, P.O. Box 5055, Boroko, Papua New Guinea. 17 pp.

Logan, A. F., and F. H. Phillips. 1977. *Hardwood Species for Reforestation in Tropical Areas*. Paper presented at the 18th Forest Products Research Conference, Melbourne, May 1977. (For authors' address, see below.)

Nicholson, D. I. 1965. A note on *Acacia auriculiformis* A. Cunn ex Benth in Sabah. *Malayan Forester* 28(3):243-244.

Phillips, F. H., and A. F. Logan. 1976. Papua New Guinea hardwoods: future source of papermaking. *Appita* 30(1):29-40.

Ratnasabapathy, M. 1974. *Acacia auriculaeformis* and *Casuarina equisetifolia*–the urban invaders. *Malayan Nature Journal* 28:18-21.

Sastroamidjojo, J. S. 1964. *Acacia auriculiformis* A. Cunn. *Rimba Indonesia* 9(3): 214-225.

Research Contacts

D. M. W. Anderson, Department of Chemistry, University of Edinburgh, West Mains Road, Edinburgh EH93JJ, Scotland (gum chemistry)

Assistant Conservator of Forests (Silviculture and Research), Forest Department, P.O. Box 1017, Kingston, Georgetown, Guyana

A. K. Banerjee, Development Manager, The Titaghur Paper Mills Co., Ltd., Raw Material and Coal Section, Chartered Bank Buildings, Calcutta 700001, India

Department of Botany, University of Malaya, Kuala Lumpur, Malaysia (M. Ratnasabapathy and B. C. Stone)

Division of Chemical Technology, Commonwealth Scientific and Industrial Research Organisation, P. O. Box 310, South Melbourne, Victoria 3205, Australia (A. F. Logan and F. H. Phillips)

*Information supplied by D.M.W. Anderson. See Research Contacts.

†As this report went to press we received information from J.R. Luton on one successful search, footnoted on page 168.

‡Information supplied by J.F.U. Zieck. See Research Contacts.

Division of Forest Research, Commonwealth Scientific and Industrial Research Organisation, Northern Territory Regional Station, P.O. Box 39899, Winnellie, Darwin, N.T. 5789, Australia (D. Cameron)

J. C. Doran, Seeds Section, Division of Forest Research, Commonwealth Scientific and Industrial Research Organisation, P.O. Box 4008, Canberra, A.C.T. 2600, Australia

C. R. Dunlop, Animal Industry and Agriculture Branch, Department of Northern Territory, P.O. Box 5150, Darwin, N.T. 5794, Australia

Forest Products Research Centre, P.O. Box 1358, Boroko, Port Moresby, Papua New Guinea (D. J. Eddowes and J. F. U. Zieck)

Forest Research Institute, Jalan Gunung Batu, P.O. Box 66, Bogor, Indonesia

Forest Research Institute, Kepong, Selangor, Malaysia (F. S. P. Ng and T. B. Peh)

Ibu Pejabat Jabatan Hutan (Forest Department Headquarters), Kuching, Sarawak, Malaysia (Hua Seng Lee and C. Phang)

Ministry of Agriculture and Forestry, Forest Department, P.O. Box 31, Entebbe, Uganda (P. K. Karani, Deputy Chief Forest Officer)

Office of Forests, P.O. Box 5055, Boroko, Port Moresby, Papua New Guinea (J. R. Luton)

Research Branch, Forest Department, P.O. Box 1407, Sandakan, Sabah, Malaysia (Tham C. K.)

M. B. Shado, Savanna Forestry Research Station, Forestry Research Institute, P.M.B. 1039, Samaru, Zaria, Nigeria

I. Soerianegara, BIOTROP-SEAMEO, Kebun Raya, Bogor, Indonesia

B. R. Thomson, Forest Research Officer, Forestry Division, Munda, New Georgia, Solomon Islands

K. F. Wiersum, Department of Tropical Sylviculture, Agricultural University, Wageningen, The Netherlands

Albizia Species

In Africa, Asia, and tropical America are found about 100 species of *Albizia*.* At least a dozen are big, compound-leaved trees that are adapted to a wide variety of soils and environments. They appear well suited to cultivation, show very rapid early growth, and seem likely to be efficient nitrogen fixers. Yet of these only two—*Albizia falcataria* and *Albizia lebbek*—have been planted extensively; the others remain very restricted in their distribution and largely untested. This chapter highlights the promise for afforestation projects

*Often misspelled *Albizzia*. Subfamily: Mimosoideae.

of members of the genus *Albizia*, so little exploited compared with *Acacia*, from which they are distinguished by taxonomists only by minute differences in flower structure.

It is generally characteristic of *Albizia* trees that, as pioneers of forest regrowth, they produce seed abundantly, establish readily in the open, and are very robust, thriving in diverse climates and altitudes. They are also easy to propagate and handle in plantation production. The roots of *Albizia falcataria* bear abundant nodules and it seems likely that the other species do too. The resulting nitrogen-fixing capacity, together with the plants' prodigious growth, make them good soil-improvement, cover, and green-manure crops. They have particular promise for reforesting sub-marginal sites, like idle and denuded hill lands. The natural drop of leaves, pods, and small branches contributes nitrogen, organic matter, and minerals to the upper soil layers. The plants' extensive surface-root systems further improve soil conditions by breaking up heavy soils and providing channels for drainage and aeration. Because of their soil-improving traits and the light shade that their airy foliage provides, *Albizia* species have been extensively planted in Southeast Asia as shade and nurse crops for coffee, cocoa, tea, patchouli, and young timber plantations, as well as for supports for pepper vines.

Most *Albizia* species are attractive evergreens with sprays of graceful foliage, small cream-white flowers, and may have long pods that rattle in the breeze. Young trees are flat-topped or funnel-shaped, but in mature specimens the branch tips droop and the trees become massive, grayish-white trunks topped by a gigantic umbrella of foliage.

Although the trees grow taller and straighter when crowded, the low crown is an adverse characteristic for a plantation species grown for timber. The trunks are thornless and usually unbuttressed. The open, spreading canopy ideally suits *Albizia* species to agroforestry: In Java, *Albizia falcataria* is already used extensively on small farms. Beneath the trees both annual and perennial crops—such as hot peppers, upland rice, pineapple, grass, banana, bamboo, coffee, or fruit trees—can grow normally, providing a productive, three-tier combination. The species also makes fine shade and avenue trees.

Different species are known to produce well in a wide range of soil types from heavy clay to volcanic ash. They grow best in fertile soil, but generally have the ability to grow rapidly on infertile sites that are not waterlogged. They tolerate acid soils (down to pH 4.5). *Albizia falcataria*, for example, has been successfully established even on the tailings left after tin mining. Furthermore, *Albizia falcataria* can be established in land lost to the tenacious weed *Imperata cylindrica*; if carefully managed, it overtops and kills this grass by cutting off its light.*

*Because of its aggressiveness, *Albizia falcataria* can be a noxious plant. It has the ability to seed in prolifically beneath competing species and then overtake and shade them out. This has occurred in at least two high-rainfall, low-elevation areas in Hawaii.

Albizia trees, like many *Acacia* species, exude a water-soluble gum if the trunk is damaged, and their barks also contain tanning compounds. At various times, *Albizia* gums and barks have found commercial use. In some species the foliage is relished by livestock. These uses deserve greater attention from researchers.

The various species produce wood with different characteristics. For example, *Albizia falcataria* wood is light, and soft; wood from *Albizia lebbek* is hard, strong, and resembles walnut. The woods are nonsiliceous, usually light colored with some open pores, and produce a sawdust that may cause sneezing.

Eleven *Albizia* species that deserve far greater recognition and more widespread testing are described below.

ASIAN SPECIES

Albizia falcataria

One of the fastest-growing trees in the world, this species* is native to eastern islands of the Indonesian archipelago (notably the Moluccas) and to New Guinea (particularly West Irian). However, in the 1870s it was spread throughout Southeast Asia from Burma to the Philippines.

The growth of *Albizia falcataria* is so rapid that the plant has been termed a miracle tree. Measurements from plantations in the Hawaiian Islands (on Kauai and Hawaii), in Malaysia, in Indonesia (on Java and Kalimantan), and in numerous Philippine locations confirm that on sites with good soil and adequate rainfall trees may reach 7 m in height in little more than a year, 13-18 m in 3 years, 21 m in 4 years, and 30 m in 9-10 years.† After this, upward growth slows down and the final height tapers off at about 45 m. In plots in the Philippines and in Indonesia stem diameters (at breast height) of the most vigorous young trees increased at about 5-7 cm per year.‡

Plantations of *Albizia falcataria* are extremely productive. On good sites the trees can be closely spaced (1,000-2,000 trees per ha), which causes the trunks to grow straight and the crown of foliage to close quickly and shade out weeds.§ In spacing and fertilizer trials, young plantations have annually

---

Albizia falcataria (L.) Fosberg. Formerly known as *Albizzia falcata* (L.) Backer and *Albizzia moluccana* Miq., also called Molucca albizzia, Moluccan sau, jeungjing, or sengon (Indonesia), batai (Malaysia), mara (Sri Lanka) and falcata.

†Walters, 1971; Chinte, 1971; Sprinz, 1977; Suharlan *et al.*, 1975.

‡Chinte, 1971, and Sprinz, 1977.

§Crown closure at the end of the first year is not uncommon.

Albizia falcataria, 9 years old, Ivory Coast. (Centre Technique Forestier Tropical)

produced in excess of 50 m^3 of wood per ha. But a mean annual increment of
25–40 m^3 per ha in an 8- to 12-year rotation is a more likely expectation.
The trees coppice vigorously so that (at least for some products) replanting is
not necessary after the first harvest.

Albizia falcataria grows so fast that it can be regarded as a cash crop; in a
World Bank-sponsored project in the Philippines, it is now being grown for
pulpwood by thousands of small holders. It is harvested after 7 or 8 years,
with subsequent harvest on an 8-year cycle from coppice growth.

The wood is soft and light colored with a specific gravity of 0.30–0.35. It is
a light- to medium-weight hardwood. In Hawaii during the early 1970s, about

Albizia falcataria. Lindbergh tree, Surigao, eastern Mindanao, Philippines, 17 years old, 96 cm diameter. Note person (circled) for scale. (I.L. Domingo)

1 million board feet of *Albizia falcataria* logs were rotary peeled and processed for core stock. The wood can also be used for making matches, match boxes, packing cases, tea chests, lightweight pallets, and shelves, and for other general uses.

However, the greatest promise for *Albizia falcataria* appears to be as a source of pulpwood. For certain grades of paper it can favorably substitute for pinewood. The fiber has an average length of 1.15 mm, with thin walls that give it flexibility and good fiber-fiber bonding in paper. The soft, low-density wood is easy to chip and the pulp is obtained in good yield with fairly

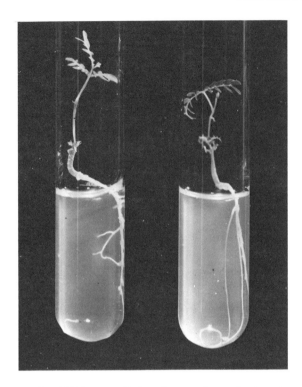

Test tube *Albizia* trees. Only a few woody species have been successfully cloned so far by the new technique of tissue culture. Shown here are plantlets recently produced from *Albizia falcataria* seed tissue at the Forest Research Institute, College, Philippines (see Research Contacts). Tissue culture is a promising technique for mass producing large numbers of superior trees, and it may prove widely applicable to *Albizia* species and related leguminous trees. (E. N. Crizaldo)

low use of chemicals. Because of its light color, only minimum bleaching is required to achieve a really good white paper. The strength properties of kraft and soda pulps are comparable to good quality eucalypt pulps.* The neutral sulfite semi-chemical process also produces pulps with excellent strength properties.

Although its geographic limits are unknown, *Albizia falcataria* seems to grow well only in the wet tropics where rainfall is 2,000–2,700 mm per year with at least 15 rain days during the driest 4 months.

Although the tree will survive on infertile sites, the exceptional growth rates mentioned above will not be achieved and fertilization may be needed.

Plantations of *Albizia falcataria* are prone to wind damage. The trees' rapid growth creates inherently weak limbs, and—with their shallow, often-exposed

*Food and Agriculture Organization of the United Nations. 1975. See Selected Readings.

roots—the trees can be completely blown over or their crowns broken if exposed to hurricane-force winds.

In cultivation, the bark and foliage can be attacked by several insects that cause defoliation and slow the tree's growth. Frequent attacks by caterpillars, monkeys, and deer have been experienced in Indonesian plantations located adjacent to rainforests; the tree recovers well from defoliations but will sprout multiple branches if the leader stem is broken.

Albizia lebbek

A quick-growing tree native to tropical Asia, Africa, and northern Australia, *Albizia lebbek** is planted as a shade tree and is already naturalized in most parts of the tropics. Its value for afforestation is not widely known; only in India is it cultivated in plantations.

When grown in the open, *Albizia lebbek* looks remarkably like the raintree (*Samanea saman*, see page 202), with a giant spreading crown. However, in the closed forest or in crowded plantations it produces a tall, straight bole. It can reach 30 m in height and a diameter of 2–3 m.

Not exacting in soil requirements, the tree can grow fairly well in laterite, sandy ground near the sea;† and in other problem soils. Much of its native habitats (northern India, for example) is characterized by extremes of climate—long, hot, dry summers and cold winters, with mean temperatures ranging from 5° to 46°C. It is found at altitudes up to 1,500 m in both dry and moist forests, with annual rainfall as divergent as 600–2,500 mm.

In addition to hardiness *Albizia lebbek* offers quick growth. In trials in Nigeria annual growth has averaged almost 1 m on deep drift sands and 1.5 m on heavy loams.‡ In India plantation trees have reached mean heights of 18 m and diameters of 66 cm in 10 years. There the trees are extensively planted along canals and roadsides, in wastelands, courtyards, and village common lands, and as a cover crop in tea and coffee plantations.

The species can be raised easily from seedlings or stump planting; even direct sowing is very successful. It coppices readily. The red-brown gum from its trunk has been used as a gum arabic substitute. Its foliage (protein content 30 percent) is lopped for fodder and also makes good green manure.

Albizia lebbek is a very promising species for fuel forests.§ The wood burns well (with a heartwood calorific value of 5,166 cal), and the trees

---

Albizia lebbek (L.) Benth. Commonly known as siris tree, kokko, East Indian walnut, lebbek, woman's tongue tree, and frywood (tropical America and West Indies).

†For example, it has survived in soils with up to 0.11 percent salt and pH 8.7.

‡Information supplied by R. W. Fishwick. See Research Contacts.

§See forthcoming companion report: *Firewood Crops: Shrub and Tree Species for Energy Production*. To order see page 329.

coppice easily. The hard, dense (specific gravity 0.55–0.90), close-grained heartwood is similar to walnut in color, with attractive black and gray streaks. It is strong and elastic and makes handsome furniture, cabinet work, and paneling. The burr wood is particularly prized for veneer.

Albizia acle

Considered one of the best cabinet woods of the Philippines, *Albizia acle** is a tree up to 1.25 m in diameter (though often short and crooked). Its hard, very durable, warm-brown wood has beautiful grain and is used for interior finish, paneling, and high-grade furniture, serving as a substitute for black walnut.

Albizia chinensis

A moderately fast-growing species of Southeast Asia, *Albizia chinensis*† is similar in appearance and properties to *Albizia falcataria*. It does not grow as tall or as fast but better resists wind damage and boring insects, is better suited to poorer sites, and provides higher-quality wood. It deserves testing in locations where *Albizia falcataria* proves unsatisfactory.

Native to mixed deciduous forests up to 1,300 m elevation as well as tropical rainforests (1,000–5,000 mm annual rainfall), *Albizia chinensis* has been recommended in Java for the reforestation of wastelands at medium altitudes. On good sites yields of 10–12 m³ per ha per year have been measured. The species is easily propagated using seedlings or stumps.

The wood is soft (specific gravity 0.30–0.45), and is light in color and weight. A little better than *Albizia falcataria* wood, it is useful for such general purposes as light furniture and planking and may be suitable for pulp and paper.

Albizia minahassae

A native of eastern Indonesia, Papua New Guinea, and Melanesia (from the Celebes to the Solomon Islands), this tree,‡ now almost unknown to foresters, is very similar in appearance to *Albizia falcataria*. *Albizia minahassae* also warrants exploratory silvicultural investigations.

Albizia acle (Blanco) Merr. Known as akle.
†*Albizia chinensis* (Osb.) Merr. (synonymous with *A. marginata* and *A. stipulata*).
‡*Albizia minahassae* Korrd. Formerly known as *Serianthes minahassae* (Koord.) Merr. et Perry.

Albizia pedicellata

Considered by some authors to be the most promising timber tree in the genus, *Albizia pedicellata** is native to small areas in western Malaysia and northern Borneo. Unlike other *Albizia* species, it grows tall and straight, with a monopodial crown. It can reach a diameter of about 2.5 m. The heartwood is hard and dark colored.

Despite its promise, this species is untried in cultivation and almost nothing is known of its silvicultural qualities. It deserves much greater attention. Research to deliberately crossbreed this species with other species of *Albizia* may produce monopodial hybrids with monopodial growth and exceptional properties.

Albizia procera

A moderately fast-growing tree widely distributed in South and Southeast Asia as well as New Guinea, *Albizia procera*† is a medium-size tree reaching an average height of about 25 m and an average diameter of 35 cm. Commonly found in low-elevation, open secondary forest up to 1,200 m in regions with a pronounced dry season, it is able to grow on stony, dry, and shallow soils and appears a useful species for testing on difficult sites.

On good sites it produces a clear but often curved bole 10–15 m long. Vigorous trees have reached 0.9–1.2 m in diameter in 12 years and up to 2 m in diameter in 30 years. On Java, annual wood production of about 10 m³ per ha has been recorded. Growth rings of 1.3 cm have been measured.

Brown with light and dark bands, *Albizia procera* wood (specific gravity 0.6–0.9) is durable and strong. It is a good cabinet and furniture wood and is often used as a substitute for walnut.

The trees are easily propagated using seedlings or stumps.

AFRICAN SPECIES

Many species of *Albizia* are native to Africa. Wood from several of them is marketed together in the timber trade under the names albizia, okuro (Ghana), ayinre, or uwowe (Nigeria), and nongo (Uganda). The species producing this timber occur in mixed stands and are difficult to tell apart. Four of them are mentioned below.

*Albizia pedicellata Baker ex Benth.
†*Albizia procera* (Roxb.) Benth. White siris tree, safed siris.

Albizia adianthifolia

A tree of the coastal, lowland, and savanna forests of West Africa, *Albizia adianthifolia** is fast to colonize any clearing and grows rapidly in its early years. Growth of 1-1.5 m annually is usual in Ghana.† The tree can reach 36 m tall with a bole 9-18 m long. Its heartwood is golden-yellow or light brown. In Nigeria the root, bark, and young shoots are widely used in traditional medicines. When damaged, the bark exudes a clear, insoluble gum.

Albizia adianthifolia, Kruger National Park, South Africa. (P. van Wyk)

Albizia ferruginea

Perhaps the largest tree in the genus, *Albizia ferruginea*‡ is a forest giant growing to 46 m in height. It is found in West Africa from Senegal to the Cameroons and in Central Africa from Uganda to Angola. It, too, is a promising afforestation species. Like most *Albizia* species the tree coppices freely. Its timber is hard, heavy, and decay-resistant, with a deep, warm, reddish-brown color. It is a general purpose hardwood.

**Albizia adianthifolia* (Schum.) W. F. Wight. Known as West African albizia.
†Taylor. 1960.
‡*Albizia ferruginea* (Guill. & Perr.) Benth.

Albizia gummifera

Widespread in East and Central Africa as well as in Madagascar, *Albizia gummifera** is found from lowland rainforests up to altitudes of 2,500 m. It seems a suitable species for afforestation projects. Its straight bole yields a golden-yellow to chocolate-brown timber that is used in Europe as a substitute for oak. It has good elastic and tensile properties and glues and lacquers well.

This species closely resembles *Albizia adianthifolia*, but has small differences in the leaflets and grows at higher elevations.

Albizia zygia

A medium-size tree (not often larger than 30 m tall and 2.4 m in diameter), *Albizia zygia*† is found scattered in secondary and high forests throughout much of tropical Africa. It is found growing from equable coastal regions to savanna woodlands with considerable dry seasons. The tree germinates and grows rapidly: 2-year-old plants can be 3 m tall.

The heartwood is pale brown and hard and makes a general-purpose timber, with uses ranging from interior joinery to structural work. Moderately fine-grained, it polishes well and has good natural durability and strength. It is a popular wood for charcoal, used extensively, for example, in Ghana, notably about Kumasi, and in Tanzania. In southern Nigeria young *Albizia zygia* leaves are eaten as cooked vegetables, especially in soups.

Selected Readings

Albizia falcataria

Anonymous. 1971. *How to Raise* Albizia falcataria. Forestry Popular Bulletin No. 7. College of Forestry, University of the Philippines, College, Laguna, Philippines. 12 pp.

Burgess, P. F. 1966. *Timbers of Sabah*. Forest Department, Sabah, Malaysia. pp. 343-347.

Chinte, F. O. 1971. Fast-growing pulpwood trees in plantations. *Philippine Forests* 5:21-26, 29.

Food and Agriculture Organization of the United Nations. 1975. *Pulping and Paper-Making Properties of Fast-Growing Plantation Wood Species*. Food and Agriculture Organization of the United Nations, Rome. pp. 33-37. (Order No. FO:MISC/75/31)

Albizia gummifera (J. F. Gmel.) C. A. Sm.
†*Albizia zygia* (DC.) Macbride.

Gerhards, C. C. 1966. *Physical and Mechanical Properties of Molucca Albizzia Grown in Hawaii.* U.S. Forest Service Research Paper FPL-55. Forest Products Laboratory, Madison, Wisconsin. 8 pp.

Peters, C. C., and J. F. Lutz. 1966. *Some Machining Properties of Two Wood Species Grown in Hawaii–Molucca Albizzia and Nepal Alder.* U.S. Forest Service Research Notes, FPL-0177. Forest Products Laboratory, Madison, Wisconsin. 17 pp.

Petroff, G., and J. Doat. 1960. *Caractéristiques Papetières de Quelques Essences Tropicales de Reboisement,* Vol. 1. Centre Technique Forestier Tropical, Nogent-sur-Marne (Seine), France, 19-36.

Skolmen, R. G. 1974. *Some Woods of Hawaii: Properties and Uses of 16 Commercial Species.* U.S. Department of Agriculture Forest Service General Technical Report PSW-8E. Pacific Southwest Forest and Range Experiment Station, Berkeley, California.

Sprinz, P. T. 1977. *Report on* Albizia falcataria *Spacing and Fertilization Study. Growth and Yield Report 77-1.* Tropical Forestry Research Center,Weyerhaeuser Company, Jakarta, Indonesia. 7 pp.

Streets, R. J. 1962. *Exotic Trees in the British Commonwealth.* Clarendon Press, Oxford. pp. 166-169.

Suharlan, A., K. Sumarna, and Y. Sudiono. 1975. *Yield Table of Ten Industrial Wood Species.* Forest Research Institute, Bogor, Indonesia.

Viado, J. 1967. Fast-growing reforestation tree species for pulp and paper manufacture. *Philippine Lumberman* 13:9, 26, 28, 32-33.

Vincent, A. J., B. A. Mitchell, and K. Sandrasegaran. 1964. Permanent sample plot information on the stocking, growth, and yield for pulpwood of Batai (*Albizzia falcata* Back.) grown in Malaya. *Malayan Forester* 27:4, 327-353.

Walters, G. A. 1971. A species that grew too fast, *Albizia falcataria. Journal of Forestry* 69:168.

Albizia lebbek

Anonymous. 1970. *Kokko (Siris).* Indian Timbers Information Series No. 6. Forest Research Institute and Colleges, Dehra Dun, India. 12 pp.

Streets, R. J. 1962. *Exotic Trees in the British Commonwealth.* Clarendon Press, Oxford.

Albizia acle, Albizia chinensis, and *Albizia procera*

Reyes, L. J. 1938. *Philippine Woods.* Technical Bulletin No. 7. Department of Agriculture and Commerce, Manila. 536 pp.

Albizia minahassae

T. C. Whitmore. 1966. *Guide to the Forests of the British Solomon Islands.* Oxford University Press, Oxford. pp. 81-82.

African *Albizia* Species

Albizia adianthifolia, Albizia ferruginea, Albizia gummifera, and *Albizia zygia*

Irvine, F. R. 1961. *Woody Plants of Ghana.* Oxford University Press, London. pp. 331-334.

Taylor, C. J. 1960. *Synecology and Silviculture in Ghana.* T. Nelson and Sons, Ltd., London and Edinburgh. pp. 213-221.

Research Contacts

Albizia falcataria

Assistant Conservator of Forests (Silviculture and Research), Forest Department, P.O. Box 1017, Kingston, Georgetown, Guyana

I. L. Domingo, Paper Industries Corporation of the Philippines, P.O. Box 502, Commercial Center, Makati, Rizal, Philippines

Forest Department Headquarters, Badruddin Road, Kuching, Sarawak, Malaysia (Hua Seng Lee, Silviculturist)

Forest Research Institute, College, Laguna 3720, Philippines (F. S. Pollisco, Director)

Forest Research Institute, Jalan Gunung Batu, P.O. Box 66, Bogor, Indonesia

Forest Research Institute, Kepong, Selangor, Malaysia

R. González-Meza, Departmento Investagaciones Forestales, Direccion General Forestal, Ministerio de Agricultura y Ganaderia, San José, Costa Rica

Institute of Pacific Island Forestry, U.S. Forest Service, 1151 Punchbowl St., Honolulu, Hawaii 96813, USA (R. G. Skolmen and C. D. Whitesell)

Ministry of Agriculture and Forestry, Forest Department, P.O. Box 31, Entebbe, Uganda (P. K. Karani, Deputy Chief Forest Officer)

Ernest Pung, Department of Land and Natural Resources, Division of Forestry, Hilo, Hawaii 96720, USA

Forest Research Centre, P.O. Box 1407, Sandakan, Sabah, Malaysia (Liew That Chim, Senior Research Officer)

Sabah Softwood Sdn. Bhd., P.O. Box 137, Tawau, Sabah, Malaysia (M. W. McMyn, Project Manager)

Jose. A. Semana, Forest Products Research and Industries Development Commission, College, Laguna 3720, Philippines

Y. N. Tamimi, Department of Agronomy and Soil Science, Hawaii Agricultural Experiment Station, 461 W. Lanikaula, Hilo, Hawaii 96720, USA

B. R. Thomson, Forest Research Officer, Forestry Division, Munda, New Georgia, Solomon Islands

K. Vivekanandan, Research Officer (Silviculture), Forest Department, P.O. Box 509, Colombo 2, Sri Lanka

R. Voss. Forest Regeneration and Research Department, Silam Forest Sdn. Bhd., W.D.T. No. 56, Lahad Datu, Sabah, Malaysia

K. F. Wiersum, Department of Tropical Sylviculture, Agricultural University, Wageningen, The Netherlands

N. Q. Zabala, College of Forestry, University of the Philippines at Los Baños, College, Laguna, Philippines

Albizia lebbek

Chief Forest Officer, Afforestation Division, Hathi Sar, Naxal, Kathmandu, Nepal

Golam A. Fakir, Associate Professor, Department of Plant Pathology, Bangladesh Agricultural University, Mymensingh, Bangladesh

R. W. Fishwick, Western Africa–Projects Department, The World Bank, A203, 1818 H Street, N.W., Washington, D.C. 20433, USA

Institute of Pacific Island Forestry, U.S. Forest Service, 1151 Punchbowl St., Honolulu, Hawaii 96813, USA (R. G. Skolmen and C. D. Whitesell)

Hassen, A. R. Musnad, Silviculturist, Arid Zone Forestry Research, Forestry Research Institute, P.O. Box 658, Khartoum, Sudan

Albizia acle

Forest Research Institute, College, Laguna 3720, Philippines (F. S. Pollisco, Director)

Albizia chinensis

Forest Research Institute, P.O. Box 273, Chittagong, Bangladesh
Forest Research Institute, College, Laguna 3720, Philippines (F. S. Pollisco, Director)

Albizia minahassae

B. R. Thomson, Forest Research Officer, Forestry Division, Munda, New Georgia, Solomon Islands
Forest Products Research Centre, Department of Forests, P.O. Box 1358, Boroko, Port Moresby, Papua New Guinea (J. F. U. Zieck)
T. C. Whitmore, Department of Forestry, University of Oxford, Commonwealth Forestry Institute, South Parks Road, Oxford OX1 3RB, England

Albizia pedicellata

Forest Research Centre, P.O. Box No. 1407, Sandakan, Sabah, Malaysia (Liew That Chim, Senior Research Officer)

Albizia procera

Forest Research Institute, P.O. Box 273, Chittagong, Bangladesh

Albizia adianthifolia, Albizia ferruginea, Albizia gummifera, Albizia zygia

Conservator of Forests, Forestry Development Investigation Branch, Government of Anambra State of Nigeria, Enugu, Anambra State, Nigeria (J. C. Okafor)
L. S. Gill, Senior Lecturer in Botany, Department of Biological Sciences, University of Benin, Benin City, Nigeria
Forest Products Research Institute, P.O. Box 63, Kumasi, Ghana (S. P. K. Britwum)
Forestry Research Institute of Nigeria, Private Mail Bag 5054, Ibadan, Nigeria

Sesbania grandiflora

Considering its many uses, it is surprising that *Sesbania grandiflora** has not been more widely exploited and researched. This small tree grows amazingly fast and provides forage, firewood, pulp and paper, food, green manure, and landscape decoration; also it appears to have much potential for reforesting eroded and grassy wastelands throughout the tropics. Although some specimens are now growing in most tropical countries, the plant's many values remain largely unrecognized.

Native to Asian countries such as India, Malaysia, Indonesia, and the Philippines, *Sesbania grandiflora* is commonly seen growing on the dikes between rice paddies, along the roadsides, and in backyard vegetable gardens.

The plant's outstanding feature is its extremely fast growth rate, especially during the first 3 or 4 years after planting. At the Ord River Irrigation Area in northern Australia, specimens of *Sesbania grandiflora*† have outgrown all other species tested, averaging heights of 4.3–5.5 m in only 1 year (some exceptional trees reached 8.3 m). Both there and in India, plantations have attained heights of about 8 m (with average diameter 10 cm and more) in as short a time as 3 years.‡ Wood yields of 20-25 m³ per ha are commonly achieved in Indonesia.§ *Sesbania grandiflora* thus promises, among other things, to be a species for short-rotation forestry in the tropics.

The species is very easy to propagate by cuttings or seedlings. It establishes readily, requires little maintenance, grows fast, and can easily be planted on a large scale by direct seeding even from the air.‖

---

*Sesbania grandiflora (Linn.) Poir., also *Sesbania formosa* (F. Mueller) Commonly called agati, bacule, katurai (Philippines), August flower (Guyana), West Indian pea tree, turi (Malaysia, Java), gallito. Subfamily: Papilionoideae.

†The species native to northern Australia has long been designated as *Sesbania grandiflora*, but on the basis of a small difference in flower structure it is classified by some botanists as *Sesbania formosa*. See Burbridge, N. T. 1965. The Australian species of *Sesbania* Scopoli (Leguminosae). *Australian Journal of Botany* 13:103-141.

‡Information from Division of Forest Research, Winnellie, Australia (see Research Contacts), and Bhat *et al.* 1971 (see Selected Readings). The Australian specimens were grown on black, poorly structured clay, pH 8.5.

§ Information supplied by K. F. Wiersum. See Research Contacts.

‖Sumarna, K., and Y. Sudiono. 1974. Regeneration sampling after aerial sowing in Balapulang forest district, Central Java. *Laporan, Lembaga Penelitian Hutan* No. 188. 21 pp.

Sesbania grandiflora. Indonesian foresters encourage the reforestation of bare land outside forest areas using *Sesbania grandiflora.* The tree can now be found along roadsides, on dikes between rice fields, and around villages and houses. This quick-growing pioneer species is harvested in 5-year rotations, particularly for firewood. (Perum Perhutani, Indonesia)

Not only can *Sesbania grandiflora* be grown under very short rotation, but it can be planted very densely. Over 3,000 stems per ha have been used both in Australia and in India.

Prolific nodulation and extremely large nodules are a dramatic feature of *Sesbania grandiflora.* Furthermore, when the plant was grown for the first time in Townsville, Australia, it nodulated readily, so that suitable strains of *Rhizobium* appear to be already widespread in tropical soils.

The wealth of uses to which this plant can be put is illustrated by the following examples.

Forage

Cattle relish the feathery leaves and the long (up to 60 cm) pods of *Sesbania grandiflora.* In parts of Java where cattle breeding is important, the tree is much planted for forage and is continually topped to keep it within the animals' reach. After cutting, shoots resprout with vigor; the plant seems irrepressible.

It has no known toxicity to cattle, and in experiments in Java 1.8 kg of fresh *Sesbania grandiflora* herbage fed daily to animals on a rice-straw diet

Sesbania grandiflora, 7 m tall after only 1 year of growth. The seed was direct-sown in deep sandy loam. East Godavari District, Andhra Pradesh, India. (A.S. Bhat)

showed growth increases comparable with those obtained by feeding formulated diets.*

Green Manure

Foliage of *Sesbania grandiflora* makes excellent green manure. The tree is planted for this purpose along rice paddies in Southeast Asia. In Java yields of 55 t green material per ha have been obtained in only 6 or 7 months. (In the same experiment, species of *Crotalaria* and *Tephrosia*, both well-known green manures, yielded only 40 and 52 t per ha, respectively.)† On Timor, *Sesbania grandiflora* grows abundantly on worn-out land left after slash-and-burn agriculture. Its extraordinary nodulation, coupled with its rapid growth, suggests that its soil-improvement qualities—though unmeasured—are exceptional.

Wood, Pulp, and Paper

Sesbania grandiflora grows to a height of 10 m with a diameter of about 30 cm. The bole is straight and cylindrical; the wood is white and soft

*Information supplied by W. J. A. Payne. See Research Contacts.
†Information supplied by K. F. Wiersum. See Research Contacts.

(density 0.42) for a heartwood, and though used for timber, it is not durable and is of little value. It has long been used as firewood in Southeast Asia and is deliberately planted in several areas in Indonesia to provide fuel. One hectare of plantation can yield 3 m^3 of stacked fuelwood in a 2-year rotation.

Recently, it has been viewed as a paper-pulp source for tropical regions. Indeed, in East Java the tree is already extensively used as a pulp source. The fiber length (1.1 mm, or about average for hardwoods used for paper) and chemical composition both appear suited to pulping. Australian researchers have suggested that *Sesbania grandiflora* logs appear to be unsuitable for pulping if the bark is left on because of gum and resin that pervade it and because of the nature and quantity of the bark. However, they conclude "that it should be possible to utilize *Sesbania grandiflora* (without bark) pulps in the production of printing papers."*

The wood is satisfactorily pulped by the sulfate process and the paper-making properties of the pulp seem adequate for a limited range of paper products. It bleaches readily to high brightness with a standard bleach sequence and should be acceptable for offset printing papers. The neutral sulfite semi-chemical (NSSC) process gives a pulp that should be suitable for the production of corrugating medium, but the pulp yield is low and severe cooking conditions are required to obtain adequate delignification.

The Australian workers have discovered that debarked *Sesbania grandiflora* and kenaf can be pulped together satisfactorily. The *Sesbania grandiflora* improved the drainage rate of the kenaf pulp without adversely affecting its strength.

The tree seems capable of producing yields at least as high as other trees now extensively grown for pulpwood.

Reforestation

In Taiwan and Indonesia, *Sesbania grandiflora* has proven useful for reforesting eroded hill regions. In East Java, where the tree is known as turi, plantations of the species have been so widely established that "turinization" projects are mounted specifically to plant it. The seeds germinate well and the seedlings grow vigorously and don't become smothered by weeds. The roots penetrate most soils. Thus it appears that the species could become valuable for reforestation throughout much of the tropics.

Food

The young leaves, tender pods, and giant flowers of *Sesbania grandiflora* are favorite Asian vegetables, used in curries and soups or fried, lightly

*Logan *et al.* 1977.

steamed, or boiled. The leaves contain over 36 percent crude protein and with their high mineral and vitamin content make a remarkably nutritious, spinach-like vetetable.

The butterfly-like flowers are perhaps the largest of any leguminous plant—up to 10 cm long. (In Martinique, they are called vegetable humming birds.) Produced year-round, the white or wine-red blooms contain a considerable amount of sugar and are used for food. A favorite throughout much of Asia (and also sold in Filipino markets in Honolulu), they are reportedly crisp and, if boiled for 1 minute, taste like mushrooms.* (Before cooking, the center part of the flower is removed to reduce bitterness.)

In some parts of Asia, the long (30 cm) narrow pods are eaten as a vegetable dish, much like string beans. They contain about 50 small seeds, which are processed and eaten like soybeans. The seeds are among the richest in protein—more than 40 percent by weight—of all legume seeds.

Other Uses

In Southeast Asia the tree is commonly planted along roadsides, fence lines, and other boundaries for beautification. With its open, spreading crown of feathery leaves, *Sesbania grandiflora* gives light shade; it also makes useful shelterbelts and is often grown as a living fence. The large, handsome flowers and long pods make it a striking ornamental.

The plant has traditionally been used as a support for pepper and betel (*Piper betle*) and sometimes for vanilla vines. The leaves drop continuously, making a thick mulch that adds nutrients to the soils and fertilizes the other crops. On the Indonesian island of Timor, the species is planted as a sacrificial "host" for the sandalwood tree, whose parasitic roots sap nourishment from the roots of any neighboring plant.

Agricultural crops continue to grow well when interplanted with *Sesbania grandiflora*, whose open crown allows sunlight to pass. This agroforestry combination is very promising, especially in areas where space is limited, for *Sesbania grandiflora* can be fitted in along fence lines or field borders where it doesn't occupy the cropland.

When cut, the bark of the tree exudes a clear gum that has been used as a substitute for gum arabic (see page 271) in foods and adhesives.

---

*In the 1920s, David Fairchild, a famous U.S. plant explorer, wrote: "As we rode through the town of Peradeniya [Sri Lanka] one day, my eye caught a large mass of white flowers hanging in a little shopkeeper's door and, as I realized the shopkeeper was not a florist, I stopped to inquire and found that these great ivory blossoms were to eat. The shopkeeper took me into his small plantation, overlooking the river, where I found two small daughters picking the blossoms for market. The flowers seemed too pretty for use as a vegetable, yet here was a plantation."

Limitations

There is no information available on the general silviculture of this plant; those who wish to grow it face considerable uncertainty.

All edible parts of the plant must be cooked before eating (see Research Needs). Some flowers are bitter and unappetizing to many people; enjoyment of them is an acquired taste. Compared with common vegetable legumes, the yield of pods is low.

The tree is frost sensitive, and at least in northern Australia, plantations have been damaged by birds (cockatoos) and grasshoppers. It is also a short-lived tree with a life span of only 20 years or so. It is not wind resistant; its brittle branches break and it is unsuitable for exposed, windy sites. It is also very susceptible to nematodes.

Although *Sesbania grandiflora* grows abundantly on the arid island of Timor, it seems best adapted to the moist tropics with annual rainfall in excess of 1,000 mm and no more than a few months of dry season.

As a forage, *Sesbania grandiflora* foliage, though more digestible than tropical grasses, seems less digestible than that of *Leucaena leucocephala* foliage (see page 131). The plants are also slower to regenerate after being browsed.

Research Needs

Sesbania grandiflora has long been considered a poor man's plant, but it appears to have characteristics that can make it a profitable tree crop with general appeal. To assess its future role, trial plantings are needed to test the production and economics of its many products in different environments. In particular, timber companies, forestry researchers, government departments, and rural development groups should establish trial plantations to produce wood products. It seems likely that in many cases the results will lead to large permanent plantations and to improved well-being for people in rural areas of the tropics and subtropics.

Basic research on the tree is also needed. Seed collections should be made throughout Southeast Asia. Samples should be maintained in safe storage at a suitably equipped facility, but field trials to compare the varieties should also be undertaken. Features to test for include rate of growth, content of canavanine (an antinutrition factor, see below), wood quality, and nutritional value.

In some ways, *Sesbania grandiflora* is a counterpart to *Leucaena leucocephala*, and much of the research recommended for leucaena in a recent NAS report* should also be applied to *Sesbania grandiflora*. The two plants

---

*National Academy of Sciences. 1977. *Leucaena: Promising Forage and Tree Crop for the Tropics.* To order see page 329.

should be compared side-by-side in some locations. Furthermore, it seems that *Anthocephalus chinensis* (a nonlegume) has comparable growth rates to *Sesbania grandiflora* and produces more satisfactory sulfate and NSSC pulps.* This species, too, should be included in any pulpwood comparison trials.

Gum arabic is now so valuable and in such short supply that tests of *Sesbania's* gum seem warranted.

Although the plant is a traditional food in Southeast Asia, recent research has detected in mature seeds the presence of canavanine, an uncommon amino acid that acts as an antimetabolite to arginine, a nutritionally important amino acid.† It is not known if the leaves, young pods, or flowers also contain canavanine, and this should be determined. Traditional cooking methods may detoxify any of the substance that may be present, but this, too, should be checked.

Animal scientists need to evaluate *Sesbania grandiflora* in cattle, pig, and poultry diets. Research should be done on making leafmeal.

Studies of the horticulture and general agronomy of the tree (e.g., planting, soil, and moisture requirements, etc.) are also needed. Studies of existing plantings should include pathology, for the tree is extremely sensitive to nematodes.

Since it has been found that the pulping and papermaking properties of some very young plantation species improve with age, specimens about 10 years old should be tested and compared with the pulping trials of the 3-year-old samples reported in the literature.

Selected Readings

There is not a single comprehensive account of this plant and its uses. Many books on tropical agriculture or tropical trees refer to it, but only sketchily.

Bhat, A. S., M. M. Menon, T. N. Soundararajan, and R. L. Bhargava. 1971. *Sesbania grandiflora* (a potential pulpwood). *Indian Forester* 97(3):128-144.

Burkill, I. H. 1935. *A Dictionary of the Economic Products of the Malay Peninsula.* Crown Agents for the Colonies, London. pp. 1997-1998.

Food and Agriculture Organization of the United Nations. 1975. *Pulping and Papermaking Properties for Fast-Growing Plantation Wood Species.* Food and Agriculture Organization of the United Nations, Rome. pp. 445-447. (Order No. FO:MISC/75/31) This gives the pulping characteristics of the wood.

Heyne, K. 1950. *De Nuttige Planten von Indonesie*, Vol. I. N.V. Uitgevery W. Van Hoeve–S. Gravenhage, Bandung. 780 pp.

Holm, J. 1972. The yields of some tropical fodder plants from northern Thailand. *Thai Journal of Agricultural Science* 5:227-236.

Holm, J. 1973. Preliminary data concerning the amount of nutrients produced by forages grown in Chiang Mai under a cut and carry system. *Thai Journal of Agricultural Science* 6:211-222.

*Logan *et al.* 1977.

†Information supplied by Professor E. A. Bell, King's College, University of London.

Holm, J. 1973. The nutritive value of 12 tropical forage plants from the Chaing Mai region of Thailand. *Landwirtschaftliche Forschung* 26(4):313-325.

Logan, A. F., P. I. Murphy, F. H. Phillips, and H. G. Higgins. 1977. Possible pulpwood resources for Northern Australia: Pulping characteristics of young *Anthocephalus chinensis* and *Sesbania grandiflora. Appita* 31(2):121-127.

Muthukrishnan, C. R., and S. Ramadas. 1974. Perennial vegetables for your kitchen gardens. *Indian Horticulture* 19(2):11-12.

Ochse, J. J. 1931. *Vegetables of the Dutch East Indies.* Department of Agriculture, Industry and Commerce, Netherlands East Indies, Buitenzorg, Java. pp. 429-430.

Research Contacts

Readers can probably get seed from their own local botanic gardens or from commercial seed suppliers in the Philippines, Indonesia, Sri Lanka, and India

D. B. Amatya, Forest Research Officer, Forest Survey and Research Office, Department of Forestry, Babar Mahal, Kathmandu, Nepal

Bhargava Consultants Pvt. Ltd., 210 Ansal Bhawan, 16 Kasturba Gandhi Marg, New Delhi 110001, India

A. S. Bhat, Bhadrachalam Paper and Board Ltd., 31 Sarojini Devi Road, Secunderabad (AP), India

A. L. Chapman, Officer in Charge, Kimberley Research Station, CSIRO Division of Tropical Crops and Pastures, Kununurra, Western Australia, Australia

Department of Botany, Kasetsart University, Bangkok, Thailand

Division of Chemical Technology, CSIRO, P.O. Box 310, South Melbourne, Victoria 3205, Australia (H. G. Higgins, F. H. Phillips, and A. F. Logan)

Division of Forest Research, Northern Territory Research Station, CSIRO, P.O. Box 39899, Winnellie, Northern Territory 5789, Australia (G. Cracium and D. Cameron)

C. R. Dunlop, Department of the Northern Territory, P.O. Box 5150, Darwin, Northern Territory, 5794, Australia

S. R. D. Guha, Cellulose and Paper Branch, Forest Research Institute, Dehra Dun, P.O. New Forest, India

Herbarium Bogoriense, National Biological Institute, Bogor, Indonesia (Endang Anggarwulan)

Chia Huang, Animal Industry Division, Joint Commission on Rural Reconstruction, 37 Nan Hai Road, Taipei 107, Taiwan

R. J. Jones, Davies Laboratory, CSIRO, Private Mail Bag, P.O. Townsville, Queensland 4810, Australia

N. S. Kaikini, IFS (Retd) Forest Advisor, West Coast Paper Mills, Ltd., Dandeli (NK) Karnataka, India

J. León, Head, Plant Genetics Resources Center, CATIE, Turrialba, Costa Rica

Livestock Breeding Station, Huai Kaeo, Chiang Mai, Thailand

G. C. Lugod, Department of Botany, College of Sciences and Humanities, University of the Philippines at Los Baños, College, Laguna, Philippines

Andree Millar, Director, National Capital Botanic Gardens, 4677 University P.O., Port Moresby, Papua New Guinea

Ministry of Agriculture and Forestry, Forest Department, P.O. Box 31, Entebbe, Uganda (P. K. Karani, Deputy Chief Forest Officer)

W. J. A. Payne, 63 Half Moon Lane, London SE24 9JX, England

H. Suijdendorp, Department of Agriculture, District Office, Carnarvon 6701, Western Australia, Australia

University of Florida Agriculture Research and Education Center, 18905 S.W. 280th St., Homestead, Florida 33031, USA

K. Vivekanandan, Research Officer (Silviculture), Forest Department, P.O. Box 509, Colombo 2, Sri Lanka

K. F. Wiersum, Department of Tropical Sylviculture, Agricultural University, Wageningen, The Netherlands

I. M. Wood, CSIRO, Division of Tropical Crops and Pastures, St. Lucia, Queensland, Australia

Other Fast-Growing Trees

Previous chapters on *Acacia auriculiformis*, *Albizia falcataria*, and *Sesbania* species and a book on *Leucaena leucocephala** have detailed some leguminous trees that grow extremely fast. Some other obscure species that have been observed to grow exceptionally fast and that deserve further testing in plantation cultivation are discussed in this chapter.

Leguminous trees are often among the first to colonize newly cleared land. Like other pioneer species, their advantages include:

• Rapid growth that enables them to overtop potential competitors and preempt their space;

• Adaptability to a wide range of sites and soils, particularly nutrient-deficient soils and marginal sites unsuited to food crops;

   • Copious seeding at an early age, often without regard to season;

   • Ability to coppice;

   • Light-colored wood; and

   • A robust, irrepressible character.

In addition, these small-tree pioneers often occur naturally in pure stands, indicating that they probably can be grown in monoculture without decimation by fungi or insects. When the advantage of nitrogen fixation is added, it can be seen that leguminous trees offer a promising field for exploratory investigations.

*National Academy of Sciences. 1977. *Leucaena: Promising Forage and Tree Crop for the Tropics.* To order see page 329.

One-year-old leucaena trees in a demonstration plot near Batangas City, Philippines. (N.D. Vietmeyer)

Acacia mangium, Gum Gum Forest Reserve, Sabah. These 9-year-old trees are 23 m tall (23 cm diameter), representing an annual production of 46 m³ per ha). It seems likely that this first--and only--experience with this straight-stemmed species is ushering in a new tropical resource. (Tham C.K.)

Some of these produce low-density wood that is of little value for construction timber or fine wood uses. In general, they are utility trees, candidates worth testing for firewood, erosion control, beautification, shade, shelter belts, utility lumber, and perhaps for pulp and paper.

The species discussed below are offered as promising candidates; researchers should look widely for other potentially useful woody legumes, too.

*Acacia mangium**

Trees often perform in unexpected ways when introduced to new locations; their growth rates, health, and utility in the natural environment are poor guides for predicting their performance when grown as exotics.

Acacia mangium Willd. Subfamily: Mimosoideae.

194

Acacia mangium exemplifies this. A decade ago, foresters in Sabah, Malaysia, introduced this tree that is native to Queensland, Australia. Despite the fact that it had never before been considered as a plantation species, they incorporated it into trials. In these tests, *Acacia mangium* has grown at a rate comparable to both *Gmelina arborea* and *Albizia falcataria* (see page 173), which are considered among the fastest-growing useful trees on earth. For example, on good sites *Acacia mangium* specimens reached 23 m tall (23 cm in diameter) in only 9 years. Untended stands of such 9-year-old trees have yielded 415 m³ of timber per ha, representing an annual production of 46 m³ per ha.*

But on poor sites *Acacia mangium* has outperformed *Gmelina arborea*, *Albizia falcataria*, *Pinus caribaea*, and other species tested. On disturbed or burned sites, on degraded lateritic clay underlain with volcanic rock, on soils so worn out that even shifting cultivation has been abandoned, and on hillslopes infested with weeds such as *Imperata* and *Eupatorium* species, *Acacia mangium* has grown vigorously, often achieving annual production in excess of 20 m³ per ha. Sabah foresters have now converted over 1,200 ha of degraded *Imperata* grassland into productive forest lands.

In plantations, *Acacia mangium* grows with clean, nearly straight stems up to 10 m long and with little taper. This good form is an advantage over its close relative *Acacia auriculiformis* (see page 165). During their first 2 years of growth in Sabah, the trees required some weeding and in some cases treatment with insecticide, but then needed little further tending. Flowering and fruiting is profuse and continuous. The trees coppice readily.

Large-diameter logs can be sawn or peeled. The hard, light-brown wood is dense, with narrow sapwood and a straight, close grain. It makes excellent particle board and could possibly be useful for furniture, cabinetmaking, and perhaps even pulp and paper.

Acacia mangium hybridizes naturally with *Acacia auriculiformis,* producing hybrids that seem to grow even faster than either parent. So far, however, the observed hybrids retain the poor form of *Acacia auriculiformis*.

The tree can be direct-sown and appears most promising for erosion control in appropriate climatic zones.

Acrocarpus fraxinifolius

This lofty tree,† both a spectacular ornamental and a promising source of timber, is native to South India, Assam, the eastern Himalayas, Burma, and

---

*Keong, Tham C. 1977.

†*Acrocarpus fraxinifolius* Wight & Arn. Also known as shingle tree, Kenya coffee shade tree, pink cedar, and red cedar. Subfamily: Caesalpinioideae.

Acrocarpus fraxinifolius, Dola Hill Forest Reserve, Zambia. (R.J. Poynton)

Sumatra. It can attain 60 m in height (sometimes as much as 45 m to the first branch), with a diameter of 3 m above its buttresses.

In trials in Malawi, Nigeria, Rhodesia, and Zambia, *Acrocarpus fraxinifolius* has proved to be the fastest-growing tree legume. Height increases of 1.3–3.0 m per year have been achieved in Zambia and in Nigeria. In Zambia a 4-year-old stand has an average height of 10.7 m (average diameter 9.5 cm), with exceptional trees reaching 15.2 m (14 cm diameter).*

The tree is remarkably free from pests and disease but a number of savanna plantations in Africa have, for unknown reasons, failed following several years of very vigorous growth. It cannot withstand prolonged drought

*Laurie. 1974.

and seems best adapted either to sites with deep soils in cool but frost-free tropical uplands or to the humid tropics with equable rainfall.

Acrocarpus fraxinifolius is easily raised from seed. Its timber is fairly hard and strong. The fresh wood, dark brown with even black stripes, has been sold as a substitute for ash or walnut in furniture making. It is also used for planking, general construction, and roofing shingles.

It sheds its leaves in the cold season; then, with returning warmth, it becomes covered with a profusion of small flowers in dense, bottlebrush clusters. The whole tree becomes a blaze of scarlet and, as one of the largest trees of South Asia, it is an unforgettable spectacle. At the peak of its flowering the new leaves begin to appear. Initially the leaves are bright crimson and for a few days a new shade of red encompasses the whole tree.

Calliandra calothyrsus

Small leguminous trees have long been popular in the tropics as ornamentals, shade trees, green manures, nurse crops, and, in some cases, fruit trees. Many have become so definitively classified for such purposes that the possibility of growing them in plantations for wood products is overlooked. *Calliandra calothyrsus** exemplifies the potential value that ornamental and utility species may have when converted to plantation crops.

Usually grown as an ornamental, *Calliandra calothyrsus* is a small Central American tree with spreading branches and spectacular flowers that resemble crimson powderpuffs. Against the handsome dark foliage these appear like balls glowing in the sunlight.† In 1936, foresters carried seed from Guatemala to Indonesia and grew the plant in trial plots. Its performance as a fuelwood source has been so exceptional that over the last 25 years *Calliandra calothyrsus* plantations have been steadily expanding and now cover more than 30,000 ha in Java. More of the trees are being planted each year on state forest and private lands.

Plantations are easily established by direct seeding or by planting seedlings or large cuttings. The trees grow with almost incredible speed, averaging heights of 2.5–3.5 m in 6-9 months. The plants can be harvested after the first year, yielding 5–20 m³ of fuelwood per ha. The cut stumps coppice readily, the sprouts often becoming 3 m tall within 6 months. The trees can continue to be annually harvested for 15–20 years, providing 35-65 m³ fuelwood per ha per year.‡

Calliandra calothyrsus Meissn. Subfamily: Mimosoideae.

†Related and little-known species that also make attractive ornamentals are: *Calliandra guildingii* Benth., the Trinidad flame bush; *Calliandra tweedii* Benth., a low tree of Guyana with showy purple stamens; *Calliandra surinamensis* Benth., which bears masses of flower balls resembling pink-to-purple paintbrushes.

‡Information supplied by Forest State Corporation (Perum Perhutani) and K. F. Wiersum. See Research Contacts.

Some Indonesian villagers now cultivate *Calliandra calothyrsus* widely on their own land, often intercropping it with food crops. The plant's value is dramatically exemplified by the village of Toyomarto in East Java. There, land that was once grossly denuded and erosion-pocked is now covered with *Calliandra* forest and is fertile once more. Today the villagers make a good living selling the firewood, actually earning more from it than from their food crops. (Perum Perhutani, Indonesia)

Even at full maturity the trees are only 10 m tall and 20 cm in diameter, so that the wood is too small for most purposes and is useful mainly as fuel. It is quite dense (specific gravity 0.5–0.8) and burns well, giving off about 4,600 cal of heat per g. In Indonesia it is mainly a source of firewood for domestic use and fuelwood for brick, tile, and lime kilns, as well as copra dryers and sugar-processing operations.

The living trees have additional utility, however. Their quick, dense growth suppresses weeds, and Indonesian foresters use *Calliandra calothyrsus* to destroy the pernicious weed *Imperata cylindrica*. The trees' abundant nodulation appears to enrich the soil in which they grow, making them useful as nurse crops or green manures. They are suitable for erosion control and will grow on eroding slopes, quickly providing cover and protection from the elements. They can also be used as firebreaks to block passage of grass fires.

Although untested as a forage source, *Calliandra calothyrsus* foliage contains 22 percent protein, is produced abundantly (7-10 t per ha, dry weight), and seems palatable to livestock.*

The plant seems extremely adaptable, thriving in a wide range of soils and at altitudes from 150 to 1,500 m. It requires 1,000 mm of rainfall annually, but can withstand several months of drought.

Dalbergia sissoo

A very adaptable tree, indigenous to northern India, Nepal, and Pakistan, *Dalbergia sissoo*† is particularly worth research attention. Its wood is strong and hard and in many ways comparable to teak. The tree grows fast and under exceptional conditions may reach 3.7 m in 1 year, 5 m in 3 years, 11 m in 5 years, and 15 m in 10 years. Even on lateritic soils trees have grown 2-3 m tall in 2 years.‡ Full-grown specimens may reach 30 m tall.

Dalbergia sissoo adapts well to widely varying sites—parks, streets, dooryards, windbreaks, dry ridges, filled areas, and river-spoil dumps—ranging in altitude from lowlands to over 1,000 m elevation. It is salt tolerant, pest resistant, and can survive temperatures from below freezing to nearly 50°C. It is a tree particularly for dry savanna woodlands (annual rainfall 700-2,000 mm) and withstands droughts of 3-4 months even during the hottest season in Sudan.

In India and Pakistan it is planted in areas too dry for teak. It is used extensively to afforest barren lands; for example, coastal sand dunes and wastelands infested with the weed lantana (*Lantana aculeata*). In the United States (Arizona and Florida) *Dalbergia sissoo* is one of the most desirable shade trees for streets and backyards.

The tree reproduces vigorously by suckers (making it useful for stabilizing eroding sites). It coppices readily and can be planted using large, stump-like cuttings.

In India it is cultivated more extensively than any species other than teak, and Pakistan has over 100,000 ha of irrigated *Dalbergia sissoo* plantations. It has grown well in a sewage-irrigated greenbelt around Khartoum, Sudan, but has been less successful in the Sahelian zone of Africa.

The wood is excellent for many purposes: furniture, cabinets, sporting goods, flooring, boats, wood carvings, and fuel. Although closely related to

*Information supplied by K.F. Wiersum.

†*Dalbergia sissoo* Roxb. Commonly known as sissoo or shisham. Subfamily: Papilionoideae.

‡Laurie, 1974; also Streets, 1962.

the rosewoods (see page 231), *Dalbergia sissoo* wood is light colored and lacks the rosewoods' striking grain. The trees also tend to have poor form.

Young branches and foliage are eaten by livestock.

Enterolobium cyclocarpum grown as an ornamental, Honolulu, Hawaii. (R.G. Skolmen)

Enterolobium cyclocarpum

Although little known elsewhere, this fast-growing species is widespread and extensively used throughout Central America from southern Mexico to northern South America, as well as in the Caribbean. Guanacaste Province in Costa Rica is named after it. It is an important species that should be propagated more intensively.

A large tree 20–30 m tall with a stout trunk sometimes over 2 m in diameter, *Enterolobium cyclocarpum** grows exceptionally fast, the diameter

*Enterolobium cyclocarpum (Jacq.) Griseb. One named variety is recognized: *Enterolobium cyclocarpum* var. *Perota schombrg. Enterolobium schomburgii* Benth. is a closely similar species that may be a variety of *E. cyclocarpum.* Commonly known as guanacaste, earpod tree, jenizero, juana costa-mahogany, caro. Subfamily: Mimosoideae.

sometimes increasing at 10 cm annually. In the forest it grows tall and long-boled, but in open sites it forms a handsome, wide-spreading crown and makes a fine shade tree. This makes it ideal for use in parks, playgrounds, and along roadsides. In pastureland it shades the livestock and sheds masses of curved, ear-shaped pods that make good forage.

A native of savanna lands, the tree can survive on very dry sites.

Enterolobium cyclocarpum wood is a rich walnut brown with intense dark stripes. In Hawaii it has been used as a substitute for monkeypod (see *Samanea saman*, page 202) in bowls and other expensive turnery items. The fine-looking lumber is useful for furniture, paneling, construction, veneer, and boat building. It is easy to work (though the dust can be an irritant), finishes to a smooth surface, and takes a high polish. It has good dimensional stability, dries without splitting or twisting, and holds its shape when manufactured despite changes in temperature and humidity. Notably durable in water, the wood is good for boatbuilding, farm troughs, and similar uses.

Mimosa scabrella, Curitibanos, Santa Catarina, Brazil. (L.E.G. Barrichelo)

Mimosa scabrella

One of the fastest growing trees of Brazil, *Mimosa scabrella** is virtually unknown elsewhere. Native to the cool, subtropical plains of southeastern Brazil, the tree grows very rapidly, attaining an amazing height of 15 m in 3

**Mimosa scabrella* Benth. (Also called *Mimosa bracatinga* Hoehne.) Known as bracaátinga or abarácaátinga. Subfamily: Mimosoideae.

years. (Intermediate growth was recorded as 5 m at 14 months and 8–9 m in 2 years.)*

The tree is hardy, fixes atmospheric nitrogen, and grows in many types of well-drained soil. It has no thorns, is easily planted by seed, and is readily cultivated in plantations, even at exceptionally close spacings.

Mimosa scabrella makes a useful ornamental, avenue tree, or living fence. It sheds large quantities of leaves that easily decompose, forming very good humus. The wood makes excellent fuel and some plantations have been harvested on rotations as short as 3 years. But the manufacture of paper pulp is perhaps the most promising use of the tree. *Mimosa scabrella* fibers average 1.17 mm long, and though its pulp is inferior to that of *Eucalyptus saligna*, it is good enough to manufacture printing and writing papers.† This, together with the tree's remarkable growth rate, makes it well worth testing outside Brazil.

Samanea saman, Raintree

Originally from the northern part of South America, primarily Venezuela, the raintree‡ is now one of the most widely cultivated trees. Its huge umbrella-shaped canopy of feathery leaves is well known in many parts of the tropics. Yet the range of products the tree offers is seldom appreciated.

Thriving in both the dry and wet tropics (usually where annual rainfall is between 600 and 2,500 mm), the tree grows rapidly. Carefully tended specimens often reach 18 cm in diameter in 5 years in Hawaii.§ It can attain great size; a famous, century-old specimen in Trinidad has a trunk 2.5 m in diameter and a canopy 45 m tall with a 55 m spread (see picture next page).

Like carob, tamarind, and some other legume trees, the raintree produces pods with edible pulp. When ripe, the pulp is sweet and sugary, with a flavor rather like licorice that is much relished by children. These pods can also be dried and ground into a meal that makes excellent animal feed. A number of South American countries have already begun exporting it.

But the raintree is best known as an ornamental shade tree. Its short main stem breaks up into massive, wide-spreading branches that create an unsurpassed canopy of shade, sometimes stretching right across wide roadways.

---

*Hoehne. 1930.

†Barrichelo and Foelkel. 1975.

‡*Samanea saman* (Jacq.) Merrill. Formerly known as *Pithecellobium saman* (Jacq.) Benth. Also called saman, samaan, algarrobo, monkeypod (Hawaii), and French tamarind. Subfamily: Mimosoideae.

§Information supplied by R. G. Skolmen. See Research Contacts.

A giant raintree dominates Queen's Park Savanna in Port-of-Spain, Trinidad. Grass grows right up to the trunk because this species' leaflets fold together at night and in wet weather, allowing the rain to fall through. (L. and M. Milne)

Farmers value the tree in their pastures, where it shades the livestock, showering down nutritious pods and fostering the growth of nearby grass (the lush green beneath the trees is one reason for the name raintree).

Although not normally considered a species for use in reforestation projects, the raintree thrives on poor soils in dry regions, is easily germinated and transplanted, and grows rapidly, suppressing grasses and weeds that compete for nutrients and light. Seed is borne in abundance while the tree is very young.

A few plantations have been established with this species. In cultivated stands at close spacings, it grows satisfactorily and branches much less than in the open, providing longer, straighter trunks.

The wood is in constant demand and always sells well. It is strong and hard and is a favorite furniture wood in the tropics because of its rich, dark colors and striking bands of cream-colored sapwood. In its properties and appearance, the heartwood resembles that of black walnut (*Juglans nigra*). The raintree has achieved its greatest recognition as a craftwood for carved bowls and turnery. Hawaii is famous for its "monkeypod" bowls, and so many local raintrees have now been felled that the wood is imported in considerable quantity from Indonesia and the Philippines. It shrinks so little that products shaped out of green wood dry without warping or splitting. It is also a durable wood and is used in boat building in Hawaii and elsewhere.

203

Schizolobium parahyba. (J. Morton)

Schizolobium Species

The two trees of this genus discussed below are pioneer species in Central and South America. Despite their extremely swift growth, they have been overlooked by professional foresters in lieu of species from other hemispheres. Nonetheless, both these plants deserve greater research attention; they could become useful sources of paper pulp produced in very short rotations.

*Schizolobium parahyba** is a strange-looking tree with a tall, slender, often-unbranched trunk topped by a huge cluster of long, fern-like leaves. From a distance it looks like a tree fern, a giant one, for *Schizolobium parahyba* sometimes attains 30 m. The tree is common in the coastal subtropical environment of southeastern Brazil from Rio de Janeiro to Rio Grande do Sul. It also occurs widely in the tropics of Central America as far

---

**Schizolobium parahyba* Vell. Blake. Sometimes incorrectly spelled *S. parahybum*. Also known as *Schizolobium excelsum* Vogel. Commonly called guapiruvu or Brazilian fire tree. Subfamily: Caesalpinioideae.

north as southern Mexico. Within this wide range of climates it is found in environments from rainforest to dry savanna, from plains to hill slopes, and from fertile to poor soils. It is obviously a very adaptable plant.

During its brief blooming season, *Schizolobium parahyba* becomes a huge mass of color, visible from a great distance; the golden blossoms occur in erect clusters 30 cm tall and it is a prized ornamental.

This tree deserves greater testing because of its exceptional ability to produce wood. In Florida, 3-year-old specimens are frequently 8 m tall. In Brazil, 8-year-old trees are normally 12.5 m tall and 21 cm in diameter,[*] amounting to over 160 m^3 of wood per ha, equivalent to an average annual growth of 20 m^3 per ha. Trees 20 years old can be 30 m tall and 80 cm in diameter. Rotations as short as 5 or 6 years have been suggested.

Little is known about this plant's silviculture, but it reproduces well and is easily cultivated. The base can be flanged but the bole is otherwise well formed, straight, and branchless.

In young specimens the wood is soft (specific gravity 0.32), almost white, and probably suitable for paper pulp. Its fibers are 1.1–1.4 mm long and 24–37 μ in diameter and have very thin walls. Although used for picture and door frames, as well as for packing cases, the wood is mechanically weak and is susceptible to decay unless treated.

A related species, *Schizolobium amazonicum*[†] is native to the hot, humid Amazon environment of the Brazilian states of Pará and Amazonas. Almost nothing is known about this tree's potential utility, but it grows with incredible rapidity. One specimen planted in Belém, Brazil, reached 4 m in height and 10 cm in diameter in 18 months.[‡] Growth is so fast that it might possibly be managed on rotations of 5 years or less.

Tipuana tipu

The tipa[§] is a handsome spreading, fast-growing tree of southern Bolivia and northern Argentina. A robust tree easily planted and cultivated, the tipa seems well suited to warm-temperate and subtropical climates worldwide. It is already grown for shade and ornament in parks and along streets in many cities in southern South America, southern France, Algeria, South Africa, and Southern California. Although not previously grown in plantations, it seems appropriate for testing in reforestation programs.

A medium-to-large thornless tree, the tipa can grow to be 40 m tall and 1.6 m in diameter. Its bole rises long and clear above the buttressed base. Its

---

[*]Anonymous. 1976.

[†]*Schizolobium amazonicum* Ducke. Known as paricá in Brazil.

[‡]Ledoux. 1976.

[§]*Tipuana tipu* (Benth.) O. Kuntze. Commonly known as tipa, tipa blanca, tipu, or tipuana.

showy, bright-yellow flowers appear in sprays at the tip of the branches and unfold their color at leafing time.

At present, tipa is nowhere abundant, but in Argentina the lumber is highly regarded for furniture and cabinetwork. It is finely striped, light colored, and finishes with a high polish. It is not resistant to decay and insects, but reportedly has potential for use in light boxing as well as in wall paneling, door frames, fine furniture, and other interior work.

Selected Readings

Acacia mangium

Keong, Tham C. 1977. *Introduction to a Plantation Species* Acacia mangium *Willd*. Pusat Penyelidikan Hutan, Sandakan, Sabah, Malaysia. 6 pp. (mimeo) Copies available from author, see Research Contacts.

Acrocarpus fraxinifolius

Laurie, M. V. 1974. *Tree Planting Practices in African Savannas*. Food and Agriculture Organization of the United Nations, Rome. pp. 55, 68-69.
Whitmore, J. L., and A. Otarola T. 1976. *Acrocarpus fraxinifolius* Wight, especie de rapido crecimiento inicial, buena forma y madera de usos multiples. *Turrialba* 26(2):201-204.

Calliandra calothyrsus

Anonymous. 1977. *The Possibility of Kaliandra Wood as a Source of Energy*. Special report of the Forest Products Research Institute, Bogor. 25 pp. (mimeo)
Suyono. 1975. Caliandra as fuel wood and forest protector. *Duto Rimba* 3:3-6, 11 and 4:9-12, 33. (in Indonesian)
Verhoef, L. 1941. Preliminary results of species trials with some legumes from tropical America. *Tectona* 34:711-736. (in Dutch)

Dalbergia sissoo

Forest Research Institute and Colleges. 1968. *Indian Timbers: Sissoo*. Information Series I. Forest Research Institute and Colleges, Dehra Dun, India. 14 pp.
Goor, A. Y., and C. W. Barney. 1976. *Forest Tree Planting in Arid Zones*. The Ronald Press, New York. pp. 390-392.
Laurie, M. V. 1974. *Tree Planting Practices in African Savannas*. Food and Agriculture Organization of the United Nations, Rome. pp. 45, 50-51, 72,78.
Streets, R. J. 1962. *Exotic Trees in the British Commonwealth*. Clarendon Press, Oxford. pp. 259-262.

Enterolobium cyclocarpum

Little, E. L., R. O. Woodbury, and F. H. Wadsworth. 1974. *Trees of Puerto Rico and the Virgin Islands*. Vol. 2. Forest Service, U.S. Department of Agriculture, Washington, D.C. pp. 258-259.
Record, S. J., and R. W. Hess. 1943 (reprinted 1972). *Timbers of the New World*. Arno Press, New York. p. 266.
Streets, R. J. 1962. *Exotic Trees in the British Commonwealth*. Clarendon Press, Oxford.

Mimosa scabrella

Barrichelo, L. E. G., and C. E. B. Foelkel. 1975. Utilização de madeiras de essências florestais nativas na obtenção de celulose. *Edicão Especial, Technologia de Celulose e Papel.* Instituto de Pesquisas e Estudos Florestais (IPEF), pp. 43-56. See Research Contacts.

Hoehne, F. C. 1930. *A Bracaátinga ou Abáracaátinga.* Secretaria da Agricultura, Industria e Commercio do Estado de São Paulo, Brazil. 47 pp.

Samanea saman, Raintree

Anonymous. 1969. *The Properties and Potential Uses of Raintree* (Samanea saman). Fiji Timbers and Their Uses Number 37. Department of Forestry, Suva, Fiji. 4 pp.

Schizolobium parahyba

Anonymous. 1925. *Schizolobium*: A promising source of pulpwood. *Tropical Woods* 2:2-5.

Anonymous. 1976. *Guapuruvu*, Schizolobium parahyba *(Vell.) Blake.* Report Number IPT/DIMAD/FC:111/1975/76. Divisão de Madeiras, Instituto de Pesquisas Tecnológicas, São Paulo, Brazil. 4 pp.

Meninger, E. A. 1962. *Flowering Trees of the World for Tropics and Warm Climates.* Hearthside Press, Inc., New York. p. 97.

Rizzini, C. T. 1971. *Avores e Madeiras Uteis do Brazil. Manual de Dendrologia Brasileiro.* Editora da Universidade de São Paulo. Published by Editora Edgard Blucher Ltda, Caixa Postal 1400, São Paulo, Brazil. pp. 127-130.

Record, S. J., and R. W. Hess. 1943 (reprinted 1972). *Timbers of the New World.* Arno Press, New York. p. 325.

Schizolobium amazonicum

Ledoux, P. V. E. 1976. Relatorio sumario sobre pesquisas referentes a *Schizolobium amazonicum* Ducke (Huber ex D.). In *Simposio Internacional Sobre Plantas de Interes Economico de la Flora Amazonica,* p. 53. Instituto Interamericano de Ciencias Agrícolas, Informes de Conferencias, Cursos y Reuniones No. 93, Turrialba, Costa Rica.

Tipuana tipu

Anonymous. 1976. *Tipuana.* Note Number IPT/DIMAD/FC:120/1975/76. Divisao de Madeiras, Instituto de Pesquisas Tecnologicas, São Paulo, Brazil. 4 pp. (mimeo)

Tortorelli, L. A. 1956. *Maderas y Bosques Argentinos.* Editorial Acme, S.A.C.I., Buenos Aires, Argentina. pp. 458-462.

Research Contacts

Acacia mangium

General Manager, Sabah Forestry Development Authority (SAFODA), Locked Bag 122, Kota Kinabalu, Sabah, Malaysia

N. Johnson, Weyerhaeuser Far East Ltd., P.O. Box 2682, Jakarta, Pusat, Indonesia

Pusat Penyelidikan Hutan (Forest Research Centre), P.O. Box 1407, Sandakan, Sabah, Malaysia (Liew T. Chim, Senior Research Officer and Tham C. Keong, Plantation Officer)

Research Director, Forestry Department, P.O. Box 269 Broadway, Brisbane 4000, Queensland, Australia (D. I. Nicholson)
Sabah Softwood Sdn. Bhd., P.O. Box 137, Tawau, Sabah, Malaysia (M. W. McMyn, Project Manager)

Acrocarpus fraxinifolius

J. Chavelas-Polito, C.E.F. "San Felipe Bacalar," Apartado Postal No. 182 Chetumal, Quintana Roo, Mexico
O. Cedeño, Apartado No. 1, Campo Experimental El Tormento, Escárcega, Campeche, Mexico
Department of Forestry, P.O. Box 30048, Capital City, Lilongwe 3, Malawi
Division of Forest Research, P.O. Box 2099, Kitwe, Zambia
Forestry Research Institute, P.O. New Forest, Dehra Dun, Uttar Pradesh, India
Forest Research Institute of Malawi, P.O. Box 270, Zomba, Malawi
Ministry of Agriculture and Forestry, Forest Department, P.O. Box 31, Entebbe, Uganda (P. K. Karani, Deputy Chief Forest Officer)
A. Otarola-Toscano, San Miguel P-8, Urbanizacion Cahuache San Luis, Lima, Peru
J. L. Whitmore, Institute of Tropical Forestry, P.O. Box AQ, Rio Piedras, Puerto Rico 00928

Calliandra calothyrsus

Department of Tropical Sylviculture, Agriculture University, Wageningen, The Netherlands (K. F. Wierşum)
Forest State Corporation (Perum Perhutani), Jalan Jenderal Gatot Subroto 17-18, Post Box 111, Jakarta, Indonesia (Soekiman Atmosoedarjo)
Hua Seng Lee, Silviculturist, Forest Department Headquarters, Badruddin Road, Kuching, Sarawak, Malaysia

Dalbergia sissoo

D. B. Amatya, Research Officer, Forest Survey and Research Office, Department of Forestry, Babar Mahal, Kathmandu, Nepal
Central Arid Zone Research Institute, Jodhpur, India (H. S. Mann, Director)
Director, Forest Planning Office, Department of Natural Resources, Box 5887, Puerta de Tierra, Puerto Rico 00906
Forest Products Research Division, Pakistan Forest Institute, Peshawar, Pakistan (K. M. Siddiqui, Director)
Forest Research Institute, P.O. New Forest, Dehra Dun, Uttar Pradesh, India
P. K. Karani, Deputy Chief Forest Officer, Ministry of Agriculture and Forestry, Forest Department, P.O. Box 31, Entebbe, Uganda

Enterolobium cyclocarpum

O. Cedeño, Apartado No. 1, Campo Experimental El Tormento, Escárcega, Campeche, Mexico
Faculty of Forestry Sciences, University of the Andes, Apartado No. 305, Merida, Venezuela
L. R. Holdridge, Tropical Science Center, Apartado 2959, San José, Costa Rica
Institute of Tropical Forestry, P.O. Box AQ, Rio Piedras, Puerto Rico 00928 (T. H. Schubert, Research Forester)
Latin American Forestry Institute, Apartado 36, Merida, Venezuela
J. A. Lewald-Caouilliez, P.O. Box 543, Guatemala City, Guatemala

Research and Training Center for Tropical Agriculture (CATIE), Forestry Department, Turrialba, Costa Rica

R. G. Skolmen, Institute of Pacific Island Forestry, U.S. Forest Service, 1151 Punchbowl St., Honolulu, Hawaii 96813, USA

Mimosa scabrella

Departamento de Silvicultura, ESALQ-USP, Cidade Universitaria, "Armando de Salles Oliviera," Caixa Postal 8191, São Paulo, Brazil

Industrias klabin do Paraná de Celulose S/A, Monte Alegre, Estado do Paraná, Brazil

Instituto de Pesquisas e Estudos Florestais (IPEF), C.P. n° 9, 13.400-Piracicaba, São Paulo, Brazil (L. E. G. Barrichelo and C. E. B. Foelkel)

Samanea saman, Raintree

Assistant Conservator of Forests (Silviculture and Research), Forest Department, P.O. Box 1017, Kingston, Georgetown, Guyana

Central Forest Experiment Station, University of the Philippines at Los Baños, College, Laguna 3720, Philippines (J. O. Sargento)

Director, Forest Planning Office, Department of Natural Resources, Box 5887, Puerta de Tierra, Puerto Rico 00906

Faculty of Forestry Sciences, University of the Andes, Apartado No. 305, Merida, Venezuela

Institute of Pacific Island Forestry, U.S. Forest Service, 1151 Punchbowl St., Honolulu, Hawaii 96813, USA (R. G. Skolmen and C. Whitesell)

Latin American Forestry Institute, Apartado 36, Merida, Venezuela

Franklin Martin, Mayaguez Institute of Tropical Agriculture, P.O. Box 70, Mayaguez, Puerto Rico 00708

F. S. P. Ng, Senior Forest Botanist, Forest Research Institute, Kepong, Selangor, Malaysia

A. W. Owadally, Conservator of Forests, Ministry of Agriculture, Natural Resources, and the Environment, Forestry Service, Curepipe, Mauritius

Schizolobium parahyba

C. B. Briscoe, c/o NBC—Jari, 1345 Avenue of the Americas, New York, New York 10019, USA

R. González-Meza, Depto. Investigaciones Forestales, Dirección General Forestal, Ministerio de Agricultura y Ganadería, San José, Costa Rica

Herbarium Bradeanum, Caixa Postal 15.005–ZC-06, 20.000 Rio de Janeiro, Rio de Janeiro, Brazil (G. F. J. Pabst, Director)

E. P. Heringer, Reserva Ecológica do 1BGE, Laboratorio de Ecología, Ed. Venâncio II-2° andar, 70.000—Brasília–D.F., Brazil

L. R. Holdridge, Tropical Science Center, Apartado 2959, San José, Costa Rica

J. Murca Pires, Instituto de Pesquisas Agropecuaria do Norte, Caixa Postal 48, Belém, Pará 66000, Brazil

C. T. Rizzini, Jardim Botanico de Rio de Janeiro, Rio de Janeiro, Brazil

Schizolobium amazonicum

P.V.D. Ledoux, Departamento de Ciencias Biológicas, Universidade Federal do Pará, Caixa Postal 691, 66000 Belém, Pará, Brazil

J. Murca Pires, Instituto de Pesquisas Agropecuaria do Norte, Caixa Postal 48, Belém, Pará 66000, Brazil

Tipuana tipu

Banco Nacional de Semillas Forestales, Servicio Forestal y de Caza, Ministerio de Agricultura, Natalio/Sanchez 20-Jesús Mariá, Lima, Peru

Los Angeles State and County Arboretum, Arcadia, California 91006, USA

R. J. Poynton, Director, Forestry Research, P.O. Box 727, Pretoria, South Africa

VI Luxury Timbers

Afrormosia

A West African tree hailed as the timber find of the century when it first entered international trade 30 years ago, afrormosia* is still not well known, but it is admired by all who are familiar with it. Indeed, on world timber markets afrormosia wood already brings some of the highest prices of any tropical hardwood. Pound for pound it is now the most valuable indigenous wood of Ghana, more costly than the renowned African mahogany (*Khaya* species).

As a result, the natural stands are being heavily cut, and because afrormosia's natural regeneration is negligible and it is not being planted on a large scale, the tree is facing economic and biological extinction. Already production in Ghana is declining. A concerted research effort on afrormosia silviculture is needed urgently.

Afrormosia wood has a texture, grain, and appearance much like that of teak. In addition, it is as durable and dimensionally stable. But afrormosia wood has higher density and is harder, stronger, finer, and more uniformly textured and lacks the oily feel of teak. It is therefore being used increasingly, not only as a teakwood substitute but for its own distinctive merits.

The brown, dark-streaked afrormosia wood undoubtedly could be used in a wide variety of products if it were more available. At present, it is principally used for shipbuilding (especially for rails and decks), furniture (some of the "teak" furniture sold in the United States is actually afrormosia), decorative veneer, high-quality joinery, decorative flooring, and shop fittings.

*Pericopsis elata (Harms) van Meeuwen. Formerly known as *Afrormosia elata* Harms. Also called kokrodua, golden afrormosia, asamela, African teak. Subfamily: Papilionoideae.

Nine-year-old plantation of *Afrormosia elata*, Ghana. (K. Tufuor)

Afrormosia is native to countries along the west coast of Africa and occurs principally in pockets of the Ivory Coast, Ghana, Gabon, and Zaire. In some areas it is common and is available in quantity; however, production today is limited mainly to the border region between the Ivory Coast and Ghana. Nowhere is the tree's regrowth adequate to sustain continued commercial production of timber.

It is a large tree with a diameter of 1–1.5 m and a height as much as 45 m, topped by a fan-shaped crown. The stem is usually straight and is often free of branches for about 30 m of its height. The trunk is normally flanged with small buttresses around the base. A gregarious plant, afrormosia is found growing in almost-uniform stands in semi-deciduous forests.

Little is known of afrormosia's genetic variation, but Ghanaian foresters have begun selection breeding.* High seed germination (87 percent) and the nursery production of seedlings have been achieved.† Afrormosia has also been propagated without difficulty using stem cuttings. The tree is known to nodulate well,‡ and its ability to supply its own nitrogen gives it a notable advantage.

*Jones. 1969.

†Information supplied by S.P.K. Britwum. See Research Contacts.

‡Masefield, G.B. 1958. Some factors affecting nodulation in the tropics. In *Nutrition of the Legumes,* ed. E.G. Hallsworth. pp. 202-215. Butterworth, London.

Although afrormosia is generally considered to be slow growing, vigorous seedlings in Ghana have reached heights of 2.1-2.7 m in their first year. (On average, however, seedlings reached only about 0.85 m.) Moreover, trees 8 years old have shown mean annual diameter increases of 3 cm.

There is far more information available about afrormosia wood than about the plant itself. The sapwood is narrow (usually less than 2.5 cm wide) and slightly lighter in color than the heartwood. When freshly cut, the heartwood is yellowish brown (teak colored), but sunlight darkens it to a pale or medium brown. The grain is straight or slightly interlocked, which produces a mottled pattern of dark, narrow stripes when the wood is quartersawn. (See color plate.)

With a specific gravity averaging 0.65, the wood is heavier and stronger than white oak. It seasons slowly but without difficulty and with little shrinking or warping and is readily worked with both hand and machine tools. Afrormosia resists wear well and is particularly noted for its resistance to decay and insect attack. It stains, polishes, turns, and glues satisfactorily.

In sum, afrormosia wood is outstanding for attractive appearance, superior strength, easy seasoning properties, good workability, high natural durability, and dimensional stability.

Limitations

Whereas teak silviculture is well known and plantations have been established in many parts of the tropics, knowledge of afrormosia silviculture is slight. Afrormosia's most serious silvicultural limitation is perhaps that—at least in the few genotypes planted so far—the leading shoot is recumbent in the young plants. Because of this, afrormosia may prove unsuitable for pure plantations.* Native trees are also commonly marred by bent and bumpy stems, low crowns, and small flanges.

In its natural habitat, afrormosia regenerates poorly. The cause has recently been traced to the seedlings' need for open sunlight. Shaded by the forest canopy, they fail to grow and nodulate.† Nurseries and young plantations therefore need open, unshaded sites.

The species seems to require annual rainfall of 750-2,000 mm and a mean annual temperature of about 26°C.

Afrormosia seeds have no dormancy period and germinate well if sown soon after collection. But they quickly lose viability and cannot be stored for more than 3 months (6 months if stratified).

---

*Information supplied by S.P.K. Britwum. See Research Contacts.
†Ampofo, 1972; also Ampofo and Lawson, 1972.

Research Needs

The first commercial lot of afrormosia wood left West Africa in 1948, and the qualities of the timber are just now beginning to be recognized. Ghana is the major exporter. But many wood-using industries in Europe are finding increasing difficulty in obtaining supplies. Other countries of West and Central Africa should recognize that afrormosia is becoming an increasingly valuable resource.

It is particularly important to begin the time-consuming process of developing afrormosia plantation techniques, especially in line- or group-enrichment planting. This would make an excellent research project for African foresters and for researchers elsewhere in the humid tropics. Basic information on afrormosia needs to be gathered to answer fundamental questions on its flowering and seeding habits, including: pollination methods; fruit ripening and frequency of seed years; seed germination; ecological requirements of young seedlings (especially to determine the light intensities that stimulate growth and reduce mortality); and its performance under plantation conditions, including methods of raising planting stock (i.e., wildings, seedlings, or vegetative propagates). Research to overcome poor seed production and low seed viability is particularly needed.

Many of the best afrormosia specimens in West Africa's native forests are being felled and the plant is failing to regenerate in most logged-over areas; immediate action must be taken to preserve afrormosia germ plasm. It is recommended that Ghana, Cameroon, Zaire, and other countries each set aside 2-3 km^2 of afrormosia forest as a conservation reserve, protected from exploitation, but available to foresters for germ plasm collection.

When considering afrormosia for culture, forest researchers should also consider test plantings of closely related species such as:

*Pericopsis angolensis,** a large tree native to hot, humid areas of Malawi, Zambia, and Rhodesia.

Pericopsis laxifolia,† whose wood is reported to be almost identical to that of afrormosia. This tree is adapted to a drier climate and is found in savanna woodlands from Senegal to the Sudan and from Cameroons to northern Zaire.

Pericopsis mooniana,‡ a highly prized wood native to Asian rainforests from Sri Lanka to New Guinea. It is fast disappearing due to lumbering and

Pericopsis angolensis Harms. Formerly known as *Afrormosia angolensis.*
†*Pericopsis laxifolia* (Benth. ex Bak.) van Meeuwen. Formerly known as *Afrormosia laxifolia* (Benth. ex. Bak.) Harms.
‡*Pericopsis mooniana* Thwaites. Known as kayu laut (Indonesia), nedun (Sri Lanka).

land clearing for rubber and oil palm plantations. The warm brown, deep red, or orange wood has attractive dark streaking. Hard, heavy, and strong, this durable fine wood is eagerly sought (notably in Indonesia) for furniture, cabinetmaking, paneling, turnery, and sliced veneers.

Selected Readings

Ampofo, S. T. 1972. The problem of natural regeneration of *Pericopsis elata* (Harms) van Meeuwen in Africa. *Ghana Journal of Agricultural Science* 5(3):241-245.

Ampofo, S. T., and G. W. Lawson. 1972. Growth of seedlings of *Afrormosia elata* Harms in relation to light intensity. *Journal of Applied Ecology* 9:301-306.

Farmer, R. H. 1975. *Handbook of Hardwoods,* 2nd ed. Building Research Establishment, Princes Risborough Laboratory, Her Majesty's Stationery Office, London. pp. 15-16.

Jones, N. 1969. Forest tree improvement in Ghana. *Commonwealth Forestry Review* 48(4):370-374.

Kukachka, B. F. 1960. *Kokrodua* (Afrormosia elata *Harms*). Foreign Wood Series No. 1978. Forest Products Laboratory, U.S. Department of Agriculture, Forest Service, Madison, Wisconsin 53705, USA. 7 pp.

Loins, J., and J. Fouarge. 1943. *Essences Forestières et Bois de Congo*, Vol. 2. *Afrormosia elata*. Institut National pour l'Etude Agronomique du Congo Belge (INEAC), Brussels, Belgium. 22 pp.

Taylor, C. J. 1960. *Synecology and Silviculture in Ghana*. T. Nelson and Sons, Ltd., London and Edinburgh. pp. 268-271.

Research Contacts

S. T. Ampofo, Cocoa Research Institute of Ghana, P.O. Box 8, Tafo, Ghana

S. P. K. Britwum, Forest Products Research Institute, P.O. Box 63, Kumasi, Ghana

Centre Technique Forestier Tropical, 45Bis, Avenue de la Belle Gabrielle, 94130 Nogent-sur-Marne, France

Commonwealth Forestry Institute, South Parks Road, Oxford OX1 3RB, England

Department of Botany, University of Ghana, Legon, Ghana

Forest Research Institute, Council for Scientific and Industrial Research, University Box 63, Kumasi, Ghana (K. Tufuor)

F. Grison, Centre de Recherches Forestières, Programme Centre et Est, BP 2102 Yaoundé, Cameroon

Houtinstituut T. N. O., Postbus 151, Delft, The Netherlands (distributes a pamphlet on afrormosia wood)

S. Jai, Taiwan Forestry Research Institute, 53, Nan-Hai Road, Taipei, Taiwan

G. W. Lawson, Department of Biological Sciences, University of Lagos, Lagos, Nigeria

Intsia Species

Throughout Southeast Asia and islands of the southwest Pacific, *Intsia** is one of the most valued timbers. It has a handsome, warm, nut-brown appearance and is highly esteemed for use where beautiful woods are appreciated: in high-quality paneling, furniture, decorative turnery, and high-grade joinery. Stronger than teak, it is a hard, stable timber that is also suitable for door and window frames, stairs, and floorings (strip or parquet; it is also used for velodrome cycling tracks in Europe). In addition, *Intsia* wood is resistant to the weather and to insect attack, making it useful for house posts.

So intensively has it been exploited that in most countries few trees are left in natural stands. Alarmed by this turn of events, some countries (Malaysia, for example) have restricted the export of *Intsia* wood. Although the wood is increasingly difficult to obtain and there is a market for all that can be harvested, there have been few systematic attempts to cultivate the species in plantations. They do not appear to be ideal for plantations, but their complete disappearance as economic plants is imminent and makes research on their silviculture urgent.

Intsia bijuga and *Intsia palembanica* differ mainly in the number of leaflets that make up their compound leaves. They are large, broad-crowned trees, sometimes exceeding 40 m in height and 1.5 m in diameter. The bole, though often short, can be as much as 25 m long. It is also often fluted, slightly crooked, and extensively buttressed. Both species are deciduous in seasonally dry areas.

Both *Intsia bijuga* and *Intsia palembanica* are native to tropical rainforests from Southeast Asia (especially in the Philippines, Thailand, Malaysia, and Indonesia) to the islands of the southwest Pacific (including Papua New Guinea, the Solomons, Fiji, and Samoa). They are essentially trees of the wet lowlands. The two species rarely grow together. *Intsia bijuga* is found in coastal areas bordering mangrove swamps, rivers, or river floodplains. *Intsia*

Intsia bijuga (Colebr.) O. Kuntze and *Intsia palembanica* Miq. (Also called *Intsia bakeri* Prain). Known commonly as merbau (Malaysia), ipil (Philippines), Moluccan ironwood, Borneo teak (U.K.), kwila (Papua New Guinea), lum-pho or lumpaw or maka-mong (Thailand), ifil or ifit (Guam), ifi-lele (Samoa), vesi (Fiji), u'ula (Solomon Islands), and go nuoc (Vietnam). Subfamily: Caesalpinioideae.

Fifty-year-old *Intsia bijuga*, Los Baños, Philippines. (N.D. Viet-meyer)

palembanica is usually found farther inland on low hillslopes or well-drained river flats. Both species tolerate a wide array of soil textures that range from sandy and gravelly soils to clay.

Both species have a pronounced taproot and this, together with their many lateral roots, enables them to exploit the minerals in a large, deep volume of soil. This helps *Intsia* trees to dominate and suppress other lowland-rainforest species, most of which have only a lateral root system.

Intsia logs are usually sound to the heart and notably free of defects, except that they may be short and somewhat out-of-round. The logs dry well with little loss in quality and with little shrinkage for such a high-density wood. They have sharply differentiated heartwood that is yellow or orange-brown when freshly cut but that in time deepens to bronze or dark red. In exposed situations, it weathers to a silvery-gray. The fresh wood is distinctive for sulfur-yellow deposits that occur in the pores. The heartwood is dense and heavy (average specific gravity 0.65).

A handsome timber, *Intsia* produces the world-renowned "merbau floors." The grain is interlocked and sometimes wavy, which gives the surface patterns of ribbons, light zigzag tracery, or, sometimes, an attractive fiddleback figure. Although of rather coarse grain and low luster, the wood takes a high polish. It also glues, stains, and turns well.

Among the most decay-resistant 'imbers known, *Intsia* wood is accepted in the Philippines—where it is known as ipil—as the standard against which the durability of other timbers is assessed. It is highly resistant to dry rot, to subterranean termites and other insects, and to fungi.

Trials in the Solomon Islands have shown that *Intsia bijuga* is easily established either from seed or as forest wildings potted in the nursery. In 1957, wildings were planted on Guadalcanal in a black alluvial valley soil, and had attained a mean height of 11 m (diameter 10 cm) by the age of 7 years, when the area was struck by cyclone. In subsequent trials planting lines were cut through logged-over rainforest overlying volcanic red clays of only moderate fertility. *Intsia bijuga* attained a mean height of 8.8 m (diameter 7.4 cm) by 8 years and showed significantly better survival and height growth in its early years than five other indigenous species on trial. The potential of the species was demonstrated by the quickest-growing trees, which added 2 m height per annum. Form of the young trees often seemed poor with a characteristic dropping leader and sinuous or forked stems, but appeared to improve and straighten with age. No pest or disease problems have been encountered in the wild or in trial plots in the Solomons.*

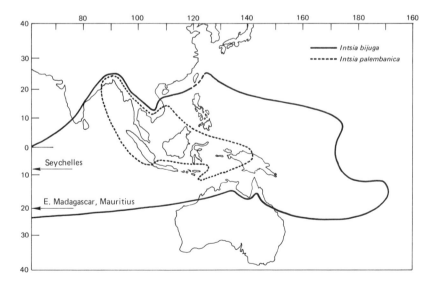

The distribution of *Intsia* species. Taken from M.M.J. van Balgooy. 1966. In *Pacific Plant Maps*. Blumea Supplement V. pp. 158-159.

*Information supplied by B.R. Thomson. See Research Contacts.

Limitations

Little is known about the potential of *Intsia bijuga* and *Intsia palembanica* as plantation crops. Information about their environmental tolerances, seeding and flowering habits, and susceptibilities to diseases and pests is uncertain. However, their growth rate appears to be slow. Further, they probably have specific soil, moisture, and climate requirements that make them potentially useful only for the wet lowland tropics and not for the vast, denuded tropical uplands where reforestation is most desperately needed.

Although the wood is nonsiliceous, it does have a moderate blunting effect on saw and plane blades. It will plane to a smooth surface, but is generally hard to work with hand tools. It is particularly difficult to cut across the grain. The wood can discolor under damp conditions, especially when it is in contact with iron.

The yellow deposits in the pores help confer insect and fungal resistance to the wood, but they are water soluble and leach out in wet conditions.

Research Needs

Although most natural *Intsia* stands are now almost worked out, large stands still exist in Indonesia's Kalimantan, Sumatra, and West Irian regions and in Papua New Guinea. These areas, along with a few locations where regeneration is occurring, provide an important source for information on varietal differences, climatic tolerances, pests, diseases, soil preferences, and growth habits. It is particularly important to study the regenerating crop. This will give an indication of propagation and site preparation requirements and of the potential of *Intsia* species as economic plantation crops. The information will also lead to methods for improving survival and regrowth of the natural stands.

Intsia trees are probably easily established, for it has been observed that in areas where logging has opened the natural forest canopy *Intsia* seedlings pop up in profusion. However, research is needed on seed germination, seedling characteristics, nodulation, nursery requirements, transplantation, and basic silvicultural requirements such as shade tolerance, optimum thinning time, planting density, and the need for intermixing with other species.

Plantation trials of both the two commercially valuable *Intsia* species should be made throughout Southeast Asia. Strains with desirable characteristics should be selected and exchanged and small plantings made in different soils and climates.

Some species of the genus *Afzelia* (also known as *Pahudia*) are closely related to *Intsia* and produce wood of similar quality. They also deserve much greater research attention than they now receive. Indeed, the genus *Afzelia* is so closely related to *Intsia* that, until recently, they were classified together as a single genus. The trees of each are similar and the timbers are of like quality. Most statements on *Intsia* also apply to *Afzelia* species.

Species worth silvicultural consideration include:

Afzelia africana, Afzelia pachyloba, and *Afzelia bipindensis,* West African timbers exported under the trade name Apa or Afzelia;

Afzelia quanzensis (sometimes spelled *cuanzensis*), the source of pod mahogany, an important timber of Central Africa in Malawi, Rhodesia, and Zambia;

Afzelia xylocarpa; and

Afzelia rhomboides (formerly called *Pahudia rhomboidea*), known in commerce as tindalo or Malacca teak and one of the most valuable and highly prized timbers of Southeast Asia.

Selected Readings

Burgess, P. F. 1966. *Timbers of Sabah*. Forest Department, Sabah, Malaysia. pp. 355-361.
Papua New Guinea, Department of Forests. 1973. *New Horizons—Forestry in Papua New Guinea*. Jacaranda Press, Brisbane, Australia.
Stadelman, R. C. 1966. *Forests of Southeast Asia*. Wimmer Bros., Memphis. 245 pp.
Streitman, H. 1972. *Kwila*. Timber Species Leaflet No. 4. Forest Products Research Centre, P.O. Box 1358, Boroko, Papua New Guinea.

Research Contacts

Fijian Forest Service, Suva, Fiji
Forest Products Research Centre, Department of Forests, P.O. Box 1358, Boroko, Papua New Guinea (P. J. Eddowes and C. R. Levy)
Forest Research Institute, Kepong, Selangor, Malaysia (F. S. P. Ng)
Forestry Research Office, Division of Forestry, Ministry of Natural Resources, Munda, New Georgia, Solomon Islands (B. R. Thomson, Forest Research Officer)
FORPRIDECOM, College, Laguna 3720, Philippines (J. P. Rojo)
S. Jai, Taiwan Forestry Research Institute, 53, Nan-Hai Road, Taipei, Taiwan
Hua Seng Lee, Silviculturist, Forest Department Headquarters, Badruddin Road, Kuching, Sarawak, Malaysia
Research Branch, Forest Department, P.O. Box 1407, Sandakan, Sabah, Malaysia
C. D. Whitesell, Institute of Pacific Island Forestry, U.S. Forest Service, 1151 Punchbowl St., Honolulu, Hawaii 96813, USA

Pterocarpus Species

Some Asian and African species of the genus *Pterocarpus** produce beautiful, highly decorative timbers that rank among the finest luxury woods in the world. Padauk, narra, and muninga—all from species of *Pterocarpus*—are some of the most famous woods in the international timber trade. The demand for these rich, dark-brown to blood-red woods—often compared with teak and mahogany—far outstrips supply. Yet none are under extensive cultivation and the native stands are fast disappearing. But though little known to the world's foresters and virtually untried in plantations, several *Pterocarpus* species appear to have the inherent qualities desirable in a reforestation crop. There are commercially valuable species native to a variety of tropical climates from rainforest to dry open savanna. Table 2 lists nine commercially valuable *Pterocarpus* species.† Modern silvicultural research might turn them into important plantation species for the tropics.

Except for *Pterocarpus indicus* (narra) and *Pterocarpus angolensis* (muninga) the literature gives no information on the cultivation of any of these species. However, prolific seed production and easy propagation is a characteristic of *Pterocarpus* species. Indeed, narra is one of the easiest trees to reproduce: it grows readily from seeds, suckers, or cuttings. With narra, *Pterocarpus dalbergioides* (Andaman padauk), and muninga, large cuttings, sometimes as tall as a man, will root, forming an "instant forest" (see illustration, page 228). In this way, waste branches from wind-blown, felled, or pruned trees can be planted (if done in the season when the sap is rising) to produce new trees.

All *Pterocarpus* species have distinctive fruits that differ remarkably from the long pods of most legumes: They are spherical and girded by a flat wing (pterocarpus means winged fruit) that gives a "flying saucer" appearance.

Root nodules have been observed on narra seedlings in the Philippines and it seems likely that other species can obtain nitrogen, at least when young, by symbiosis with *Rhizobium* bacteria.

*Subfamily: Papilionoideae.
† Others include *Pterocarpus pedatus* (Vietnam and Khmer Republic) and *P. mildbraedii.*

In isolation these trees may assume an undesirable, open spreading form with short bole and low branching; in plantations, however, narra, at least, produces trees with long straight boles, the small branches dropping of their own accord. It seems likely that the other species may react similarly.

Growth rates for these trees are little known. Statements in the literature conflict, some claiming rapid growth, others slow growth. It seems likely that they grow somewhat more slowly than mahogany (*Swietenia macrophylla*), but that in favorable locations growth can be moderately fast. In trials in the Solomon Islands on degraded, potassium-deficient soils narra trees grown from cuttings have reached 2-3 m in their first year.* A plot of narra established in Zanzibar (from cuttings 0.6 m long) reached 8 m in height in 5 years.† In the Philippines 7 year old narra trees can have a diameter of 30 cm.‡ Andaman padauk planted on lateritic soils in Madras, India, established rapidly and reached a height of 23 m and a girth of 56 cm in 16 years. §

Generally the *Pterocarpus* timbers are deep red or reddish purple. For furniture, cabinetwork, joinery, carvings, parquet, flooring, decorative paneling, plywood, and boat building, they are unsurpassed. Medium-to-heavy woods with a handsome, fine-grained appearance, they take a high polish and are stable, strong, durable, and easily worked.

The young leaves of many of the species are edible. *Pterocarpus soyauxii*, *Pterocarpus santalinoides*, and *Pterocarpus mildbraedii* are very important sources of green vegetables and forage in southeastern Nigeria. Young narra leaves are sometimes eaten in the Philippines.

Pterocarpus trees are also choice ornamentals. For most of the year their attractive canopy provides shade and beautification. They create scant litter, their branches seldom break, and they will arch over wide roadways, producing cool, beautiful avenues. Narra is widely planted in parks and avenues in Southeast Asia and to a lesser extent in Florida and Puerto Rico. The trees also produce annual showy masses of bright yellow blooms that, upon falling, create a golden carpet beneath the trees. New leaves follow immediately, so that shade is quickly restored. *Pterocarpus erinaceus* is particularly worth testing as an ornamental in appropriate dry savanna country. Each year it provides a great profusion of golden-yellow flowers that completely cover the tree.

More specific information on some of the better-known timber species is given below.

*Information supplied by B. R. Thomson. See Research Contacts.
†Streets. 1962.
‡Information supplied by J. P. Rojo. See Research Contacts.
§Streets. 1962.

TABLE 2 Species of *Pterocarpus* that produce high-quality furniture woods.

SPECIES	NATIVE HABITAT	COMMON NAME	
Asia			
Pterocarpus dalbergioides	South Asia	Andaman padauk; andaman redwood; vermilion wood	One of the most sought after of all tropical hardwoods.
P. indicus	Southeast Asia	Narra	One of the classic furniture woods of the Orient.
P. macrocarpus	Burma; Thailand; Indochina	Burma padauk	Luxury wood, well-streaked orange-yellow to red or red-brown.
P. marsupium	India; Sri Lanka		In Southern India, most important timber after teak and blackwood (*Dalbergia latifolia*, see page 232). Much in demand.
P. santalinus	India	Red sandalwood	Fragrant red heartwood. Scent resembles sandalwood.
Africa			
Pterocarpus angolensis	Southern Africa; Tanzania; Zaire	Muninga	Tree of dry, open woodlands. Less dense wood than *P. indicus* but properties similar. Important export timber.
P. erinaceus	Senegal to Central African Empire		Widespread savanna tree. Heartwood rich brown, mottled with darker streaks.
P. osun and *P. soyauxii*	Nigeria to Zaire	African padauk; barwood	Heartwood has striking deep-red color, makes excellent furniture wood and decorative veneer. Highly prized.

*Pterocarpus indicus**

In the Philippines, narra wood is the choicest timber for furniture, cabinet-work, paneling, carvings, and flooring. In Malaya, Sabah, Indonesia,and Papua New Guinea, it is considered to be the finest indigenous furniture wood. It is a lustrous and decorative wood noted for taking a high polish. In contact with water, it gives off an iridescent blue-green glow; cups turned from narra wood were once considered gifts fit for royalty. It is still in great demand for expensive furniture and is sometimes sold as mahogany—Tenasserim mahogany.

Narra is the national tree of the Philippines and its wood is an important export.

Pterocarpus indicus (narra). (Philippine National Oil Company)

*Pterocarpus indicus Willd. Also known as narra, angsana (Malaysia), Papua New Guinea rosewood (Papua New Guinea), amboyna wood (burr-figured wood), liki (Solomon Islands), sena (Java, Sumatra, Moluccas), and linggoa (Indonesia). This species occurs in genotypes that were until recently designated as distinct species (see Rojo. 1972. Selected Readings). Two of these are *P. indicus* Willd., forma *indicus* (formerly known as Blanco's narra *P. blancoi* or as hairy narra *P. pubscens*) and *P. indicus* Willd. forma *echinatus* (Pers) Rojo (formerly known as *P. vidalianus*).

The heartwood from rapidly growing trees is golden brown and known as yellow narra; that from slower growing trees is red or red-brown and called red narra. The wood is also often yellow or bright red with black striping. The grain is frequently crossed, wavy, or interlocked, producing an attractive pattern in the finished wood. It has a pleasant, persistent odor suggesting rose, cedar, sandalwood, or camphor, and is sometimes marketed under the name rosewood.

Pterocarpus indicus is lofty, handsome, broad crowned, heavily branched, and often reaches a height of 40 m. The bole can be 20 m tall and 1–2 m in diameter (breast height). It is usually irregular and fluted, with a smooth, light-yellow bark.

*Pterocarpus angolensis**

The premier timber of East and Central Africa, muninga has a well-deserved, worldwide reputation. The wood varies from brick red to pale brown, golden brown and chocolate and is one of the most valuable timbers

Pterocarpus angolensis: Infulene Plantation, Mozambique. (R.J. Poynton)

*Pterocarpus angolensis DC. Timber marketed internationally under name of muninga. Also known as bloodwood.

found in Africa. A teak-like wood, it is easily worked, shrinks little on drying, and is strong and durable, resisting both borers and termites. It takes a fine polish and is handsomely figured with golden, yellow, or reddish streaks. It is used mainly for furniture, general joinery, carvings, parquet flooring, paneling, plywood, and boat building.

The muninga tree is native to savanna woodland and coastal plains. Although it can be planted as large cuttings, as mentioned above, attempts to grow it in plantations have so far met with little success.

Pterocarpus dalbergioides *

A native of South Asia, this tree produces Andaman padauk, one of the most famous tropical timbers. Although little tested in plantations, the species showed vigorous growth when introduced to very poor soil on Zanzibar. This, together with the exceptional quality of its wood, has led one prominent author to conclude that this species has high potential as a crop for laterite soils in high rainfall areas where teak grows poorly.†

The heartwood ranges in shade from red-brown to warm red and may have red or black streaks. It is easy to season and is very hard and strong. It is used mainly in veneers, paneling, furniture, interior fittings, balustrades, and turnery. (See color plate.)

Pterocarpus soyauxii ‡

Found in rainforests from Nigeria to Zaire, this tall, straight-boled tree has blood-red heartwood that is an important export of countries such as Cameroon and Gabon. There has been little attempt to introduce it into plantations even though it is readily propagated from seed and is widely planted by African villagers for its edible leaves and shoots. These greens contain about 30 percent protein and are eaten in soups and in "fufu" with pounded yams, cocoyams, and cassava, especially during the dry season when annual vegetable crops are not available.

Red dye extracted from the heartwood is used extensively in Europe to color foods such as tomato ketchup. The timber has a brilliant red hue, though it fades on exposure and needs a protective coating. (See color plate.)

Pterocarpus dalbergioides Roxb.
†Streets. 1962.
‡*Pterocarpus soyauxii* Taub. Timber is marketed under the names barwood, redwood, Gabon padauk, African coralwood, African padauk.

Pterocarpus erinaceus*

Timber from this small tree (reaching 17 m tall and 2.3 m in girth) is virtually unknown to commerce. But it is a beautiful rich, rose-red or dark-brown wood mottled with dark streaks. It has been overlooked because larger timber trees have been widely available in its native habitat. Although found throughout West Africa from Senegal to Gabon, this hard, attractive timber is currently produced mainly in Togo and Nigeria.

Pterocarpus erinaceus is a tree of dry, open savanna forests. It thrives on shallow soils and in areas with moderately long dry seasons. Its leaves make fairly good fodder (with 19 percent protein), and the trees are deliberately planted for this purpose. Once established, they require little attention and readily regenerate after cutting for forage or wood. As previously noted, this species is also an attractive ornamental, especially when bedecked in its copious racemes of bright golden-yellow flowers.

Limitations

Success in cultivating plantations of *Pterocarpus* species will probably be largely determined by site conditions. Each type of tree has specific requirements. For example, narra grows best on deep, fertile, well-drained soils at elevations less than 600 m and seems to require annual rainfall of more than 1,500 mm.

Although widely considered to be fairly disease- and pest-resistant plants, hundreds of narra specimens grown during the last century as roadside trees in Penang, Malacca, and Singapore died of an unknown cause, probably a disease. Although narra is a wind-firm tree, it has been injured by typhoons in the Philippines.

Narra trees in plantations typically grow with a long, sweeping, bent leader sometimes producing forks that often disappear as the tree gradually straightens with age. Untended individual trees develop poor form and have low branches. They also sometimes grow prominent buttresses (which are made into exquisitely patterned table tops), as well as fluted and twisted boles; large trees are often hollow. On poor soils the trees may be stunted. Similar problems may be encountered with the other *Pterocarpus* species.

Research Needs

Despite their commercial importance, *Pterocarpus* species have been almost entirely overlooked by science; only one research paper on *Pterocarpus* silviculture has been published in the past 8 years.

---

*Pterocarpus erinaceus Poir. Also known as African or Senegal rosewood, apepe, madobia.

"Instant" *Pterocarpus* trees have been produced in the Philippines. Big branches (2 m long and 10 cm diameter) of *Pterocarpus indicus* were dipped in a solution of rooting hormone for 24 hours and then directly planted in the field. Roots and shoots developed profusely. This innovative system saves the years of delay normally involved in waiting for a seedling to reach this size. (E.N. Crizaldo, M.V. Dalmacia, and Z. Genil, Forest Research Institute, College, Laguna, Philippines)

Narra is the best-known species, but all those listed in Table 2 deserve research.

These *Pterocarpus* species should be tested as plantation crops, much of which can be done in regions where the species are indigenous. In addition, trials should be established to determine the environmental tolerances and productivity differences between the individual species.

Information on the cultural requirements of *Pterocarpus* species under plantation conditions is badly needed. Forestry researchers are encouraged to undertake the comprehensive trials necessary for establishing commercial plantations. The investigators must consider:

- Acquisition of superior varieties (by selection and hybridization);
- Performance in different ecological zones and in various soil types;

- Identification and control of serious pests and diseases;
- Seed production, handling, and storage (including seed orchard establishment, seed collection, and seed pretreatment);
- Silvicultural methods of reproduction (natural and artificial as well as nursery and plantation requirements); and
- Management (economic rotation and harvesting, for example).

Nodulation has been found in narra seedlings and it is important to investigate the other species to see if they too make use of *Rhizobium* for nitrogen supplies.

Further investigation of the propagation of *Pterocarpus* species using large cuttings (truncheons) is needed. The use of rooting hormones may facilitate this technique and extend its use to species other than narra, muninga, and Andaman padauk.

Selected Readings

Bryce, J. M. 1967. *The Commercial Timbers of Tanzania*. Forest Division, Ministry of Agriculture and Cooperatives, United Republic of Tanzania. pp. 95-96.

Burgess, P. F. 1966. *Timbers of Sabah*. Forest Department, Sabah, Malaysia. pp. 343-347.

Burkill, I. H. 1935. *Dictionary of the Economic Products of the Malay Peninsula*, Vol. 2. Crown Agents for the Colonies, London. pp. 1829-1832.

Claveria, J. R. 1952. Notes on narra (*Pterocarpus* spp.). *The Philippine Journal of Forestry* 7(1/4):31-40.

Farmer, R. H. 1972. *Handbook of Hardwoods*, 2nd ed. Building Research Establishment, Princes Risborough Laboratory, Her Majesty's Stationery Office, London. pp. 138-139, 162-164.

Forest Products Research and Industries Development Commission. n.d. *Narra*. Philippine Timber Series No. 13. College, Laguna E-109, Philippines.

Jay, B. A. 1072. *Timbers of West Africa*. Timber Research and Development Association, Hughenden Valley, High Wycombe, England.

Keay, R. W. J., C. F. A. Onochie, and D. P. Stanfield. 1964. *Nigerian Trees*, Vol. 2. Federal Department of Forest Research, Ibadan, Nigeria. pp. 145-151.

Papua New Guinea, Department of Forests. 1973. *New Horizons—Forestry in Papua New Guinea*. Jacaranda Press, Brisbane, Australia.

Rojo, J. P. 1972. *Pterocarpus—Revised For the World. Phanerogamarum Monographie Tomus V*. Verlag Von J. Cramer, GMBH, 6901 Leutershausen, Federal Republic of Germany.

Streets, R. J. 1962. *Exotic Trees in the British Commonwealth*. Clarendon Press, Oxford. pp. 655-657.

Research Contacts

Forest Research Institute, P.O. New Forest, Dehra Dun, Uttar Pradesh, India (*P. marsupium, P. dalbergioides, P. santalinus*)

P. K. Karani, Deputy Chief Forest Officer, Ministry of Agriculture and Forestry, Forest Department, P.O. Box 31, Entebbe, Uganda

A. Kumar, Research Assistant, Seed Testing Laboratory, Forest Research Institute, P.O. New Forest, Dehra Dun, Uttar Pradesh, India (*P. santalinus*)

S. Jai, Taiwan Forestry Research Institute, 53, Nan-Hai Road, Taipei, Taiwan

Hua Seng Lee, Silviculturist, Forest Department Headquarters, Badruddin Road, Kuching, Sarawak, Malaysia

Office of the Conservator of Forests, Forest Department, P.O. Box 509, Colombo 2, Sri-Lanka (*P. marsupium*)

Royal Forest Department, Paholyothin Road, Bangkok 9, Thailand (S. Nicharat, Chief, Botany Section [*P. indicus* and *P. macrocarpus*])

B. R. Thomson, Forest Research Officer, Forestry Division, Munda, New Georgia, Solomon Islands

Pterocarpus indicus

Forest Products Research Centre, Department of Forests, P.O. Box 1358, Boroko, Port Moresby, Papua New Guinea (J. F. U. Zieck, P. J. Eddowes, and C. R. Levy)

Forest Products Research and Industries Development Commission, College, 3720 Laguna, Philippines (J. P. Rojo)

Forest Research Institute, College, Laguna 3720, Philippines (F. S. Pollisco, Director)

Forest Research Institute, Jalan Gunung Batu, P.O. Box 66, Bogor, Indonesia

Forest Research Institute, Kepong, Selangor, Malaysia (F. S. P. Ng)

Research Branch, Forest Department, P.O. Box 1407, Sandakan, Sabah, Malaysia

Pterocarpus angolensis

Division of Forest Research, Box 2099, Kitwe, Zambia.

Faculty of Agriculture and Forestry, University of Dar-es-Salaam, P.O. Box 643, Morogoro, Tanzania (J. F. Redhead, Professor)

Forest Department, P.O. Box 228, Ndola, Zambia (D. E. Greenwood)

Officer in Charge, National Herbarium and National Botanic Garden, P.O. Box 8100, Causeway, Salisbury, Zimbabwe-Rhodesia

I. M. Shehaghilo, Forester–Silviculture Seeds Section, Forest Department, Ministry of Natural Resources and Tourism, P.O. Box 95, Lushoto, Tanzania

Pterocarpus angolensis, Pterocarpus soyauxii

Centre Technique Forestier Tropical 45[Bis], Avenue de la Belle Gabrielle 94130 Nogent-sur-Marne, France

Department for Silviculture, Faculty of Agriculture, B.P. 30 Yangambi, Sous Region de la Thsopo, Zaire

Service des Eaux et Forêts, Ministere du Developpement Rural, Bamako, Mali (M. Jean Djigui Keita, Directeur)

Pterocarpus soyauxii, Pterocarpus erinaceus, Pterocarpus osun

Federal Department of Forest Research, P.M.B. 5054, Ibadan, Nigeria

B. N. Okigbo, International Institute of Tropical Agriculture, P.M.B. 5320, Ibadan, Nigeria

Conservator of Forests, Forestry Development Investigation Branch, Government of Anambra State of Nigeria, Enugu, Anambra State, Nigeria (J. C. Okafor)

Pterocarpus macrocarpus

S. Boonkird, Deputy Director, Forest Industry Organization, Ministry of Agriculture and Cooperatives, Rajadamndern Nok Avenue, Bangkok 1, Thailand

S. Kittinanda, Director, National Forest Land Management Division, Royal Forest Department, Ministry of Agriculture and Cooperatives, Paholyothin Road, Bangkok 9, Thailand

Rosewoods

A dozen or so species of the genus *Dalbergia** produce the rosewood timber so renowned for its rich colors, beautiful grain, pleasant fragrance, and superlative technical qualities. Rosewood species have long been sought by makers of fine furniture. Brazilian rosewood (*Dalbergia nigra*) was already an item of commerce 300 years ago, and Brazilian tulipwood† is characteristic of classic French furniture, especially that of the Napoleonic era. Today, rosewoods are among the most esteemed and costly timbers in the world.

Rosewoods are richly variegated and uncommonly beautiful. Although each is different, as a group they comprise woods with shades of yellow, chocolate brown, red, and violet—all irregularly and conspicuously streaked with dark red, black, or purple. Freshly cut, the wood has a mild, lasting, rose-like scent that gives it its name.

Wherever *Dalbergia* trees grow, their woods are recognized as one of the best timbers of the region: Brazilian rosewood in Brazil, cocobolo in Central America, Honduras rosewood in Belize, grenadilla in East Africa, blackwood (Indian rosewood) in India, and others in Madagascar and Southeast Asia (see Table 3). Some are so valuable that even tiny logs less than 2 m long and 10 cm in diameter are exported.

Although widespread, today the trees are nowhere abundant; all the accessible stands have long been logged out and rosewood has become very scarce.

*Actually, some 250 *Dalbergia* species are known. Most are tropical shrubs or vines. Subfamily: Papilionoideae.

†From *Dalbergia frutescens* (Vell.) Britt.

TABLE 3   Some *Dalbergia* species that produce luxury timbers with remarkable coloration.

Species	Common Name	Native Habitat	Environment	Heartwood Color
Africa				
Dalbergia africana	Pau santo africana	Equatorial and South West Africa	Highland savanna	Dark brown, with irregular black streaks
D. baronii	Palissandre voamboana	Madagascar (East)	Tropical rainforest	Gray-buff to dark brown
D. greveana	Palissandre violet	Madagascar (West)	Tropical savanna	Purple-brown
D. melanoxylon	East African blackwood; Senegal ebony	Sudan to South Africa; Senegal	Dry, often rocky sites	Dark, purplish brown
Asia				
D. cochinchinensis	Thailand rosewood; payoong; tracwood	Thailand; Indochina	Dry and moist evergreen forests	Brownish red
D. cultrata	Burma blackwood; yindaik	Burma	Lowland and dry, upland mixed forests	Black, with dark, purple streaks
D. latifolia	Indian rosewood; Bombay blackwood; East Indian blackwood	Indian Subcontinent	Dry savanna	Gold-brown to rose-purple, or deep purple, streaked with black
D. oliveri	Burma rosewood; tamalan	Upper Burma; Thailand	Dry hillsides, often on laterite	Rich red
D. sissoides	Malabar blackwood;	Southern India	Hill slopes up to 600 m	Purple mixed with dark brown

Brazil

Species	Common names	Location	Habitat	Color
D. cearensis	Brazilian kingwood	Ceara, Brazil	Dry savanna	Brown, with fine stripes of black or deep violet
D. decipularis	Brazilian tulipwood; Sebastião-de-Arruda	Bahia, Brazil	Dry forests	Pinkish-yellow with wine-colored stripes
D. frutescens (Vell.) Britt. var. tomentosa	Brazilian tulipwood	Bahia, Brazil	Coastal rainforest	Bright yellow or pink with red or purple streaks
D. nigra	Brazilian rosewood; Bahia rosewood; Rio rosewood	Coastal Brazil: Bahia, Rio	Coastal rainforests	Brown, red, or violet, streaked with black
D. spruceana	Amazon rosewood; jacaranda do Para	Lower Amazon Brazil	Dry sites	Rich golden brown, streaked with red or violet

Central America

Species	Common names	Location	Habitat	Color
D. retusa	Cocobolo; Nicaraguan rosewood	West coast Central America; Mexico; Panama	Coastal lowlands and hillslopes	Rainbow hued to deep red
D. stevensonii	Honduras rosewood; hagaed wood	Belize	Riverain and dryer areas	Pinkish-brown to purple; irregular light and dark zones
D. turcurensis	Rosewood; granadillo	Guatemala; Honduras; Belize; Mexico	Riverain and dryer areas	Orange to brown with violet or purple striping

Since the timber is in great demand, *Dalbergia* trees would seem to be worth cultivating. But outside of India and Java, there are no plantations or trial plantings. Indeed, rosewoods have been so neglected by science that the strength properties and structure of most of them have never been measured. Given research attention, these legumes might once more become important economic crops for the tropics.

Dalbergia latifolia, Tamil Nadu, India. (Forest Research Institute, Dehra Dun, India)

The woods differ in color, but they share most other gross properties. The trees that produce them are also much alike. They are medium size, reaching

25-35 m tall, with irregular-shaped boles 1-2 m in diameter. They have large, leathery leaflets and clusters of white or yellow pea-like flowers that give rise to thin, flat pods containing a single seed. A few species are native to tropical rainforest regions, but most come from savanna regions with long dry seasons.

Only the heartwood yields quality timber. It seasons slowly but with little warping, splitting, or cracking. During seasoning, shrinkage is slight, comparable to that of mahogany (*Swietenia macrophylla*), a wood noted for its unusually low and uniform shrinkage. In manufactured objects, the wood is exceptionally stable and holds its shape, making it much esteemed for patternmaking. It is hard, heavy, and strong. Indian rosewood (*Dalbergia latifolia*), for example, is 2.5 times harder and 25 percent stronger than oak. Specific gravity of rosewood varies from 0.75-1.22, usually falling between 0.85 and 1.1.

Dalbergia heartwoods are not difficult to work.* They saw and machine satisfactorily and can be carved more intricately and to greater depth than perhaps any other wood. Their grain is either straight or wavy, with a surface texture that is uniform and moderately coarse. Rosewoods stain well and polish to a rich, lustrous finish.

The timber is unusually durable. Researchers have found that one species, *Dalbergia retusa*, secretes compounds of a type not found in any other plant genus that act as potent bactericides, fungicides, and algicides. These substances are highly toxic to termites, mosquito larvae, the confused flour beetle (one of the most widespread and injurious insect pests of cereal products), and marine borers. *Dalbergia retusa* is an exceptionally good timber for marine use.† The compounds contain only carbon, hydrogen, and oxygen and may be less broadly toxic, less persistent, and more biodegradable than pesticides now in use. With slight structural changes, they can sterilize, repel, or inhibit the growth of other insect pests.‡

With their variegated colors, rosewoods make striking veneers and paneling. They are in demand for fine furniture, cabinetmaking, and sounding boards for high-quality musical instruments (e.g., pianos, clarinets, guitars), jewelry cases, canes, moldings, and interior trim in boats.

---

*An exception to this and many other descriptions in this chapter is *Dalbergia melanoxylon*, a small, often misshapen tree (less than 7.5 m tall) yielding short (1-1.5 m long) logs that are often defective. The wood is very difficult to season and work, but it is one of the most valuable timbers of East Africa and makes the finest clarinets, oboes, bagpipe chanters, nightsticks, and bearings.

†It was the most bioresistant wood out of 97 Panamanian woods tested for resistance to termites, teredo worms, fungi, and other organisms. Bultman. 1977.

‡Information supplied by L. Jurd, U.S. Department of Agriculture, ARS, Western Regional Research Laboratory, Berkeley, California 94710, USA.

Limitations

Except for *Dalbergia latifolia*,* almost nothing is known about the cultural requirements of rosewoods, not even whether they are suitable for cultivation.

The trees are slow in forming heartwood. Thus, even large logs often lose much of their volume when the valueless sapwood is removed.

In some species it is thought that only old (and often defective) stems give the fragrant, richly colored timber.

Sawdust from *Dalbergia retusa* causes an irritating dermatitis in some people; susceptible workmen must be protected.

It is reported that, at least for *Dalbergia nigra*, the color is most pronounced if the tree is girdled and the wood left to season before felling.

Although among woods of comparable density and hardness rosewood is easy to work, it is more difficult, and dulls cutting edges more readily, than softer woods.

Research Needs

The commercially valuable *Dalbergia* species are slow-growing trees, but due to the value of their timber, efforts should be made to extend their cultivation. Trials are recommended in native habitats and in comparable environments elsewhere in the tropics.

There are pioneering plantations of *Dalbergia latifolia* in India and Java. But for the other species, research is needed on such basic cultural practices as seed collecting and handling, germination, nursery handling, transplanting, plantation spacing, maintenance, and pest control.

Information is also needed on the basic physiology of the trees, especially their nodulation and nitrogen-fixing ability, as well as on the physiology of heartwood production and the reason why wood from old, defective trees has the best color.

In Brazil, *Machaerium* species—close relatives of *Dalbergia*—are also exploited for their heartwood, which, though lighter colored and not as highly figured, resembles rosewood. Researchers are encouraged to consider *Machaerium* species in their *Dalbergia* research.

Selected Readings

Bultman, J. D., ed. 1977. *Proceedings of a Workshop on the Biodeterioration of Tropical Woods: Chemical Basis for Natural Resistance.* Marine Biology and Biochemistry

Dalbergia sissoo, a related species is quite well known in plantations (see page 199), but this fast-growing species produces a light and uniformly colored wood, quite unlike the rosewoods.

Branch, Ocean Sciences Division, Naval Research Laboratory, Washington, D.C. 20375, USA. 93 pp.

Deshmukh, D. K. 1975. Regeneration of rosewood (*Dalbergia latifolia*, Roxb.). *Myforest* 11(2):87-93.

Farmer, R. H. 1972. *Handbook of Hardwoods*, 2nd ed. Building Research Establishment, Princes Risborough Laboratory, Her Majesty's Stationery Office, London. pp. 43, 184-185.

Forest Research Institute and Colleges. 1973. *Indian Timbers: Rosewoods*. Information Series 11. Forest Research Institute and Colleges, Dehra Dun, India. 13 pp.

Pearson, R. S., and J. P. Brown. 1932. *Commercial Timbers of India*. Central Publication Branch, Government of India, Calcutta. pp. 368-373.

Record, S. J., and R. W. Hess. 1943 (reprinted 1972). *Timbers of the New World*. Arno Press, Inc., New York. pp. 252-258.

Rizzini, C. T. 1978. The discovery of Sebastião-de-Arruda, a fine Brazilian wood that was botanically unknown. *Economic Botany* 32:51-58.

Streets, R. J. 1962. *Exotic Trees in the British Commonwealth*. Clarendon Press, Oxford. pp. 259-262.

Research Contacts

R. C. Koeppen, Center for Wood Anatomy Research, Forest Products Laboratory, U.S. Department of Agriculture, Forest Service, P.O. Box 5130, Madison, Wisconsin 53705, USA

S. K. Purkayastha, Officer-in-Charge, Wood Anatomy Branch, Forest Research Institute, P.O. New Forest, Dehra Dun, Uttar Pradesh, India

Brazilian Rosewoods

Centro de Pesquisas do Cacau, Ilbéus, Bahia, Brazil (A. C. Leão, and S. G. da Vinha).

E. P. Heringer, Reserva Ecológica do IBGE, Laboratório de Ecologia, Ed. Venâncio II-2° andar, 70.000–Brasilia–D.F., Brazil

Carlos T. Rizzini, Jardim Botanico do Rio de Janeiro, Rio de Janeiro, Braz

Emilio Rotta, rua Bom Jesus 650–Juveve, 80.00–Curitiba, Paraná, Brazil

Dalbergia retusa

Instituto Nicaraguense de Tecnología Agropecuaria, Apartado Postal 453, Kilometro 12 Carretera Norte, Managua, Nicaragua

Dalbergia latifolia

Forest Research Institute, P.O. New Forest, Dehra Dun, Uttar Pradesh, India

Forest Survey and Research Office, Department of Forestry, Babar Mahal, Kathmandu, Nepal (D. B. Amatya, Research Officer)

K. A. Kushalappa, Silviculturist, Forest Department, Karnataka Government, Malleswaram P. O., Bangalore 560 003, Karnataka, India

S. N. Rai, Silviculturist, Karnataka Forest Department, Southern Zone, Madikeri 571201, Karnataka, India

Dalbergia oliveri, Dalbergia cochinchinensis

Swat Nicharat, Chief, Botany Section, Silvicultural Division, Royal Forest Department, Paholyothin Road, Bangkok 9, Thailand

Dalbergia cochinchinensis

Forest Industry Organization, Ministry of Agriculture and Cooperatives, Rajadamndern Nok Avenue, Bangkok 1, Thailand (Sa-Ard Boonkird, Deputy Director)

S. Kittinanda, Director, National Forest Land Management Division, Royal Forest Department, Ministry of Agriculture and Cooperatives, Paholyothin Road, Bangkok 9, Thailand

Dalbergia melanoxylon

Officer in Charge, National Herbarium and Botanic Garden, P.O. Box 8100, Causeway, Salisbury, Zimbabwe-Rhodesia

B. Ramanonjiarisoa, Department of Botany, University of Massachusetts, Amherst, Massachusetts 01003 USA

I. M. Shehaghilo, Forester–Silviculture Seeds Section, Forest Department, Ministry of Natural Resources and Tourism, P.O. Box 95, Lushoto, Tanzania

VII Miscellaneous

Ornamentals

The family Leguminosae includes some of the most glorious of flowering plants. Many are tropical or subtropical trees, and a number of countries have chosen a showy legume as a national flower or tree.*

The expansion of cities and highways has resulted in an ever-increasing need for shade and beautification. Cement walls reflect up to 60 percent of the incident sunlight—partly as light, partly as heat. Road surfaces, depending on type, reflect 25–45 percent of the sunlight. In warm climates there is often no respite from the sun for months on end, with the intense glare verging on the threshold level above which vision is damaged. This unrelenting glare and heat, along with urban blight, can be factors in civil unrest; the increase of urban discontent in the hot season has been noted in many parts of the world.

Trees reduce these damaging light intensities. On a hot afternoon when the tropical sun is beating down mercilessly, a person standing beneath a tree can be relatively comfortable, for dense foliage absorbs about 70 percent of the sun's rays, reflects 17 percent, and transmits only about 13 percent.† Within the tree-shaded microclimate, temperatures are lower and the light less blinding.

---

*Including Brazil (Brazil-wood or pau-brasil, *Caesalpinia echinata*), New Zealand (unofficial, kowhai, *Sophora* species), Australia (golden wattle, *Acacia pycnantha*), Argentina (el seibo, *Erythrina crista-galli*), Barbados (pride of Barbados, *Caesalpinia pulcherrima*), Philippines (molave or narra, *Pterocarpus indicus*), Hong Kong (Hong Kong orchid tree, *Bauhinia blakeana*), and Thailand (ratchapruck, golden shower, *Cassia fistula*).

†Chaphekar, S.B., and S.S. Kulkarni. 1973. Light, heat and roadside plants. *Indian Forester* 99(9):579-581.

In cities and villages, along roadsides, in private gardens or public parks, and in schools and universities, ornamental plants have always been contributing factors in helping people take pleasure in their environment. Yet the provision of these important amenities is often overlooked, especially in developing countries, where funds are limited. Cultivation of trees and shrubs can be a major "appropriate technology" for such countries, requiring little or no foreign exchange or technical support and using indigenous skills. Many ornamentals have functional value beyond the aesthetic; some can also provide fodder, honey, soil stabilization, soil improvement, wood, and food and shelter for birds and other wildlife, as well as the standard benefits of reducing wind, noise, heat, and dust and giving privacy and protection to dwellings. It has been calculated that one shade tree has the cooling equivalent of four room air conditioners.

In addition, some tropical and subtropical countries are airfreighting millions of dollars worth of flowers each year to North America and Europe. There is a large market for flowering plants, especially during northern winter months when ornamentals cannot be locally grown. Warm-climate countries such as Brazil, Israel, Ivory Coast, and Kenya are already taking advantage of this and are reaping considerable export earnings.

This chapter outlines leguminous ornamentals that deserve greater recognition and use throughout the tropics.

Acacia Species

The billowing blossoms of *Acacia* trees are a conspicuous feature of the Australian and African countryside.* Of the 800 or so *Acacia* species, several dozen produce such masses of flowers that the trees become bent with their weight. Most of these establish easily from seed, grow quickly, and flower at an early age. With their considerable drought tolerance, most will thrive where dry seasons are long.

The flowers, often yellow, cluster at the branch ends in either balls or catkin-like spikes. They are sweet scented and may remain in bloom for several weeks. The trees are generally small and often display attractive, silver-colored foliage. Neat and graceful, they are well suited to private gardens.

In Australia, ornamental *Acacia* species are found in all the states and appear on the national coat of arms. Some flower so prolifically that Australians call them "golden showers." Among the most attractive† are:

Acacia baileyana F. Muell. Cootamundra wattle. One of the loveliest of all *Acacia* species; highly prized as an ornamental and street tree in eastern

*Subfamily: Mimosoideae. In Australia they are known as wattle trees, in Africa as thorn trees.

‡See also *Acacia pendula* (page 146).

Australia. Elegant, round-headed small tree with branches sweeping the ground and feathery, silver-gray foliage concealing each branchlet. In spring it provides a show of brilliant, bright-gold flowers. Grows quickly (1.4 m per year for first few years) but dies after 15–20 years. Valuable for interplanting with slow-growing ornamentals. (See color plate.)

Acacia drummondii **Lindl.** One of the daintiest of all shrubby acacias, with an attractive open habit (1–2 m tall) and finely divided blue-gray or green, feathery leaves. Its masses of golden spikes make it a striking sight in season. Requires well-drained soil. A perfect garden shrub. (See color plate.)

Acacia podalyriifolia **A. Cunn.* ex G. Don.** Queensland silver wattle. One of the most accommodating, quick-growing, and attractive ornamental acacias. A small slender tree with profuse deep-golden flower heads in short, dense clusters. Suitable for climates with 675–1,150 mm annual rainfall and for light to medium soils. Good for open terrain, for instance, near coasts or on mountains. Often short lived, but especially useful for quick-growing temporary cover.

Acacia prominens **A. Cunn. Ex G. Don.** (*A. linifolia Willd.* var. *prominens*) Golden rain wattle. A shrub or small tree with weeping-willow-like drooping branches and light-green foliage. Flower heads in dense clusters, very profuse and—unlike most *Acacia* blossom—unaffected by rain. Sweetly scented. A well-grown specimen in full bloom is a magnificent spectacle.

Acacia pycnantha **Benth.** The golden wattle. Australia's national flower. Occurs as either a shrub or small (3–6 m high), open-crowned tree. In flower, it becomes a mass of showy golden blossoms. Drought tolerant and prized by Australians as an ornamental species for areas with hot, dry summers and annual rainfall from 300 to 650 mm. Bark contains more tannin than other acacias, but the tree's small size reduces its commercial value. Will grow in shallow soils, is an excellent sand binder, and is suitable for coastal and mountain plantings. (See color plate.)

Afgekia sericea

A twining, quick-growing climber, *Afgekia sericea*† was first collected by botanists only 50 years ago. Although native to savanna country of Thailand, the plant grows vigorously and flowers year-round in Singapore, so it seems suited to both dry and wet tropics. Among its beautiful foliage, *Afgekia*

---

*Formerly spelled *A. podalyriaefolia*.
†*Afgekia sericea* Craib. Subfamily: Papilionoideae.

sericea produces giant trusses (sometimes 60 cm long) of cream and pink flowers with pink bracts covered with silky hairs. Each flower cluster continues blooming for several weeks. Propagated by seed, this plant deserves much wider recognition and use. (See color plate.)

Amherstia nobilis

This plant, among the most beautiful in the vegetable kingdom, merits widespread planting. But *Amherstia nobilis** has proved difficult to establish and propagate and presents a major horticultural challenge.

A small tree growing to 12 m tall, it blooms most of the year. In its native Burma, where it is considered sacred, handfuls of its flowers are offered before images of Buddha. Individual flowers have wide-spreading crimson petals, though the upper ones are tipped with gold. These blossoms hang like a glowing mobile sculpture enhanced by the background of handsome dark foliage. (See color plates.)

The feathery leaves have whitish undersides and are up to 1 m long. *Amherstia* is deciduous, and when its new leaflets emerge they have a pinkish-copper color that gradually changes to rich bronze and finally green, making the plant exceptionally colorful even before the flowers appear.

Amherstia requires a warm, moist climate as well as shade and protection from severe winds. It has been cultivated successfully in botanic gardens in the Philippines, India, Sri Lanka, Hawaii, Jamaica, Trinidad, and Brazil, but attempts in other parts of the tropics so far have failed.

Since the plant seldom sets seed, propagation is usually by means of layering or, less often, by cuttings.

Barklya syringifolia

One of the loveliest of Australian trees, *Barklya syringifolia*† is also one of the least known outside its native coastal districts of southern Queensland and northern New South Wales. It is a tall tree, sometimes reaching 20 m, with dark evergreen foliage. Each summer it erupts in a brilliant display of small, bright, yellow-orange flowers clustered at the branch tips in sprays 15-18 cm long. This is a tree to brighten residential areas in warm climates. Although it grows slowly and requires moist, rich soil, it well deserves more widespread trials. (See color plate.)

Amherstia nobilis Wall. Subfamily: Caesalpinioideae.
†*Barklya syringifolia* F. Muell. Subfamily: Uncertain; traditionally it is placed in Papilionoideae, but some botanists now suspect that it may be allied to the genus *Bauhinia* in Caesalpinioideae.

Bauhinia Species

The genus *Bauhinia** contains about 200 species scattered throughout the tropics, about 50 of which have been cultivated as ornamentals. A number of them are considered to be among the most attractive of all flowering plants. These trees, shrubs, and woody vines bear prolific clusters of flowers, many of which strikingly resemble orchids. Colors range from pure white through shades of yellow, rose, and lavender to deep red and purple. The "orchid trees" bloom at different seasons; combined plantings can give virtual year-round color. There is scope for hybridization to enhance their attractiveness even further.

The plants grow well in a wide range of poor soils—alkaline or acid, rocky or sandy—but soils must be well-drained. They establish readily from seed and require little maintenance. The leaves, flower buds, flowers, young shoots, and young pods of some of the species are eaten as vegetables.

Bauhinia purpurea, Bauhinia variegata, and *Bauhinia monandra* are already widely planted throughout the tropics. (See color plate.) Some lesser-known species of singular beauty follow.

Bauhinia blakeana **Dunn.** The single most spectacular *Bauhinia*, a sterile hybrid from Hong Kong. Its fragrant flowers, up to 15 cm across, are brilliant deep crimson. Not yet common in the tropics, it has become a popular tree in south Florida in recent years. Produces no seed and is propagated by cuttings and air-layering. (See color plate.)

Bauhinia corymbosa **Roxb.**† The great 19th-century botanist Sir Joseph Hooker termed this "one of the most beautiful of climbers," but it is still not well known in most tropical areas. A native of South China, it bears masses of fragrant, rosy-pink flowers, each set off by three bright red stamens. *Bauhinia glauca,* an almost identical species, is found in South China, Southeast Asia, and Burma.

Bauhinia kochiana **Korth**‡. One of the few high climbers from the jungles of Southeast Asia that have been brought into cultivation. Has glossy green leaves and large racemes of flowers. At first opening each flower is golden yellow, but over a period of days a red color diffuses outwards from the petal veins until the whole flower is a rich, deep, orange-scarlet. At any one time, flowers of different colors may be seen in the same bunch. (See color plate.)

---

*Pronounced baw-*hin*-ee-ah. Also known as orchid flowers and orchid trees. The double-lobed leaves resemble a cloven hoof-print and the plants are sometimes called cow-hoof, camel-foot, and similar names. Subfamily: Caesalpinioideae.

†Also known as *Phanera corymbosa* (Roxb.) Benth.

‡Also known as *Phanera kochiana* Benth.

Bauhinia tomentosa L. St. Thomas bush. A handsome shrub or small tree (1.5–5 m tall) worthy of more extensive cultivation. Native to Sri Lanka, India, and South China. Bears yellow or cream-colored drooping, bell-shaped flowers up to 10 cm across. It is popular in Hawaii, commonly cultivated and naturalized in the West Indies, and has been grown in southern Florida since 1880.

Bolusanthus speciosus, Rhodesian Wisteria Tree

One of the most beautiful of bluish-blossomed plants, the Rhodesian wisteria tree* produces drooping clusters of mauve-purple flowers resembling wisteria. (See color plate.) Native to savannas of southern Africa (Swaziland, northern Transvaal, and Rhodesia), it is a small tree (up to 6 m tall with trunk diameter to 15 cm) with glossy, dark-green leaves and a wood so decay resistant and so in demand for fence posts that in many areas the tree has disappeared due to overcutting. When planted in deep, fertile soil the tree reaches good size in 4–5 years; it is recommended for test planting in small yards or along highways in tropical and subtropical regions. Some specimens are already well established in southern Florida.

Lonchocarpus and *Millettia* are related genera whose species also have deep-blue or purple flowers. They, too, are worth examining by horticulturists searching for attractive ornamental tropical trees.

Brownea Species

Brownea† is a genus of 25 small slow-growing trees and shrubs that are endemic to northern South America (especially Venezuela and Colombia) and the West Indies. All are magnificent in bloom and deserve more widespread cultivation.

Great, globular, rhododendron-like flower heads grow from the branches and branchlets and even from the trunks. They are red or pink, though one white species is known. Even when not blooming they are handsome plants, with slender trunks and long, spreading branches.

Another attractive feature is the brilliant coloring of the new leaves. When the leaves first develop they are pink, purple, or red, often spangled with white. At first they dangle limply, but later they stiffen, straighten, and change to the green of mature foliage.

Some examples of *Brownea* species that make beautiful ornamentals for tropical parks, gardens, or arbors are:

Bolusanthus speciosus (Bolus) Harms. Subfamily: Papilionoideae.
†Subfamily: Caesalpinioideae.

Brownea grandiceps Jacq. Rose-of-Venezuela: rose-of-the-mountain. A Venezuelan tree to 12 m tall, with spectacular flower heads (often 20 cm across) tightly packed with many deep-pink or red blossoms. "The flowers around the edge open first, then others, the flowering moving gradually toward the center, tier above tier, until at last the whole mass becomes a globe of living and glowing crimson."* (See color plate.)

Brownea macrophylla Linden. A viny tree (it prefers to rest its branches on neighboring trees) of the dense Colombian forest known as the rouge-puff. Fire-red flower heads made up of 30–50 flowers erupt from the trunk and branches, sometimes almost hiding the tree itself. (See color plate.)

Brownea capitella Jacq. Has orange-red flower heads, the largest produced by this genus. One of the spectacles of the world-renowned botanic gardens in Trinidad. At present, rarely cultivated elsewhere.

Butea monosperma, Flame-of-the-Forest

An ugly, crooked, medium-size (5–15 m tall) tree, flame-of-the-forest† is transformed by spectacular flowers each spring. Seen in the sunlight, the massed crown of blossoms suggests a forest in flames. (See color plate.)

A native of Sri Lanka, India, and Burma, the tree has been spread eastward as far as Papua New Guinea and China.

Leaves are shed during cold or dry weather, exposing the twisted, misshapen trunk and branches. Then, with returning warmth or moisture, there begins "a vermilion riot of bloom, great stiff clusters of pea-like flowers, red shaded with orange, hanging from leaf axils and branch tips, each individual blossom more than [5 cm] long. Each petal is softly hairy so that it shines and shimmers like silver in the sunlight, and the color contrasts vividly with the jet black or bottle green, velvety calyxes."‡

Hindus consider the flame-of-the-forest sacred to Brahma and use its wood in religious ceremonies and for sacred utensils. Followers of the gods Siva and Vishnu mark their foreheads with bright yellow and deep orange-red dyes extracted from the flowers. Scattered throughout India is a yellow-flowered variety that has seldom been cultivated.§

---

*Menninger. 1962.

†*Butea monosperma* (Lam.) Taub. (*Butea frondosa* Roxb.) Known in India as palas or dhak. Subfamily: Papilionoideae.

‡Menninger. 1962.

§Maheshwari, J.K. 1971. A yellow-flowered variety of the "flame of the forest." *Indian Forester* 97(1):70-71. (More information can be obtained from J.K. Maheshwari, National Botanic Gardens, Lucknow-1, Uttar Pradesh, India.)

At the end of the flowering season, the leaves develop. When young, they are a beautiful pale, bronze-tinged green.

The flame-of-the-forest is difficult to propagate and grow. However, it has been successfully established in Israel, Nigeria, and Florida. It is propagated by seed and is slow growing. It survives in saline and badly drained soils on which few trees will grow. Birds are its chief pollinators. It is important to India's lac industry, which produces most of the world's shellac. The lac insect frequents the tree and punctures young twigs, causing the sticklac gum to exude. Of all lac trees, flame-of-the-forest yields the most sticklac per hectare.

Three or four other members of the genus *Butea* deserve testing as ornamentals. One is *Butea superba* Roxb., a woody climber (with stems as thick as a man's leg) from India, Burma, and Thailand that has flowers fully as showy as those of flame-of-the-forest.

Camoensia maxima

A lofty climber from Angola, Zaire, and Equatorial Guinea, this robust vine* produces some of the largest individual flowers of any legume. Milky-white or cream-colored and edged in gold, they are up to 28 cm long and hang in great profusion from the plant. During evening hours they are exceedingly fragrant, making this a desirable plant for an arbor. (See color plate.)

Cassia Species, Shower Trees

With about 600 species, *Cassia*† is the fourth-largest leguminous genus, and many of its species are distinguished by their delicate beauty and floral brilliance. Sometimes known as shower trees, they have striking, fragrant flowers that hang in graceful sprays 30 cm or more long. They occur in various translucent colors in yellow, white, rose, red, or purple, solid or mixed. Most have yellow blossoms—pale primrose to rich gold—but a dozen or more pink-flowered species are much sought after. Several species are already cultivated but deserve wider recognition. Others remain an almost untapped resource of beauty.

The ornamental *Cassia* species are small or medium-size deciduous trees that come from all parts of the tropics. They are adaptable and grow well in a wide range of elevations, soils, temperatures, and rainfalls. (There are species, for example, that withstand temperatures from −5 to 50°C and 200–3,000

Camoensia maxima Welw. ex Benth. & Hook. Subfamily: Papilionoideae.
†Subfamily: Caesalpinioideae.

Luxury timbers. Top: *Afrormosia elata, Dalbergia frutescens, Dalbergia nigra*. Bottom: *Intsia bijuga, Pterocarpus soyauxii, Pterocarpus dalbergioides*. (E. S. Ayensu)

Clockwise from top: *Acacia baileyana*, *Acacia drummondii* (Canberra Botanical Gardens), *Barklya syringifolia* (A. N. Rodd), *Acacia pycnantha* (Canberra Botanical Gardens).

Clockwise from top: *Amherstia nobilis* flower (K. B. Sandved) and pod (V. L. Saplala), *Butea monosperma* (K. B. Sandved), *Afgekia sericea* (Narong Chomchalow).

Clockwise from top left: *Bauhinia kochiana* (Parks and Recreation Department, Singapore), a street of *Bauhinia* trees, Natal, South Africa (S. Eliovson), *Clianthus formosus* (Robin Smith), *Brownea grandiceps* (K. B. Sandved), *Bauhinia blakeana* (N. D. Vietmeyer), *Brownea macrophylla* (C. Clift), *Clianthus puniceus* (Robin Smith), *Bolusanthes speciosus* (P. van Wyk).

Clockwise from top: *Camoensia maxima* (K. B. Sandved), *Cassia spectabilis* (E. S. Ayensu), *Erythrina poeppigiana* (Compania Shell de Venezuela), *Erythrina mildbraedii* (E. S. Ayensu), *Mucuna novo-guineensis* (Parks and Recreation Department, Singapore), *Schotia brachypetala* (P. van Wyk), *Colvillea racemosa* (S. Eliovson).

Clockwise from top: *Peltophorum africanum* (P. van Wyk), *Saraca indica* (N. D. Vietmeyer), *Sophora microphylla* (J. A. Rattenbury), *Strongylodon macrobotrys* (R. J. Seibert).

mm of annual rainfall.) Propagated by seed, most grow rapidly. They bloom in the hot season and for best growth require sunny sites.

In some species, the pods that hang conspicuously from the branches enclose a pulp containing purgative glucosides used as a laxative. Two low, shrubby species produce senna leaves and senna pods that have long been important commercial drugs. The bark of *Cassia* trees often contains much tannin, used by the tanning industry. Some of the species are useful for firewood plantations.

Cassia fistula (the golden shower, or Indian laburnum), *Cassia grandis* (pink shower or horse cassia), *Cassia javanica* (apple-blossom shower), and *Cassia nodosa* (pink-and-white-shower) are now well known throughout the tropics, but some lesser-known species with equal or greater beauty are:

Cassia renigera **Benth.** A small tree of northern Burma, grown in gardens in the Malay Peninsula. Similar to *Cassia nodosa*, but the flowers are more showy and a richer pink.

Cassia agnes **(DeWit) Brenan.*** A pink-blossomed species native to Indochina.

Cassia spectabilis **DC.** A fast-growing tree (to 20 m). Native to central and northern South America. Flowers all year, producing masses of bright-yellow blossoms in giant congested bunches 15–60 cm long. (See color plate.) With its spreading crown, it makes a useful shade tree.

Cassia **hybrids.** Crossbreeding *Cassia* species produces sterile hybrids with flowers sometimes more handsome than those of the parents. Multicolored, they are known as rainbow showers. The *Cassia fistula* x *Cassia nodosa* hybrid is already commercially available in Hawaii. Further crossbreeding is a promising research area for horticulturists.

The species listed above are for humid tropical regions, but *Cassia* species are also among the most attractive shrubs of dry regions of Central Australia. Ornamentals popular around Outback homesteads and worthy of testing in the dry tropics elsewhere include:

Cassia sturtii (see page 124).

Cassia nemophilia **A. Cunn. ex Vogel** (also known as *Cassia eremophila* **A. Cunn. ex R. Br.**) Desert cassia. A small quick-growing, ground-hugging bush, annually bespangled with brilliant yellow blossoms. Very widely distributed in the arid, semiarid, and subhumid regions of inland Australia. Livestock relish the foliage. A weed in some farmlands, it has become a nuisance.

*Often misnamed *Cassia javanica.*

Cassia artemisioides **Gaud, ex DC.** Silver cassia. Seldom more than 1.5 m tall, this bush has silver-gray leaves and golden-yellow flowers. It thrives where rainfall is as low as 200 mm annually and tolerates extended droughts.

Clianthus Species

The genus *Clianthus* contains four species, two of which, *Clianthus formosus* and *Clianthus puniceus*, are striking ornamentals. (See color plate.)

Clianthus formosus (G. Don.) Ford. & Vickery,* Sturt's desert pea or glory pea, has foliage coated with silky, silvery hairs and bright-scarlet flowers with glossy black centers.† A low, sprawling, fast-growing evergreen shrub, the plant occurs wild in poor, sandy soils over a wide area of arid and semiarid Central Australia, including some of the fiercest environments in the world. Yet after a rain its large (up to 8 cm long) flowers light up the barrenness with a spectacular display. This is an ornamental worth testing in subtropical and arid zones elsewhere.‡ It is hardy and withstands 11°C frost. Seeds germinate freely (after scarification) but the plant is difficult to cultivate. It will not tolerate any disturbance to its roots and thus cannot be transplanted, nor does it endure waterlogging; it must always be grown in sand or other completely draining soil. However, for half a century in England it has been standard practice to graft it onto *Colutea arborescens* to provide a most attractive basket plant that lasts for several years. To horticulturists *Clianthus formosus* presents a challenge well worth the effort.

By contrast, *Clianthus puniceus* Banks & Soland, the red parrotsbeak or kakabeak, is cultivated in a range of soils. It is an established ornamental and is native to temperate and subtropical areas of New Zealand. It is a fast-growing, shrub (1-4 m tall), with attractive light-green foliage and flamboyant flowers that hang clustered beneath the branches. The flowers, up to 9 cm long, are cardinal-red, rose-pink, or white. They look like the wide-open beaks of a bird. Considered New Zealand's most attractive shrub, the kakabeak is fairly widely grown in European greenhouses and in California and the southern United States. It is almost unknown in the wild state and is classified as an endangered species.

Colvillea racemosa

A tree for parks and wide roadways, this little-known, showy-flowered tropical tree§ is a worthy rival of its famous close relative, the royal poinciana

---

*Formerly known as *Clianthus dampieri* A. Cunn. Subfamily: Papilionoideae.

†Color forms exist with flowers from almost pure white to pale pink, red, and even purple, many without the black center.

‡Recently introduced in Israel, the plant is performing well unirrigated at Beer-Sheva (200 mm rainfall). Information supplied by M. Forti. See Research Contacts.

§*Colvillea racemosa* Boj ex Hook. Known as Colville's glory. Subfamily: Caesalpinioideae.

or flamboyant tree (*Delonix regia*). Both are natives of Madagascar, and with their half-drooping shape and feathery leaves they look alike when not in bloom. But when the red-and-white blossoms of the flamboyant have faded and gone, *Colvillea racemosa* bursts forth in clusters of burnt-orange flowers that festoon the branches—often a dozen bunches to a limb. The cylindrical racemes can be 20 cm long and look like hanging bunches of orange-colored grapes. (See color plate.) When spent, the blossoms fall, spreading an orange carpet beneath the tree.

This fairly slow-growing tree is cultivated like the flamboyant. It has been cultivated in Hawaii since 1918 and there are a number of mature specimens scattered around southern Florida. Elsewhere, it is not common outside of botanic gardens and fanciers' collections.

Erythrina Species, Coral Trees

Though common in the tropics, *Erythrina* species,* widely known as coral trees, still have much untapped potential as ornamentals. Over 100 species are known, native to North and South America, Australia, Africa, and Asia. Among the most brilliantly flowered of trees, the majority have blood-red or red-and-yellow flowers borne in clusters at the branch tips.

Most coral trees are thorny, though practically thornless types are also known. They are among the easiest of plants to grow; seeds germinate well and the young plants grow vigorously. Sections of stem—even large ones—take root readily and become living, colorful, and long-lasting fence posts.

In some parts of the tropics *Erythrina* species are used to shade plantation crops, especially vines like pepper, betel, and grape that use the tree trunks as support. *Erythrina edulis* has large, soft, succulent seeds that are cooked and eaten in South America, though the raw seeds of many other species are poisonous. Three species in Central America have edible leaves that are added to stews and other cooked dishes.

Within the genus there are unlimited possibilities for hybridization, which may well yield vigorous crosses with exceptional characteristics.

Many *Erythrina* species make worthy ornamentals, though they shed their leaves and may be bare for long periods. A few outstanding examples are:

Erythrina coralloides **A. DC.** One of the showiest of flowering trees, it is known as the naked coral tree because it blooms brilliant red for 2 months before leaves appear. The blossoms stand upright on the branch tips like scarlet candles. The tree easily adapts to most not-too-wet soils in Southern California and similar climates.

*Subfamily: Papilionoideae.

Erythrina caffra **Thunberg.** A commanding sight at any season, its fresh green crown provides an umbrella of shade for 9 months. Then, over the winter and early spring months the leafless tree becomes a canopy of orange-red blossoms. A native of southern Africa, it is now also the official tree of the City of Los Angeles, California.

Erythrina humeana **Spreng.** Spectacular vermilion-flowered shrub from southern Africa (South Africa, Swaziland, Mozambique, and Rhodesia).

Erythrina mildbraedii (*Erythrina senegalensis* **DC**). Senegal coral tree. Native to savannas of West Africa, this easy-to-cultivate, quick-growing, large shrub deserves more widespread use. It flowers profusely (often twice a year) and is a handsome sight, its bare branches covered in red flowers. (See color plate.)

Erythrina speciosa **Andrews.** This small (3–4 m tall) Brazilian tree produces racemes of flowers, like crimson candelabra glowing in the sunlight. Each year these spectacular blossoms enshroud the trees before the leaves form. The plants are easy to propagate; branches stuck in the ground take root and grow vigorously. The species has long been cultivated in Portugal and Madeira.

Erythrina poeppigiana (**Walpers**) **O. F. Cook.** Mountain immortelle, anauca. Native of Andean foothills in Peru and widely grown in highlands of South America and West Indies, as well as in Africa and Malaysia, where it was introduced as shade for coffee and cacao. Reaches 22 m in height. Has dazzling orange flowers. (See color plate.)

Erythrina verna **Vell.** (*Erythrina mulungu* **Mart.**). Mulungu. Deep-red flowers. Trunk surrounded by light-yellow cork that is soft, flexible, and appears to have considerable commercial potential. Native of cerrado regions of South America, where poor soils and extended dry seasons are fatal to most plants.

Lysidice rhodostegia

A medium-size tree from the Canton area, *Lysidice rhodostegia** is one of southern China's most conspicuous flowering trees. The fragrant flowers form spreading clusters that cover the treetop. The petals are violet and the protruding stamens pure white; at the base of the flower are whorls of red and pink leaf-life calyxes and bracts that remain for weeks after the blossoms have faded.

**Lysidice rhodostegia* Hance. Subfamily: Caesalpinioideae.

Propagated from seed, this is still a rare plant outside China. It grows best in humid tropical and subtropical lowlands and has been successfully introduced into Hawaii, Cuba, southern Florida, and Trinidad.

Maniltoa Species

These rare shrubs and trees* are highly recommended for trials as decorative or shade trees. Native to New Guinea, the plants have been cultivated at the Botanic Gardens in Bogor, Indonesia, and Papua New Guinea, but apparently nowhere else.

Maniltoa flowers come clustered in pink or white bulb-shaped heads somewhat like those of *Brownea* species (see page 244) and about 10 cm in diameter. The young leaves are also attractive; they first appear as a pink flush of drooping leaflets that arise from cone-shaped buds.

Moldenhauera floribunda

A relative of the well-known flamboyant tree (*Delonix regia*), *Moldenhauera floribunda*† is one of Brazil's noblest ornamentals. It is native to forests near Rio de Janeiro and São Paulo. During summer months the tree is covered with yellow flowers in dense clusters near the branch tips. Although unknown outside Brazil, this fairly fast-growing tree is recommended for trials in parks and gardens throughout the subtropics and tropics.

Mucuna Species

When in bloom, the woody climbing vines of the genus *Mucuna* are one of the most dramatic sights among all the world's plants. Some bear brilliantly colored flowers in long pendant trusses or in glowing orbs as large as a man's head. However, they have been largely neglected by horticulturists.

Perhaps the most spectacular of these species are:

Mucuna novoguineensis. ‡ A native of New Guinea, which climbs high into the rainforest canopy. Its crimson or orange-scarlet flower clusters can be 60

---

*Maniltoa schefferi K. Schum, *Maniltoa gemmipara* Scheff., and other *Maniltoa* species. Subfamily: Caesalpinioideae.

†*Moldenhauera floribunda* Schard. Subfamily: Caesalpinioideae.

‡*Mucuna novoguineensis* Schaeff. (Often wrongly called *Mucuna bennettii* F. Muell.) Subfamily: Papilionoideae.

cm long, bearing 40 or 50 flowers along the entire length. They make an unforgettable sight as they drape the forest with color.* (See color plate.)

Mucuna brachycarpa **Rech**. A native of Bougainville, has scented, golden-yellow flower clusters up to 30 cm long. At present it is cultivated only in Papua New Guinea; cultivation should be attempted in other parts of the lowland tropics.

Mucuna rostrata Benth. Native to Trinidad, Panama, and northern South America, it has spectacular clusters of yellow flowers.

Peltophorum Species

Closely related to the flamboyant tree, these vigorous umbrella-shaped trees† are among the best choices for producing shade quickly. In addition, they erupt into delightfully fragrant yellow flowers that stand erect in great sprays all over the top of the tree. When fully opened, the flowers have crinkled golden petals and orange-tipped stamens. The display is heightened by the dense green foliage behind it. The examples mentioned below both require well-drained, rather dry soils. Both are recommended for widespread use as shade and ornamental trees. (See color plate.)

Peltophorum africanum **Sond**., African wattle, builbos or huilboom. A deciduous, thornless tree, widely dispersed throughout dry bush country in Angola, South Africa, Botswana, Rhodesia, Mozambique, and Zambia, it grows to 15 m tall and has silvery-gray, acacia-like foliage. When in flower this is one of the most striking of Central African trees. For several spring and early-summer months, it splashes yellow throughout the countryside. The pods are much favored by cattle. The tough heartwood is used for axe handles and other small objects. A good shade tree, this is said to be a perfect avenue tree. It is somewhat frost tolerant. Seeds germinate readily and the trees grow quite fast (about 1.3 m annually for the first 4 years‡).

Peltophorum pterocarpum(DC.) **K. Heyne**, Copperpod, yellow flame or yellow poinciana. A straight-trunked, dense-crowned tree sometimes reaching 50 m. Native to Southeast Asia (from Indochina and the Philippines to the northern tip of Australia). Commonly grown in tropical Africa, Hawaii,

---

*More information on this and other *Mucuna* vines is given in Herklots, 1976, and Menninger, 1970.

†Subfamily: Caesalpinioideae.

‡P. van Wyk. 1972. *Trees of the Kruger National Park*. Purnell and Sons (Pty) Ltd., Cape Town, South Africa.

southern Florida, Central America, and some islands of the West Indies. Good shade, windbreak, or avenue tree with its quick growth and spreading crown. Each year for several weeks in summer the crown is transformed to golden yellow; a few weeks later it has purple-brown pods projecting out all over the tree, making it colorful in a different way. However, it is totally or nearly leafless all winter. Used to shade coffee and cacao plantations. Resistant to wind damage and not attacked by boring beetles. Cattle will eat the leaves. The wood is good for both furniture and fuel. Reportedly, this tree is useful for reclaiming wastelands covered with *Imperata cylindrica.*

Pithecellobium grandiflorum, Lace Flower Tree

A native of warmer parts of Australia's east coast (Queensland and northern New South Wales), this evergreen tree* can reach 15 m tall. Even while a small shrub, it produces its masses of flower clusters (up to 8 cm wide) at every branch tip. The powderpuff blossoms, scented like honeysuckle, have crimson stamens projecting beyond the pale yellow petals.

The light, soft wood is beautifully patterned and polishes well. It is sold under the names marble wood or tortoise shell-tulip wood and is used for indoor paneling or decorative trays and boxes.

Sabinea carinalis

Dominica's finest flowering tree is the shrubby or middle-sized *Sabinea carinalis*,† which produces such a carnival of red blossoms in the spring that it is now popular as an ornamental throughout the entire West Indies.‡

The plant's feathery leaves are shed in winter and it is before they are replaced that the copious clusters of scarlet, butterfly-shaped blossoms appear in bunches along the branches.

Saraca indica, Asoka

Both Hindus and Buddhists revere this small Indian tree.§ To Hindus the asoka is a symbol of love and is used in celebrations dedicated to the god of

---

*Pithecellobium grandiflorum Benth. The lace flower tree. Subfamily: Mimosoideae.

†*Sabinea carinalis* Briseb. Subfamily: Papilionoideae.

‡Menninger. 1962. See Selected Readings.

§*Saraca indica* L. Known as asoka (Sanskrit), askok, or ashok (Hindi), sok (Thailand), soko (Indonesia), or sorrowless tree. Subfamily: Caesalpinioideae.

love. To Buddhists the tree is sacred because Gautama Buddha himself is believed to have been born beneath its shade. Consequently, the flowers are much used for temple decoration. They are especially appealing at night, when they exude a delicate scent.

The flowers spring in great profusion directly from the trunk, branches, and twigs in small, compact clusters. Initially yellow, they deepen through orange to red. (See color plate.)

The leaves, like those of *Amherstia* and *Brownea* (see above), first hang in limp, grayish-pink or purplish-red tassels, but soon stiffen and turn green. The pods are purple.

Common in gardens all over India, particularly near temples, the asoka thrives best in sheltered, shady sites, especially near water, in wet or monsoonal lowlands (below 500 m).

There are some 20 other species in the genus *Saraca*. Throughout the year they are spectacular and have been called "glittering ornaments of the moist forests of Asia," but are little known elsewhere. Frequently, especially after short spells of dry weather, new, brightly colored leaves emerge in limp, dangling tassels ("angel's handkerchiefs") that paint the tree pink or purple for several days before stiffening and turning green. At other seasons (often twice a year) the brilliantly colored bunches of fragrant flowers change the trees to red or yellow. In turn, they give way to large, colored (often purple), pods. Three splendid examples are:

Saraca thaipingensis **Cantley**. Yellow saraca. A native of Taiping, Malaysia, this small (6 m tall) tree produces a profusion of flowers that open yellow, change to apricot-yellow and, finally, to deep yellow with a blood-red eye.

Saraca declinata **Miq**. The red saraca of Malaysia, Thailand, and Indonesia. A beautiful sight with its huge heads of flowers that change from yellow to brick red. The pods are bright red.

Saraca palembanica **(Miq.) Baker**. Pink saraca, a native of Indonesia now found also in Malaysia. The light-yellow flowers darken to orange, then—at least in some types—to deep red.

Schotia brachypetala, Fuchsia Tree

Essentially a bushveld plant, the shapely and beautiful fuchsia tree* is native to Rhodesia, Mozambique, South Africa, Swaziland, Botswana, and South West Africa. Although a popular ornamental in this region and in the French and Italian Rivieras, it is little known elsewhere. A small tree (height

Schotia brachypetala Sond. Also known as huilboerboon, boerboon. Subfamily: Caesalpinioideae.

to 12 m, trunk to 18 cm diameter) with a spreading crown and drooping branch tips, the fuchsia tree in bloom is a memorable sight. Just before flowering, most of its leaves fall; then dense clusters of deep-red tubular flowers appear. With their long, protruding red stamens, they resemble fuchsia flowers. (See color plate.) Nectar showers down when a branch is shaken. The new foliage also has great beauty. As the leaf buds form and open the tree takes on shades of rose, ruby-red, and copper, gradually ending up a fresh, light-green color. The seeds are much infested by insects, but those that escape germinate readily. This plant usually grows slowly, but transplants easily. It is frost sensitive.

Sophora Species, Kowhais

New Zealand's most popular small tree—and its unofficial national flower—the kowhai, *Sophora microphylla* Ait.,* is widely planted in parks and gardens. In the spring, usually before the leaves are formed, the tree blooms in profusion; sulfur-yellow blossoms hang in clusters, turning the tree to a mass of gold. (See color plate.)

Reaching to 10 m tall or more, this graceful, often weeping tree is found all over New Zealand (as well as in Chile) and deserves to be better known in warm temperate and subtropical areas elsewhere.

Some near-relatives also make fine ornamental trees. All produce trumpet-like flowers varying from pale yellow to deep gold. *Sophora tetraptera* J. Miller, also called kowhai, grows in eastern sections of New Zealand's North Island.†

Related North American species with promise as ornamentals for arid regions are *Sophora secundiflora* (Ort.) DC. and *Sophora gypsophila* Turner & Powell. Both have attractive foliage and bear masses of fragrant purple flowers. *Sophora secundiflora*, the mescal bean, is already widely used as an ornamental in the arid southwest of the United States.

Strongylodon macrobotrys, Jade Vine

Commonly called the jade vine, this vigorous perennial climber‡ with its thick, twisted, rope-like stems is native to the Philippines and is found spreading over the canopy of high trees in damp ravines and forests. Its flowers are

*Subfamily: Papilionoideae.

†Godley, E.J. 1975. Kowhais. *New Zealand Native Heritage* 5(65):1804-1806. Copies available from author, see Research Contacts.

‡*Strongylodon macrobotrys* A. Gray. Subfamily: Papilionoideae. This section is mainly based on Steiner, M.J. 1959. The Philippine jadevine. *National Horticultural Magazine* (Philippines) 38:42-45.

large (6-8 cm long) and crescent shaped and occur in long pendant trusses. Up to 1 m long, these clusters are sometimes packed with almost 100 flowers. Their color is most unusual: a luminous, jade-like, bluish-green. Flowering often continues year-round in the Philippines. Each inflorescence stays in flower 3-4 weeks. The falling blossoms produce thick aqua-blue carpets on the ground. (See color plate.)

The leaves are reddish when young and dark green and glossy when mature. Pods are about the size of a child's head. The plant is best propagated by seed, though the seed does not remain viable for long. Flowers are not produced until 3 years after planting.

Although formerly this plant could be admired only in the Philippines, in recent years it has been cultivated in botanic gardens in Papua New Guinea, Indonesia, Singapore, and even in a greenhouse at Kew Gardens in England.

The Philippine jade vine is only one of 20 *Strongylodon* species that are found from Madagascar to Northern Australia and the Philippines (which boasts 10 species). The others are even less well known, and yet they also appear to be promising ornamentals. *Strongylodon lucidus* has coral-red flowers and occurs from Hawaii to Ceylon; *Strongylodon caeruleus*, with bluish-purple flowers, is being grown at the College of Forestry Nursery, Los Baños, Philippines.

Selected Readings

Ornamental Horticulture Abstracts. A new monthly journal describing the latest research concerning annual and herbaceous ornamentals, bulbs and tubers, lawns and sport turf, aquatic plants, foliage and house plants, and ornamental trees and shrubs. Annual subscription, 12 issues, $36.00. Published by Commonwealth Agricultural Bureaux, London. Available through the United Nations from UNIPUB, Box 433, Murray Hill Station, New York, New York 10016, USA.

Blatter, E., and W. S. Millard. 1954. *Some Beautiful Indian Trees*, 2nd ed. (rev. W. T. Stern). Bombay Natural History Society, Bombay, India.

Bor, N. L., and M. B. Raizada. n.d. *Some Beautiful Indian Climbers and Shrubs.* Bombay Natural History Society, Bombay, India.

Eliovsen, S. 1975. *Shrubs, Trees and Climbers.* Macmillan South Africa (Publishers), Johannesburg. 269 pp.

Esteva, F. O. 1969. *Arboles Ornamentales y Otras Plantas del Tropico.* Ediciones Armitano, Caracas, Venezuela.

Herklots, G. 1976. *Flowering Tropical Climbers.* Dawson Science History Publications, Folkestone, Kent, England.

Karschon, R., and G. Schiller. 1976. Forest trees as ameliorators of heat stress of man in a Mediterranean environment. In *Trees and Forests for Human Settlements*, pp. 382-387. Centre for Urban Forestry Studies, University of Toronto, 203 College Street, Toronto, Ontario, Canada M5S 1A1.

Menninger, E. A. 1962. *Flowering Trees of the World for Tropics and Warm Climates.* Hearthside Press, Inc., New York. 336 pp.

Menninger, E. A. 1970. *Flowering Vines of the World.* Hearthside Press, Inc., New York. 410 pp.

Morton, J.F. 1971. *Exotic Plants.* Golden Press, Western Publishing Co., New York. 160 pp. [1973. *Plantes Exotiques.* Editions des Deux Coqs d'Or, Paris (in French). 1977. *Tropisch Bloemen.* Delphin Verlag, Stuttgart and Zurich (in German).]

Pertchik, B., and H. Pertchik. 1951. *Flowering Trees of the Caribbean.* Rinehart and Company, New York. 125 pp.

Schiller, G., and R. Karschon. 1974. Microclimate and recreational value of tree plantings in deserts. *Landscape Planning* 1:329-337.

Research Contacts

Many of the species in this chapter have been introduced to botanic gardens and nurseries throughout the tropics; readers wishing to obtain seed should first check locally. If this is unsuccessful, botanic gardens and commercial nurseries in the species' country of origin may be able to help. Addresses can usually be obtained through the appropriate embassy or consulate. Some institutions and research scientists with knowledge of the plants are listed below.

Acacia Species

Many commercial seed suppliers in Australia's mainland states can supply germ plasm for these, also specialty seedsmen in California.

D. B. Amatya, Forest Research Officer, Forest Survey and Research Office, Department of Forestry, Babar Mahal, Kathmandu, Nepal

Botanic Gardens, George St., Brisbane, Queensland, Australia (H. Caulfield, Curator)

Canberra Botanic Gardens, City Parks Administration, P.O. Box 158, Canberra City, A.C.T. 2601, Australia (John Wrigley, Curator)

John C. Doran, Seeds Section, Division of Forest Research, CSIRO, P.O. Box 4008, Canberra, A.C.T. 2600, Australia

Harold L. Lyon Arboretum, University of Hawaii at Manoa, 3860 Manoa Road, Honolulu, Hawaii 96822, USA (*A. podalyriifolia*)

P. K. Karani, Chief Research Officer, Ministry of Agriculture and Forestry, Forest Department, P.O. Box 31, Entebbe, Uganda

Hua Seng Lee, Silviculturist, Forest Department Headquarters, Badruddin Road, Kuching, Sarawak, Malaysia

Longwood Gardens, Kennett Square, Pennsylvania 19348, USA

Los Angeles State and County Arboretum, Arcadia, California 91006, USA (*A. podalyriifolia*)

A. W. Owadally, Conservator of Forests, Ministry of Agriculture, and Natural Resources, and the Environment, Forestry Service, Curepipe, Mauritius

Afgekia sericea

Botanical Gardens, Parks and Recreation Department, Cluny Road, Singapore 10, Singapore

C. Chermserivathana, Botanical Section, Department of Agriculture, Bang Khen, Bangkok 9, Thailand

Narong Chomchalow, Applied Scientific Research Corporation of Thailand, 196 Pahalyothin Road, Bang Khen, Bangkok 9, Thailand

Swat Nicharat, Chief, Botany Section, Silvicultural Division, Royal Forest Department, Bangkok 9, Thailand

Amherstia nobilis

Botanic Gardens, Lae, Papua New Guinea
Herbarium Bradeanum, Caixa Postal 15.005–ZC-06, 20.000 Rio de Janeiro, RJ, Brazil
   (G. F. J. Pabst, Director)
Indian Botanic Gardens, Botanical Survey of India, P.O. Botanic Gardens, Howrah, W.
   Bengal, India
A. H. M. Jayasuriya, Research Officer, National Herbarium, Peradeniya, Sri Lanka
V. L. Saplala, Green and Grow, Inc., Pansol, Calamba, Laguna, Philippines
H. Valmayor, Department of Horticulture, College of Agriculture, University of the
   Philippines at Los Baños, College, Laguna, Philippines

Barklya syringifolia

Botanic Gardens, George St., Brisbane, Queensland, Australia (H. Caulfield, Curator)
S. L. Everist, 13 Sunset Avenue, Bongaree, Bribie Island 4507, Queensland, Australia
Society for Growing Australian Plants, P.O. Box 809, Fortitude Valley, Queensland
   4006, Australia (Lorna Murray, Secretary)

Bauhinia Species

D. B. Amatya, Forest Research Officer, Forest Survey and Research Office, Department
   of Forestry, Babar Mahal, Kathmandu, Nepal
Botanical Gardens, Parks and Recreation Department, Cluny Road, Singapore 10, Singa-
   pore
Director of Agriculture and Fisheries, Canton Road Government Offices, 393 Canton
   Road, 12th Floor, Kowloon, Hong Kong (*B. blakeana*)
Harold L. Lyon Arboretum, University of Hawaii at Manoa, 3860 Manoa Road, Hono-
   lulu, Hawaii 96822, USA
Herbario Alberto Castellanos, Departamento de Conservacão Ambiental–FEEMA, C.P.
   23011 ZC-08, 20.000 Rio de Janerio, RJ, Brazil
A. H. M. Jayasuriya, Research Officer, National Herbarium, Peradeniya, Sri Lanka
Hua Seng Lee, Silviculturist, Forest Department Headquarters, Badruddin Road, Ku-
   ching, Sarawak, Malaysia
Mayaguez Institute of Tropical Agriculture, P.O. Box 70, Mayaguez, Puerto Rico 00708
A. W. Owadally, Conservator of Forests, Ministry of Agriculture, Natural Resources, and
   the Environment, Forestry Service, Curepipe, Mauritius
V. L. Saplala, Green and Grow, Inc., Pansol, Calamba, Laguna, Philippines
United States Department of Agriculture, Subtropical Horticulture Research Unit,
   13601 Old Cutler Road, Miami, Florida 33158, USA (P. Soderholm)

Bolusanthus speciosus

Longwood Gardens, Kennett Square, Pennsylvania 19348, USA
Ministry of Agriculture, Department of Research and Specialist Services, Branch of
   Botany, Herbarium and Botanic Gardens, P.O. Box 8100, Causeway, Salisbury,
   Zimbabwe-Rhodesia
National Botanic Gardens of South Africa, Kirstenbosch Botanic Garden, Private Bag
   X7, Claremont 7735, South Africa

Brownea Species

B. grandiceps

Assistant Conservator of Forests (Silviculture and Research), Forest Department, P.O.
   Box 1017, Kingston, Georgetown, Guyana

Fairchild Tropical Garden, 10901 Old Cutler Road, Miami, Florida 33156, USA
Harold L. Lyon Arboretum, University of Hawaii at Manoa, 3860 Manoa Road, Honolulu, Hawaii 96822, USA
A. H. M. Jayasuriya, Research Officer, National Herbarium, Peradeniya, Sri Lanka
Mayaguez Institute of Tropical Agriculture, P.O. Box 70, Mayaguez, Puerto Rico 00708
A. W. Owadally, Conservator of Forests, Ministry of Agriculture, and Natural Resources, and the Environment, Forestry Service, Curepipe, Mauritius
P. Byrne, Assistant Secretary—Horticulture, Department of Primary Industry, P.O. Box 2417, Konedobu, Papua New Guinea
Andree Millar, Director, National Capital Botanic Gardens, 4677 University P.O., Port Moresby, Papua New Guinea

B. macrophylla

Fairchild Tropical Garden, 10901 Old Cutler Road, Miami, Florida 33156, USA
Instituto de Ciencias Naturales de la Universidad Nacional, Apartado Aereo 7495, Bogota, Colombia
A. H. M. Jayasuriya, Research Officer, National Herbarium, Peradeniya, Sri Lanka
Longwood Gardens, Kennett Square, Pennsylvania 19348, USA

B. capitella

Forestry Division, Long Circular Road, St. James, Port-of-Spain, Trinidad, West Indies (S. Faizool, Assistant Conservator of Forests)

Butea monosperma

D. B. Amatya, Forest Research Officer, Forest Survey and Research Office, Department of Forestry, Babar Mahal, Kathmandu, Nepal
Department of Botany, University of Calcutta, 35, Ballygunge Circular Road, Calcutta—700 019, India
Indian Botanic Gardens, Botanical Survey of India, P.O. Botanic Gardens, Howrah, W. Bengal, India
National Botanic Gardens, Rana Pratap Marg, Lucknow, India
A. W. Owadally, Conservator of Forests, Ministry of Agriculture, and Natural Resources, and the Environment, Forestry Service, Curepipe, Mauritius
United States Department of Agriculture, Subtropical Horticulture Research Unit, 13601 Old Cutler Road, Miami, Florida 33158, USA (P. Soderholm)

Camoensia maxima

Botanical Gardens, Parks and Recreation Department, Cluny Road, Singapore 10, Singapore
Forestry Division, Long Circular Road, St. James Port-of-Spain, Trinidad, West Indies (S. Faizool, Assistant Conservator of Forests)
Hope Botanic Gardens, Kingston 6, Jamaica
A. H. M. Jayasuriya, Research Officer, National Herbarium, Peradeniya, Sri Lanka
Longwood Gardens, Kennett Square, Pennsylvania 19348, USA
Royal Botanic Gardens, Kew, Richmond, Surrey TW9 3AE, England

Cassia Species

The following contacts are knowledgeable about various ornamental *Cassia* species.
Agricultural Experiment Station Botanical Garden, Rio Piedras, Puerto Rico 00928
D. B. Amatya, Forest Research Officer, Forest Survey and Research Office, Department of Forestry, Babar Mahal, Kathmandu, Nepal

Assistant Conservator of Forests, Silviculture and Research, Forest Department, P.O. Box 1017, Kingston, Georgetown, Guyana

P. Byrne, Assistant Secretary–Horticulture, Department of Primary Industry, P.O. Box 2417, Konedobu, Papua New Guinea

Charleville Pastoral Laboratory, Charleville 4470, Queensland, Australia (*C. sturtii, C. nemophila,* and *C. artemisoides*)

Department of Botany, University of Calcutta, 35, Ballygunge Circular Road, Calcutta 700 019, India

Desert Botanical Garden, P.O. Box 5415, Phoenix, Arizona 85010, USA (*C. artemisoides, C. nemophilia,* and *C. sturtii*)

Herbario Alberto Castellanos, Departamento de Conservacão Ambiental–FEEMA, C.P. 23011 ZC-08, 20.000 Rio de Janeiro, RJ, Brazil

Herbarium of the Northern Territory, Animal Industry and Agriculture Branch, Department of the Northern Territory, Alice Springs, N.T. 5750, Australia (*C. sturtii, C. nemophilia,* and *C. artemisoides*)

I.B.D.F. Jardim Botanico do Rio de Janeiro, Rua Jardim Botanico 1008, 20.000 Rio de Janeiro, ZC-20, GB, Brazil

Indian Botanic Gardens, Botanical Survey of India, P.O. Botanic Gardens, Howrah, W. Bengal, India

A. H. M. Jayasuriya, Research Officer, National Herbarium, Peradeniya, Sri Lanka

Hua Seng Lee, Silviculturist, Forest Department Headquarters, Badruddin Road, Kuching, Sarawak, Malaysia

Los Angeles State and County Arboretum, Arcadia, California 91006, USA

Andree Millar, Director, National Capital Botanic Gardens, 4677 University P.O., Port Moresby, Papua New Guinea

Ministry of Agriculture, Department of Research and Specialist Services, Branch of Botany, Herbarium and Botanic Garden, P.O. Box 8100, Causeway, Salisbury, Zimbabwe-Rhodesia

A. W. Owadally, Conservator of Forests, Ministry of Agriculture, and Natural Resources, and the Environment, Forestry Service, Curepipe, Mauritius

Ray A. Perry, Chief, Division of Land Resources Management, CSIRO, Private Bag, P.O. Wembley, W.A. 6014, Australia

Carlos M. García, Head, Forest Planning Office, Department of Natural Resources, Box 5887, Puerto de Tierra, Puerto Rico 00906

V. L. Saplala, Green and Grow, Inc., Pansol, Calamba, Laguna, Philippines

K. Vivekanandan, Office of the Conservator of Forests, P.O. Box 509, Colombo 2, Sri Lanka

Clianthus Species

Many commercial nurseries in Australia and New Zealand sell seed of Sturt's desert pea and kakabeak, respectively. Listed below are botanists and horticulturists actively engaged in research on these species.

Sturt's Desert Pea

Arthur B. Court, Registrar of Australian Cultivars, Canberra Botanic Gardens, P.O. Box 158, Canberra City, A.C.T. 2601, Australia

M. Forti, Research and Development Authority, Ben-Gurion University of the Negev, P.O. Box 1025, Beer-Sheva, Israel

Longwood Gardens, Kennett Square, Pennsylvania 19348, USA

T. R. N. Lothian, Director, Botanic Garden, North Terrace, Adelaide, South Australia 5000, Australia

West Australian Wildflower Society (Inc.), P.O. Box 64, Nedlands, Western Australia 6009, Australia

John Wrigley, Curator, Canberra Botanic Gardens, P.O. Box 158, Canberra City, A.C.T. 2601, Australia

New Zealand Kakabeak

E. J. Godley, Director, Botany Division, Department of Scientific and Industrial Research, Private Bag, Christchurch, New Zealand
Otari Native Plant Museum, Wellington City Corporation, Parks Department, P.O. Box 2199, Wellington, New Zealand

Colvillea racemosa

Fairchild Tropical Garden, 10901 Old Cutler Road, Miami, Florida 33156, USA
Forestry Division, Long Circular Road, St. James Port-of-Spain, Trinidad, West Indies
A. W. Owadally, Conservator of Forests, Ministry of Agriculture, and Natural Resources, and the Environment, Forestry Service, Curepipe, Mauritius

Erythrina

The following contacts have experience with growing various ornamental *Erythrina* species.
Assistant Conservator of Forests (Silviculture and Research), Forest Department, P.O. Box 1017, Kingston, Georgetown, Guyana
Botanic Gardens, George St., Brisbane, Queensland, Australia (H. Caulfield, Curator)
Harold L. Lyon Arboretum, University of Hawaii at Manoa, 3860 Manoa Road, Honolulu, Hawaii 96822, USA
Herbarium, Department of Biology, P.O. Box 4820, University, Papua New Guinea
Herbario Alberto Castellanos, Departamento de Conservacão Ambiental–FEEMA, C.P. 23011 ZC-08, 20.000 Rio de Janeiro, RJ, Brazil
I.B.D.F., Jardim Botanico do Rio de Janeiro, Rua Jardim Botanico 1008, 20.000 Rio de Janeiro, ZC-20, GB, Brazil
A. H. M. Jayasuriya, Research Officer, National Herbarium, Peradeniya, Sri Lanka
N. Lackhan, Director, Northern Range Reafforestation Project, St. Joseph Farm, St. Joseph, Trinidad, West Indies
Hua Seng Lee, Silviculturist, Forest Department Headquarters, Badruddin Road, Kuching, Sarawak, Malaysia
Andree Millar, Director, National Capital Botanic Gardens, 4677 University P.O., Port Moresby, Papua New Guinea
Ministry of Agriculture, Department of Research and Specialist Services, Branch of Botany, National Herbarium and National Botanic Garden, P.O. Box 8100, Causeway, Salisbury, Zimbabwe-Rhodesia
National Botanic Gardens, Rana Pratap Marg, Lucknow, India
National Botanic Gardens of South Africa, Kirstenbosch Botanic Garden, Private Bag X7, Claremont 7735, South Africa
K. Williams, Waimea Arboretum, Waimea, Oahu, Hawaii 96796, USA
A. W. Owadally, Conservator of Forests, Ministry of Agriculture, and Natural Resources, and the Environment, Forestry Service, Curepipe, Mauritius
Pacific Tropical Botanical Garden, P.O. Box 340, Lawai, Kauai, Hawaii 96765, USA (N. L. Theobald, Director)
Peter H. Raven, Missouri Botanical Garden, 2315 Tower Grove Ave., St. Louis, Missouri 63110, USA

Lysidice rhodostegia

Director of Agriculture and Fisheries, Canton Road Government Offices, 393 Canton Road, 12th Floor, Kowloon, Hong Kong
Harold L. Lyon Arboretum, University of Hawaii at Manoa, 3860 Manoa Road, Honolulu, Hawaii 96822, USA
A. H. M. Jayasuriya, Research Officer, National Herbarium, Peradeniya, Sri Lanka
Longwood Gardens, Kennett Square, Pennsylvania 19348, USA

Maniltoa Species

Kebun Raya Bogor, P.O. Box 110, Bogor, Indonesia (Didin Sastrapradja, Director)
Andree Millar, Director, National Capital Botanic Gardens, 4677 University, P.O., Port
    Moresby, Papua New Guinea
P. Byrne, Assistant Secretary–Horticulture, Department of Primary Industry, P.O. Box
    2417, Konedobu, Papua New Guinea

Moldenhauera floribunda

Herbarium Bradeanum, Caixa Postal 15.005–ZC-06, 20.000 Rio de Janeiro, RJ, Brazil
    (G. F. J. Pabst, Director)

Mucuna Species

Botanic Gardens, Lae, Papua New Guinea
P. Byrne, Assistant Secretary–Horticulture, Department of Primary Industry, P.O. Box
    2417, Konedobu, Papua New Guinea
G. A. C. Herklots, Vanners, Chobham, Woking, Surrey GU24 8SJ, England
A. H. M. Jayasuriya, Research Officer, National Herbarium, Peradeniya, Sri Lanka
Longwood Gardens, Kennett Square, Pennsylvania 19348, USA (*Mucuna rostrata*)
Andree Millar, Director, National Capital Botanic Gardens, 4677 University P.O., Port
    Moresby, Papua New Guinea
National Herbarium of Trinidad and Tobago, Department of Biological Sciences, Uni-
    versity of the West Indies, St. Augustine, Trinidad, West Indies (*Mucuna rostrata*)
A. W. Owadally, Conservator of Forests, Ministry of Agriculture, and Natural Resources,
    and the Environment, Forestry Service, Curepipe, Mauritius
V. L. Saplala, Green and Grow, Inc., Pansol, Calamba, Laguna, Philippines
Bernard Verdcourt, Royal Botanic Gardens, Kew, Surrey, Richmond TW9 3AE, Eng-
    land (*Mucuna* taxonomy)

Peltophorum Species

P. africanum

Director, Botanical Research Institute, Private Bag X101, Pretoria 0001, South Africa
Harold L. Lyon Arboretum, University of Hawaii at Manoa, 3860 Manoa Road, Hono-
    lulu, Hawaii 96822, USA
Los Angeles State and County Arboretum, Arcadia, California 91006, USA
Ministry of Agriculture, Department of Research and Specialist Services, Branch of
    Botany, National Herbarium and National Botanic Garden, P.O. Box 8100, Causeway,
    Salisbury, Zimbabwe-Rhodesia
National Botanic Gardens of South Africa, Kirstenbosch Botanic Garden, Private Bag
    X7, Claremont 7735, South Africa
A. W. Owadally, Conservator of Forests, Ministry of Agriculture, and Natural Resources,
    and the Environment, Forestry Service, Curepipe, Mauritius
P. van Wyk, Chief Research Officer, Kruger National Park, Skukuza, South Africa

P. pterocarpum

Hua Seng Lee, Silviculturist, Forest Department Headquarters, Badruddin Road, Ku-
    ching, Sarawak, Malaysia
Andree Millar, Director, National Capital Botanic Gardens, 4677 University P.O., Port
    Moresby, Papua New Guinea
National Botanic Gardens, Rana Pratap Marg, Lucknow, India
F. S. P. Ng, Senior Forest Botanist, Forest Research Institute, Kepong, Selangor,
    Malaysia

Philippine National Herbarium, National Museum, Manila, Philippines
Carlos M. García, Head, Forest Planning Office, Department of Natural Resources, Box 5887, Puerto de Tierra, Puerto Rico 00906
V. L. Saplala, Green and Grow, Inc., Pansol, Calamba, Laguna, Philippines
K. Vivekanandan, Research Officer (Silviculture), Office of the Conservator of Forests, P.O. Box 509, Colombo 2, Sri Lanka

Pithecellobium grandiflorum

Botanic Gardens, George St., Brisbane, Queensland, Australia (H. Caulfield, Curator)
Selwyn L. Everist, 13 Sunset Avenue, Bongaree, Bribie Island 4507, Queensland, Australia

Sabinea carinalis

Assistant Conservator of Forests (Silviculture and Research) Forest Department, P.O. Box 1017, Kingston, Georgetown, Guyana
Botanic Gardens, St. George's, Grenada, West Indies
Division of Agriculture, Government Headquarters, Roseau, Dominica, West Indies
Forestry Division, Botanic Gardens, Roseau, Dominica, West Indies (C.C. Maximea, Chief Forestry Officer)
Hope Botanic Gardens, Kingston 6, Jamaica

Saraca Species

D. B. Amatya, Forest Research Officer, Forest Survey and Research Office, Department of Forestry, Babar Mahal, Kathmandu, Nepal
Fairchild Tropical Garden, 10901 Old Cutler Road, Miami, Florida 33156, USA
Harold L. Lyon Arboretum, University of Hawaii at Manoa, 3860 Manoa Road, Honolulu, Hawaii 96822, USA
A. H. M. Jayasuriya, Research Officer, National Herbarium, Peradeniya, Sri Lanka
Kebun Raya Bogor, P.O. Box 110, Bogor, Indonesia (Didin S. Sastrapradja, Director)
Swat Nicharat, Chief, Botany Section, Silvicultural Division, Royal Forest Department, Bangkok 9, Thailand
V. L. Saplala, Green and Grow, Inc., Pansol, Calamba, Laguna, Philippines
H. Valmayor, Department of Horticulture, College of Agriculture, University of the Philippines at Los Baños, College, Laguna, Philippines

Schotia brachypetala

Director, Botanical Research Institute, Private Bag X101, Pretoria 0001, South Africa
Los Angeles State and County Arboretum, Arcadia, California 91006, USA
Ministry of Agriculture, Department of Research and Specialist Services, Branch of Botany, National Herbarium and National Botanic Garden, P.O. Box 8100, Causeway, Salisbury, Zimbabwe-Rhodesia
National Botanic Gardens of South Africa, Kirstenbosch Botanic Garden, Private Bag X7, Claremont 7735, South Africa
United States Department of Agriculture, Subtropical Horticulture Research Unit, 13601 Old Cutler Road, Miami, Florida 33158, USA (P. K. Soderholm)
P. van Wyk, Chief Research Officer, Kruger National Park, Skukuza, South Africa

Sophora Species

E. J. Godley, Director, Botany Division, Department of Scientific and Industrial Research, Private Bag, Christchurch, New Zealand

Harold L. Lyon Arboretum, University of Hawaii at Manoa, 3860 Manoa Road, Honolulu, Hawaii 96822, USA
Otari Native Plant Museum, Wellington City Corporation, Parks Department, P.O. Box 2199, Wellington, New Zealand
David Northington, Department of Biological Sciences, Texas Tech University, Lubbock, Texas 79409, USA
A. W. Owadally, Conservator of Forests, Ministry of Agriculture, and Natural Resources, and the Environment, Forestry Service, Curepipe, Mauritius
J. A. Rattenbury, Associate Professor, Department of Botany, The University of Auckland, Private Bag, Auckland, New Zealand

Strongylodon macrobotrys

Botanic Gardens, Lae, Papua New Guinea
Botanical Gardens, Parks and Recreation Department, Cluny Road, Singapore 10, Singapore
Department of Horticulture, University of the Philippines at Los Baños, College, Laguna, Philippines (H. Valmayor)
Harold L. Lyon Arboretum, University of Hawaii at Manoa, 3860 Manoa Road, Honolulu, Hawaii 96822, USA
Kebun Raya Bogor, P.O. Box 110, Bogor, Indonesia (Didin Sastrapradja, Director)
Longwood Gardens, Kennett Square, Pennsylvania 19348, USA
A. W. Owadally, Conservator of Forests, Ministry of Agriculture, and Natural Resources, and the Environment, Forestry Service, Curepipe, Mauritius
Pacific Tropical Botanical Garden, Box 340, Lawai, Kauai, Hawaii 96765
Philippine National Herbarium, National Museum, Manila, Philippines
R. M. Polhill, Royal Botanic Gardens, Kew, Surrey, Richmond TW9 3AE, England
V. L. Saplala, Green and Grow, Inc., Pansol, Calamba, Laguna, Philippines

Sunnhemp

Cultivated in India since ancient times, sunnhemp* remains second only to jute as the Subcontinent's source of bast fiber. Traditionally, sunnhemp has been considered a good fiber for the manufacture of twine and cord, canvas,

---

Crotalaria juncea L. Also known as sannhemp, Indian hemp, Madras hemp. Subfamily: Papilionoideae.

Mature sunnhemp growing at Texas A & M University, College Station, Texas, USA. (United States Department of Agriculture)

fishing nets, mats, rugs, and sacks. But recent research has demonstrated its potential for pulp and paper. The bast fiber shows good pulping characteristics, yielding a pulp that appears suitable for a wide range of uses. Used in paper, it imparts high strength as well as scuff and tear resistance.*

Because it is a legume that nodulates freely, sunnhemp grows on poor soils and requires little or no nitrogen fertilizer. Some strains can be grown in soils infested with root-knot nematodes that may destroy similar bast fiber crops such as kenaf, ramie, and roselle.

Each year about 130,000 tons of sunnhemp fiber are produced (mainly in India, Pakistan, Brazil, and Bangladesh), much of it for export to Europe or the United States. However, there has never been any significant plant breeding done on sunnhemp. Germ plasm has not been collected and varieties with predictable qualities are not available; consequently, yields remain low compared with kenaf, a nonlegume competitor for which cultivars exist. Yet

*For information on the papermaking potential of *Sesbania bispinosa,* a similar, and even less well known leguminous annual, see page 287.

Manually separating sunnhemp fibers, northern India. (Sunnhemp Research Station, Pratapgarh, Uttar Pradesh, India)

sunnhemp is a crop that deserves research attention, not only to benefit the countries and farmers that now produce it, but also to enable its cultivation to expand into new regions.

Sunnhemp is normally a shrubby, many-branched plant, but when it is grown in dense stands it has a single spindly stem that can be 3 m tall. It is an annual that grows vigorous lateral roots and a long taproot that exploits subterranean moisture, conferring some drought resistance on the plant. On rootlets near the soil surface are produced many nodules that are well branched and up to 2.5 cm in diameter. Although adapted to a hot climate, the plant will endure slight frost.

To obtain the fiber for cordage or textiles, the plants are traditionally processed in the same way as jute. Bundles of freshly harvested stems (with the roots and tops cut off) are soaked in water for a week. During this time, microorganisms decompose much of the soft tissue (a process called retting). The bark can then be peeled away and, by repeated beating and washing, the fibers separated from it.

Sunnhemp textile fiber is whitish-gray or yellow and comes in hanks 1-2 m long. The fiber is reported to be more durable than jute and to have a greater tensile strength. The strength increases when wet and the fiber resists degradation caused by moisture, mildew, and saltwater.

The cleaned cordage fiber represents about 8 percent of the weight of the dried stem. Yields of 300-900 kg of dry fiber per ha are average, but researchers in Brazil have obtained dry-fiber yields of 2,000 kg per ha.*

*Information supplied by A.L. de Barros Salgado. See Research Contacts.

Decorticating sunnhemp in Brazil. (Instituto Agronômico, Campinas, Brazil)

The high cellulose (45–60 percent) and low ash content of sunnhemp fiber has long made it a choice for cigarette and high-grade tissue paper. The fiber is soft and only slightly lignified; it pulps readily and in high yield (53–54 percent by the sulfate process). Individual papermaking fibers are 3.4–8 mm long and 13–50 μ wide (lumen width 7–8 μ), with cell walls 6–7 μ thick. For large-scale pulp and paper manufacture, the plant can be machine harvested and the whole stalk (containing both bast fiber and shorter wood fiber) can be pulped. The pulp has bursting and tearing strengths similar to those of commercial mixed hardwood pulp, but it has considerably higher folding endurance.*

Sunnhemp is easy to grow. It thrives on almost any type of soil that is not waterlogged. It is easily established from seed. The seedlings appear above ground in about 3 days and rapidly produce a thick ground cover that smothers competing weeds. After planting, no care is needed until harvest time. The complete mechanization of the culture and harvesting offers no difficulties.

When the seeds are planted inoculation is unnecessary; cowpea-type rhizobia that nodulate sunnhemp are present in most soils. The roots nodulate freely and, given adequate phosphate, one hectare of sunnhemp can add up to 300 kg of nitrogen to the soil.† For this reason the plant is a valuable soil builder, used even more widely as a green manure than a fiber crop. As manure, the plants are plowed into the soil when 2–2½ months old (they decompose more rapidly at this young age). Green matter yields of 18–27 t

*Cunningham *et al.* 1978.
†Rao and Sadasivaiah. 1968.

per ha are average. In many parts of the tropics sunnhemp is grown in rotation with rice, maize, tobacco, cotton, and other crops and it is also sometimes grown together with sugarcane, pineapples, and coffee or used as a cover crop in plantations and fruit orchards.

Limitations

The lack of both a systematic germ plasm collection and of a classification of lines is the major limitation to the spread and more intensive utilization of sunnhemp.

Partly due to the lack of cultivars, the growth of a stand of sunnhemp is often not uniform, which contributes to low yield and weed competition. But even the best plants now available yield less than competing crops such as kenaf.

Available sunnhemp strains have a tendency to bend and break (lodge) when the plants get tall. This complicates harvesting.

Although the plant grows vigorously in almost any soil, in heavy clays the fiber produced is coarse and its yield low. As a fiber crop sunnhemp should be grown on light, loamy, well-drained soils.

Many disease organisms—including viruses, fungi, insects, and nematodes—have been found on sunnhemp but seem to cause little economic damage. In India, a few, such as wilt and caterpillars of the sunnhemp moth *Utetheisa pulchella*, can become serious. In Brazil, the only disease affecting the crop is a fungus *Ceratocystes fimbriata*. If it becomes too severe, sunnhemp fields are fallowed or planted with other crops for 3 years.

Although sunnhemp will grow in warm temperate regions, most varieties set seed only in the tropics and subtropics. This latitude dependence means that any breeding or seed production must be done outside the temperate zone.

The dried leaves and stems are fed to cattle, but the literature contains conflicting statements on the forage value of fresh sunnhemp foliage. Under some conditions it seems to become toxic.

Research Needs

Sunnhemp will never realize its worldwide potential until a comprehensive plant breeding program is mounted. There is variability among the lines found on the Indian Subcontinent, and they need to be collected, compared, and classified. Improved types suited to specific localities need to be selected. The plant breeders' targets should be to select for high fiber yield (almost no information is available on differences in bast fiber content between different sunnhemp lines), early maturity, stronger stems, and resistance to disease.

Experimentation is also needed to determine more precisely the environmental and cultural requirements of the crop.

Harvesting and handling methods need improvement. End-use applications need further testing, and the economics of producing the crop should be analyzed.

Given research, sunnhemp may prove to be a useful forage; it grows fast, can yield two crops a year (if cut 30 cm from the ground), and in India has outyielded alfalfa (lucerne).* In South Africa, sunnhemp hay has been fed to cattle at levels of about 10 percent of the diet. But as already noted, sunnhemp appears to be mildly toxic under some conditions. Research is needed to identify the toxins, their effects, and their means of detoxification. It is also important to identify which parts of the plant are toxic, as well as varietal, seasonal, and environmental differences in toxin levels.

Selected Readings

Cunningham, R. L., T. F. Clark, and M. O. Bagby. 1978. *Crotalaria juncea*—Annual source of papermaking fiber. *Tappi* 61(2):37-39.

Demsey, J. 1975. *Fiber Crops*. University of Florida Book, Gainesville, Florida 32603, USA. pp. 417-447.

Heyne, K. 1950. *De Nuttige Planten van Indonesia*, Vol. 1. N. V. Utigevery W. Van Hoeve—S. Gravenhage, Bandung, Indonesia, 780 pp.

Kirby, R. M. 1963. *Vegetable Fibres*. Leonard Hill, London.

Nieschlag, H. J., G. H. Nelson, I. A. Wolff, and R. E. Perdue. 1960. A search for new fiber crops. *Tappi* 43:993-998.

Rao, B. V. V., and T. Sadasivaiah. 1968. Studies on nitrogen mobilization through phosphate fertilizing of a legume in the Bangalore red soil. *Mysore Journal of Agricultural Science* 2(4):251-256.

Reddy, M. R. 1968. Sunn-hemp hay can cut down concentrate needs of cattle. *Indian Farming* 18(6):45-46.

Salgado, A. L. B., L. A. C. Lovadini, J. M. Pimentel, and W. Gimenez. 1972. *Instruções Para a Cultura da* Crotalária júncea. Instituto Agronômico, Campinas, Brazil (see address below). 21 pp.

Singh, B. N., and S. N. Singh. 1936. Analysis of *Crotalaria juncea* with special reference to its use in green manure and fibre production. *Journal of American Society of Agronomy* 28:216-227.

White, G. A., and J. R. Haun. 1965. Growing *Crotalaria juncea*, a multi-purpose legume, for paper pulp. *Economic Botany* 19:175-183.

Research Contacts

Fibrous Products Research, Northern Regional Research Center, U.S. Department of Agriculture, 1815 N. University St., Peoria, Illinois 61604, USA

Institute for Crops and Pastures, Private Box X116, Pretoria, South Africa 0001 (J. W. Snyman)

Instituto Agronômico, Caixa Postal 28, Campinas, Estado de São Paulo, Brazil (A. L. de Barros Salgado)

*Reddy, 1968 (see Selected Readings), reports exceptional per-hectare forage yields of 5.19 t dry matter, 749 kg digestible crude protein, and 3,855 kg total digestible nutrients.

Joint Commission on Rural Reconstruction, 37 Nan Hai Road, Taipei 107, Taiwan
P. K. Karani, Deputy Chief Forest Officer, Ministry of Agriculture and Forestry, Forest
   Department, P.O. Box 31, Entebbe, Uganda
Sunnhemp Research Station, Pratapgarh, Uttar Pradesh, India
G. A. White, Germplasm Resources Laboratory, U.S. Department of Agriculture, Agri-
   cultural Research Center, Beltsville, Maryland 20705, USA

Gums

A surprisingly large number of plants produce the complex carbohydrates known commercially as gums. Much used in medicines since ancient times, gums have recently gained considerable importance in some of the world's largest industries. Chemically, gums are complex polysaccharides. Some are completely soluble in water, dissolving to give clear solutions, while others absorb water and swell to form gelatinous mucilages. Their commercial value is evident from the wealth of uses to which they are put, including the following:

• As major components of adhesives, including those widely used on postage stamps;
• To impart smoothness and stability to bakery products and lengthen their shelf life;
• To give body and smooth texture to confections (by acting as emulsifying, binding, and thickening agents and by preventing sugar from crystallizing);
• As a foam stabilizer in beer, to provide the long-lasting head found in some brands;
• To provide the ultra-smooth consistency of high-quality ice cream;
• To act as a purifier in winemaking and as an emulsifier in certain soft drinks, cosmetic lotions, ointments, and detergents; and
• As a vital ingredient in float-processing minerals and in assaying minerals, foundry sands, ceramic glazes, and printing inks.

In addition, gums are used to impart luster to silk and other fine textiles; for sizing paper; as a granulating agent in fertilizers; as a binder in explosives; and as a pigment-suspending element in paints and polishes. Medicinally, gums are important for soothing inflammations of the intestinal mucosa and to cover inflamed or burned skin.

In light of the importance of gum, the amount of research devoted to improving the cultivation and production of gum crops has been minuscule. Until recently, the actual species that produce some commercially available gums were not known with any degree of certainty. Even today, we are ignorant of the physiological processes and causes of natural gum formation, and agronomic techniques for producing most of the crops have only recently been systematically studied. In fact, the deliberate cultivation of some of the plants (for example *Astragalus* species, discussed below) has yet to be attempted. Moreover, there have been few concerted attempts to systematically screen plants in search of new gum sources, and it seems likely that a number of future gum crops await discovery.

For purposes of investigation, perhaps the most potentially important gum-producing plant family is the Leguminosae. Many legumes produce gums either in their seeds (see, for example, carob, page 109; tamarind, page 117; *Prosopis* species, page 153; and raintree, page 202) or as an exudate when their bark is damaged (see, for example, *Acacia auriculiformis*, page 165; *Sesbania grandiflora*, page 185; and *Pterocarpus* species, page 221). Seed gums seem particularly rich in the leguminous genera *Cassia, Acacia, Crotalaria, Indigofera,* and *Sesbania.* Copious gum exudates from tree barks are found among others in *Acacia, Albizia, Astragalus, Bauhinia,* and *Caesalpinia.* One formerly obscure legume, guar (*Cyamopsis tetragonoloba*), is increasingly cultivated in India and the United States, and guar seed gum is becoming an important commodity in international trade.* Others could follow and this chapter highlights some promising examples described below.

Acacia senegal

Acacia senegal† is native to hot, dry, and barren regions of Africa and the Middle East. When this spiny, gnarled tree's branches or stems are wounded, the tissues beneath the bark bleed a viscous gum that dries to walnut-size

---

*Guar's promise is described in a companion report: National Academy of Sciences. 1974. *Underexploited Tropical Plants with Promising Economic Value.* To order see page 329. More details of this exciting crop are given in a forthcoming book: Whistler, R., and T. Hymowitz. 1979. *Guar: Production, Nutrition and Industrial Use.* Purdue University Press, Lafayette, Indiana 47907, USA.

†*Acacia senegal* (L.) Willd. (Formerly also known as *Acacia verek* Guill. and Perr.) Subamily: Mimosoideae.

Gum arabic tree. (A. G. Seif-el-Din)

globules on the bark. Known internationally as gum arabic,* this is perhaps the most commercially important natural gum. About 40,000 tons are produced annually.

Brittle and glass-like, the dry gum dissolves in water slowly, giving a translucent, viscous, acidic solution that is virtually tasteless. The Egyptians used it in medicines and ceramic pottery over 4,000 years ago. Since biblical times Europe has imported it from Sudan and Arabia (hence the name). Today, at least 10 countries produce it commercially: Sudan (which provides 75–85 percent of the world's supply), Mauritania, Senegal, Mali, Nigeria, Niger, Chad, Tanzania, Ethiopia, and Somalia.

In areas of Africa too dry for general agriculture and livestock, gum arabic is often the principal source of revenue for seminomadic African people. Much gum arabic is still gathered largely at random from *Acacia senegal* plants growing wild and untended, though trees in the Sudan are grown commercially in plantations ("gum gardens") and are deliberately tapped by slitting the bark. An average annual yield is 250 g of gum per tree.

Often the most abundant plant in dry, sandy, thorn-scrub areas, *Acacia senegal* is found in a belt 300 km wide along the southern frontier of the Sahara Desert, from Mauritania to Sudan, Ethiopia, and Somalia. It also grows in East Africa as far south as Mozambique, the Transvaal, and Natal;

---

*Also known as Senegal gum, Sudan gum, gum hashab (Arabic), and Kordofan gum, as well as by many other names in local vernacular.

Sorting gum arabic, Sudan. (UN photo issued by FAO)

along the southern coast of Arabia and Iran; and in Pakistan and western India.

In addition to producing gum, *Acacia senegal* is a useful plant for dry environments. In the Virgin Islands and Puerto Rico it is grown as an ornamental. In India and the Sudan it has proved useful for windbreaks. Its pods and foliage provide good fodder for livestock, the tough wood of its taproot and stem is used for tool handles, and a strong fiber can be obtained from the long, flexible, surface roots. Furthermore, the dense wood yields excellent charcoal, and the trees enrich the soil through their ability to fix nitrogen.

The plant thrives on rocky hills, dry sandy flats, or dunes where the annual rainfall is between 200 and 350 mm. It can yield well even where the soil is worn out and unable to support other crops.

A dearth of knowledge about its physiology, agronomy, environmental tolerances, and other aspects is a major factor in limiting more rational exploitation of *Acacia senegal.* Currently, gum arabic production is highly labor intensive. The trees are tapped, the gum-tears picked, and, where grading is practiced, every tear is color sorted entirely by hand.

Different races or subspecies of *Acacia senegal* and of other *Acacia* species occur in different regions. Some have flat crowns while others have rounded ones; some produce much gum, others none. Little is yet known about these races and their genetic effects on gum yield and quality.

Research to improve and streamline the production of gum arabic is badly needed, with a goal of changing it from a haphazard effort to a well-organized, systematic occupation. This will involve genetic improvement of the plant, chemical stimulants for greater production, scientific management of plantations, development of more systematic grading procedures, production of a more uniform product, and development of new ways of using gum arabic as a chemical raw material. The producing countries, all among the most impoverished of developing nations, lack sufficient research facilities and technical manpower to accomplish this. For their own benefit as well as to help satisfy the world's need for gum, international attention is needed. Much of the needed research can be done in arid regions and in scientific laboratories in the developed countries.

Research into the causes and physiology of gum production is needed. For example, it is not known whether gum exuded from bark wounds is the normal reaction of a healthy tree or a result of bacteria or fungi that infect the wound. A goal of this research should be to find ways to increase gum yield.

The remarkable root system of *Acacia senegal.* The deep taproot (severed) extends down to the water table; widespread lateral roots take advantage of light rain showers. Kordofan Province, Sudan Republic. (G.E. Wickens)

In a given population, some trees of *Acacia senegal* produce gum more readily than others. Yields from individual trees vary from a few grams to about 10 kg per tree. There is also evidence that individual trees produce gums with slightly different chemical properties. Much more research is needed into this than is currently in progress, as well as more widespread selection and replication of the best races.

Other *Acacia* Species

Over 100 species of *Acacia* are known to exude copious amounts of gum when their bark is damaged. These plants tend to grow in inhospitable areas where conventional agriculture is not feasible and where poverty is rife and economic development extremely difficult. The development of these species as gum sources could bring employment and improved welfare to local inhabitants.

Six species* whose gums appear to have commercial promise and that deserve exploratory research attention from industrial chemists and agronomists are:

Acacia auriculiformis. See page 165.

Acacia berlandieri Benth. Native to southern Texas and adjacent areas of northern Mexico, this drought-tolerant shrub is the most common and conspicuous *Acacia* in the area. It frequently occurs together with cactus, *Prosopis* species (see page 153), and other desert-adapted plants. It yields gum freely, especially when the trees are pruned or sprayed. The gum is brownish, but it has good solubility in water and its general properties closely resemble those of gum arabic. This, together with the plant's drought hardiness, makes the gum of *Acacia berlandieri* well worth research attention.

Acacia hebeclada DC.† Found in dry areas of southern Africa south of Rhodesia, this bush (sometimes a small tree reaching 7 m in height) produces a gum of unique composition that should interest many industries. It is a strongly acidic gum (containing about 33 percent uronic acid), with a protein content of about 9 percent, and many methoxyl groups (about 2.5 percent).

The spiny bush bears yellow-white flower heads and thick gray pods that usually do not hang but stand upright on the branches.

Acacia mellifera (Vahl.) Benth. This species is native to a vast area stretching from Arabia and Egypt to South Africa (a distinct subspecies *Acacia*

*Selected by Professor D.M.W. Anderson. See Research Contacts.
† Also known as *Acacia stolonifera* Burch.

mellifera spp. *detinens* [Burch.] Brenan is prevalent from Zambia southwards). It grows as a shrub or small tree, sometimes reaching 9 m tall. Its hard, clean-burning wood is a valued cooking fuel in rural areas. Its cream or white flowers attract bees (important to honey production) and its foliage provides valuable shade and fodder for livestock. The gum exudate from *Acacia mellifera* has only recently been analyzed, but its remarkable properties could give it a commercial future. It is viscous, contains protein (8–9 percent), and is acidic (with about 21 percent uronic acid groups). Despite its usefulness, this is a prickly plant whose impenetrable thickets are sometimes a nuisance.

Acacia saligna (Labill.) H. Wendl.* A bushy shrub native to poor sandy and clay soils of Western Australia, it is extremely rugged and widely planted for coastal sand dune fixation in North Africa, the Middle East, South Africa, and some Mediterranean countries; for gully erosion control in Uruguay; and for ornamental purposes in Australia. It grows rapidly and tolerates drought, fire, calcareous soils, and salt winds.† Damaged bark exudes copious amounts of a light-colored, water-soluble gum that is very acidic (27 percent uronic acid). Such an acid stable gum seems to have exceptional promise for use in pickles and other acidic foodstuffs.

Acacia victoriae. See page 148.

Astragalus species

Of all natural gums, tragacanth, obtained from *Astragalus* species,‡ is the most expensive, now selling at over $48 per kg. But although it has been an item of commerce since at least three centuries before the Christian era, today it is a vanishing commodity. Despite conservation laws, the plants that produce it are disappearing because heavy tapping weakens them, reduces seed production, and depletes the natural stands. Yet except for a few brief test plantings in California and Arizona, the cultivation of gum tragacanth has never been attempted.

Gum tragacanth's properties are unique. Although many people have predicted the complete demise of its trade, various industries have found it

---

*Formerly known as *Acacia cyanophylla* Lindl.

†Because of this irrepressible nature it has become a rampant weed in South Africa.

‡Notably *A. adscendens* Boiss., *A. echidnaeformis* Sirjaev, *A. gummifer* Labill., and *A. microcephalus* Willd. Subfamily: Papilionoideae. A common Persian name for the plants is "gommer," from which European terms gomma (Italian and Spanish), gomme (French), and gum derive. The Iranian desert city of Qum (Qom) is named because it has long been a gum tragacanth market.

Azerbaijan, Iran. *Astragalus* species that are the source of gum tragacanth. (H.S. Gentry)

indispensable to their products and are prepared to pay enormous prices to get it.

When water is added gum tragacanth swells to form a gel. Highly viscous solutions result even when the gum is in very low concentrations. The better grades contribute thickening without sliminess, are colorless and tasteless, and resist thermal or acidic degradation. Major current uses are in pharmaceuticals and cosmetics; as a thickening agent in syrups, dressings, and sauces; as an industrial textile sizing; and as an adhesive for cigar wrapper leaves.

Gum tragacanth is produced from small *Astragalus* bushes that thrive in arid locations in the mountains of Iran, Iraq, and Turkey,* as well as in the Soviet Union, Pakistan, Afghanistan, Syria, Israel, and Greece. Before World War I, Turkey was the world's major supplier; today, Iran is.

The gum is collected from wild bushes, usually in a haphazard way by nomads and villagers of the region. Production is thus unsystematic and largely uncontrolled. It takes place in remote and inhospitable semideserts, making collection and transportation difficult. The bushes are widely scattered and tricky to harvest, each yielding only about 15–25 g per tapping season. It is not surprising, therefore, that gum tragacanth production is declining; a natural resource is running out.

Amazingly, after 3,000 years of using gum tragacanth, we are still unsure of the identity of the species that produce the gum; even the environmental and genetic factors that enhance gum yield and gum quality are unknown.

The best gum comes from small, pincushion-like plants that can be covered by a hat. These develop a mass of gum in the center of the root. Summer heat

---

*Like tarwi (page 86), these are not strictly tropical plants but are included here because of their potential value to cooler developing countries.

The spiraling exudate of gum tragacanth, Isfahan, Iran. (H.S. Gentry)

swells this cylinder of gum and if the stem is slit, a stream of soft gum pushes out in the form of a ribbon. Although most gum is produced in the root of the plant, inferior grades may be found in the older branches.

The overwhelming limitation to the gum tragacanth trade is that its only source, the wild plants in Iran and Asia Minor, is becoming exhausted. In the absence of attempts to improve gum production, there is a complete lack of knowledge of how to cultivate the gum-producing *Astragalus* plants. However, a test planting in California demonstrated that several high-elevation species would grow there with ordinary gardening care. In their second year they flowered and produced seed, and small samples of gum were obtained.* Cultivation, especially with modern mechanized methods, would greatly reduce the labor required of tribesmen for gathering gum from scattered wild plants.

The plants can be propagated from seed. Test plantings should be started in the semiarid areas that have environments homologous to the highlands of Asia Minor, Iran, and Afghanistan. The hinterlands of Southern California and the highlands of Arizona and New Mexico and similar climatic areas in South America (Chile, Argentina, etc.), Australia, Southern Africa, and Asia appear propitious. Areas with early summer rains are to be avoided, as rains wash away the exuded ribbons of gum. Trial cultivation of different genotypes should seek varieties that are good yielders of high-quality gum. Once these are identified, plant breeding through selection and hybridization can be expected to produce cultivars with several times the productive capacities of the maltreated wildlings that now supply this valuable gum to the world.

*Information supplied by H.S. Gentry. See Research Contacts.

Sesbania bispinosa. (I.P. Abrol)

Sesbania bispinosa

World demand for guar gum is increasing, but the occurrence of an almost identical gum in the seeds of *Sesbania bispinosa** is little known outside two or three research laboratories in India and Pakistan. *Sesbania bispinosa* is extremely versatile, producing a wide variety of useful products that complement its value as a gum source; it is also quick growing, well adapted to difficult soils, and appears easy to produce on large scale with little care or investment. It richly deserves increased attention from horticulturists and the gum industry.

Sesbania bispinosa is normally shrub-like, but in crowded stands grows a straight, slender stem that may reach 4 m tall. A prickly-leaved annual, it is native to tropical and subtropical areas of the Indian Subcontinent but has been distributed to parts of tropical Africa, Southeast Asia, China, and the West Indies. It appears to nodulate vigorously and improve soil fertility. On the Subcontinent, it is a choice green manure, particularly because its fast growth (5- to 6-month maturing time) allows it to fit into existing crop rotation.

Sesbania bispinosa (Jacq.) W.F. Wight. Often designated as *Sesbania aculeata* Pers. In India known as dhaincha (name also used for other *Sesbania* species) and in Pakistan as jantar. Subfamily: Papilionoideae.

Unlike other legumes, it will grow on saline and alkaline wastelands and wet, almost waterlogged soils, an extremely important capability, for such areas often remain barren for want of suitable crops.

Sesbania bispinosa seeds are a little smaller than those of guar,* but the composition of the two is roughly the same. Gum comprises 30–42 percent of each seed's weight. Like guar gum, that from *Sesbania bispinosa* is a viscous, water-soluble galactomannan (with a 5:1 ration of mannose to galactose) mucilage, very low in protein, oil, or fiber impurities. On drying, the gum produces a smooth, light-colored, coherent, and elastic film of a type needed for sizing textiles and paper products and for thickening and stabilizing solutions.

The seeds are easily harvested, and yields of 1,500 kg per ha have been reported when the plants are judiciously topped to force branching and greater flower production.†

In the face of competition from guar, *Sesbania bispinosa* is worth developing as a gum source because its exceptional adaptability (it has grown well even in southern Italy‡) may allow its production in areas where guar fails and because this multipurpose plant has other uses that add to its potential as a new crop. The seed kernel is protein rich and the meal remaining after gum extraction contains 58 percent protein and 15 percent oil. Although this product is not highly palatable to livestock, it has been experimentally added to cattle and poultry feeds with some success. More testing seems warranted.

By-products are also obtained from other parts of the plant:

• The fresh young foliage is palatable to livestock and boosts the growth of both cattle and sheep;
• The stems make useful firewood; and
• The stem also provides bast fiber (9 percent yield) used in fishing nets, gunny sacks, and sails and is said to be stronger than jute.

On top of all that, *Sesbania bispinosa* has exciting potential as a source of pulp for paper products and construction materials. This is even less developed than the seed gum. Nonetheless, the plant does produce a pulp closely similar to that of eucalyptus, poplar, and birch, some of the best short-fiber pulps known.‡ The pulp is superior to that of most annual crops. Fiber length averages 0.96 mm and the pulp is formed in high yield and has good bleachability. A rayon grade pulp can be made, and the fiber looks particularly promising for fiberboard, hardboard, and particleboard. Yields of 46–60 t of

---

*More information on guar is given in a companion report: National Academy of Sciences. 1975. *Underexploited Tropical Plants with Promising Economic Value.* To order see page 329.

†Hussain and Ahmad. 1965.

‡Information supplied by L. Markila. See Research Contacts.

fiber (bone dry) per ha per harvest seem attainable with irrigation and good management.* Furthermore, because of the plant's short growing season two (or perhaps more) harvests per year are feasible.

Research on pulp production from *Sesbania bispinosa* is urgently needed. Problems are similar to those being tackled in projects producing pulp from other annuals and include developing economical methods for harvesting, handling, and debarking the stems.

The living plant is used to provide windbreaks, hedges, erosion control, and provide shade and cover for crops. The plant is ornamental and, as already mentioned, is a useful green manure for increasing soil fertility, especially on saline and wet soils. It is also reportedly excellent for suppressing vigorous weeds such as *Imperata cylindrica* that now grip so much of the tropics as green deserts.†

Before *Sesbania bispinosa* can be fully exploited as a gum source, research is needed to:

- Select high-yielding varieties with uniform qualities;
- Optimize cultivation practices;
- Improve techniques for milling the gum on a commercial scale; and
- Fully determine the gum's functional properties and the extent of its commercial viability.

In introducing this plant to new areas much care should be exercised. It grows fast, seeds freely, and reportedly has become a noxious weed in rice paddies in some areas. Related species such as *Sesbania cannabina, S. paludosa, S. aegyptiaca (S. sesban)*, and *S. speciosa* also seem worth considering in projects researching *Sesbania bispinosa*.

Selected Readings

Acacia senegal

Adamson, A. D., and J. M. L. Bell. 1974. *The Market for Gum Arabic.* Tropical Products Institute, Ministry of Overseas Development, London.
Anderson, D. M. W., 1977. Water-soluble plant gum exudates—Part 1: gum arabic. *Process Biochemistry* 12(10):24-25, 29.
Awouda, E. H. M. 1974. *Production and Supply of Gum Arabic.* Khartoum, Sudan.
Brenan, J. P. M. 1959. *Flora of Tropical East Africa. Leguminosae-Mimosoideae.* Crown Agents for Overseas Government and Administrations, London. pp. 92-94.
Glicksman, M. 1969. *Gum Technology in the Food Industry.* Academic Press, New York.

*Information supplied by L. Markila. See Research Contacts.

†Whyte, R.O., G. Nilsson-Leissner, and H.C. Trumble. 1953 (reprinted 1966). *Legumes in Agriculture.* Food and Agriculture Organization of the United Nations, Rome. p. 322.

Kaul, R. N., and Man Singh Manomar. 1966. Germination studies on arid zone tree seeds. I. *A. senegal* Willd. *Indian Forester* 92(8):499-503.

Obeid, M., and A. Seif-el-Din. 1971. The effect of simulated rainfall distribution at different isohyets on the regeneration of *Acacia senegal* (L.) Willd. on clay and sandy soils. *Journal of Applied Ecology* 8(1):203-209.

Seif-el-Din, A., and M. Obeid. 1971. Ecological studies of the vegetation of the Sudan. II. The germination of seeds and establishment of seedlings of *Acacia senegal* (L.) Willd. under controlled conditions in the Sudan. *Journal of Applied Ecology* 8(1):919-201.

Seif-el-Din, A., and M. Obeid. 1971. Ecological studies of the vegetation of the Sudan. IV. The effect of simulated grazing on the growth of *Acacia senegal* (L.) Willd. seedlings. *Journal of Applied Ecology* 8(1):211-216.

Astragalus species

Gentry, H. S. 1957. Gum tragacanth in Iran. *Economic Botany* 2(1):40-63.

Whistler, R. L., and J. N. BeMiller, eds. 1973. *Industrial Gums: Polysaccharides and Their Derivatives*, 2nd ed. Academic Press, New York.

Sesbania bispinosa

Abrol. I. P., and D. R. Bhumbla. 1971. Start with dhaincha on saline sodic soil *Sesbania aculeata* reclamation. *Indian Farming* 21(2):41-42.

Bhardwaj, K. K. K. 1974. Note on the distribution and effectiveness of Rhizobium of *Sesbania aculeata* Poir in saline-alkali soils. *Indian Journal of Agricultural Science* 44(10):683-684.

Chela, K. S., and Z. S. Brar. 1973. Green-manuring popular again. *Sesbania aculeata, Cyamopsis tetragonoloba, Crotalaria juncea. Progressive Farming* 10(3, 9.3. 4):11.

Farooqi, M. I. H., and V. N. Sharma. 1972. *Sesbania aculeata* Pers. seeds—new source for gum. *Research and Industry* 17:94-95.

Gillett, J. B. 1963. Sesbania in Africa. *Kew Bulletin* 17(1):91-158.

Hussain, A., and M. Ahmad. 1965. *Sesbania aculeata*—a promising new crop in West Pakistan. *World Crops* 17:28-31.

Hussain, A., and D. M. Khan. 1962. Jantar (*Sesbania aculeata*)—a source of protein supplement and industrial raw material. *West Pakistan Journal of Agricultural Research* 1(1):31-35.

Hussain, A., and D. M. Khan. 1962. Nutritive value and galactomannan content of jantar—*Sesbania aculeata* and *Sesbania aegyptica. West Pakistan Journal of Agricultural Research* 1(1):36-40.

Katiyar, R. C., and S. K. Ranjhan. 1969. Yield and chemical composition of dhaincha (*Sesbania aculeata*)—its nutritive value for sheep. *Indian Journal of Dairy Science* 22(1):33-36.

Khan, A. A., and A. H. Awan. 1967. Salinity tolerance character of dhaincha (*Sesbania aculeata*). *West Pakistan Journal of Agricultural Research* 5(3):135-136.

Mazumdar, A. K., A. Day, and P. D. Gupta. 1973. Composition of dhanchia fibre (*Sesbania aculeata* Pers.). *Science and Culture* 39(10):473-374.

Razzaque, M. A., and A. B. Siddique. 1971. Pulping and paper making experiments on dhaincha (*Sesbania cannabina*). *Science and Industry* 8:315-319.

Research Contacts

Acacia senegal

D. M. W. Anderson, Department of Chemistry, University of Edinburgh, West Mains Road, Edinburgh, EH9 3JJ, Scotland, United Kingdom (Gum chemistry)

J. P. M. Brenan, Royal Botanic Gardens, Kew, Richmond, Surrey TW9 3AE, England (Taxonomy)

Central Arid Zone Research Institute, Jodhpur, Rajasthan, India (H. S. Mann and R. S. Paroda) (Establishment of *Acacia senegal* plantations for soil conservation, fuel and fodder.)

Centre Technique Forestier Tropical, 45 BIS, Avenue de la Belle Gabrielle, 94130 Nogent-sur-Marne (Val-de-Marne), France (R. Catinot)

Ministry of Agriculture, Food and Natural Resources Research and Education Institute, P.O. Box 658, Khartoum-Soba, Sudan

M. Obeid, Gezira University, Wad Medani, Sudan

A. G. Seif-el-Din, Senior Gum Research Officer, P.O. Box 302, El Obeid, Sudan

Tropical Products Institute, 56-65 Gray's Inn Road, London WC1X 8LU, England (Post-harvest utilization)

Water and Forestry Branch, Ministry of Rural Development, Government of Senegal, Dakar, Senegal (Gives courses on gum arabic production for students of the Sudan-Sahelian region.)

Other *Acacia* species

For information on the gums of these species contact Professor D. M. W. Anderson, Department of Chemistry, University of Edinburgh, West Mains Road, Edinburgh, EH9 3JJ, Scotland

Astragalus species

Howard S. Gentry, Desert Botanical Gardens, P.O. Box 5415, Phoenix, Arizona 85010, USA

Harold Jabloner, Hercules Incorporated, Research Center, Wilmington, Delaware 19899, USA

Roy Whistler, Department of Biochemistry, Purdue University, Lafayette, Indiana 47907, USA

Sesbania bispinosa

Ayub Agricultural Research Institute, Lyallpur, Pakistan

Division of Soils and Agronomy, Central Soil Salinity Research Institute, Karnal 132001, Haryana, India (I. P. Abrol)

P. C. D. Gupta, Jute Technological Research Laboratory, 12 Regent Park, Tollygunge, Calcutta 40, West Bengal, India

L. Markila, Pulp and Paper Branch, Forest Industries Division, FAO, Via delle Terme di Caracalla, 00100-Rome, Italy

National Botanic Gardens, Rana Pratap Marg, Lucknow, India (T. N. Khoshoo and M. I. H. Farooqi)

National Bureau of Plant Genetic Resources, Indian Agricultural Research Institute, New Delhi 110012, India (K. L. Mehra, Director)

Punjab Agricultural University, Ludhiana, 141004 Punjab, India (Kartar Singh Chela and Zora Singh Brar)

Tropical Products Institute 56-62 Gray's Inn Road, London WC1X 8LU, United Kingdom (W. S. Matthews)

Roy Whistler, Department of Biochemistry, Purdue University, Lafayette, Indiana 47907, USA

George A. White, Germplasm Resources Laboratory, U.S. Department of Agriculture, Agricultural Research Center, Beltsville, Maryland 20705, USA

Green Manure, Soil Reclamation, and Erosion Control

Restoration and maintenance of soil fertility is a basic and critical environmental problem. It is especially serious in developing countries, many of which suffer poor productivity because their soils lack plant nutrients and humus.

Mineral fertilizers are easy to handle and produce quick results. However, their efficacy does not diminish the usefulness—and generally unrecognized potential—of organic fertilizers. Optimum yields are obtained by complementing mineral fertilizers with organic manures. Nevertheless, in recent years the use of organic materials in agriculture has decreased, even in countries with long traditions of organic manuring.

Legumes are a good source of organic matter for manure. Their fresh foliage usually contains from 0.5 to 1 percent nitrogen. The foliage of vigorous perennial legumes may accumulate 100–600 kg of nitrogen per ha. When incorporated into soil, it improves fertility, moisture, nutrient retention, and general tilth. At the same time, by improving soil structure, it can also retard erosion.

The costs and long-term effects of mineral fertilizer make it increasingly important to reexamine green manure crops, especially for fragile farming ecosystems in the tropics. Leguminous candidates for testing include species of *Cajanus, Canavalia, Crotalaria, Desmodium, Erythrina, Lablab, Leucaena, Lupinus, Mucuna, Pueraria, Sesbania,* and *Tephrosia.*

Used with discretion, many legumes are valuable for initial plantings on bare grounds, wastelands, or sand dunes. Once established, they can create conditions that induce other species to grow well. They act as pioneers, preparing difficult sites for farming or forestry.

This chapter demonstrates, pictorially, the use of legumes for green manure and for the reclamation of worn-out, eroding, and toxic soils. Some of the examples are from temperate zones, but they exemplify the results that can be expected in tropical and arid zones with the use of appropriate leguminous species.

Pueraria phaseoloides used as a cover crop near Belem, Brazil. In tropical regions like this, rainfalls of 20 cm per hour are frequent and more soil is gouged out by falling raindrops than by runoff water. Densely growing leguminous plants then become particularly valuable. They provide nitrogen and humus, but ab⌄ve all, they shield the soil surface from erosion by wind and water. (A. van Wambeke)

The use of the densely matted velvet bean *Mucuna pruriens* as a green manure and soil protector, eastern Mexico. Sustaining agricultural yield in the heat, humidity, and heavy rainfall of the lowland tropics is a particular problem. Exposed soils rapidly lose their productive capacity; organic matter decomposes fast, nutrients leach away, soils compact, and populations of weeds, pests, and diseases build constantly because there is no cold or dry season to kill them back. The velvet bean is an exceptionally promising pulse and cover crop for such areas. It is productive, hardy, adapted to widely different conditions, and resists diseases and pests. By growing a crop of velvet bean and sword bean (see page 54) to restore productivity to their fields, farmers in southeastern Mexico reduce fallow periods from 5 years to one growing season.

The seeds of some velvet bean genotypes are a new-found source of L-Dopa, a drug used in treating Parkinson's disease. A related species, *Mucuna sloanei*, is grown as a pulse crop in the extreme heat and humidity of eastern Nigeria. Since few other food crops survive in such conditions, the species deserves widespread testing and research. (S. R. Gliessman and R. Garcia E., Colegio Superior de Agricultura Tropical, Cardenas, Tabasco, Mexico)

The simultaneous cultivation of beans and maize is an ancient practice in Central America. Even Mayan farmers knew that the bean plant *(Phaseolus vulgaris)* helped maintain high maize yields. On many small farms in Latin America these crops are still grown together. Each can be planted at its own optimum density. Maize yields are not diminished, so the farmer gets the beans as a bonus. (Rodale Press)

Living mulches at the Centro Internacional de Agricultura Tropical (CIAT), Cali, Colombia. Left: A field of maize planted through perennial peanut *Arachis prostrata*. Right: Rice growing in a living mulch of *Desmodium triflorum*. Living mulches are a promising new method for increasing vegetable production in the tropics. A carpet-like cover of low-growing plants enhances vegetable yield and shortens the growing season by conserving soil moisture, reducing leaching, suppressing weeds, and by making soil temperatures more equable. Compared with other mulches, the use of living plants is cheap. At the International Institute for Tropical Agriculture in Ibadan, Nigeria, equipment to plant vegetable seedlings right through the living "carpet" is being designed. (K. O. Rachie and B. N. Okigbo)

294

Mulch *in situ*. International Institute of Tropical Agriculture, Ibadan, Nigeria. Cowpea *(Vigna unguiculata)* and maize established by zero tillage through a mulch of dead Brazilian lucerne *(Stylosanthes guianensis)*. In this modification of a living mulch, the cover crop is killed with herbicide and the vegetable crop is planted into the residue. (G. F. Wilson)

Strip-mined land, before and after planting with *Coronilla varia*, Hanna, Ohio, USA. *Coronilla varia* (crownvetch) has risen, in four decades, from complete obscurity to one of the most important soil-stabilizing legumes in the United States. The plant protects hundreds of miles of highway embankments and has been used to turn mine spoil into grazing land. It is being tested internationally and holds promise for the tropics, especially for cool highlands (F. V. Grau)

Black locust (*Robinia pseudoacacia*) growing vigorously on extremely steep, infertile mine spoil, Raleigh County, West Virginia, USA. After 4 growing seasons the trees have reached 4 m in height and, except for a small, very stony area, the slope is completely stabilized by the trees. (Soil Conservation Service, U.S. Department of Agriculture)

The use of *Leucaena leucocephala* to reclaim highly aluminous soil, Weipa, northern Australia. The site is on a former bauxite mine, and the leucaena is being tested as a nurse crop for African mahogany (*Khaya* species), which is planted between the leucaena trees. (COMALCO, Weipa, North Queensland, Australia)

Legumes as reforestation aids, Southern Alps, New Zealand. In the high country of New Zealand seed of legumes, grasses, and trees are combined and spread from the air. The resulting mixture of vegetation stabilizes eroding mountain slopes, improves fertility, and helps establish forests. The tree seedlings grow through a "carpet" of legumes and grasses that protects and nurtures them while they are young and vulnerable to harsh weather and erosion. The technique is described in *What's New in Forest Research*, Number 33, January 1976, available from Forest Research Institute, Private Bag, Rotorua, New Zealand. (A. H. Nordmeyer)

Lespedeza bicolor and *L. thunbergii*. Known in South Korea as "miracle plants," these leguminous bushes rapidly cover bare ground. Their long, shallow roots bind and hold down soil. Prolific root nodules provide nitrogen and their protein-rich foliage is fed to livestock. Foresters plant *Lespedeza* species around pine seedlings to protect the soil, provide plant nutrients, and produce forage and firewood until the forest is established. The dense wood of the small stems is eagerly sought for cooking fuel and it is a well-established Korean practice to plant *Lespedeza* species along ridges as a firewood crop. The flowers are a source of a honey known throughout the country. Although Korea has temperate climate, these plants could prove useful in cool tropical highland regions. Other *Lespedeza* species as well as *Amorpha fruticosa* (foreground) are used for the same purposes. (T. Bok Lee, Kwanak Arboretum, College of Agriculture, Seoul National University, Suwon, Korea)

The use of leguminous trees to shade plantation crops, New Britain, Papua New Guinea. Here *Leucaena leucocephala* is grown as a canopy above cacao plants. The trees shade the sensitive cacao leaves from the heat and desiccation of the tropical sun. Also, the falling, nitrogen-rich foliage provides humus and nutrients to the crop beneath. (Department of Primary Industries, Papua New Guinea)

Three-dimensional agriculture. In Bajo Chino, CATIE, Costa Rica, coffee and trees are grown together. The coffee is planted in the shade of the leguminous tree *Erythrina poeppigiana* (pollarded trunks with young branches, see also page 252). Towering above both is *Cordia alliodora* (wide trunks), whose timber is highly esteemed for fine furniture and house construction. (G. Budowski)

The use of legumes to establish forests on pure sand, Northland, New Zealand. First the dunes are stabilized with a grass (marram grass, *Ammophila arenaria*). Lupins are then sown between the grass and quickly come to dominate it (see background). . . .

. . . Pine seedlings are planted into the lupin cover. They grow well because lupins are legumes and provide nitrogen and organic matter to the sand. . . .

. . . The pines come to dominate the lupins. . .

. . . eventually producing a productive forest. (Forest Research Institute, Private Bag, Rotorua, New Zealand)

Indigofera spicata (I. endecaphylla) used as live, maintenance-free cover for pond embankments. (Fish Culture Experiment Center, Universidad de Caldas, Manizales, Colombia)

Diphysa robinioides used as a living fence in Costa Rica. Leguminous trees are commonly used as living fence posts in Central America. The fence provides protection and shade for animals, but in addition the branches and the foliage can be continuously harvested for cuttings (for more live fence posts), forage, firewood, or green manure. (G. Budowski)

Leguminous trees used to support climbing crops. In these experiments very dense plantings of *Leucaena leucocephala* were used as low-cost stakes for yams at Ibadan, Nigeria (left) and pole beans at Cali, Colombia (right). The tree's roots did not seriously interfere even with the yams. In both cases leucaena foliage was harvested for forage or green manure, an additional benefit over normal staking. (International Institute of Tropical Agriculture and K. O. Rachie)

Acacia saligna fixing moving sand dunes near Tripoli, Libya. This is an extremely hardy leguminous Australian shrub that can survive in, and stabilize, shifting sand dunes. Here it is shown within squares of grass stems placed in the sand to slow the sand's movement until the shrub's roots are established. *Acacia saligna* (see page 284) is also a promising source of gum. (FAO)

Gliricidia sepium (G. maculata) grown as a firebreak, Central Java, Indonesia. This and other fast-growing leguminous trees have the vigor to outcompete weeds such as *Imperata* grass. In the shade of the trees the weeds die, leaving almost nothing that can sustain a grass fire. (Perum Perhutani, Jakarta)

Lambs grazing a pasture of legume (white clover, *Trifolium repens*) and grasses among pine seedlings (*Pinus radiata*) planted 6 months earlier. Agroforestry, the combination of tree crops and agriculture, has an important future, particularly in the tropics, and leguminous plants seem destined to be an important part of it. (New Zealand Forest Service)

304

Appendix A

Comparative Nutritional Values

Crude Chemical Composition of Food and Forage Species.*

Species	Part†	Calories	Protein g	Fat g	Total Carb. g	Fiber g	Ash g
Acacia albida	P		11.5	01.4	55.1	23.4	03.2
Acacia aneura	L		13.2	02.2	51.5	27.9	05.0
Acacia pendula	L		13.2	03.4	46.2	29.6	07.8
Acacia senegal	P		22.0	01.0	30.9	39.0	07.1
Acacia tortillis	P		17.8	01.7	54.6	17.5	08.4
Apios americana	R		17.5		57.1		04.7
Arachis hypogaea	L	320	20.5	02.8	69.3	21.4	07.4
(peanut)	S	587	24.8	47.9	24.6	03.1	02.7
Canavalia ensiformis	S	393	23.7	03.6	68.9	08.6	04.1
(jackbean)	S	389	27.4	02.9	66.1	08.3	03.6
	GF	324	21.0	02.6	71.0	15.8	05.2
	GF	377	23.7	01.8	69.3	15.8	05.2
Canavalia gladiata	S	375	32.0	00.7	63.5	13.7	04.2
(swordbean)	GF	315	25.9	07.4	67.6	13.9	04.6
	GS		23.7	01.8	56.1	13.2	05.2
Cassia sturtii	L		12.6	02.3	63.3	13.4	08.4
Ceratonia siliqua	A	203	05.1	01.6	91.2	08.7	02.4
(carob)	S		19.9	02.8	66.8	08.6	03.4
	F		05.3	03.0	42.6	10.7	03.3
Cordeauxia edulis (ye-eb)	S	446	12.1	13.4	71.6	01.6	02.5

*Compiled by James A. Duke, U.S. Department of Agriculture.
†A=aril, DS=dry seed, F=fruit, GS=green seed, GF=green fruit, I=inflorescence or flower, L=leaf, P=pod, R=root, S=seed, Sp=sprout, LC=leaves cooked

Species	Part	Calories	Protein g	Fat g	Total Carb. g	Fiber g	Ash g
Desmanthus virgatus	L		22.4				
Desmodium discolor	L		20.9	03.0	38.1	27.3	10.9
Desmodium nicaraguense	L		22.5				08.6
Flemingia vestita	R		09.3	02.3	83.9	01.1	03.1
Gleditsia triacanthos (Honeylocust)	P		14.3	01.9	60.8	18.4	04.7
Glycine max (soybean)	GS	436	40.8	17.9	35.8	06.0	05.3
(yellow)	S	444	39.0	19.6	35.5	04.7	05.5
(black)	S	439	38.0	17.1	40.3	04.9	04.6
	S	445	37.1	19.7	37.3	05.2	05.5
	Sp	335	41.7	09.7	43.3	03.8	05.4
Kerstingiella geocarpa	S	386	21.5	01.2	73.9	06.1	03.6
Lablab purpureus	GF	312	25.0	02.7	65.2	16.1	07.1
(lablab bean)	S	382	25.1	01.7	68.9	07.8	04.0
	S	381	25.5	01.1	69.6	09.6	03.6
	S	380	24.5	01.4	69.9	07.8	04.3
	GF	312	24.8	02.4	65.6	15.2	07.2
	L	284	22.0	03.7	55.9	61.4	12.8
Leucaena leucocephala	L	332	14.2	03.9	74.7	08.8	07.3
(leucaena)	GF	306	43.5	04.7	45.6	19.7	06.2
Lupinus mutabilis	S	440	47.8	17.8	30.4	07.7	03.6
(tarwi)	S	513	32.2	32.6	32.2	07.1	03.0
	GS	441	48.0	17.8	31.5	02.1	02.8
Medicago sativa (alfalfa)	L	301	34.7	02.3	54.9	17.9	08.1
Pachyrizus erosus	R	359	10.7	00.8	83.9	04.6	04.6
(yam bean)	R	357	11.0	00.6	84.4	09.1	03.9
	GF		19.1	02.2	73.5	21.3	05.1
Phaseolus acutifolius (tepary bean)	S	378	24.5	01.5	65.5	03.7	04.6
Phaseolus coccineus	S	385	23.1	02.1	70.7	05.5	03.9
(runner bean)	GS			00.5		18.5	04.3
	F		17.8	02.4	71.5	04.6	03.8
Phaseolus lunatus	S	384	25.0	01.6	70.3	04.9	03.9
(lima bean)	S	388	22.2	01.5	73.2		03.4
	GS	377	26.6	01.6	66.6	03.2	05.1
	Sp	306	36.1	02.2	55.6	01.7	06.1
	L	286	21.4	00.0	60.7		17.9
Prosopis alba	F		09.7	02.3	46.9	38.0	03.1

Species	Part	Calories	Protein g	Fat g	Total Carb. g	Fiber g	Ash g
Prosopis chilensis	L		28.4	09.2	34.3	26.8	01.5
Prosopis pallida	F		10.3	00.7	58.6	26.7	03.8
Prosopis tamarugo	GF		11.9	01.7	51.5	28.8	06.1
Psophocarpus	GF	321	26.9	03.8	62.7	21.8	06.4
tetragonolobus	GF	324	18.1	01.0	75.2	15.2	05.7
(winged bean)	S	450	36.4	18.8	40.5		04.4
	S	447	35.0	17.8	43.4	11.1	04.1
	R	370	11.4	02.4	82.6	06.1	03.7
	L	313	33.4	03.3	56.7		06.7
Psoralea esculenta			13.1		66.7		03.1
Pterocarpus sp.	L	340	36.1	08.8	50.2	12.2	04.9
Pueraria lobata	LC	327	03.6	00.9	88.2	70.0	07.3
	R	359	06.7	00.3	88.4	02.2	04.4
Sesbania grandiflora	L	321	36.3	07.5	46.1	09.2	09.2
	I	345	14.5	03.6	77.3	10.9	04.5
Sphenostylis	S	391	21.1	01.2	74.1	05.7	03.2
stenocarpa	R	366	10.8	00.6	86.3	01.1	02.3
(African yam bean)							
Tamarindus indica	I	375	12.5	09.0	7.50	06.0	03.5
(tamarind)	L	342	23.3	04.0	70.7	05.7	02.6
	L	332	14.1	03.6	75.1	18.7	07.3
	F	343	10.1	01.0	83.8	42.4	05.0
Tylosema esculentum	S	560	29.5	42.8	24.3	20.5	03.2
(marama bean)	L	307	16.1	00.4	74.6	25.5	09.0
	R	46	08.1	01.8	56.3	22.8	10.2
Vigna aconitifolia (moth bean)	S		26.5	01.2	63.2	05.0	03.9
Vigna umbellata (rice bean)	S	390	21.5	01.2	71.6	03.4	02.3
Vigna vexillata	R		14.5	00.9	58.2		03.8
Voandzeia subterranea (bambara groundnut)	S	412	17.8	06.7	72.2		03.3

Appendix B

Contributors

The Research Contacts listed at the end of each chapter contributed greatly to this report. In addition the following people contributed.

A. F. ANGULO, Centraal Proefdierenbedrijf-TNO, Zeist, The Netherlands

E. S. AYENSU, Director, Endangered Species Program, Smithsonian Institution, Washington, D.C., USA

J. R. BAGGETT, Department of Horticulture, Oregon State University, Corvallis, Oregon, USA

HERBERT G. BAKER, Professor of Botany, University of California, Berkeley, California, USA

J. P. BARBOSA, Universidade de Fortaleza, Fortaleza, Ceará, Brazil

T. BARETTA-KUIPERS, Instituut voor Systematische Plantkunde, Botanisch Museum en Herbarium van de Rijksuniversiteit, Te Utrecht, The Netherlands

RUPERT BARNABY, Research Associate, The New York Botanical Garden, Bronx, New York, USA

C. W. BARNEY, Department of Forest and Wood Sciences, Colorado State University, Fort Collins, Colorado, USA

E. A. BELL, Professor, School of Biological Sciences, University of London, King's College, London, England

F. A. BISBY, Department of Biology, The University, Southampton, England

E. G. BOLLARD, Director, Plant Diseases Division, Department of Scientific and Industrial Research, Auckland, New Zealand

DONALD BOULTER, Science Laboratories, University of Durham, Durham, England

BERNARD BROWN, S. B. Penick Co., Lyndhurst, New Jersey, USA

G. W. BUTLER, Assistant Director-General, Department of Scientific and Industrial Research, Wellington, New Zealand

BILLY E. CALDWELL, Head, Department of Crop Science, North Carolina State University, Raleigh, North Carolina, USA

ANNETTA CARTER, Research Associate, University of California, Berkeley, California, USA

WONG KAI CHOO, Department of Agronomy and Horticulture, University of Agriculture, Serdang, Selangor, Malaysia

J. COPPEN, Tropical Products Institute, London, England

DERMOT COYNE, Department of Horticulture, University of Nebraska, Lincoln, Nebraska, USA

ELMO W. DAVIS, McCormick and Company, Hunt Valley, Maryland, USA

ALICIA AREVALO DE DELGADE, Naturalist, Guayaquil, Ecuador

D. A. V. DENDY, Head of Cereals and Rural Technology Sections, Tropical Products Institute, Oxfordshire, England

R. DENNIS, Department of Plant Sciences, University of Arizona, Tucson, Arizona, USA

RAJAMMAL P. DEVADAS, Principal, Sri Avinashilingam Home Science College, Coimbatore, India

R. DEVRED, Research Development Centre, Food and Agriculture Organization, Rome, Italy

H. C. D. DE WIT, Professor, Landboushogeschool, Laboratorium voor Plantensystematiek en Geografie, Foulkesweg, Wageningen, The Netherlands

Division of Horticultural Research, Commonwealth Scientific and Industrial Research Organization, Merbein, Victoria, Australia

J. W. DOLLAHITE, Veterinary Medical Officer, United States Department of Agriculture, Agricultural Research Service, Southern Region, College Station, Texas, USA

JAMES SHOLTO DOUGLAS, Afforestation Officer and Acting Projects Officer, Sudan Council of Churches, Khartoum, Sudan

SYDNEY DRAPER, Agriculture and Rural Development Department, The World Bank, Washington, D.C., USA

HAROLD E. DREGNE, International Center for Arid and Semi-Arid Land Studies, Texas Tech University, Lubbock, Texas, USA

W. G. DYSON, Centro Agronómico Tropical de Investigación y Enseñanza, Turrialba, Costa Rica

The East-West Center, Honolulu, Hawaii, USA

K. W. ENTWISTLE, James Cook University, Townsville, Queensland, Australia

R. E. ERICKSON, Givaudan Corp., Clifton, New Jersey, USA

A. M. EVANS, Department of Applied Biology, University of Cambridge, Cambridge, England

NORMAN R. FARNSWORTH, Professor of Pharmacognosy, University of Illinois at the Medical Center, Chicago, Illinois, USA

RAMON FERREYRA, Director, Museo de Historia Natural "Javier Prado," Universidad Nacional Mayor de San Marcos, Lima, Peru

TARCISO DE SOUSA FILGUERIAS, Oregon State University, Corvallis, Oregon, USA

LLOYD FREDERICK, Department of Agronomy, Iowa State University, Ames, Iowa, USA

G. FREGTAG, Mayaguez Institute of Tropical Agriculture, Mayaguez, Puerto Rico

F. M. A. GEURTS, Senior Agronomist, Department of Agricultural Research, Royal Tropical Institute, Amsterdam, The Netherlands

Ghana Herbarium, University of Ghana, Legon, Ghana

L. S. GILL, Department of Biological Sciences, University of Benin, Benin City, Nigeria

JUAN RAMON ACEBES GINOVES, Departamento de Botánica, Universidad de la Laguna, Tenerife, Spain

J. S. GLADSTONES, Institute of Agriculture, University of Western Australia, Perth, Australia

R. J. GOODLAND, The World Bank, Washington, D.C., USA

G. Y. GOOR, Tel Aviv, Israel

JOHN W. GREAR, Associate Professor and Curator, Department of Botany, University of Toronto, Toronto, Canada

D. J. HAGEDORN, Department of Plant Pathology, University of Wisconsin, Madison, Wisconsin, USA

P. HANELT, Akademie der Wissenschaften der DDR, Zentralinstitut für Genetick und Kulturpflanzenforschung, Gatersleben, Germany

M. W. HARDAS, Head, Division of Plant Introduction, Indian Agricultural Research Institute, New Delhi, India

JAMES A. HARDING, Environmental Horticulture, University of California, Davis, California, USA

JACK HARLAN, University of Illinois, Urbana, Illinois, USA

J. A. HART, Botanical Museum, Harvard University, Cambridge, Massachusetts, USA

R. HEGUAUER, Laboratorium voor Experimentale Plantensystematiek, Leiden, The Netherlands

M. HOLLE, Lima, Peru

A. M. IBRAHIM, Agricultural Research Service, United States Department of Agriculture, Salinas, California, USA

Instituto Technologico y de Estudios, Superiores de Monterrey, Monterrey, N.L., Mexico

HOWARD S. IRWIN, President, The New York Botanical Garden, Bronx, New York, USA

DUANE ISELY, Professor of Botany, Iowa State University, Ames, Iowa, USA

SOEMARTONO JAKARTA, Horticultural Research Institute, Jakarta, Indonesia

D. JELLIFFE, School of Public Health, University of California, Los Angeles, California, USA

J. KELLY, Vegetable Crops Department, University of Florida, Gainesville, Florida, USA

J. P. KERR, Plant Physiology Division, Department of Scientific and Industrial Research, Palmerston North, New Zealand

ALBERT E. KRETSCHMER, JR., Professor of Agronomy, Agricultural Research Center, University of Florida, Fort Pierce, Florida, USA

JAMES A. LACKEY, Iowa State University, Ames, Iowa, USA

E. LAING, Pro-Vice-Chancellor, University of Ghana, Legon, Accra, Ghana

KAI LARSEN, Professor of Botany, Botanical Institute, University of Aarhus, Risskov, Denmark

SUPEE S. LARSEN, Botanical Institute, University of Aarhus, Risskov, Denmark

COLIN A. LEAKEY, The Close, Cambridge, England

HERMÕGENES DE F. LEITÃO FILHO, Instituto de Biologia, Universidade Estadual de Campinas, Campinas, São Paulo, Brazil

W. A. LOEY, Animal Research Institute, Department of Primary Industries, Brisbane, Australia

R. F. LOGAN, Professor, Geography, University of California, Los Angeles, California, USA

K. LOSINS, Department of Genetics, The University of Alberta, Edmonton, Alberta, Canada

C. MAINIER, IPT, Cidade Universidade Estadual de Campinas, São Paulo, Brazil

R. MARECHAL, Faculte des Sciences Agronomiques de l'Etat, Gembloux, Belgique

G. B. MASEFIELD, Department of Agricultural Science, University of Oxford, Oxford, England

ROGERS McVAUGH, Curator of Vascular Plants, University of Michigan Herbarium, Ann Arbor, Michigan, USA

WILLEM MEIJER, Associate Professor of Botany, University of Kentucky, Lexington, Kentucky, USA

A. M. W. MENNEGA, Instituut voor Systematicshe Plantkunde, Botanisch Museum en Herbarium van de Rijksuniversiteit, Te Utrecht, The Netherlands

C. C. MEYR, Department of Botany, The Hebrew University, Jerusalem, Israel

G. O. MOTT, Agronomy, University of Florida, Gainesville, Florida, USA

B. R. MASLIN, Botanist, Western Australian Herbarium, South Perth, Western Australia, Australia

J. NIELSEN, Botanical Institute, University of Aarhus, Risskov, Denmark

A. J. OAKES, Research Agronomist, Germplasm Resources Laboratory, United States Department of Agriculture, Agricultural Research Service, Beltsville, Maryland, USA

Y. P. de CASTRO PÁSZTOR, Pesquisador Cientifico, Instituto Florestal, São Paulo, Brazil

V. PLITMANN, Department of Botany, The Hebrew University, Jerusalem, Israel

HUGH POPENOE, International Programs in Agriculture, University of Florida, Gainesville, Florida, USA

ROBERT F. RAFFAUF, Department of Medicinal Chemistry and Pharmacology, Northeastern University, Boston, Massachusetts, USA

G. RANGASWAMI, Vice Chancellor, Tamil Nadu Agricultural University, Coimbatore, India

R. REID, Experimental Officer, Plant Introduction, Commonwealth Scientific and Industrial Research Organization, Townsville, Queensland, Australia

DAVID H. REMBERT, JR., Associate Professor, University of South Carolina, Columbia, South Carolina, USA

LOUIS B. ROCKLAND, Chemist, United States Department of Agriculture, Berkeley, California, USA

J. H. ROSS, Royal Botanic Gardens and National Herbarium, South Yarra, Victoria, Australia

NABIEL A. M. SALEH, National Research Center, El Dokki, Cairo, Egypt

S. C. SCHANK, Professor of Agronomy, University of Florida, Gainesville, Florida, USA

JOEL SCHECHTER, Director, Research and Development Authority, Ben-Gurion University of the Negev, Beer-Sheva, Israel

A. SCHREIBER, Botanische Staatssammlung, München, West Germany

BERNICE G. SCHUBERT, Curator, The Arnold Arboretum of Harvard University, Cambridge, Massachusetts, USA

T. H. SCHUBERT, Institute of Tropical Forestry, United States Department of Agriculture, Rio Piedras, Puerto Rico

R. E. SCHULTES, Botanical Museum, Harvard University, Cambridge, Massachusetts, USA

A. T. SEMPLE, Lyons, Colorado, USA

A. K. SHARMA, Department of Botany, University of Calcutta, Calcutta, India

ARMANDO S. SHIMADA, Head, Department of Animal Nutrition, Instituto Nacional de Investigaciones, Pecuarias, S.A.G., Ganadería, Mexico

K. B. SINGH, International Crops Research Institute for the Semi-Arid Tropics, Hyderabad, India

WERTIT SOEGENG-REKSODIHARDJO, Pioneer Hi-Bred International, Inc., Tropical Research Station, Jamaica, West Indies

C. H. STIRTON, Pretoria, Republic of South Africa

M. S. SWAMINATHAN, Director General, Indian Council of Agricultural Research, New Delhi, India

E. T. THEIMER, International Flavors and Fragrances Corp., Rumson, New Jersey, USA

J. S. THOMPSON, Horticultural Research Station, Department of Agriculture, Gosford, New South Wales, Australia

K. THOTHATHRI, Editor of Publications, Botanical Survey of India, Howrah, India

G. TOUZINSKI, Northern Regional Research Center, United States Department of Agriculture, Agricultural Research Service, Peoria, Illinois, USA

D. E. TSURIELL, Chairman, International Cooperation Study Group on Sand Dune Reclamation and Management, Haifa, Israel

OSCAR VILEHEZ LARA, Universidad Nacional Agraria, La Molina, Lima, Peru

J. WASSINK, Wood Specialist, Royal Tropical Institute, Amsterdam, The Netherlands

R. W. WEAVER, Department of Soil and Crop Science, Texas A & M University, College Station, Texas, USA

DEANE F. WEBER, Microbiologist, Cell Culture and Nitrogen Fixation Laboratory, Beltsville, Maryland, USA

JÜRGEN K. P. WEDER, Oberassistant, Institut für Lebensmittelchemie, Technische Universitat München, Germany

F. W. WENT, Desert Research Institute, University of Nevada, Reno, Nevada, USA

ROY L. WHISTLER, Department of Biochemistry, Purdue University, West Lafayette, Indiana, USA

RICHARD P. WUNDERLIN, University of South Florida, Tampa, Florida, USA

Appendix C

Biographical Sketches of Panel Members

JOHN PATRICK MICKLETHWAIT BRENAN is Director of the Royal Botanic Gardens, Kew. He received the degrees of M.A. in 1943 and B.Sc. in 1954 from Oxford University. He worked at the Imperial Forestry Institute at Oxford until 1948, when he left to join the staff of the Herbarium at the Royal Botanic Gardens. He is also a Visiting Professor of the University of Reading. His research has been mainly on the taxonomy of tropical African plants, with special emphasis on the Leguminosae, particularly the Mimosoideae; he has written revisions of his work covering much of eastern and southern tropical Africa. In 1965 he became Keeper of the Herbarium at the Royal Botanic Gardens and became Director in 1976.

JAMES L. BREWBAKER is Professor of Horticulture and Genetics at the University of Hawaii. He received a B.A. degree in 1948 from Colorado University and his Ph.D. in plant breeding from Cornell University in 1952. Before joining the faculty of the University of Hawaii in 1961, he was employed by the University of the Philippines and the U.S. Atomic Energy Commission. His research has focused on crop genetics and breeding, with emphasis on maize, leucaena, and other tropical plants. He directs work in Hawaii on forest legume and maize improvement.

JAMES A. DUKE is Chief of the Plant Taxonomy Laboratory, Plant Genetics and Germplasm Institute of the Agricultural Research Service, U.S. Department of Agriculture. After completion of his Ph.D. in botany at the University of North Carolina in 1960, Dr. Duke joined the Missouri Botanical Garden, working his way up to assistant curator concerned primarily with the economic flora of Panama and Peru. After joining USDA in 1963, he studied the economic flora of Puerto Rico and Thailand. He then joined Battelle Memorial Institute for 5 years, largely doing field work on the sea level canal program in Panama and Colombia. Currently, he is developing

314

a computerized file on the ecology, utilization, and geography of economic plants.

E. MARK HUTTON retired as Chief, CSIRO, Division of Tropical Crops and Pastures, Brisbane, Australia, in March 1977. After completing his B.Ag.Sc. degree at Adelaide University in 1933, he worked with the South Australian Agricultural Department, then Roseworthy College, where his cereal breeding research earned an M.Sc. in 1940. From 1941 to 1953 he was at CSIRO, Division of Plant Industry, Canberra, and in 1951 received a D.Sc. from Adelaide University for research on inheritance of virus resistance in potatoes and tomatoes. While at Canberra he commenced breeding research in pasture plants, continuing this in Brisbane from 1954 to 1977 with tropical species. Concentrating on legumes, he bred Siratro, now widely used in pastures throughout the tropics, and has continued research on breeding legumes for acid tropical soils. He has traveled widely in the tropics lecturing and consulting on pasture and cattle production and has written numerous papers. He was president of the XI International Grassland Congress held in Australia in 1970 and has received a number of honors.

THEODORE HYMOWITZ is Professor of Plant Genetics, Crop Evolution Laboratory in the Department of Agronomy, University of Illinois. He received a B.S. from Cornell University in 1955, an M.S. from the University of Arizona in 1957, and a Ph.D. in plant breeding and genetics in 1963 from Oklahoma State University. Dr. Hymowitz has made extensive legume seed collections in many tropical and subtropical countries. His current research interests are with the origin and domestication of legumes, germ plasm resources, and the inheritance of chemical components of seed. He has been a Fulbright Scholar to India, an exchange scientist to Australia, and a member of the NAS winged bean panel. He is a Fellow of the American Association for the Advancement of Science.

RAYMOND J. JONES is a Senior Principal Research Scientist with the CSIRO Division of Tropical Crops and Pastures and Officer in Charge of the CSIRO Davies Laboratory, Townsville, Australia. He was graduated from the University College of Wales, Aberystwyth, with a B.Sc.(Hons), in 1953. From 1956 to 1960 he worked in Kenya for the British Colonial Service. In 1960 he joined the then CSIRO Division of Tropical Pastures in Brisbane, undertaking research on the growth and management of tropical legumes and animal production from legume-based and nitrogen-fertilized grass pastures. In 1973 he received a Ph.D. in agronomy from the University of New England, Armidale.

ROBERT C. KOEPPEN is Project Leader in charge of the Center for Wood Anatomy Research at the U.S. Forest Products Laboratory in Madison,

Wisconsin. He received a Ph.D. from the University of Wisconsin at Madison in 1962. Since that time he has worked as a wood anatomist at the Forest Products Laboratory, specializing in the identification of tropical woods from all parts of the world. He also serves as a Lecturer in Forest Products at the University of Wisconsin at Madison. His wood anatomy research has been concentrated in the area of tropical legumes, and monographic studies have been published on several South American genera. From 1973 to the present, he has also served as a tropical woods resource specialist for the U.S. Agency for International Development, and assignments have taken him to tropical regions throughout the world.

JEAN H. LANGENHEIM is Professor of Biology and has been Chairman of the Department of Biology at the University of California, Santa Cruz. She received a Ph.D. from the University of Minnesota in 1952 in plant ecology and paleobotany. At Harvard University, where she was Radcliffe Institute Scholar and Research Fellow in The Biological Laboratories from 1962 to 1966, she began an intensive chemical and ecological study comparing fossil resins (amber) with modern resins. This led to long-range field and laboratory investigation of tropical resin-producing leguminous trees. Her studies include an analysis of the ecological role of resin compounds in tropical ecosystems as well as their potential as a renewable forest product resource. She has been Secretary and is currently Vice President for Education of the Organization for Tropical Studies and has served on the U.S. National Academy of Sciences and Brazilian CNP Scientific Advisory Committee. She is also a member of the Scientific Advisory Committee of the Environmental Protection Agency.

JORGE LEÓN is head of the Crop Genetic Resources Program at the Tropical Agricultural Research and Training Center (CATIE) at Turrialba, Costa Rica. He received a Ph.D. degree from Washington University in 1953 and until 1962 worked at Turrialba on improvement of coffee and other tropical crops. From 1962 to 1968 his activities were concentrated on Andean crops and from 1968 to 1976 on genetic resources at the FAO headquarters in Rome.

JAMES C. MOOMAW is Director of the Asian Vegetable Research and Development Center (AVRDC) in Taiwan. He received a Ph.D. in botany from Washington State University in 1956 and then served on the University of Hawaii staff doing research on tropical pasture legumes and grasses. Joining the staff of the Rockefeller Foundation in 1961, he served as the first agronomist at the International Rice Research Institute in the Philippines working on rice production and multiple cropping. After 2 years in Sri Lanka with the IRRI Outreach Program, he joined the International Institute of Tropical Agriculture in 1970, serving successively as Rice Agronomist, Leader of the Farming Systems Program, and Director of Outreach Programs. Dr. Moomaw became Director of AVRDC in 1975.

BEDE N. OKIGBO is Deputy Director General of the International Institute of Tropical Agriculture (IITA), Ibadan, Nigeria. He graduated from Washington State University with a B.S. in agronomy and entomology and received an M.S. in 1956 and Ph.D. in 1959 in agronomy (crop production and ecology) from Cornell University. He was lecturer and then Professor, Head of the Department of Plant/Soil Science (1961-1973) and Dean, Faculty of Agriculture (1965-1971), University of Nigeria, Nsukka. While at the university, he lectured at various times on economic and agricultural botany, genetics and plant breeding, statistical methods for biology students, and field plot technique and the development of agriculture and crop production. He has published many articles on crop production of maize, yams, cassava, and miscellaneous crops and has recently written on farming systems in the tropics. From July 1973 to April 1977, he was Assistant Director of the Farming Systems Program at IITA. He has served as a member of the Economic Advisory Council (1975-1976) and Chairman, Agricultural Research Council of Nigeria (1975-1977). Now a member of the National Science and Technology Development Agency (NSTDA), he has been elected Fellow of the Science Society of Nigeria and of the Nigerian Academy of Science.

ANTONIO M. PINCHINAT received his Ph.D. degree in crop science from Michigan State University in 1964. Following his graduation, he went to work for the Interamerican Institute of Agricultural Science (IICA). There he served as Professor of Plant Breeding and Crop Improvement Specialist at the Graduate School and Research Center now known as CATIE (Centro Agronomico Tropical de Investigacion y Ensenanza), in Turrialba, Costa Rica, carrying out extensive agronomic work in food grain legumes. In 1976 he became IICA's Regional Director for the Antilles Zone, supervising and coordinating agricultural production and research programs in cooperation with national institutions within the Zone.

DONALD L. PLUCKNETT is Professor of Agronomy and Soil Science at the College of Tropical Agriculture, University of Hawaii. He received B.S. and M.S. degrees in agriculture and agronomy from the University of Nebraska in 1953 and 1957, respectively, and a Ph.D. in tropical soil science from the University of Hawaii in 1961. He has worked extensively in tropical crop and pasture research and has had broad international experience in tropical agriculture. He has been a consultant for many international groups, including work for the Ford Foundation on the Aswan Project in Egypt, for FAO, AID, and the South Pacific Commission. From 1973 to 1976 he was Chief of the Soil and Water Management Division, Office of Agriculture, Technical Assistance Bureau, Agency for International Development, Washington, D.C. In 1976 he was awarded AID's Superior Honor Award for his activities in international development. In June 1977, he was Chairman of a vegetable farming systems delegation to the People's Republic of China, sponsored by the Committee for Scholarly Communication with the People's Republic of China. He has served on several National Academy of Sciences study panels.

KENNETH O. RACHIE is Associate Director General of the Centro Internacional de Agricultura Tropical in Cali, Colombia, with overall responsibilities for research at this center, one of 10 such centers in tropical developing countries around the world. He earned a Ph.D. in agronomy and plant breeding at the University of Minnesota in 1954. From 1955 to the present he has been employed by the Rockefeller Foundation with assignments in several developing countries including Iraq, Mexico, India, Uganda, Nigeria, and Colombia. During this period he has been active in genetic improvement and agronomic research on forages, sorghums, millets, pigeon peas, cowpeas, and other basic food crops of the lowland tropics. He has been involved in collecting and assembling germ plasm of sorghum, millets, pigeon peas, and cowpeas and has contributed numerous articles and chapters in scientific and technical journals on these crops, including a series of monographs on millet species of importance in the developing tropics.

GUILLERMO SANCHEZ RODRIGUEZ is head of a collection, introduction, evaluation, and seed production program of tropical forage legumes and of a research and demonstration dairy program under irrigated mixed pastures in Guerrero State, Mexico. Both programs belong to a fideicommissum between the World Bank and the Bank of Mexico. He is also working on the collection and evaluation of Mexican legumes with forage potential, with particular emphasis on species and strains of the genus *Leucaena*. He received a B.S. in agriculture and animal production from the Escuela Nacional de Agricultura de Chapingo in 1973.

SETIJATI SASTRAPRADJA received a Ph.D. in botany from the University of Hawaii in 1967. Upon returning to Indonesia she rejoined the research staff of the National Biological Institute, Bogor, Indonesia. In 1973 she was appointed Director of that institute, a post she still holds. Dr. Sastrapradja has been involved in tropical legume research since 1969. Her major interest is plant genetic resources of minor food legumes such as *Canavalia, Psophocarpus,* and *Mucuna.* In addition, she is interested in tropical tuber crops and fruits. In 1976 she received a medal from the Indonesian government for her contribution to the development of sciences in Indonesia.

YUSUF N. TAMIMI is Professor of Soil Science at the University of Hawaii. He received his B.S. degree in agriculture from Purdue University in 1957, an M.S. in soils from New Mexico State University in 1960, and a Ph.D. in soils from the University of Hawaii in 1963. He conducts research on forest tree fertilization, forest soils, mineral cycling in forest stands, pasture management, and soil fertility on row crops. He also teaches courses on tropical soils, soil chemistry, and soil fertility.

CRAIG D. WHITESELL is the Principal Silviculturist, timber and watershed resource development research, Institute of Pacific Islands Forestry in Honolulu, Hawaii, for the United States Forest Service. He received his B.S.F. in forest management from West Virginia University and his M.F. in silviculture and soils from Duke University. For the past 15 years he has worked in Hawaii with forest species to be used for reforestation, type conversion, fuel-breaks, watershed protection, and timber production.

NOEL D. VIETMEYER, staff director for this study, is a Professional Associate of the National Academy of Sciences. Recipient of a Ph.D. in organic chemistry from the University of California, Berkeley, he has been staff officer for a number of NAS studies that have drawn attention to little-known plants that could well become future crops.

Index of Plants

Advisory Committee on Technology Innovation

Members

GEORGE BUGLIARELLO, President, Polytechnic Institute of New York, Brooklyn, New York, *Chairman*

HAROLD E. DREGNE, Director, International Center for Arid and Semi-Arid Land Studies, Texas Tech University, Lubbock, Texas

FRANÇOIS MERGEN, Pinchot Professor of Forestry, School of Forestry and Environmental Studies, Yale University, New Haven, Connecticut

E. R. PARISER, Senior Research Scientist, Department of Nutrition and Food Science, Massachusetts Institute of Technology, Cambridge, Massachusetts (member through 1977)

HUGH POPENOE, Director, International Programs in Agriculture, University of Florida, Gainesville, Florida

CHARLES A. ROSEN, Staff Scientist, Stanford Research Institute, Menlo Park, California (member through 1977)

VIRGINIA WALBOT, Assistant Professor, Department of Biology, Washington University, St. Louis, Missouri (member through 1977)

Board on Science and Technology for International Development

DAVID PIMENTEL, Professor, Department of Entomology and Section of Ecology and Systematics, Cornell University, Ithaca, New York, *Chairman*

Members

RUTH ADAMS, Editor, *The Bulletin of the Atomic Scientists*, Chicago, Illinois (member through December 1977)

EDWARD S. AYENSU, Director, Office of Biological Conservation, Smithsonian Institution, Washington, D.C.

PEDRO BARBOSA, Department of Entomology, University of Massachusetts, Amherst, Massachusetts

DWIGHT S. BROTHERS, International Economist and Consultant, Fairhaven Hill, Concord, Massachusetts

JOHN H. BRYANT, Chairman, Committee on International Health, Institute of Medicine, *ex-officio*

GEORGE BUGLIARELLO, President, Polytechnic Institute of New York, Brooklyn, New York

ELIZABETH COLSON, Department of Anthropology, University of California, Berkeley, California

CHARLES DENNISON, Consultant, New York, New York (member through December 1977)

BREWSTER C. DENNY, Dean, Graduate School of Public Affairs, University of Washington, Seattle, Washington

Board on Science and Technology for International Development
(JH-217D)
Office of International Affairs
National Research Council
2101 Constitution Avenue, Washington, D.C. 20418, USA

How to Order BOSTID Reports

Reports published by the Board on Science and Technology for International Development are sponsored in most instances by the U.S. Agency for International Development and are intended for free distribution primarily to readers in developing countries. A limited number of copies are available without charge to readers in the United States and other industrialized countries who are affiliated with governmental, educational, or research institutions, and who have professional interest in the subjects treated by the report. Requests should be made on the institution's stationary.

Single copies of published reports listed below are available free from BOSTID at the above address while the supplies last.

Energy

19. **Methane Generation from Human, Animal, and Agricultural Wastes.** 1977. 131 pp. Discusses means by which natural process of anaerobic fermentation can be controlled by man for his benefit and how the methane generated can be used as a fuel.

33. **Alcohol Fuels: Options for Developing Countries.** 1983. 128 pp. Examines the potential for the production and utilization of alcohol fuels in developing countries. Includes information on various tropical crops and their conversion to alcohols through both traditional and novel processes.

36. **Producer Gas: Another Fuel for Motor Transport.** 1983. 112 pp. During World War II Europe and Asia used wood, charcoal, and coal to fuel over a million gasoline and diesel vehicles. However, the technology has since been virtually forgotten. This report reviews producer gas and its modern potential.

38. **Supplement to Energy for Rural Development: Renewable Resources and Alternative Technologies for Developing Countries.** 1981. 240 pp. Updates the 1976 BOSTID publication and offers new material on direct and indirect uses of solar energy. Provides index to both volumes.

39. **Proceedings, International Workshop on Energy Survey Methodologies for Developing Countries.** 1980. 220 pp. Report of a 1980 workshop organized to examine past and ongoing energy survey efforts in developing countries. Includes reports from rural, urban, industry, and transportation working groups, excerpts from 12 background papers, and a directory of energy surveys for developing countries.

Technology Options for Developing Countries

8. Ferrocement: Applications in Developing Countries. 1973. 89 pp. Assesses state of the art and cites applications of particular interest to developing countries — boat building, construction, food and water storage facilities, etc.

14. More Water for Arid Lands: Promising Technologies and Research Opportunities. 1974. 153 pp. Outlines little-known but promising technologies to supply and conserve water in arid areas. (French language edition is available from BOSTID.)

21. Making Aquatic Weeds Useful: Some Perspectives for Developing Countries. 1976. 175 pp. Describes ways to exploit aquatic weeds for grazing, and by harvesting and processing for use as compost, animal feed, pulp, paper, and fuel. Also describes utilization for sewage and industrial wastewater treatment. Examines certain plants with potential for aquaculture.

28. Microbial Processes: Promising Technologies for Developing Countries. 1979. 198 pp. Discusses the potential importance of microbiology in developing countries in food and feed, plant nutrition, pest control, fuel and energy, waste treatment and utilization, and health.

31. Food, Fuel, and Fertilizer for Organic Wastes. 1981. 150 pp. Examines some of the opportunities for the productive utilization of organic wastes and residues commonly found in the poorer rural areas of the world.

34. Priorities in Biotechnology Research for International Development: Proceedings of a Workshop. 1982. 261 pp. Report of a 1982 workshop organized to examine opportunities for biotechnology research in developing countries. Includes general background papers and specific recommendations in six areas: 1) vaccines, 2) animal production, 3) monoclonal antibodies, 4) energy, 5) biological nitrogen fixation, and 6) plant cell and tissue culture.

Plants

16. Underexploited Tropical Plants with Promising Economic Value. 1975. 187 pp. Describes 36 little-known tropical plants that, with research, could become important cash and food crops in the future. Includes cereals, roots and tubers, vegetables, fruits, oilseeds, forage plants, and others.

22. Guayule: An Alternative Source of Natural Rubber. 1977. 80 pp. Describes a little-known bush that grows wild in deserts of North America and produces a rubber virtually identical with that of the rubber tree. Recommends funding for guayule development.

25. Tropical Legumes: Resources for the Future. 1979. 331 pp. Describes plants of the family Leguminosae, including root crops, pulses, fruits, forages, timber and wood products, ornamentals, and others.

37. The Winged Bean: A High Protein Crop for the Tropics. (Second Edition). 1981. 59 pp. An update of BOSTID's 1975 report of this neglected tropical legume. Describes current knowledge of winged bean and its promise.

47. **Amaranth: Modern Prospects for an Ancient Crop.** 1983. Before the time of Cortez grain amaranths were staple foods of the Aztec and Inca. Today this extremely nutritious food has a bright future. The report also discusses vegetable amaranths.

Innovations in Tropical Reforestation

26. **Leucaena: Promising Forage and Tree Crop for the Tropics.** 1977. 118 pp. Describes *Leucaena leucocephala*, a little-known Mexican plant with vigorously growing, bushy types that produce nutritious forage and organic fertilizer as well as tree types that produce timber, firewood, and pulp and paper. The plant is also useful for revegetating hillslopes, providing firebreaks, and for shade and city beautification.

27. **Firewood Crops: Shrub and Tree Species for Energy Production.** 1980. 237 pp. Examines the selection of species suitable for deliberate cultivation as firewood crops in developing countries.

35. **Sowing Forests from the Air.** 1981. 64 pp. Describes experiences with establishing forests by sowing tree seed from aircraft. Suggests testing and development of the techniques for possible use where forest destructions now outpaces reforestation.

40. **Firewood Crops: Shrub and Tree Species for Energy Production.** Volume II. 1983. A continuation of BOSTID report number 27. Describes 27 species of woody plants that seem suitable candidates for fuelwood plantations in developing countries.

41. **Mangium and Other Fast-Growing Acacias for the Humid Tropics.** 1983. 63 pp. Highlights ten acacias species that are native to the tropical rain forest of Australasia. That they could become valuable forestry resources elsewhere is suggested by the exceptional performance of *Acacia mangium* in Malaysia.

42. **Calliandra: A Versatile Small Tree for the Humid Tropics.** 1983. 56 pp. This Latin American shrub is being widely planted by villagers and government agencies in Indonesia to provide firewood, prevent erosion, yield honey, and feed livestock.

43. **Casuarinas: Nitrogen-Fixing Trees for Adverse Sites.** 1983. These robust nitrogen-fixing Australasian trees could become valuable resources for planting on harsh, eroding land to provide fuel and other products. Eighteen species for tropical lowlands and highlands, temperate zones, and semiarid regions are highlighted.

Managing Tropical Animal Resources

32. **The Water Buffalo: New Prospects for an Underutilized Animal.** 1981. 118 pp. The water buffalo is performing notably well in recent trials in such unexpected places as the United States, Australia, and Brazil. Report discusses the animal's promise, particularly emphasizing its potential for use outside Asia.

44. **Butterfly Farming in Papua New Guinea.** 1983. 36 pp. Indigenous butterflies are being reared in Papua New Guinea villages in a formal government program that both provides a cash income in remote rural areas and contributes to the conservation of wildlife and tropical forests.

45. **Crocodiles as a Resource for the Tropics.** 1983. 60 pp. In most parts of the tropics crocodilian populations are being decimated, but programs in Papua New Guinea and a few other countries demonstrate that, with care, the animals can be raised for profit while the wild populations are being protected.

46. **Little-Known Asian Animals with a Promising Economic Future.** 1983. 124 pp. Describes banteng, madura, mithan, yak, kouprey, babirusa, Javan warty pig and other obscure, but possibly globally useful wild and domesticated animals that are indigenous to Asia.

General

29. **Postharvest Food Losses in Developing Countries.** 1978. 202 pp. Assesses potential and limitations of food-loss reduction efforts; summarizes existing work and information about losses of major food crops and fish; discusses economic and social factors involved; identifies major areas of need; and suggests policy and program options for developing countries and technical assistance agencies.

30. **U.S. Science and Technology for Development: Contributions to the UN Conference.** 1978. 226 pp. Serves the U.S. Department of State as a major background document for the U.S. national paper, 1979 United Nations Conference on Science and Technology for Development.

The following topics are now under study and will be the subjects of future BOSTID reports:

- **Leucaena: Promising Forage and Tree Crop for the Tropics** (Second Edition)

- **Jojoba**

For a complete list of publications, including those that are out of print and available only through NTIS, please write to BOSTID at the address above.